University of Michigan Publications

HISTORY AND POLITICAL SCIENCE

VOLUME IX

THE ANGLO-FRENCH TREATY OF COMMERCE OF 1860 AND THE PROGRESS OF THE INDUSTRIAL REVOLUTION IN FRANCE

BRIGHT   COBDEN   CHEVALIER
Discussing the Treaty of Commerce of 1860
(From an old photograph given to the author)

THE ANGLO–FRENCH TREATY OF
COMMERCE OF 1860
AND THE
PROGRESS OF THE INDUSTRIAL
REVOLUTION IN FRANCE

BY

ARTHUR LOUIS DUNHAM

1971

OCTAGON BOOKS
New York

Reprinted 1971
by special arrangement with The University of Michigan Press

OCTAGON BOOKS
A Division of Farrar, Straus & Giroux, Inc.
19 Union Square West
New York, N. Y. 10003

Library of Congress Catalog Card Number: 77-159180

ISBN-0-374-92411-2

Printed in U.S.A. by
NOBLE OFFSET PRINTERS, INC.
NEW YORK 3, N. Y.

To

EDWIN FRANCIS GAY

PREFACE

THE object of this book is to consider the Anglo-French Treaty of Commerce of 1860, first, as a rather unusual episode in secret diplomacy and, secondly, as one of the factors that stimulated the development of the industrial revolution in France. I have not attempted to study at length the effects of this agreement as a precedent in tariff history because the evolution of those French industries which were most affected by the Treaty seemed to me of greater importance and wider interest.

The first seven chapters of the book, which deal with the negotiation of the Treaty, were written as a thesis for the degree of Ph.D. at Harvard University and are here published virtually unaltered. English historians have, almost without exception, described the Treaty as the achievement of Richard Cobden, with the assistance of Michel Chevalier. I have endeavored to show that the initiative was taken by Chevalier, and that in the subsequent negotiations he and Cobden worked together in real coöperation and with mutual appreciation. Next to them in importance came Gladstone, whose influence from the beginning was vital, but has never been adequately recognized. The fourth figure, Napoleon III, remains, as in life, somewhat of a mystery. If he ever wrote down his opinions or orders concerning the Treaty, the documents have not been preserved. I can say only that after many years of investigation I am of the opinion that the Emperor favored a really moderate tariff for France.

In the next seven chapters, which are studies of the development of French industries in the nineteenth century, an attempt is made to estimate the influence upon them of the Treaty of 1860. The conclusions are necessarily inadequate. Reliable evidence is scanty and the effects of a commercial treaty cannot be set down with precision. The three remaining chapters deal with the return of France to high protection, a reaction which developed slowly from 1870 to 1892 and was due to a combination of political and economic factors. The later phases of this movement have been fully described by earlier writers, but the opening onslaught of Thiers, which failed completely, and the period that followed when the cause of protection in France was weaker than ever before, have not previously been dealt with adequately.

Throughout the book so much use has been made of unpublished material in private papers or government archives, or of books that are little known, that I have given a critical bibliography of great length, as well as a list of books and articles. This list includes, however, with few exceptions, only those sources from which evidence or information that could be used in this book was actually obtained.

The list of my personal obligations is so long that it cannot be given fully here. This book is the result of nearly nine years of somewhat interrupted study and writing. It grew from a suggestion by Professor Gay of Harvard University regarding the part played by Chevalier in the negotiation of the Treaty. Ever since, his advice, encouragement, and friendship have been a never failing source of inspiration. The book is dedicated to him as an expression of my deep appreciation. Another economic historian whose friendship has lightened the labors of research abroad and whose advice and active assistance have been invaluable is Charles Schmidt, formerly on the staff of the Archives Nationales and now Inspector General of French Archives.

For the use of material drawn from private papers I gratefully acknowledge the kind permission of the representatives of the Cobden family, the Gladstone Trustees, and Sir Bernard Mallet in England; and, in France, of Madame Maxim Renaudin and Mademoiselle Flourens, granddaughters of Michel Chevalier.

The whole or parts of several of the chapters of this book have been published in periodicals. For permission to reprint these I am indebted to the editors of the *American Historical Review*, the *Nineteenth Century and After*, the *Quarterly Journal of Eco-*

nomics, the *Economic Journal*, the *Economic History Review*, and the *Journal of Economic and Business History*.

During the two years that I spent in Europe collecting material for this book I received much advice and assistance from librarians and government officials in the British Museum, the Bibliothèque Nationale, and the archives in London and Paris. I wish in particular to express my gratitude to M. Rigaud of the Ministère des Affaires Étrangères, and MM. Martin and Feller of the Bibliothèque Nationale. Much time was spent also in research at Harvard University, where every facility was put at my disposal by Mr. Walter Briggs, of the Widener Library. For assistance in obtaining access to private papers or to official papers not open to the public I am greatly indebted to Mr. Maurice Léon of New York, M. Max Lazard and Dr. Pierre Lepaulle of Paris, and Dr. G. P. Gooch and the late Lord Phillimore of London.

Valuable advice and criticsm have been given me by Professor Henri Hauser of the University of Paris, Dr. J. H. Clapham, now professor of Economic History, and Mr. G. M. Trevelyan, now regius professor of Modern History at Cambridge University; the late Professor Archibald C. Coolidge, Professor W. C. Abbott, and Mr. R. I. Lovell of Harvard University; the late Professor C. H. Van Tyne of the University of Michigan, and my former colleague here, Professor W. A. Frayer.

I wish to express my gratitude to Dean G. Carl Huber and the Executive Board of the Graduate School through whom the publication of this book under the auspices of the University of Michigan was made possible; to the editor, Dr. Eugene S. McCartney; and to Mr. Dwight C. Long, of the University of Michigan, who has made the index and given valuable assistance in preparing the manuscript for the press.

The frontispiece is from a photograph, the gift of Thomas Potter, Esq., who was in Paris during the treaty negotiations and carried some of the notes exchanged between his father's friend, Cobden, and Chevalier.

ARTHUR LOUIS DUNHAM

ANN ARBOR, MICHIGAN
October 12, 1929

CONTENTS

xi

THE ANGLO–FRENCH TREATY OF COMMERCE OF 1860 AND THE PROGRESS OF THE INDUSTRIAL REVOLUTION IN FRANCE

ABBREVIATIONS

Works referred to by *op. cit.* are cited in full at the first references to them in each chapter.

The following abbreviations are employed throughout the volume:

Arch = Archives Nationales
F. O. = Foreign Office
J. des écon. = Journal des économistes
Min. Aff. Étr. = Ministère des Affaires Étrangères
Parl. Paper, Commerc. = Parliamentary Paper, Commerc.

INTRODUCTION

THE treaty of commerce signed by Great Britain and France in 1860 was an event of importance in the history of both countries. On the side of England it marked the practical completion of the gradual adoption of free trade which had been begun by Huskisson nearly forty years before, whereas on the side of France it was only the first decisive step in a reduction which was not desired to go beyond the limits of moderate protection. The French Government hoped that the stimulus of British competition would compel French manufacturers to improve their methods and use machinery, and would thus serve to bring down the cost of living and strengthen the position of France in international trade. For both countries the impelling force was the rising tide of the industrial revolution.

This treaty was negotiated chiefly by two idealists who were the leaders of the free trade cause in their respective countries. Their object was to obtain as near an approach to free trade as possible on the ground that this would promote peace between nations. We know now that they were mistaken in believing that a notable increase in international trade would prevent war, but they were perfectly sincere in their belief. They hoped also that lower tariffs would raise the standard of living for the working classes. Chevalier, at least, thought that the treaty with England should be only the first and most important of a network of commercial treaties through which the tariff level of Europe would be progressively lowered. His wish was fulfilled and many other treaties on the model of the Anglo-French agreement were concluded by both France and England.

It is doubtful whether the Chevalier-Cobden treaty influenced appreciably the general development of British industries, but in France it was of very real significance. Though England had been able to reduce her tariff progressively by legislation France had not. In France public opinion was still so hostile to any drastic lowering of the tariff that action was possible only through the treaty-making powers of the Emperor, as had been proved by the government's failure to secure the passage of a very moderate bill a few years before. Through a treaty alone, therefore, could the moribund French industries be revived by the salutary pressure of foreign competition. It is for this reason that the agreement planned by Chevalier was a decisive step in the progress of the industrial revolution in France.

CHAPTER I

ANGLO-FRENCH TARIFF HISTORY AND
COMMERCIAL NEGOTIATIONS, 1786–1860

THE first serious attempt to negotiate a treaty that would
help to maintain peace between the old enemies facing
each other across the English Channel through facilitating
a great increase in trade was made in the brief interval between
the American and the French revolutions. It was successful,
and had that interval been longer the Treaty of 1786 would
probably have brought valuable and enduring benefits to both
countries, and would have made unnecessary the negotiation
of a new treaty after the lapse of three quarters of a century.

Conditions in both France and England favored a mutual reduction of tariffs in the late eighteenth century. Many of the
advisors of Louis XVI were Physiocrats or were greatly influenced by that school of economic thinkers, while their most
brilliant pupil, Adam Smith, had influenced many of the leaders
in England through his *Wealth of Nations* published in 1776.
Both the French and British governments had additional reasons
for favoring a commercial rapprochement. The War of the
American Revolution had left England with a heavy debt and a
crying need for new markets to replace the monopoly in her
colonial trade, which she thought had been lost irretrievably,
although subsequent events proved that the economic independence of the United States was not won until the War of 1812.
England's new premier, Pitt, seeking to aid both the revival
of British trade and the depleted exchequer, renewed the attempt
of Walpole to increase the revenue by reducing customs duties,
and included a commercial treaty with France as one of the
features of his reform of the tariff in order to get compensation
from the French. Like his predecessor, Lord Shelburne, he was
a disciple of Adam Smith. On the French side Vergennes, al-

though a follower of Turgot, who believed liberty vital to commerce, favored a commercial treaty with England chiefly from political motives. He feared that England was planning to renew the war and avenge her defeats as soon as she could complete her financial convalescence. A treaty of commerce, he thought, would probably prevent this and assure a solid and permanent peace. But he was handicapped by the opposition of the majority of the French chambers of commerce and of the French diplomatic representatives in England, Comte d'Adhémar and M. de Barthélemy, and by the mutual dislike and suspicion of the peoples of the two countries. Rayneval, to whom Vergennes assigned the task of negotiating the treaty, was also a disciple of the Physiocrats, who taught that agriculture must be favored at all costs and that the government should consider the consumer before either the manufacturer or the trader. In a memorandum to the Council of State in May, 1786, he said: "The system of prohibitions encourages smuggling. It is, therefore, essentially vicious because it prevents the legitimate operations of commerce and curtails the public revenue without helping the consumer."

Pitt on his side had to meet the opposition of Parliament and of his Minister of Foreign Affairs, Marquis Carmarthen, so that he was obliged virtually to direct the negotiations himself. He delayed their commencement, therefore, until he had made a thorough investigation of both British and French industries, a wise precaution which was neglected by France. Finally, in March, 1786, he sent over William Eden to begin serious negotiations. After some haggling both the French and British governments declared their desire to abolish prohibitions and any duties levied exclusively on Franco-British trade. The treaty was signed on September 26, 1786, and three months later the two governments executed a supplementary convention fixing various duties not given in the treaty itself.

The most important products affected by the treaty were wine, spirits, beer, textile manufactures, pottery, glass, and iron. French wine coming directly to Great Britain was to pay no more than Portuguese wines then paid, but England reserved the right to decrease further the duties on Portuguese wines under the Methuen Treaty of 1703, without giving any equivalent concession to the French. Eden gave Rayneval to understand that this reservation would not be made use of, but the British Government did take advantage of it and thus deprived France of one of the chief benefits she had expected to derive from the treaty. This misunderstanding is important as a precedent, for in 1860 we find Cobden assuring the French Government of a low duty on wine, which he was unable to induce his own government to adopt. Under the Treaty of 1786 the British duty on French spirits fell from 9 shillings 7 pence per gallon to 7 shillings. Beer was to be taxed 30 per cent in both countries. A maximum duty of 10 per cent was charged in either country on hardware, cutlery, and miscellaneous metal wares; and a similar duty of 12 per cent on cottons, woollens, porcelain, earthenware, and glass. Silk and all goods mixed with silk remained mutually prohibited. On linens, beer, glass, mirrors, and iron England reserved the right to levy increased duties as compensation for excise taxes, and France made similar reservations respecting cotton goods, iron, and beer. All products not specified were to receive most-favored-nation treatment, which meant that neither signatory would grant any other country more favorable rates upon them than it gave to the other party to the treaty. If new concessions were given by either France or England to a third power, they would automatically be extended to the other with two important exceptions. France stipulated that this provision should not apply to the Family Compact with Spain of 1761 and England made a similar exception of the Methuen Treaty with Portugal.

In general the Treaty of 1786 was received with satisfaction in England because British commercial interests, which had been consulted regarding the duties, received far more than they had expected. But in Parliament, Pitt, like Gladstone in 1860, encountered strong opposition, and he had no great speaker such as Gladstone to help him against the greatest orators of the day, Fox, Burke, and Sheridan. The chief basis of attack against both treaties was the alliance with France and, though France was not considered as dangerously militaristic in 1786 as in 1860, the fortification of the port of Cherbourg was denounced in both years as a direct threat to the security of England.[1]

In France there was no parliament to endorse or oppose the Eden-Rayneval Treaty and it could not easily be judged by its effects because three years after it came into operation it was virtually abrogated by the outbreak of the French Revolution. There can be no question, however, that French manufacturers labored under great handicaps in the competition that was forced upon them. They were hampered by the tariff barriers within their country, by the restrictions of the guild system which were still in force, and by their almost complete ignorance of the kinds and qualities of British goods. Of the machines then used in England only the spinning jenny had gained a firm foothold in France, so that the output of mechanically spun yarn was negligible. England had further advantages in cheaper coal, in cheaper and better wool, and in an organization of commercial travelers who knew the needs of French consumers. In addition, England had a strong government which executed strictly her customs regulations, but the French administration was weak and unable to stop widespread frauds by British exporters. Yet despite all these disadvantages and the even more serious fact that the financial situation of France was growing steadily worse, French manufacturers were not ruined by British competition.

Vergennes had predicted that the operation of the Treaty of 1786 would give a severe shock to French industry, but would be a stimulant that was badly needed. This prediction seems to have been correct. Sixteen years later, during the brief interlude in the long years of war between France and England, Chaptal, the Minister of the Interior, recommended to Napoleon the conclusion of a new treaty of commerce with England similar to the agreement negotiated under his predecessor Vergennes.

---

[1] M. F. Dumas, *Étude sur le traité de commerce de 1786 entre la France et l'Angleterre.* The text of the treaty is given in more convenient form in de Clercq, *Receuil des traités de la France,* I, 146. See *Cambridge History of British Foreign Policy, 1783-1919,* I, 170.

He estimated that in the three years following 1786 French exports of wine to England had doubled and those of spirits tripled. Though British exports to France were much larger than French shipments to England, this was explained by England's rôle as a great carrying nation. A large part of French imports from England was thus the product of neither British industry nor British agriculture; and, furthermore, the amount of these shipments decreased notably each year. The judgment of Chaptal was that the British were becoming accustomed to French wines and spirits and that they would have provided an important and permanent market. On the other hand, the French liking for cheap British textiles declined steadily. It is interesting to note that French merchants made their shipments on orders from British customers, whereas British merchants, in textiles at least, sent their goods to France without orders because overproduction in England made it impossible to sell them at home. The result was a sharp drop in British textile prices and the failure of many British firms between 1787 and 1789. This overproduction in England also appears to have been the chief cause of the widespread undervaluation of British goods declared at the French customs. Here again it can only be repeated that this policy hurt the British merchants as well as the French, as is shown by the large number of bankruptcies in England. In France no single branch of industry was ruined and industry in general seems to have been notably stimulated by the competition which induced French manufacturers to study and copy British goods with gratifying success.[2]

The commercial relations of France and England and the whole tariff policy of France were changed radically by the wars of the French Revolution. The hostility of Europe to the growing strength of that movement forced its leaders to adopt a belligerent policy in order to save themselves from destruction by the restoration of Bourbon absolutism. They met the threat

[2] Dumas, *op. cit.;* Jean A. C. Chaptal, " Un Projet de traité de commerce avec l'Angleterre sous le Consulat," *Revue d'économie politique*, February, 1893, VI, 83–98. Chaptal was a grandson of Napoleon's minister.

of foreign intervention in the spring of 1792 by a declaration of war and by the mobilization of a revolutionary army, and on the outbreak of actual hostilities they prepared to utilize also the economic resources of France. Great Britain was soon recognized as the most determined enemy of revolutionary France and a series of statutes was passed with a view to depriving her of the valuable French market for her goods. The fact that the exclusion of British goods might injure French consumers even more than British manufacturers and merchants was not appreciated. Everything was subordinated to the great aim of ruining the banker of the allies and the organizer of their coalitions by striking at his trade. Thus the Law of October 9, 1793, forbade the importation of any British merchandise. This economic offensive was relaxed for a time under the Directory, but was resumed with renewed vigor under the Consulate. The Decree of June 20, 1803, forbade the importation of all goods from British colonies or coming directly or indirectly from England, while on July 20 French ports were closed to all ships which had touched at a British port. In 1806 and 1807 Napoleon issued the well-known Berlin and Milan decrees proclaiming the blockade of England and directing the seizure of any ship that had touched at a British port or submitted to inspection by the British authorities.[3]

The effect of these sweeping measures was mitigated, in practice, by smuggling and by importation under licenses issued by the Emperor. Their chief interest to us lies in the fact that under them France again grew accustomed to the prohibition of manufactures imported from England and that a system devised as an instrument of war became so firmly established that it was regarded as necessary to safeguard the prosperity of French industry. Many an industry had grown strong through the monopolies created by the isolation of France under the revolutionary and Napoleonic system and was able on the fall of the Empire to exert political pressure effectively. The manufacturers, especially those of textile and iron goods, were supported in their opposition to any change in

[3] Auguste Arnauné, *Le Commerce extérieur et les tarifs de douane* (Paris, 1911).

French commercial policy by the personnel of the administration trained in the application of prohibitions and by the landowners interested in the production of wool or the exploitation of forests for fuel. With the Restoration the prohibitions, which had been applicable mainly to British goods, were extended to the goods of all nations; but this change was less important in practice than in theory, because, even under the Empire, most manufactures likely to be imported were the products of British industry or trade.

There is some reason to believe that the Bourbons, upon their return to France, would have been glad to moderate somewhat the severity of the system of prohibitions, but Louis XVIII was a shrewd politician. As in politics he tried to steer a middle course, so in the economic field he was anxious not to arouse opposition unnecessarily, for he knew that his hold upon the throne was none too strong and he did not wish to start again upon his travels. Under the restricted suffrage the Chambers were controlled by the great landed proprietors, but the leaders of certain industries, such as iron and cotton, were strong enough to command respect. Hence it was natural for the government to extend the protective system to agricultural products such as wool, flax, and cereals, and, in compensation, to cotton. Coal was taxed on its importation under a complicated system of duties which favored the remote fields of Prussia, discriminated somewhat against the neighboring mines of Belgium, and bore heavily on coal brought in by sea. By this means a blow was aimed at England and an inducement was offered to French manufacturers to continue to use wood as fuel. For iron a tariff was devised that would preserve intact for French ironmasters the complete monopoly of the home market. The danger of an invasion from Sweden and Russia which, like France, used chiefly wood for smelting and refining, was averted by raising the duty on bar iron from 10 per cent to approximately 50 per cent. Then it was discovered that the British were shipping iron smelted with coal across the Channel, so a special duty was imposed on such iron amounting to no less than 120 per cent. In this way the French ironmasters were fully protected, the owners of forests, including the Crown and many of the nobles, were assured of the continuance of large profits, and the progress of metallurgy in France was almost completely checked.[4]

Under the July monarchy the government showed clearly that it desired a more moderate tariff, but it was largely dependent on the political support of the manufacturers. Hence, although much was said about reductions, little was done. The duties on wool were brought down one third, the duty on iron smelted with coal one fourth, that on cotton, whether of long or short staple, was decreased to 20 francs. In addition, permission was granted to import very fine cotton yarn, which was not spun in appreciable quantities in France, and coarse linens. With a few unimportant exceptions these reductions comprise all the reforms of the Government during the reign of Louis Philippe. In the last year, it is true, the Guizot ministry introduced a more comprehensive bill affecting nearly half the articles in the French tariff, but the report of the Chamber's committee, headed by Thiers and Casimir Périer, was so hostile that it was dubbed by Chevalier "un monologue de l'intérêt privé en contemplation devant lui-même," and the committee took care to present its report so late in the session that there was no time for discussion.[5]

The Revolution of 1848 brought no change in tariff policy, although it replaced by an assembly elected through universal suffrage the legislature controlled by the landowners and manufacturers through a restricted franchise based on a property qualification. The new body was distinctly hostile to tariff reform and no popular demand arose to make action necessary. In consequence, the old tariff remained with its chaotic mixture of high duties and prohibitions.[6] The continuance of this system meant that iron, coal, and machinery, the vitamins of industry, could be imported only at great cost. As a result the industrial revolution made slow progress in France. Methods of smelting

[4] Arnauné, *op. cit.*, pp. 156–168; Léon Amé, *Étude économique sur les tarifs de douanes* (Paris, 1876), I, 143–160.

[5] Amé, *op. cit.*, I, 251.

[6] Charles Coquelin, " Les Douanes et les finances publiques," *Revue des deux mondes*, XXII (May 1, 1848), 362.

and refining iron were not improved appreciably and the construction of railroads was slow and expensive.

While France was thus maintaining almost intact her virtually prohibitive tariff, England was making rapid progress toward the adoption of complete free trade, so that the divergence in the tariff policies of the two countries became steadily greater. England had secured commercial supremacy in the eighteenth century. To this she now added industrial supremacy secured through the introduction of machinery and large scale production. The inevitable result was the free trade movement supported by the merchants and the newly enfranchised manufacturers who needed new markets for the goods their machines were turning out in ever increasing quantities. The first steps toward a drastic reduction of the British tariff were taken by Huskisson who in the Act of 1825[7] removed the prohibition on the importation of wool and greatly decreased the duties on many raw materials and on some partly manufactured goods. He was followed after some years by Sir Robert Peel, who decided to remove all prohibitions, make the duties on raw materials merely nominal, or, when possible, abolish them; reduce the duties on all partly manufactured goods; and on wholly manufactured goods levy duties of approximately 20 per cent. The loss in revenue was to be made up by an income tax and a small duty on the exportation of coal, although the latter was repealed soon after its imposition because it proved injurious and annoying. Before his defeat, after the repeal of the Corn Laws in 1846, Peel had abolished import duties on four hundred and thirty articles which brought in little revenue, had removed the qualified prohibition of the exportation of machinery, and had secured the free admission of wool and cotton.[8] His work was continued by Gladstone in his first great budget in 1853,[9] until

---

[7] Leone Levi, *History of British Commerce and of the Economic Progress of the British Nation 1763–1870* (London, 1872), pp. 162–169; also British Statutes at Large, X, 304, 6 George IV, c. 104 and c. 111.

[8] There were four of Peel's tariff acts, of which the most important were the act of July 9, 1840 (Statutes at Large, XVI, 219) and the Act of August 5, 1845 (Statutes, XVII, 884).

[9] Act of August 8, 1853 (Statutes, XXI, 490).

the British tariff contained only a moderate number of very low duties, with the exception of taxes imposed on certain commodities primarily for revenue. In addition to throwing open her markets to foreign goods England also opened her ports to foreign ships through the repeal of the Navigation Laws in 1849 and the removal of restrictions on the coastal trade in 1854.[10]

In neither England nor France, as we have seen, did these developments in tariff policy provide a suitable basis for a new commercial agreement of any real significance. Hence it is not surprising to find that, although the two governments exchanged notes on the subject from time to time and on several occasions appointed commissions to negotiate, they accomplished practically nothing. Before the free trade movement in England had made great progress the British Government was willing to discuss adjustments of tariff duties and navigation dues of limited scope, which was the only modification of existing arrangements the French were prepared to consider. One result of this attitude was a navigation treaty in 1826 which provided that each nation should give the ships of the other, and the goods imported in them, the same treatment in the matter of navigation dues and surtaxes as its own ships received in the ports of the other nation. This applied, however, only to ships engaged in the direct trade between France and England. The treaty contained no specific tariff clauses, but authorized the prohibition by France of the importation of all products from Asia, Africa, or America, transported wholly under the British flag.[11]

No commercial negotiations were seriously considered by either government until 1838 when, as the result of a long dispute over French import duties on flax yarn and linen, France suggested the appointment of commissioners to discuss commercial relations and tariffs. England agreed and discussions began

---

[10] Act of June 26, 1849, 12 and 13 Victoria, c. 29, and the Act of March 23, 1854 (Statutes, XXII, 11).

[11] Lewis Hertslet, *A Complete Collection of the Treaties and Conventions, and Reciprocal Regulations at present subsisting between Great Britain and Foreign Powers and of the Laws, Decrees and Orders in Council, concerning the same* (London, 1827–1907), III, 123.

in January, 1839, were adjourned for a time, and then resumed the following year, when a tentative tariff convention was drawn up, but never signed because of a sharp disagreement between the two governments over Mehemet Ali in the Near East. Negotiations were renewed in 1843, but no agreement could be reached, probably because France had settled her tariff controversy with Belgium and did not, therefore, feel the need of strengthening her commercial position by an understanding with England. No very important concessions had been offered by either the French or the British. England had agreed to reduce somewhat her duties on French wines, spirits, silks, and artificial flowers, and on the class of goods known as *Articles de Paris*, which included toys, haberdashery, and imitation jewelry; and she had consented to allow the exportation of machinery for spinning flax under a merely nominal duty, a concession that involved no real loss of revenue because the British prohibition was being evaded through the smuggling in of machines by French manufacturers. The French on their side agreed to admit at a duty of 30 per cent pure woollens, flannels, and woollens mixed with silk or linen, but offered no concession on cottons, coal, or iron.[12]

In 1852 France was again involved in a tariff controversy with Belgium which was settled only by the Treaty of 1854 and again we find her discussing tariff adjustments with England. But by this time the British had gone so far toward free trade that they would consider only a treaty of broad scope, whereas the French wanted, as before, an agreement on a few points only which would place them in a stronger position for bargaining with the Belgians. Once the agreement with Belgium had been reached France lost interest in the discussion with England. The

---

[12] Hertslet, Memorandum for F.O. on commercial negotiations of England with France, 1830–1855, in F.O., 97–207; also Min. Aff. Étr., memoranda and documents, Angleterre, 94; memorandum by de Clercq on the negotiation of the Treaty of 1860 prepared December, 1859, p. 96; and Arch. Nat., F 12–2684, unsigned memorandum giving the terms of the proposed convention of 1840 in eight articles together with the opinions of the French commissioners of whom the chief was Gréterin, Director of Customs. England was represented by Lytton Bulwer and G. R. Porter.

only real change in the French position as compared with that of 1840 was that in the 'fifties she offered the British reductions in the duties on iron and coal. This was because France was finding it difficult to build her railroads, owing to the limited resources and antiquated equipment and methods of her iron-masters.

The futility of all these commercial negotiations between 1815 and 1859 seemed to indicate that the best way to lower the French tariff with a view to aiding the development of industry and of an adequate system of transportation would be by legislation. We know that this was the opinion of the strong government established by Louis Napoleon through the reaction from the disorders of 1848 and the memory of his famous uncle. We may well ask also whether the triumphant free trade movement in England did not weaken the position of the protectionists in France by starting a similar agitation on the southern shore of the Channel, and thus make easier the passage of a law to repeal the prohibitions and reduce some of the really prohibitive duties. France had had many promi-nent free traders when she negotiated the Treaty of 1786 with England. Had they changed their opinions during the succeed-ing generations of revolution and commercial isolation or had they brought forth descendants able to fight for free trade as soon as a favorable opportunity should present itself?

The first manifestation of any considerable body of opinion favoring free trade in France after 1815 came in 1842, when a treaty of commerce was negotiated with Belgium and there was a renewal of the proposal of a customs union between the two states which had been made shortly after the Belgians had won their independence from the Dutch and the great powers had denied them a king from the house of Orleans then reigning in France. The proposed union was now supported by a number of French chambers of commerce representing the industries of wine, silks, woollens, and Paris manufactures (cabinet ware, perfumery, imitation jewelry, toys, etc.), and by the French economists through their organ, the *Journal des économistes*, founded in 1841. The protectionists, led by Mimerel, a cotton manufacturer of Roubaix, retorted by organizing in 1842 the Comité pour la Défense du Travail National and by founding the *Moniteur industriel*. They denounced the new treaty, signed in July, 1842, as one of those schemes "qui frappent les industries une à une, au lieu de les atteindre en masse et qui produisent un mal dont nous n'avons déjà que trop d'exemples." They met with great success, for the plan for a customs union was quickly dropped and the opposition to the treaty in the Chambers was so strong that the Government did not secure its ratification until 1845, when it was about to expire. In 1843 the Mimerel Committee went on to denounce the renewed commercial negotiations with England saying, "England asks that we open our frontiers to her only because she must destroy our prosperity in order to relieve her own great distress," to which Wolowski replied that one did not generally begin an effort to increase trade by ruining one's customers. In the same year the protectionist committee issued a manifesto opposing any reform of the tariff which the free traders answered with declarations in favor of freer international trade by the chambers of commerce of Lyon, Bordeaux, ·Marseille, St. Étienne, Nîmes, Montpelier, Bayonne and Arras; while Wolowski, in the *Journal des économistes*, thanked Mimerel and his committee for arousing this reaction.[13]

The free trade cause soon afterward found a leader in Frédéric Bastiat, who had spent his life in managing his estate at Mugron in the Landes, but had read widely and well and had kept in close touch with English thought. He began writing articles on economic questions as early as 1834, and ten years later published an article in the *Journal des économistes* on the "Influence of the English and French Tariffs," in which he stated that England, through free trade, was lowering her prices and securing cheaper labor, whereas the commercial policy of France was producing exactly the opposite effects; and he warned his countrymen that, if this went on, England would soon drive France from all foreign markets.[14] In 1845 Bastiat came to

[13] L. F. R. Wolowski, *J. des écon.*, Series I, VI, 377–392.
[14] A. Bouchié de Belle, *Bastiat et le libre-échange* (Paris, 1878), pp. 192–216.

Paris in order to organize the free trade movement in France and began to pour forth a veritable flood of pamphlets. He used both facts and humor effectively, even going so far as to write a petition to the Government on behalf of the candle-makers protesting against intolerable competition by the sun "in flooding the national market with light at a marvelously low cost." He made known to France the work of the Anti-Corn Law League in England, both through his pamphlets and through his book *Cobden et la ligue, ou l'agitation anglaise pour la liberté des échanges,* in which he translated and analyzed the chief speeches of Cobden and his friends.[15]

Bastiat's success in France was speedy. On February 18, 1846,[16] he organized at Bordeaux an Association for Free Trade which, in its manifesto, declared that it intended to work by all legal means for the reform of the tariff and the abolition of prohibitions and protective duties. Expressions of sympathy were received from Marseille, Havre, Nantes, and Lyon. The Central Association was organized at Paris on July 1, 1846,[17] by Bastiat, Blanqui, Dunoyer, Léon Faucher, Horace Say, the Duc d'Harcourt, and others. On August 18 [18] the Association gave a banquet in honor of Richard Cobden, at which there took place the meeting of Cobden and Michel Chevalier which was to bear such rich fruit fourteen years later. Soon afterward the Association held its first public meeting, which was followed in September by a second meeting at which Chevalier was one of the chief speakers. The Association declared that it favored a tariff for revenue only, and announced its opposition to any form of protection and its desire for free trade regardless of reciprocity. It would support no party, class, province, or industry and wished only to popularize the principle of free trade, leaving the initiative in its application to the Government. Its views were expressed in its weekly organ, *Le Libre échange,* edited by Bastiat.[19] During the autumn branches were organized at Marseille, Lyon, and Havre.[20]

---

[15] Arnauné, *op. cit.,* p. 241.
[17] *Ibid.,* XIV, 305.
[19] Bouchié de Belle, *op. cit.,* pp. 232–238.
[16] *J. des écon.,* Series I, XIII, 405.
[18] *Ibid.,* XV, 179.
[20] *J. des écon.,* Series I, XV, 361.

The protectionists replied to this outburst of activity by a great meeting held at Lille in October, 1846, when a Committee of Fifty was formed to represent all French industries in view of their attack by Paris, Bordeaux, and Marseille. Roubaix soon afterward called an anti-free trade meeting and voted to form a committee to support the Central Committee at Paris. The Central Committee itself was reorganized and strengthened by the creation of a permanent subcommittee consisting of Odier, Lebeuf, and Mimerel to direct activities and organize branches. Active support was voted by the Comité des Industriels de l'Est of Mulhouse, and by enthusiastic meetings at Valenciennes, Elbeuf, Amiens, and Tourcoing,[21] and the *Moniteur industriel* was joined by *Le National* and *La Presse*.[22]

Even more effective support of the protectionist cause came from the Revolution of February, 1848, with its socialistic tendencies and its attacks on private property. The economists, who had led the battle for tariff reform, now joined the conservatives in fighting the radicalism of the Second Republic. Bastiat's Association pour la Liberté des Échanges and its organ, *Le Libre échange*, disappeared in the confusion and no successful attempt to revive them was made until after the victory of 1860. The free trade cause had succeeded in appealing to few beyond the economists and some of the commercial interests. Only the wine and silk industries and the larger ports were favorable, and even these showed no unanimity and no persistence in fighting for their views. The chief effect of the agitation in France was to unite the vast majority of French manufacturers into a compact organization opposed to all reform of the tariff, but the mass of public opinion remained either indifferent, or favorable to the protectionists. Arnauné shows clearly how different was the situation in France from that in England:[23]

"We have no landed aristocracy with immense estates. Our land is in the hands of a peasant democracy. The duties on the products of agriculture and on livestock seem to be imposed, not in the interest of a few great landowners, but for the benefit of a whole nation of farmers, both large and small. This is apparently one of the reasons why associations formed to check the rising price

---

[21] *J. des écon.*, XV, 378.   [22] *Ibid.*, XV, 423.   [23] Arnauné, *op. cit.*, p. 245.

of food in France have invariably failed. Similarly, a multitude of small-scale producers shared in the protection of industry because of its being much less concentrated than in England. In fact, French industry was split up into a very large number of enterprises the majority of which were workshops operated by the owner and his family and producing chiefly for consumers within the country and often in the nearest local market. These manufacturers could not have the boundless ambitions of English industrialists. The small scale of their operations forced them to restrict their plans to the conservation of their local clientèle. They thought far more of excluding foreign competition than they did of extending their markets and of competing with the foreigner in his own country. The workmen were no less devoted to the system of prohibitions than were the landowners and manufacturers. The argument of the defense of national labor was fully appreciated by them. They felt the same fear of the importation of foreign goods as they did of the introduction of machinery. They thought only of the danger to their wages and could conceive of no other results from the abolition of prohibitions or the increasing use of machinery than a decrease in the demand for labor, unemployment, and misery. Thus propaganda for free trade found no support in any class of the population.[24] On the contrary all classes believed they had an interest in the maintenance of prohibitions."

The first event after the Revolution of 1848 was the sudden action of Sainte-Beuve, which startled even the surviving advocates[25] of free trade. On February 5, 1851,[26] he proposed, in the Assemblée Législative, a new tariff which should abolish all export duties, all the protective import duties on foodstuffs and raw materials, and all the prohibitions, but on partly manufactured goods the duties were not to exceed 10 per cent and on wholly manufactured goods 20 per cent. Exceptions were to be made only for iron and sugar, which were to have protective duties. As was to be expected, this bill was reported unfavorably by the commission of the Chamber, and, under the leadership of Thiers, the Assembly voted 428 to 199 to refuse to discuss it.[27] The Government through its Minister of Finance, Fould, expressed its disapproval of Sainte-Beuve's bill as embodying the principle of free trade, but significantly hinted at the desirability of some reform of the tariff:

[24] This is an exaggerated statement since several chambers of commerce, the larger ports, and a number of manufacturers had supported tariff reform.
[25] Bastiat died in 1850.
[26] *J. des écon.*, Series I, XXVIII, 203.
[27] *Ibid.*, XXIX, 243.

" The principle of free trade is that each country produce only what nature permits it to produce at the lowest price. We emphatically reject this principle as being incompatible with the independence and security of a great nation; as inapplicable to France because it would destroy our finest industries. Our tariff undoubtedly contains many useless and archaic prohibitions and we think that they should be stricken out. Protection through the tariff is necessary for our industries. We do not mean by this that protection should be blind, fixed, or excessive, but that the principle of protection should be firmly maintained. The proposal of M. de Sainte-Beuve demolishes this principle and its consideration would alarm the whole country." [28]

The Government did not, however, support the protectionists in their violent attack on the economists in the press and it ignored the demand of the *Moniteur industriel* for the dismissal of the professors Chevalier and Blanqui.[29]

After the establishment of the Second Empire in December, 1852, the Government revived the Conseil Supérieur du Commerce to give advice on the negotiation of commercial treaties and on other projects affecting the tariff.[30] The majority of the new members appointed were clearly protectionist, but there was a strong minority favoring tariff reform consisting of de Morny,[31] the Emperor's brother; de Parieu, a member of the Council of State; Duffour-Dubergier who, as mayor of Bordeaux, in 1846 had presided over the first meeting of the Free Trade League organized in that city; Legentil, president of the Chamber of Commerce of Paris; Gautier; and d'Eichthal. In November, 1853, the Council appointed a committee to study the coal and iron tariffs, and on the 14th this committee recommended reforms which were embodied in the Decree of the 22d.[32] For coal the zones were retained, but the duty on importations by sea from Dunkirk to the Sables d'Olonne was reduced from 0.55 to 0.33 franc per 100 kg.; that on importations by land, by the same

[28] *J. des écon.*, XXX, 245.
[29] *Ibid.*, XXIX, 262.
[30] *Ibid.*, XXXIV, 315–316.
[31] Arch. Nat., F 12–2514. Report of Sessions of Conseil Supérieur du Commerce, November 14 and 16, 1853. De Morny spoke of the need to spur foreign competition, November 14, and voted the same day with the minority for a greater reduction in the iron tariff.
[32] Arch. Nat., F 12–2514. See also *Bulletin des lois*, CLXXVIII, 958.

amount;[33] that on coal brought in by sea south of the Sables d'Olonne, from 0.33 to 0.165 franc.[34] For iron and steel similar reductions were made and further, but smaller, reductions were to become effective January 1, 1855. Thus for cast iron the duty of 7.70 francs for importations by sea was decreased to 5.50, but in 1855 there was to be a uniform duty on all cast iron of 4.40 francs, the existing rate on cast iron from Belgium alone. For bar-iron the distinction between iron smelted by wood and by coal was abolished and the duties of 18.25 and 20.50 francs reduced to 13.20 francs, with a further reduction in 1855 to 11 francs. Cast steel then paid 132 francs per 100 kg., and raw steel paid 66. These rates were replaced by a uniform duty of 44 francs to be reduced in 1855 to 33 francs. Of all these reductions the most important was that on bar-iron, since this included rails and made possible for the first time the importation in quantity of English rails on which the old duty of 20.50 francs (about 100 per cent) had been prohibitive. These rails were badly needed, since the French ironmasters had been quite unable to meet the rapidly increasing demand.

A long succession of decrees followed, of which we may note the Decree of August 29, 1855,[36] reducing the duties on machinery, and that of October 17 [37] of the same year, admitting free raw materials for shipbuilding. Another decree issued on January 19, 1856,[38] reduced heavily the duties on raw wool and replaced the ad valorem charge by a duty on weight. All these decrees were issued under the authority of the Acts of 1814 and 1836 permitting such action in emergencies, and they were ratified by sullen Chambers in the Tariff Acts of July 26, 1856,[39] and April 18, 1857.[40]

Meantime the Government had secretly laid its plan for a far more thorough reform of the tariff. Napoleon III was in a much stronger position relative to the Chambers than were his

---

[33] Decree of September 14, 1852, had raised the duty on Belgian coal from 0.15 to 0.30 franc.

[34] *J. des écon.*, Series I, XXXVII, 447.

[35] *Ibid.*, XXXVII, 466–467.

[36] *Bulletin des lois*, CLXXXVI, 301.

[37] *Ibid.*, p. 435.

[38] *Ibid.*, CLXXXVIII, 43.

[39] *Ibid.*, CXC, 375.

[40] *Ibid.*, CXCII, 657.

royal predecessors, for after the Coup d'État he had restored many of the features of the old imperial constitution; nevertheless his government moved cautiously. The idea of abolishing the prohibitions was proposed first in correspondence between the Ministers of Foreign Affairs,[41] Finance, and Commerce [42] (Brennier, Fould, and de Persigny). All three approved of abolition in principle, but de Persigny felt that French industry was not yet ready to meet the competition of stronger industrial states such as England, Belgium, and the Zollverein, with their negligible duties on raw materials, because of the recent economic crisis in France; while the Government could not yet afford to sacrifice so much revenue. But the result of this correspondence was the submission by the Government to the Council of State on May 1, 1852, of a plan for abolishing sixteen prohibitions on imports and practically all those on exports; admitting two hundred and forty-one articles free; and reducing the import duties on ninety-seven others. This was virtually the very moderate bill of 1847, but the Council of State could not reach any agreement on it, one party holding that the plan was too bold, while the other thought it excessively timid in its avoidance of all really important reforms.

In 1853 de Persigny was succeeded as Minister of Commerce by the strongly protectionist Magne,[43] but two years later Magne was moved to the Ministry of Finance and his place taken by Rouher, who soon resumed the study of the question of abolishing the prohibitions. The Government felt stronger through its success in the Crimean War, while the strength of French industry seemed to have been shown at the Exposition of 1855 in Paris. A new bill was submitted to the Council of State early in 1856, and with its approval was introduced in the Corps Législatif on June 9. The moment chosen was, however, most inopportune, for the session was drawing to a close, while the various decrees modifying the tariff which had been submitted

---

[41] Amé, *op. cit.*, I, 269.

[42] Arch. Nat., F 12-2488. Ministère de l'Intérieur, Bureau de Commerce; "Note sur le système commercial de France," March 19, 1853; Fould to de Persigny, January 24, 1852, and the reply of de Persigny, December 2.

[43] Amé, *op. cit.*, I, 269-275.

for ratification earlier in the year had met with so cold a reception that the real opposition of the Chambers to any tariff reform was clear. The bill proposed the replacement of the prohibitions by high protective duties, but the excitement aroused by its introduction was so great, that on the 22d the Government introduced an amended bill raising even higher the protective duties. Woollens were now to be admitted under a duty of 30 per cent ad valorem, cottons at 35 per cent, clothing 40 per cent, and even the coarsest yarns were to pay 1.20 francs per kilogram. Cast iron was to pay 4.80 francs per 100 kg. and the largest iron bars 12 francs. Other prohibitions were to be replaced by specific duties of from 30 to 50 per cent.

The protectionists had been dozing in complete security. Only a few months before the Committee for the Protection of National Labor had assured the faithful that no important change in protective legislation was being prepared. The morale of the rank and file had sunk so low that on March 7 the Committee sent out an appeal to its local branches:

"It is the duty of these committees to sustain wavering convictions, to urge perseverance on those who weary of the struggle, and above all to recall the essential solidarity of all branches of national labor. If individual claims are pressed against the general interest, the committees must fight them and remind everyone of his duty. They must prevent the expression of differences of opinion by individuals which would tend to discredit or ruin in the estimation of the public the whole system of protection, by making everyone understand that in objecting to the protection given his neighbor he is endangering the protection which he himself enjoys. They must, in short, maintain discipline in the ranks, see that no one is disloyal to the spirit and aims of this association, and use their influence to prevent opponents or doubtful friends from entering the chambers of commerce and the consultative chambers of arts and manufactures which form the official representation of industry."

This appeal produced its effect when the storm broke without warning on June 9. The Central Committee leapt into action. On the 10th,[44] it wrote to the branch committees that it was working hard to meet the danger and urged them to give prompt assistance by flooding the Government with petitions showing the lack of protection from which each industry would suffer.

[44] *Moniteur industriel,* June 15, 1856.

The response was quick. Chambers of commerce, departmental councils, and groups of manufacturers vied with each other in their appeals to the Government and the Chambers,[45] while the Central Committee, supported by delegates from the principal industries affected, kept in constant touch with the commission appointed by the Corps Législatif to examine the bill, and also distributed appeals and pamphlets to the deputies of the Chamber as a whole. The lobbying was so successful that the Committee and its assistant industrial delegates reported that the Commission of the Corps Législatif had received them with the greatest cordiality and listened attentively to all their criticisms of the bill. "This attempt," wrote the Committee, "failed rather sadly and we have every reason to hope that in view of this experience the attempt will not be made again." [46]

But the victory in the Corps Législatif did not satisfy the protectionists, for they feared the reintroduction of the bill at the next session. So the agitation continued and spread through the manufacturing districts. The workmen were told that tariff reform meant free trade, which would bring industrial paralysis with declining wages, if not general unemployment. To the declaration of the Customs Service that duties exceeding 30 per cent merely encourage smuggling it was replied that it had been shown that the cotton industry could not be protected with a duty of less than 40 per cent; "why, then, remove this prohibition since, under present conditions, the only results would be the ruin of the industry and the loss of all revenue to the Government by the triumph of smuggling?" [47]

But the climax in sophistry was reached by the *Moniteur industriel* when it declared in an editorial that prohibitions had never been erected into a system in any country. "We are not concerned here with the system of prohibitions. This system does not exist in our country. We are concerned with the protective system and with its radical modification through the abolition of those prohibitive measures whose maintenance has

---

[45] June 22. See *Moniteur industriel,* July 3, 1856.
[46] *Ibid.*
[47] *Ibid.,* July 9, 1856. Report of Mimerel to Conseil Général du Nord.

been believed necessary until now for the purpose of protection and not of prohibition." [48]

The success of the protectionist agitation gives the impression that virtually the whole country had a hand in it and that public sentiment was universally hostile to the bill. This is just the impression the Central Committee wished to produce, although it was a great exaggeration. Letters and editorials in the newspapers, the votes of the Conseils Généraux of the Departments in the summer of 1856, and the strenuous efforts made by the protectionists themselves testify to this exaggeration. Most parts of the country favored protection, it is true, but they did not favor the indefinite continuance of prohibitions. The Mimerel Committee for the Defense of National Labor was supported in its agitation almost entirely by the cotton, woollen, and metallurgical industries and true zeal for the maintenance of prohibitions was widely displayed only in Flanders and Normandy.[49]

The activity of the protectionists procured the defeat of the bill introduced in the session of 1856, but it did not bring the Government's surrender on the principle of the necessity for abolishing prohibitions. This was shown first by the Decree of July 27, 1856, appointing a committee of the Conseil Supérieur du Commerce to study the condition of the various French industries and advise the Government concerning the amount of protection needed by each.[50] When it was seen that, in spite of this decree, the agitation continued, the Government issued a more definite statement of its position on October 17: [51]

" The progress of French industry had been shown so clearly at the Universal Exposition of 1855 that the moment seemed opportune for replacing the prohibitions in our tariff laws by protective duties. This was a great step toward the goal which should be sought by all peoples. In fact, the development of commercial activity and of international relations paves the way for the progress of civilization. Profoundly convinced of this, the Government had introduced in the Corps Législatif a bill repealing all the prohibitions. This bill could not be brought to a vote in the last session and the Government, desiring adequate

---

[48] See *Moniteur industriel*, June 22, 1856.
[49] *J. des écon.*, Series II, XII, 157.   [50] *Journal des débats*, July 29, 1856.
[51] *Ibid.*, October 18, 1856.

advice, decided to begin an official investigation of these questions. Alarmist reports were, however, spread throughout the country and made use of by the interested parties. His Majesty wished to have a very careful study made of the complaints which had reached him and, therefore, directed the Minister of Commerce to examine them. Having been enlightened by the Minister's report on the true position of French industries the Emperor decided to modify the bill introduced in the Corps Législatif so as to have the repeal of prohibitions take effect only after July 1, 1861. A bill to this effect has been sent to the Council of State. French industries, warned of the firm intentions of the Government, will have ample time to prepare themselves for the new commercial régime."

The Government kept its word and during the next two years merely issued a few decrees making slight reductions in the tariff. But it had gained only a truce in its war with the protectionists and had set a bad example by its partial surrender.

" If the Administration had not thought it necessary to draw back in the face of the opposition aroused by its proposed reform," wrote Amé in 1858,[52] " the manufacturers who threatened to close their workshops would probably have given way before embarking on so dangerous a course of action. In any case the postponement of tariff reforms merely sets the difficulties aside without solving them. At the approach of 1861 plenty of reasons and pretexts will be found for the opinions held and we shall see the renewal of the manifestations that caused the Government to hesitate in 1814 and in 1834 as it did in 1856."

Amé did not have to wait long to see the fulfillment of the prophecy. In February, 1859, the Government submitted to the Conseil d'État a bill to abolish the sliding scale of duties on cereals which had been suspended by successive decrees since August, 1853,[53] and word went out that it was planning to open an investigation preparatory to repealing the prohibitions in 1861. The protectionists had no intention of being caught napping again and promptly set out to arouse a new agitation which they knew would greatly embarrass the Government on the eve of the war against Austria. On May 12, Mimerel and his colleagues, Feray, Talabot, and Seillière, issued a manifesto to their followers to report the results of their campaign.[54]

" The Committee of the Association, having heard at its meeting on March 24 last the report dealing chiefly with the questions of cereals and of prohibitions, instructed its officers to take the steps necessary to enlighten the Government

---

[52] Amé, *op. cit.* (ed. 1860), pp. 303–304.
[53] Amé, *op. cit.* (ed. 1876), I, 281.
[54] *Moniteur industriel,* May 15, 1859.

regarding the dangers of the present situation and to ask that it be kind enough to take the only action possible to maintain employment by reassuring agriculture and industry. We hasten to inform you that the steps we took, supported by petitions from all the great industrial centers, have been crowned with complete success. We asked that, while retaining the right to revise the tariff at a convenient time, the Government now postpone indefinitely action on the bill to repeal prohibitions and the formal investigation that had been planned. This request, which was particularly opportune under existing circumstances and which was endorsed by the Senate's Committee on Petitions, was favorably received by the Government."

This report was quite accurate, for on the very day on which it was written the Government issued a decree ending the suspension of the sliding scale of duties on corn and withdrawing its bill for the abolition of these duties; and on the previous day [55] Rouher had sent a significant reply to a letter from the chamber of commerce of Lille regarding the abolition of prohibitions. He said that the Enquête of 1834 showed that the abolition of a few prohibitions did no harm and that the whole system ought to go. At that time the most bitter opponents of the Government's bill had asked only for delay in abolition and this had been more than granted since twenty-five years had passed. Other warnings had been given by the Bill of 1847, which proposed to abolish several prohibitions, and by the declaration of the Minister of Finance in 1851 that several antiquated prohibitions should go. After referring to the Bill of June, 1856, and the declaration of October 17 of the same year, Rouher stated that the Government had planned to open an *enquête* in October, 1859, on the seventeen products in the bill of 1856 in connection with which the abolition of prohibitions had aroused no protest. In 1860 a bill would have been presented covering these products and a second *enquête* opened on the products, such as textiles, regarding which the opposition had been strongest, after which, in 1861, a second bill would have been drafted. But the Government recognized that recent complications in foreign policy made such an investigation inopportune and it therefore planned to postpone it and, in consequence, to postpone also the abolition of prohibitions.

[55] *Journal des débats*, May 17, 1859.

Thus the protectionists won another signal victory, and by the same methods that brought success three years before. In the confidence of their strength they had not feared even the inconsistency of opposing in 1859 the very *enquête* they had so eagerly demanded in 1856. They asked and secured the indefinite postponement of the abolition of prohibitions, thinking that this would give them complete security; whereas, in reality, this very uncertainty enabled the Government eight months later to say that no promise had been made regarding the date of abolition other than the assurance that it would not be before July 1, 1861. Another factor of even greater importance did not enter into their calculations at this time, although they had thought of it in 1843 and again in 1852, and that was, that the Government might achieve its ends through a treaty of commerce. Fortunately for the cause of tariff reform in France there was an economist who had a keener memory. He had predicted the failure of the attempt made in 1856 to abolish prohibitions by law and had stated that this desirable reform could be achieved only through a treaty which the Emperor could sign and promulgate by his authority alone. This economist was observing the situation as closely as ever in 1859 and in July of that year he began on his own responsibility the secret negotiations which ended six months later in the treaty with England.

CHAPTER II

MICHEL CHEVALIER

OF THE two principal authors of the Anglo-French Treaty of 1860, Richard Cobden is by far the more widely known. His name is associated with free trade in all the civilized countries of the world because the first great victory for tariff reform was won by the Anti-Corn Law League in England under his leadership. Cobden was, therefore, a man of international fame in Europe fourteen years before 1860, and many books had already been written about him at the time of his death in 1865. Since that time his life has been the subject of two very able biographers: Lord Morley, who wrote *The Life of Richard Cobden* in 1879, and Hobson, who followed in 1918 with *Richard Cobden, the International Man.* His French collaborator, on the other hand, though already a distinguished writer and economist, was not well known outside his own country before 1860. Though generally recognized as the leader of the French free traders as early as 1852, he had not acquired an international reputation, as had his English friend, because the French Free Trade League had met only with defeat. In 1860 the French author of the Treaty acquired little merit in the eyes of the majority of his countrymen and few writers thereafter concerned themselves with the important, but unofficial, part he had played, because the Treaty was not generally popular in France; while in England, where it was popular, its successful conclusion was ascribed entirely to Cobden. The life of the French negotiator was, however, one of great activity and interest and only through a knowledge of it can anyone understand the influence he exercised in inducing the British and French governments to begin the negotiations which led to the Treaty of 1860.

Michel Chevalier was born on January 13, 1806, at Limoges, where his father was collector of indirect taxes. He attended the Lycée there until he was seventeen, when he went to Paris and entered the École Polytechnique, from which he was graduated with high distinction. He was sent by the Government as a mining engineer to Lille, where he attracted attention through his enthusiasm for technical investigations and through his writings on the application of science to industry.[1]

" He saw industry wholly absorbed in empiricism, seeking the path to follow without confidence in its strength, energetic only in complaints and above all as lacking in dignity because it demanded help from the Government instead of standing on its own feet. His aim was to raise it up, to enlighten it regarding its power, to restore to it the belief in its mission, and to show it by conclusive examples at the price of what effort domination in this world is founded and maintained. He believed in the idea which he has supported ever since, that in industry as elsewhere the convenient posts are neither the most honorable nor the most secure because true success is insured only by a constant struggle."[2]

Chevalier's idealism showed itself at this time in his active interest in two religious movements. In 1827 he joined a group of young men who revived the old order of the Templars because the Church did not satisfy their religious aspirations, while the free-masons and Carbonari were regarded as definitely anti-religious. Two years later he helped Laurent and Auguste Comte revive *L'Organisateur*, which Saint-Simon had attempted to establish in 1819 as the journal for the expression of his ideals.

Henri de Rouvroy, Comte de Saint-Simon, believed in action, but he spent his life as a dreamer trying to evolve a theory for the rule of the world by wise men. He believed that a nation is only an industrial society, and that men's efforts should be directed solely toward the most favorable organization of industry. He regarded it as his mission to transfer power, without the use of violence, from the nobles, clergy, and soldiers to the manufacturers who would be guided and inspired by wise men and artists. On his death in 1825, Saint-Simon had achieved none of his aims and had gathered about him only a

[1] Say and Chailley, *Nouveau dictionnaire d'économie politique*, I, 410 (article on Chevalier by his son-in-law, Paul Leroy-Beaulieu); also *Journal officiel*, December 9, 1889 (address by Jules Simon before the Institute).
[2] Louis Reybaud, *Économistes modernes* (Paris, 1862), p. 175.

tiny group of disciples, of whom the most prominent were Augustin Thierry and Auguste Comte. They were joined the day after their master's funeral by Enfantin and together they founded, in June, 1825, *Le Producteur* which they published until October, 1826. There they declared that industry must be ruled by authority and not by liberty or individual initiative, which had caused so much suffering and strife. Every man would be given the task for which he was best fitted. Barriers between nations, such as tariffs, must be overthrown, and the perfect distribution of goods must be achieved through the improvement of means of transportation, such as railroads, and through the organization of credit by the creation of banks.

The economic and social ideas of the Saint-Simonians became gradually enveloped, however, in an ever denser cloud of religious sentiment, and in 1829 a church was organized, and in the following year the leaders began to preach before the public in a hall in the Rue Taitbout. By this time the sect had some three hundred members, among whom were Michel Chevalier and his younger brother Auguste, Gustave d'Eichthal, Le Play, Émile and Isaac Pereire, Edmond Talabot, and Arlès-Dufour. Saint-Simon was declared the successor of Christ, and under the direction of the two Fathers Enfantin and Bazard, the sect tried to create a new religion. Discussions over theology and ritual accomplished little, however, and, when the position of woman in the Saint-Simonian church was taken up, Bazard withdrew and started a schism which soon proved fatal. Enfantin, with a remnant of forty disciples, of whom the chief was now "Père" Michel, retired to a house in Menilmontant where he proceeded to organize the new society and await the coming of the woman-messiah. Discussion about liberalizing the institution of marriage and open advocacy of the abolition of private property alarmed the Government which, in August, 1832, seized the papers of the Saint-Simonians and brought Enfantin and Michel Chevalier to trial on a formal charge of violating Article 291 of the Penal Code, which forbade the holding of meetings of more than twenty people. They were found guilty and sentenced to one year in prison, which they began to serve in

December. This blow completely disorganized the Saint-Simonian Church which, soon afterward, was formally dissolved by Enfantin, who released his followers from their vows of obedience.[3]

Michel Chevalier had joined the Saint-Simonian sect in 1829, but had retained his post at Lille until December, 1830, when he was called to Paris by Enfantin to take charge of the *Globe*, which had been bought to replace the former paper, *L'Organisateur*, as the official organ of the Saint-Simonians. Here Chevalier denounced tariffs and declared that no country should be tributary to another, because an exchange of products meant, not the exploitation of either party, but the benefit of both. The idea of the development of means of communication, as first expressed in *Le Producteur*, was taken up by him and carried further in the proposed "Système de la Méditerranée," [4] which was to insure quick and frequent communication between the occident and the orient by means of a network of railroads connecting at the head of each gulf with steamship lines, while the whole was to be financed by chains of banks. His ability as a writer won him a position on the staff of the *Journal des débats*, in the spring of 1833,[5] while he was still in prison. Soon after his release in June of that year, when he had served only half his sentence, he was sent by the Government to study the development of railroads and other means of communication in the United States.

Chevalier remained two years in America, where he threw himself with enthusiasm into the study of our expanding civilization. The letters he sent to the *Journal des débats* from January 1, 1834, to October 22, 1835, describe not only the development of railroads and other means of communication, but also the banking system and social and political conditions. In general, the young engineer was filled with admiration of what he saw, but, as a former Saint-Simonian, he noted with alarm a widespread lack of respect for authority. The letters were

---

[3] Sebastien Charléty, *Histoire du Saint-Simonisme (1825–1864)*, (Paris, 1896).
[4] Published in the *Globe*, January and February, 1832.
[5] Reybaud, *op. cit.*, p. 177.

published in two small volumes in 1836, and were followed in 1840 by two large quarto volumes on the development of means of communication in the United States. As a result of the publication of his American letters, Chevalier, in 1836, was given a position on the staff of the *Revue des deux mondes*. In the following year the French Government sent him to England to study the commercial crisis and the development of the railroads, but soon after his arrival he was thrown from a carriage and so seriously injured that he had to give up his mission and return to France. In 1838 he published a volume entitled *Des intérêts matériels en France. Travaux publics. Routes, canaux, et chemins de fer*, in which he offered to the timid Government a comprehensive program of development which included a network of railroads closely resembling that which was constructed in the early years of the Second Empire. Under the protection of Count Molé he was appointed to the Council of State and the Conseil Supérieur du Commerce; but his administrative career, begun with so much promise, ended abruptly on the fall of Molé in March of the following year.[6]

In 1840 Chevalier was appointed professor of political economy at the Collège de France, a post which he held for twelve years. As a teacher he retained very largely the interests of his youth. He continued to advocate the development of lines of communication, popular banks, and technical schools, his ideal being the replacement of the old directing class, which had had a classical education, by a new class composed of engineers and leaders of industry. He lectured also on problems of currency and on the relation of political economy to morality and to social welfare. In short, though he had discarded the strange religious ideas of the Saint-Simonians together with their belief in communism, he had retained their ideas regarding industry and the majority of economic questions, and above all their keen interest in moral progress and the welfare of the masses. The new professor was also a disciple of Jean Baptiste Say, who had taught at the Collège de France from 1830 to 1832. Say, by assimilating the ideas of Adam Smith, as well as those of the Physiocrats, had

[6] Say and Chailley, *op. cit.*, I, 411.

done much to give political economy the unity and organization of a science. In his theory of markets he had advocated closer international relations and free trade, although, like his predecessors in France, he thought that the foundation of national prosperity lay in the development of agriculture rather than of industry. Say declared that protection increases production in the protected country, but, since it restricts importations, it does more harm than good, because importations increase national production even more by creating a larger body of consumers through the greater cheapness of goods, and by stimulating domestic production in order to pay for the goods imported. Free trade, therefore, would result in the maximum national production at the lowest cost, for by it a country would obtain all goods and produce only those in whose production it excelled.[7]

In his lectures Chevalier showed the influence of Say, but kept the point of view of a Saint-Simonian who was interested primarily in the welfare of the working classes and in the development of industry. He declared that freedom of labor was the necessary concomitant of political liberty, for in France the abolition of the guilds had been contemporaneous with the political declaration of the rights of man. Isolation had been the dominant idea in the foreign policy of states on the hypothesis that the interests of different states were incompatible (which was true, said Chevalier, when each was trying to seize the territory of others); and, in like manner, the principle of isolation had determined their economic policy. Political economy, on the contrary, teaches that the civilized states form one great body whose members must communicate freely and profit by the special advantages of each. The problems of the individual are concerned with the liberty of the producer, the right to property, and the equality of all before the law. The first is violated if the worker is forbidden to buy where he likes the materials and tools he needs; the second is violated if he cannot dispose of the fruits of his labor as he pleases; and equality is denied if he

[7] A. Arnauné, *Le Commerce extérieur et les tarifs de douane* (Paris, 1911), p. 232.

is forced to buy dearly from a neighbor what he could purchase cheaply from a foreigner, for he then pays his neighbor a tax which he does not owe him. The labor of a country is a means to provide for the needs of that country and unless it does so more efficiently than foreign labor it is not truly national.[8]

In 1845 Michel Chevalier married Emma Fournier, the daughter of a wealthy manufacturer of cloth of Lodève, in the Department of Hérault; and in the same year he was elected to the Chamber of Deputies by the Department of Aveyron. In the following year he took a prominent part in the organization of the French Association for Free Trade, urging France to follow England's example and gradually lower her customs barriers. Absolute free trade, he said, is a Utopia, but France should try to approach it. This open attack on protection caused Chevalier's defeat when he sought reëlection to the Chamber, the majority of the voters supporting the protectionist candidate Cabrol, director of the iron foundries of Decazeville.[9]

After the outbreak of the Revolution of 1848, Chevalier attacked the communism advocated by Louis Blanc in a course of lectures to working-men in the Rue Montesquieu, and in a series of letters published in the *Journal des débats* under the title "L'Organisation du travail et la question des travailleurs." As a result of these attacks he was dismissed from his chair at the Collège de France by the Provisional Government, but he was soon reinstated by a vote of the National Assembly. Two years later the three leading professors of political economy in Paris, Chevalier, Wolowski, and Blanqui were attacked by the protectionists because they lectured on the advantages of free trade. At a meeting of the Conseil Général de l'Agriculture, des Manufactures, et du Commerce, under the presidency of the protectionist Dumas, Minister of Agriculture and Commerce, the following resolution was introduced:

"That political economy be no longer taught only in the light of the theory

---

[8] M. Chevalier, *Cours d'économie politique fait au Collège de France* (Paris, 1842–50), I, 144–164 (Introductory Lecture 1847).

[9] *Élections dans le Départment de l'Aveyron, 1846,* a pamphlet giving speeches of Chevalier and Cabrol and newspaper articles on their campaign.

of free trade as it has been until now, but in the light of facts and of the legislation regulating French industries; that when he occupies a public chair and is
paid by the state the professor must refrain scrupulously from impairing in the
slightest degree respect for laws now in force; from arousing by his discourses
defiance, division, and hatred among his fellow-citizens; from attacking the
foundations of society as now constituted. Above all he must say nothing that
might encourage disobedience to the laws of the state or opposition to their en-
forcement."

Michel Chevalier replied to this attack at the meeting of the
Conseil Général, of which he was a member, in a speech which
showed the strength of his convictions. He admitted that the
professors of political economy at Paris frequently advocated free
trade and denounced protection in their lectures, because by
doing so they were teaching what they believed to be the truth
and what they thought would promote the welfare of their
country. In this they were not violating the law, as their
opponents claimed, but were merely availing themselves of the
privilege of free discussion which was recognized in all civilized
countries; and when they attacked the protective system they
did so with the assent of the Government because it had known
their views regarding the tariff when it appointed them to their
chairs at Paris. Finally, free trade could not rightly be described
as in contradiction with the French law because the Constitution
guaranteed liberty of labor to every citizen and no man could
be said to work freely unless trade was free.

"This resolution reproaches us," continued Chevalier, "with a refusal to
consider facts. What do we call facts? I do not believe there are any facts in
commercial legislation more important than the recent history of the tariff.
This history shows that the protective system, which was formerly accepted in
good faith as one of the causes of prosperity, is now recognized, even by most
governments, as being nothing but a cause of impoverishment. During the last
decade we have seen most governments, with the exception of the French, modify
broadly their tariffs and move toward the system of free trade. We have never
said that a complete change must be made immediately; far from that. We
have said that it is necessary to proceed cautiously with due consideration of the
interests involved; that the transition from the now discredited system of protection to the only good system, that of free trade, must be made gradually.
All the governments are doing this. . . .

"It is under these circumstances, when the cause of protection is morally
lost, for a cause is lost when it is opposed by the principles and experience of

nearly all peoples; it is then that you are asked, gentlemen, to endorse by your resolution this system and to compel its instruction by professors who are firmly convinced that it is wrong. The moment and the audience are badly chosen. . . . You believe yourselves strong, as you are; you have abundant capital, you are enlightened, you are regarded with the consideration felt naturally for the owners of large establishments; you are powerful, but truth is more powerful than you and principles are stronger. The protective system in France cannot be maintained intact either by the proposed resolution or by anything else. Its hour has struck in our country because other nations have given us the example of abandoning it. The breach was made by the new law on navigation voted by the English parliament on June 26, 1849. The only possible reply to this is reciprocity. After that the protective system in France will collapse like a house of cards." [10]

In 1852 Chevalier attacked the protectionist system with even greater vigor and with a thoroughness that made him the leading champion of free trade in France. In his *Examen du système commercial connu sous le nom de système protecteur*, which he had begun to write in the summer of 1851 as a reply to the attack on the tariff bill of Sainte-Beuve, he gave, for the first time, a constructive plan for the reform of the French tariff. He repeated his declaration that the change should be made gradually. The first step, he declared, should be the abolition of all prohibitions with the exception of those on gunpowder, firearms, and playing cards, which had not been imposed for commercial reasons. The Government should promptly abolish also the duties on foodstuffs and raw materials such as coal, cotton, wool, hemp, flax, silk, raw hides, and raw cast iron. This would be in accordance with the method followed by England, with the spirit of the French Tariff of 1791, and with the policy begun by Belgium after 1848. After a brief delay textile yarns and dyestuffs should be admitted free, as in England. In the interest of general production, iron and steel ought to be free, but because of the large number of manufacturers of bar-iron in France, the Government should, for the present, merely make a heavy reduction in the existing duties, abolish the distinction between iron smelted with coal and with wood, and fix the date when all

---

[10] *Moniteur*, May 13, 1850. This prints the text of the resolution and Chevalier's speech at the meeting of May 6. The resolution was passed in a modified form.

prohibitions should cease. On manufactured goods the duties which were then so high as to be prohibitive should be reduced until French industry felt foreign competition, after which further reductions should be made at intervals until the rates charged were duties for revenue only. On few products could a duty exceeding 30 per cent ever be justified. To help French industry through the period of transition the Government ought to begin at once to use extensively the power given it under the Act of 1836 to admit free all materials employed in the manufacture of goods for exportation.

" Since it would be dangerous to postpone action further I urge the Government to write into our laws the principle of free trade, provided its application is made slowly with allowance for a period of transition of sufficient length. The English took twenty-two years, beginning with Huskisson in 1824 and ending with Peel in 1846, to pass from protection, which was almost as extreme as that affecting our commercial laws and interests now, to the relatively great freedom which they enjoy at present. Let us not quibble over a few years more or less. We may take the same time for our evolution toward free trade even if England's experience could enable us to move with greater knowledge and speed and even if the manifest progress of our industries should embolden us. In any case let us begin and with determination." [11]

In closing, Chevalier quoted Napoleon, who said at St. Helena: "We should fall back upon the free navigation of the seas and the complete freedom of trade throughout the world"; [12] and he then appealed to his successor, Napoleon III, to carry out his program.

Chevalier's liberalism in economic problems did not extend to political questions. Being a former Saint-Simonian, he favored a strong government as the best instrument for the realization of economic and social reforms. The followers of Saint-Simon had planned to reorganize society on an industrial and communistic basis for what they considered the welfare of the masses and, though they did not approve of using physical force, they asserted that the heads of the new state ought to decide for what

[11] Chevalier, *Examen du système commercial connu sous le nom de système protecteur* (2d edition, Paris, 1853), pp. 311–312.

[12] *Ibid.*, and Comte de Las Cases, *Memorial de Sainte Helène* (Paris, 1842), I, 688.

work each member of the state was best fitted. The fact that such a government would inevitably be a political despotism, however benevolent in its economic and social views, did not trouble them at all.   Hence we should not share in the amazement of Chevalier's new colleagues in the Institute and of his old friends in the Société d'Économie Politique, when he openly expressed his approval of the Coup d'État by signing the register at the Élysée on December 2, 1851.[13] He never became a Bonapartist, however, and never sought high office, which he could almost certainly have obtained by a little subservience and flattery.   He chose to remain independent, but he did support the new government and render it signal service in promoting economic reforms; and his support received quick recognition, for in January, 1852, he was appointed a member of the revived Conseil d'État in the Section of Public Works, Agriculture, and Commerce, of which Magne was president.[14] He accepted the appointment, although it meant resigning his chair at the Collège de France, since no member of the Council could hold another salaried post under the Government.

Chevalier was now in a highly responsible position in the Government which gave him an opportunity to use his influence effectively in promoting tariff reforms; and it was not long before the Government showed that it meant to have the power to make such reforms.   Eleven months later, in December, 1852, the Second Empire was proclaimed and shortly afterward the Senate, which had been called in special session, adopted by a vote of 64 to 7 a decree giving the Emperor the power to sign commercial treaties without the assent of the Chambers, such treaties having the force of law with respect to any modifications of the tariff which they involved.[15] Under Article VI of the Constitution of January 14, 1852, the Prince-President had been given power to sign all treaties of peace, alliance, and commerce, and the Sénatus-Consulte of December 23 was asked

---

[13] Jules Simon, in *Journal officiel*, December 9, 1889, p. 6132.
[14] *J. des écon.*, XXXI, 228.
[15] *Ibid.* XXXIV, 74–96.   Gives the report of the Senate's commission presented by Troplong, December 21, 1852.

for only because this power had been questioned in the Corps Législatif. Like so many of the provisions of the Constitution of 1852, Article VI had its prototype in Napoleonic legislation, for the Sénatus-Consulte of the 16th Thermidor Year X (August 4, 1802) gave the First Consul the right to ratify all treaties on the advice of the Privy Council, stipulating only that they should be brought to the attention of the Senate before promulgation. Article XIV of the Charte of 1814 gave the king the right to make all treaties and the government of the Restoration assumed that it had inherited all the powers of the Empire; but the Chamber, under the leadership of Casimir Périer, voted that under Article XXXIV of the Act of December 17, 1814,[16] tariff laws could be modified without the consent of the Chambers only temporarily, or in emergencies, and that sooner or later such changes must be submitted for ratification. This decision was reluctantly accepted by Louis XVIII, and, in turn, by the July Monarchy, so that the power of the ruler to sign commercial treaties or otherwise permanently modify the tariff at his discretion remained in abeyance from the fall of the First Empire until the accession of Napoleon III. It was not used at once, even under the Second Empire, but it remained in full force on the statute book and by its exercise in 1860 the commercial treaty with England was made possible. The Emperor now had the necessary power, and in Michel Chevalier he had the statesman who saw when that power could wisely be used.

[16] *Bulletin des lois*, XLVI, 529.

CHAPTER III

THE TREATY PROPOSALS OF CHEVALIER

REPEATED efforts to improve the commercial relations of France and England had been made by diplomacy during the one hundred and forty years since the Treaty of Utrecht, yet nothing really constructive had been accomplished. Neither government seemed eager to do anything, and no expression of public opinion in France or England called for a commercial entente. The great agitation for free trade in England did win a decisive victory in 1846, but no one then urged international coöperation for the extension of the reform to other countries. The English leader, Richard Cobden, on the contrary, declared that free trade was a good thing in itself and should be sought for its own sake without any thought of compensation from other countries. England had just lowered her tariff barriers without asking the intentions of other powers. Let the continental countries follow her example and win for themselves the benefits she had gained by her own unaided efforts. This was the gospel Cobden preached when he came to France in the summer of 1846, flushed with his recent victory; but, despite the organization of the Free Trade League at Paris, his work aroused no national response and it seemed as if he had received merely the personal homage which he could justly claim, without effectively promoting the cause he sought to serve.

Yet during Cobden's visit to France there was sown the seed that bore fruit fourteen years later in the Anglo-French Treaty of Commerce. It was at the great banquet offered him by the Association for Free Trade at Paris on August 18, 1846, that Cobden met Michel Chevalier.[1] Neither of them has left us an account of the meeting, but we know that it marked the beginning of a friendship that grew ever closer until it was broken

[1] *J. des écon.*, XV, 179.

by Cobden's death. There is no record of another meeting between the two economists before Chevalier's second trip to England in October, 1859, when Cobden had already become converted to the idea of a treaty of commerce; and the correspondence between them is far from complete, owing to the loss of many of Cobden's letters. Yet from the letters which have been preserved we can trace the interchange of ideas between the Frenchman, who saw that tariff reform could be won for his country only through England's coöperation, and his friend across the Channel, who slowly yielded to his arguments until, in the autumn of 1859, he gave his services to the cause of international friendship with a zeal which undermined his health, but which secured the signature of the Treaty of 1860.

The first letters in the Cobden-Chevalier correspondence that have come down to us are all by Chevalier and begin in 1852, when he was the acknowledged leader of the free trade cause in France, and a member of the Council of State. On September 18, 1852,[2] he wrote to Cobden from his home at Lodève in the Cévennes:

" In this great cause we in France are making slight progress in official circles. Among the public we are making converts. Most of the great newspapers favor the revision of the tariff and some of them openly advocate the principle of free trade. This is a complete novelty. The Chamber of Deputies (Corps Législatif), I have reason to believe, has a strongly protectionist majority. In any event the present time differs from the reign of Louis Philippe in that the Government could overcome the opposition of the Chamber of Deputies if it really wished to. The question is, therefore, what policy the Government has in mind. The Prince-President inclines towards protection. I have made sure of this through repeated attempts to influence him towards liberty. Nevertheless he is so anxious to promote the welfare of the people that I am certain he would go very far indeed in the promotion of liberty [free trade] if he were urged to by his Ministry. Unfortunately the Cabinet is sharply divided on the question. The Minister of Finance [Bineau] is an intriguer who has close connections with the ironmasters and the owners of timber. He is our opponent. The Minister of the Interior,[3] who has influence, wavers, but is inclined to be rather suspicious of

[2] Cobden Papers M. C. D., 80–1861, p. 170. These papers are in the possession of the Cobden family in London, by whose kind permission I was given access to them.

[3] De Persigny. If this is an accurate statement of his views in 1852, they underwent a remarkable change, for the policy of partial reforms of the tariff

us. The Minister of State [Fould], whom in other respects I admire, is more inclined toward free trade than the others, largely because of his dislike of the Minister of Finance. There remains as a possibly decisive factor the question of balancing the budget. . . . However, I have noticed from various indications that the public has begun to take an interest in the question. For example, the book I published on it at the beginning of the year is already out of print."

During the autumn of 1852 Chevalier continued to write frequently to Cobden. He spoke of the attitude of the Conseils Généraux of the Departments toward tariff reform and told him how the Council of Hérault, of which he was president, voted unanimously for free trade, the three manufacturers who were members making no objection. Chevalier kept up the good work and obtained a similar vote from his Council at every annual meeting until the signature of the Treaty of 1860, and he also saw to it that the votes were reported in the Parisian press. His next long letter to Cobden was written soon after the proclamation of the Second Empire in December, 1852.[4] "The new Emperor," he wrote, "has encountered keen opponents on the part of the protectionists in the senate in preparing the Sénatus-Consulte for the revision of the constitution of January 14, 1852. They did everything possible to prevent the abolition of an article giving the Prince the power to negotiate treaties of commerce without having to submit them subsequently to the Chambers. Through the stupidity of the Minister of State, who is the leader of the senate, prominent protectionists secured places on the committee of the senate preparing the report on the proposed Sénatus-Consulte. . . . In the end the personal influence of the Emperor secured the approval by the Committee of the Sénatus-Consulte containing the article on treaties of commerce." Chevalier went on to speak of the strongly protectionist speech made by the First President of the Senate, Troplong, during the deliberations on the Sénatus-

by decree was initiated in November, 1853, while de Persigny was still Minister of the Interior, and Chevalier calls his retirement in June, 1854, a great blow to the free trade cause. After that time Chevalier always refers to de Persigny as one of the strongest champions of free trade as well as of the English alliance.

[4] Chevalier to Cobden, December 31, 1852. Cobden Papers M. C. D., 80–1861, p. 175.

Consulte, and of his reply in a letter printed in the *Journal des débats*. "I am none the less convinced," he told Cobden, "that free trade will be triumphant in France very soon. The Government is being pushed hard in that direction in spite of itself."

During the next three years Chevalier continued to write frequently, but there were no significant events in the fight for free trade in France which he could report. The policy of the Government was indecisive and variable, seeming to depend on the opinions of the minister who, at the moment, had the greatest influence over the Emperor. De Persigny evidently made up his mind that a reform of the tariff was needed, for Chevalier called his retirement from the Ministry of the Interior in June, 1854, a severe blow to the free trade cause. This was partly counteracted a few months later, however, by the appointment of de Morny,[5] an avowed free trader, as president of the Corps Législatif. The protectionists, in the meantime, had been doing their best to arouse opposition in France against England. Chevalier wrote to Cobden that they were quite as bad as the people in England who lived in constant dread of a French invasion. He suggested that the best way to combat this jingoism would be a demonstration in England in favor of reducing the duty on French wines. Cobden replied that he thought it might be a good thing to propose to Gladstone, then Chancellor of the Exchequer, the reduction of the British duty on wines to 1 franc, provided France, on her side, would so lower her tariff as to make possible the importation of English iron. Chevalier wrote in reply that the Minister of Finance approved of Cobden's plan; that he had gone so far as to write about it to Walewski, the French ambassador to England, and even to instruct an agent of the Council of State who was going to England to speak to Walewski about it.[6] The scheme came to nothing, although, unfortunately, the Cobden-Chevalier corre-

[5] Comte de Morny, son of Queen Hortense and Comte Flahault, was recognized by the Emperor, in private life, as his brother. Both he and Prince Napoleon were strong free traders and both had great influence over Napoleon III.

[6] Chevalier to Cobden, January 22, October 8, and October 15, 1853. Cobden Papers M. C. D., 80–1861, pp. 198–216.

spondence gives no explanation of its failure. England did not lower her wine duties and there is no reason to believe that the French reduction of iron duties, by the Decree of November 22, 1853, was the result of Cobden's suggestion to Chevalier.

At the beginning of 1856 the Crimean War was drawing to a close. Cobden had opposed it openly from the beginning with a courage that commands our admiration, and both he and Chevalier were eager to do anything they could to hasten the end of hostilities. They approved the alliance of France and England so far as it meant the rapprochement of the two peoples, but they felt that a true international friendship could not be based on partnership in war. They hoped that an early termination of the war would enable them to make the Franco-British alliance a truly popular one by placing it upon a foundation of peace. The chief difficulty to be overcome was England's strong desire to keep on fighting until a great British victory had been won, the capture of Sebastopol being regarded chiefly as a triumph for France. Chevalier felt that the friendship of the two peoples would be permanently strengthened if the negotiations for peace were used as an opportunity to secure a treaty of commerce, and he wrote to Cobden to urge the conclusion of such a treaty. His letters are of great significance, for they show that the first proposal of a treaty was made by him spontaneously in 1856, four years before the Cobden-Chevalier Treaty was actually signed.

Chevalier wrote that the cause of peace had almost been won in England:

"Let us profit by this to bind together the two great countries of the Occident by the ties of commerce. I repeat that we shall not enter seriously and effectively on the path of free trade, however advantageous that might be for France, except through a treaty of commerce signed with a foreign power. The Corps Législatif knows very little about these matters and is led by a number of prohibitionists, who will object to everything if the question is submitted to the Chamber, and the only way to avoid submitting it is to proceed through a treaty. The constitution expressly gives this power to the Government.

"Now you are the only power with whom a serious treaty could be made. In my opinion, it would not be necessary for you to give us special and exclusive advantages, nor for us to give any to you. It would suffice for each of the two contracting parties to make reductions in its general tariff. This would meet the objection you raise. A substantial reduction of your duty on wine would be an argument with which our government could reply to the clamor which the people might raise, and which the Corps Législatif certainly would raise, over a noteworthy reduction of our duty on iron, over the removal of the duties on coal, and over the repeal of all the prohibitions. If the Emperor would do me the honor of listening to me he would do all that. He would issue a provisional decree embodying all these things and the press would, almost unanimously, support him. The matter would be submitted to the Corps Législatif in such a way that they could not discuss it for a year and a half or two years, and then everything would be irrevocable. But I am not heard, and in this matter ineffective and unwise advice is listened to. For this reason, although no one has yet mentioned it, the only way remaining open is that of a treaty of commerce, and of a treaty with you." [7]

A few days later Chevalier wrote again:

" The present moment is an admirable one for a treaty of commerce. Your Minister of Foreign Affairs, Lord Clarendon, is coming to Paris, where he will have friendly interviews with our Minister every day. He will also see the Emperor. The most enlightened members of the Government here will realize the value of a close connection with you through commercial ties as a means of checking the anti-English propaganda people are now trying to spread. The opportunity should not be missed.

" It is true that our public is growing more enlightened and that people are much more nearly ready to repudiate the system of prohibitions than they were two or three years ago. But the official bodies cling to their prejudices and errors, and the Corps Législatif, especially, remains ardently protectionist. Our Government is not unaware of this, and it would, therefore, be likely to find the expedient of a commercial treaty acceptable.

" It seems to me that it would be a good idea for you to offer this suggestion to Lord Clarendon. He will think it over, and once he is in Paris, will see what can be done. I, on my side, will speak of it confidentially to one or two of our Ministers. You know that, in my opinion at least, it would be possible to adopt a plan whose form would meet all the objections from your side of the water; I mean, that the treaty, although concluded between England and France, would deal with the general trade of both parties, and not exclusively with their trade with each other.

" The French public would be grateful for a provision opening the British territory to our wine. The peace seems to me to make such an article possible. France could abolish the duties on coal, and reduce notably those on iron, steel, and machinery. In addition, she ought to remove all the numerous prohibitions from her tariff.

[7] Chevalier to Cobden, February 2, 1856. Cobden Papers M. C. D., 80–1861, p. 238.

" Lord Clarendon began his career by coming here to study our tariff; he would crown it worthily by helping us today to remove every deplorable obstacle to the growth of our national prosperity." [8]

Cobden replied promptly to these two letters of his friend in France, but his letter has been lost,[9] so that we can form an idea of his opinions on the matter only from a third letter of Chevalier's:

" I received yesterday your letter of the — . I beg you to note two things in regard to this subject: (1) I understand perfectly, and it would be clearly understood here, that while reducing greatly the duty on wine, the British Government leaves untouched the duties on *eaux de vie* and spirits. To us who drink Bordeaux or Burgundy the difference between wine and spirits is so great that a change in the wine duty would not seem to us to imply in any way a change in the duties on *eaux de vie* or spirits in general. (2) I am myself so thoroughly convinced of the advantages of free trade that I do not think we need compensation from you or from any other people for the removal of the innumerable prohibitions that disfigure our tariff and for the reduction or abolition of the excessive duties to be found in it. In my own eyes these measures would not be, or would be only secondarily, concessions made to the foreigner; they would be measures intrinsically and directly useful to France in a high degree, for it is the French people that suffers most heavily from the follies of protection.

" But the immense majority of the French people, though they have made considerable progress in recent years, would still regard any modification of the French tariff as a concession to the foreigner, far more than as the first recognition of a great national interest hitherto sacrificed to private interests whose existence was often only imaginary. This is why you must expect our Government, speaking from the point of view of French public opinion, to ask Lord Clarendon, when a treaty of commerce is mentioned, whether, as I hope, there is to be a big reduction in the duty on our wines; for, as a matter of fact, this is about the only change there remains for you to make. I know that Lord Clarendon could reply that the British Government has made of its own volition since 1846 what, in the protectionist language, would be called immense concessions to France; but the relations of the Government here with the protectionist party are such, and the promises made to that party in 1852 were so emphatic, that it would be very difficult for the Government to do what should be done in the direction of free trade if you, on your side, did not do something for wine. And, after all, it seems to me that if things were done gradually the financial difficulty for your Government would not be insurmountable.

---

[8] Chevalier to Cobden, February 7, 1856. Cobden Papers M. C. D., 80–1861, p. 241.

[9] This loss is probably explained by the fact that many of Chevalier's papers were burned after the death of his widow in 1913.

"Since you have told me that it would be agreeable to Lord Clarendon to see me I shall not fail to wait upon him." [10]

Chevalier's attempt to negotiate a treaty of commerce in 1856 failed because of the opposition of Lord Palmerston, the head of the British Cabinet. The fact that such an effort was made never became public, but Chevalier described what happened to a friend in Paris, in a letter written several years later.

"In 1856, while the treaty of March 30 was being negotiated, Lord Clarendon was one of the British plenipotentiaries. I was acquainted with him and knew how devoted he was to the cause of free trade. I profited by his stay in Paris to talk over with him a treaty of commerce with England, but it was quite unofficial and between ourselves. I had no diplomatic powers. I induced him to write to Lord Palmerston, who was then Minister of Foreign Affairs, to tell him that by reducing notably the duty on French wines he would touch the heart of the French Government and dispose it to modify its tariff. Lord Palmerston replied that wine in England was a luxury, that by reducing the duties on it he would diminish the revenue; in short, he refused. The matter rested there." [11]

Chevalier did not lose courage because of his failure to start negotiations for a treaty of commerce; nor did he give up his plan when the Government failed to pass its bill for the abolition of prohibitions in June, 1856. He wrote to Cobden that he was disgusted at the weakness shown by the Government in giving in so easily to the opposition of the protectionists, but he said one important result had been achieved in that the Government had at last been forced openly to oppose the supporters of prohi-

[10] Chevalier to Cobden, February 16, 1856. Cobden Papers M. C. D., 80–1861. The three letters written by Chevalier to Cobden in February, 1856, together with the other letters of Chevalier, Cobden, and Gladstone quoted in this chapter, with the exception of two of the letters of Chevalier to his wife, were published in the *Nineteenth Century and After* (London), November, 1922, in my article on "The Origins of the Anglo-French Treaty of 1860."

[11] Chevalier to M. Devinck, April 29, 1867. Flourens Papers, cahier No. 4, p. 108. The term "Flourens Papers" is used to designate the Chevalier Papers formerly in the possession of his late daughter, Mme. Émile Flourens, through whose kind permission they were inspected, and now in the possession of his granddaughter Mlle. Flourens. The letters of Chevalier to his wife in October, 1859, are in the possession of another granddaughter, Mme. Maxim Renaudin, and are here referred to as the "Renaudin Papers." Both collections of papers are in Paris.

bitions. He told Cobden that the inability of the Government to secure a substantial reform of the French tariff through legislation left a treaty of commerce as the only resource, and he said he felt it would be possible for England to make such a treaty and that he was certain it would not fail in France. Nothing could be done, however, so soon after the Government's defeat and its promise not to repeal the prohibitions before 1861, and Chevalier saw clearly he must wait for a more favorable opportunity.

Three years passed before an opportunity came to repeat the proposal of a treaty of commerce between France and England. Anglo-French relations had not been cordial during that time, for a large part of English opinion resented the conclusion of the Treaty of Paris on March 30, 1856, on the ground that it ended the war prematurely before the Russian army had been defeated in a predominantly British victory. French irritation against England was aroused by the hatching in England of Orsini's plot to assassinate the Emperor. Lord Palmerston's attempt to satisfy the French by introducing a Conspiracy Bill to prevent England from remaining the asylum of plotters like Orsini caused the fall of his Government in February, 1858. The succeeding Derby ministry was anti-French and feeling between the two countries began to run high. Many people in England thought Louis Napoleon was planning an invasion of their island and corps of volunteers were organized throughout the country. When Palmerston returned to power in June, 1859, he made no effort to improve this situation and continued the Government's support of the volunteer movement. He also advocated increased armaments and heavy expenditure for strengthening coastal fortifications. When it came to diplomacy, however, his Government tended to support France rather than Austria. But the feature of the new situation created by Palmerston's return to power, which made possible a revival of the proposed commercial negotiations with France, was the smallness of the new government's majority in Parliament. As a result of this, Lord Palmerston found himself dependent on the political support of, the Manchester School led by Cobden and Bright. Cobden refused the Prime Minister's offer of the presidency of the Board of Trade, to Chevalier's disappointment, but he remained a person of considerable influence at Downing Street.

The first step in the chain of events following the return to office of Lord Palmerston was a speech in the House of Commons on July 21, when John Bright rose to protest against the perpetual attacks on the French Government and Emperor in the British press: "Now I shall not go," he said, "into the question of whether we are really going to be invaded. I am told so much has been said about it that the French really believe we are making this outcry to cover our design of invading them." He went on to show how France had joined England against Russia in the Crimea, against China, and against Naples; and that it seemed clear that the most conspicuous desire of the Emperor ever since his accession had been to ally himself with England. The mutual suspicion of the French and English peoples was ridiculous, for the French and their Emperor were just as eager for peace as the English.

"I would say to the French Government: 'We are but twenty miles apart, yet the trade between us is nothing like what it ought to be, considering the population in the two countries, their vast increase in productive power, and their great wealth. We have certain things on this side which now bar intercourse between the two nations. We have some remaining duties which are of no consequence either for revenue or protection, which everybody here favors giving up; but they still interrupt trade between you and us. We will reconsider these and remove them. We have also an extraordinarily heavy duty upon one of the greatest products of the soil of France — upon the light wines of your country.' The only persons with whom the French Emperor cannot cope are the monopolists of his own country. If he could offer to his nation thirty million English people as customers, would not that give him an irresistible power to make changes in the French tariff which would be as advantageous to us as they would be to his own country? I do believe that if that were honestly done, done without any diplomatic finesse, and without obstacles being attached to it that would make its acceptance impossible, it would bring about a state of things history would pronounce to be glorious." [12]

Bright's purpose in making this speech was to relieve the existing tension in Franco-British relations by means of a notable

[12] Hansard's Parliamentary Debates, III Series, Vol. CV.

reduction in the remaining duties in the British tariff, many of which bore heavily on French goods. Though he hoped that such spontaneous action by England would induce Napoleon III to lower some of his duties on British goods, he did not propose to make British action contingent on reciprocal concessions by France. He stated his position clearly when it was challenged by Lords Palmerston and John Russell, and he denied any intention of proposing a treaty of commerce. But Chevalier had once before proposed a treaty of commerce and was only waiting for a favorable opportunity to do so again. When he read Bright's speech he felt that the time for action had come and he said so in his next letter to Cobden. He did not meet Cobden on his brief trip to England in August, 1859, but he continued to urge his views by correspondence.[13] Cobden objected that a treaty was opposed to the principles on which the great English tariff reform of 1846 had been based. These required, said he, that all nations be treated alike in commercial matters, whereas a treaty with France would constitute a private agreement by England with that country alone. But Chevalier persuaded him that the treaty could be so framed that England would extend to all nations the modifications in her tariff which she conceded to France, whereas France would make reductions in favor of England only.[14]

Cobden was impressed by Chevalier's arguments and promptly consulted the only member of the Government in whom he had complete confidence. On September 5, he wrote to Gladstone, who had resumed his old post as Chancellor of the Exchequer: "The fact is I wish to have a little talk with you about the trade with France. My good friend M. Chevalier insists very

[13] Chevalier in his letter to Bonamy Price of January 8, 1869, printed in an appendix in Price's *The Principles of Currency* (Oxford, 1869), says that he did see Cobden in England in August, 1859; but Cobden, in a letter to Chevalier on September 14, 1859, printed in Frond's *Panthéon des illustrations françaises du XIXᵉ siècle* (Paris, 1869), Vol. XVI, says: "I was sorry to miss seeing you in England." I accept the statement in the contemporary letter as being the more accurate.

[14] Chevalier to Bonamy Price, January 8, 1869. A manuscript copy of the letter in the hand of Chevalier's daughter, Mme. Paul Leroy-Beaulieu, who generally acted as his secretary, is in the Flourens Papers.

pertinaciously that the Emperor cannot reduce his duties unless you help him by a corresponding movement. How you are to do so and fulfil Lord Clarence Paget's promise to keep fifty line-of-battle ships, I don't know! My daughters are in Paris and I shall spend a part of the winter there, and if I can be of any use to you in the way of inquiry I shall be glad." [15] Two days later Gladstone replied with a cordial invitation and on the 12th Cobden was at Hawarden. [16] Gladstone shared the dislike of Cobden and the other English free traders for commercial treaties because these had always been restricted bargains; but he also remembered that his master Peel had been prepared to negotiate such treaties if they promised to lead to constructive tariff reforms. He felt that Chevalier's suggestion offered an opportunity for a really constructive treaty of broad scope and said promptly that it ought to be acted upon. [17]

Cobden was impressed by Gladstone's advice, as he had been by Chevalier's, but again was not wholly convinced of its wisdom. His orthodoxy in questions of free trade was too strong to be so quickly abandoned, even when such a change of attitude would further another cause dear to his heart, the promotion of international peace. His state of mind on leaving Hawarden is reflected in the letter he wrote to Chevalier the next day from Manchester:

" It would of course be agreeable to me to see your Ministers of State. But I attach very little importance to such interviews; for there is always a latent suspicion that I, as an Englishman, in recommending other governments to adopt free trade principles am merely pursuing a selfish British policy. Thus my advice is deprived of all weight and even my facts are doubted. Now, the honest truth is, that I feel no present solicitude for an extension of our foreign trade,

[15] Cobden to Gladstone, September 5, 1859. Gladstone Papers. Permission to see the papers of Mr. Gladstone, at Hawarden, was kindly given by the Gladstone trustees.

[16] Gladstone says in his diary, September 12, 1859: " Mr. Cobden arrived. Several hours walk and talk with him; " September 13: " Further conversation with Mr. Cobden on tariff relations with France. We closely and warmly agreed." These entries were copied for me by Mr. Henry Gladstone's secretary, since the diary is not open to inspection.

[17] John Morley, *The Life of Richard Cobden* (London, 1879), pp. 702–705. See also John Morley, *The Life of William Ewart Gladstone* (3 vols. in 2, London, 1911), II, 18–21; J. A. Hobson, *Richard Cobden, the International Man* (London, 1918), p. 243.

in so far as the material or pecuniary interests of this country are concerned. We have as much to do as we can accomplish. It is very difficult to manage matters with the working classes owing to the great demand for their labor. I am afraid we shall have 'strikes' in all directions, and if we were to have any sudden and great expansion of demand from abroad, it would probably throw the relations of capital and labor into great confusion. Therefore, I repeat, we have no necessity for opening new markets in France or elsewhere with a view to promoting our material prosperity, *the only limit to which is the supply of labor and raw material.*

"But on totally different grounds I should be glad to see a removal of the impediments our foolish legislation interposes to the intercourse between the two countries. I see no other hope but in such a policy for any permanent improvement in the political relations of France and England. I utterly despair of finding peace and harmony in the efforts of Governments and diplomatists. The *people* of the two Nations must be brought into mutual dependence by supplying each other's wants. There is no other way of counteracting the antagonism of language and race. It is God's own method of producing an *entente cordiale*, and no other plan is worth a farthing. It is with this view that I hope to see our Government greatly reduce the duties on wines and other French products. And it is only with this view that I feel any interest about your following our example. If I thought I could promote a similar spirit in any of your statesmen, I should be very glad to have an interview with them. But to have any chance of success it is necessary that they should previously understand that I am not a *commis voyageur* travelling abroad for the sale of British fabrics." [18]

Less than a month after his talk with Gladstone and his letter to Chevalier in which he never mentioned a treaty of commerce, Cobden was an ardent advocate of Chevalier's plan. Few of his letters at this time have been preserved and those do not discuss economic principles or the question of the French treaty. It seems probable, therefore, that long reflection and further letters from Chevalier sufficed to induce Cobden to abandon his rigidly orthodox principles regarding free trade. As soon as he had abandoned them, however, he threw himself with enthusiasm into the cause and Chevalier was obliged to urge restraint and moderation where he had formerly tried to convince and encourage. On October 9, the two friends met in London, Chevalier having come, ostensibly, to preside over the meeting at Bradford of a society working for the adoption of the metric

---

[18] The full text of this letter was printed in Frond, *op. cit.*, Vol. XVI. It was written by Cobden to Chevalier on September 14, 1859. The greater part of the letter is quoted by Hobson.

system in England, although the true object of his visit was the negotiation of the treaty of commerce. He remained only thirteen days in England, but in that brief period he secured the acceptance of his plan by the Chancellor of the Exchequer, together with an offer of tariff concessions by England which could serve as a basis for negotiation, and he also won the support of Bright and de Persigny. The letters he wrote to his wife almost daily during his trip were, fortunately, preserved by her, so that an account of these preliminary negotiations can be based on the contemporary evidence of Chevalier himself.

On the day of his arrival in London Chevalier wrote to Mme. Chevalier that he had just received the visit of his witty, kind, and loyal friend Cobden. They spent most of the day together and thought of going to Tunbridge Wells to see de Persigny, but had to give up the idea. They talked about free trade, English policy, and that of the Emperor, of whom Cobden declared himself a strong supporter. Chevalier wrote to his wife that he was eager to have the Emperor see Cobden, for he was sure that his friend would have a strong influence on Napoleon. Cobden, on his side, was eager to have Chevalier go to Rochdale to get the advice of Bright, who wanted to get in touch with him.[19]

The support of Bright was easily won, for Cobden had often spoken to him of his correspondence with Chevalier, and on his request Bright sent the French statesman a cordial invitation to come to see him. This Chevalier did on the 13th and next day he wrote to Mme. Chevalier:

"He is heartily in favor of the plan I have for reducing the French customs duties, while, at the same time, calling for great concessions on the part of England. He will support the scheme in Parliament. He wants the duty on wines to be reduced to one sixth of its present amount, and in this he is entirely disinterested for he drinks only water. He is so thoroughly convinced of the benefits of free trade that he calls it 'The Faith.' For him it is a religion." [20]

Meantime Cobden had arranged for an interview between Chevalier and Gladstone, and had then gone to see Lord Palmerston and Lord John Russell, the foreign secretary. The Prime

[19] Chevalier to Mme. Chevalier, October 9, 1859. Renaudin Papers.
[20] October 14, 1859.

Minister gave his consent to the proposed negotiations in Paris, and Lord John approved the plan, offered the friendly services of the British Embassy in Paris, and wrote to Gladstone that the matter could be brought before the Cabinet whenever he wished.[21] By this time Chevalier had returned to London, and on the 15th he met Gladstone. He wrote to his wife on the following day:

"Yesterday I spent the day well. I had another and a long interview with Cobden, and one of the utmost importance with Gladstone. I believe I shall have rendered a great service to the Emperor if —. Details tomorrow. I must leave for the country — I'm going to Ascot [to see the great free trader Benjamin Smith, M.P.], then I return here tomorrow to complete what has been begun so happily — complete it in so far as it depends upon those here."

Next day he continued:

"I was well satisfied with what I had done whether by my own efforts or through my friends and I remain so after reflection. If this is accomplished — and there is lacking only the consent of a single person, the one most interested of all in seeing it adopted — it will be the greatest thing I have done in my whole life. On Thursday I am to see a certain person [de Persigny] on the subject and day after tomorrow I shall dine with several people who will give their support." [22]

Chevalier never wrote the promised details regarding his decisive interview with Gladstone to his wife, but he has left us a full account in a letter written twelve years later to Gladstone himself. He began by reproaching Gladstone for omitting, in a recent speech, his name as one of the authors of the Treaty of 1860, when he had mentioned the Emperor Napoleon III, Cobden and himself.

"On the evening of Saturday, October 15, 1859, there was an interview at your official residence between you and a Frenchman, an interview arranged by Cobden. This Frenchman said to you: 'I am, as you know, a free trader who has never despaired of success in his country. I believe that the time has come. I have not been sent by the Emperor, who does not know that I am in England. But various circumstances make me believe that at the present moment he would accept the proposal of a treaty of commerce with you by which, availing himself of the power given him by the constitution to act without the coöperation of the Chambers, he would abolish all the prohibitions affecting English goods and

---

[21] Russell to Gladstone, October 15, 1859. Gladstone Papers.
[22] October 16 and 17, 1859. Renaudin Papers.

replace them by duties of approximately thirty per cent; provided that you, on your side, reduce heavily the duties on wines and abolish the duties on silk goods, articles of fashion, gloves, etc.' You asked this Frenchman if he was sure the Emperor could legally sign a treaty without any legislative sanction, and he assured you that the Emperor could do so. You then told him what you were prepared to do for manufactured goods and for wines. It was very broad and liberal.[23]

" On leaving you he went to find Cobden who was waiting for him at the Athenaeum and who was very much pleased. On Monday both left to meet again in Paris. They saw the Emperor separately on the same day, made to him the proposal which he accepted while enjoining secrecy from his own ministers except two. The treaty resulted from this after a series of conferences at which this Frenchman was present and in which he took an active part. Cobden never doubted that in everything done to get these negotiations under way this Frenchman played a part equal to his own. This opinion is accepted by the majority of your compatriots who know about the matter. After the treaty the Emperor made him a Senator and a Grand Officer of the Legion of Honor. This Frenchman, my dear and illustrious colleague[24], was my humble self. I even had to convert Cobden to the idea of a treaty of commerce which at first was repugnant to him.

" In your speech of June 14 and in others before it you refrained from mentioning my name among those of the authors and initiators of the treaty. I attribute this to your having thought that when I came to London in October, 1859, I was merely obeying an order from the Emperor. The supposition is plausible, but the truth is that in this case I had no orders except those which I gave myself. I do not speak in this way to disparage the Emperor. He was then very well disposed; he rendered a very great service to the good cause. Now he is unfortunate and calumniated. But the fact is that while personally he contributed much to the treaty, he did not take the initiative, and in this I am justified in claiming an important part. Pray consult your own memory." [25]

Cobden had seen de Persigny before Chevalier returned to London from Bradford on October 14. On the 20th, Chevalier himself saw the ambassador, whose support he felt to be essential for the success of his plan, for de Persigny was one of the few men who were so intimate with Louis Napoleon that they dared to speak freely to him. He had been a faithful supporter of the

---

[23] Gladstone agreed to all the concessions asked for by Chevalier and said England would reduce the duty on French wine from 6s. to 2s. per gallon. See Chevalier to Price, January 8, 1869. Flourens Papers.

[24] Gladstone was a corresponding member of the Institut de France.

[25] Chevalier to Gladstone, June 19, 1872. Gladstone Papers.

Emperor during the long years of his exile and imprisonment. He was, furthermore, known to be in favor of tariff reform in France and he had had a share in initiating the policy of partial reforms by decree which began in November, 1853, when he was still Minister of the Interior. Chevalier wrote to his wife from de Persigny's office immediately after the interview: "But it was not he who needed to be convinced. He will surely be at Paris during the festivities at Compiègne. And then! And then! —." [26]

Chevalier had thus secured all the support he could hope for in England and, as his letters show, he appreciated the importance of his success. But now, on the eve of his return to his own country, he began to think of the far greater obstacles which must be overcome there, and, in particular, he felt grave concern over the uncertainty of the nature of the Emperor's reception of his plan, for he knew that nothing could be done in France without the Emperor's approval. He had assumed a grave responsibility in opening even wholly unofficial negotiations with the British Chancellor of the Exchequer, for the repudiation of his action by Napoleon III would probably make any commercial negotiations between France and England impossible for some time to come. On the 21st he wrote to Madame Chevalier from London:

"We shall see what the result of this will be. The best plans often fail. The obstacles seem to have been removed, but mere chance, the thoughtlessness of one man, or the whim of another may ruin everything. I have no illusions. I shall have done my duty. No one will be able to say that I have worked in my own interest. I have been much pleased with Auguste [his brother]. He wanted to leave Paris in order to come here. I stopped him yesterday by a telegram." [27]

From the 22d until the 27th of October, Chevalier was in Paris securing the acceptance of his plan by Rouher, the Minister of Commerce, and the Emperor. On his arrival in France he wrote to his wife who was complaining of his long absence:

[26] October 20, 1859. Renaudin Papers.

[27] Auguste Chevalier was private secretary to Louis Napoleon from the beginning of his presidency until the Coup d'État. In 1859 he was a deputy.

" Through my friends and by my own efforts I have succeeded in negotiating unofficially with the English Government a treaty of commerce which should be an event in the history of our country, and a most happy one. I have not yet seen anyone here about it. M. de P'y [de Persigny] is strongly in favor of the plan and will come over to use his influence. I could not see M. Rouher this morning. When I reached the Ministry it was nearly ten o'clock and he had already left for St. Cloud. — If the Emperor neglected this opportunity it would be a grave mistake."

On the next day he wrote that Cobden, who had come to Paris on the 18th, had received a splendid letter from Gladstone. "The game has opened extremely well. I shall speak of the matter to M. Rouher tomorrow morning. —— I am wondering whether I ought not to see the Emperor to tell him of the state of public opinion in England. But I feel little inclination to see him for the present. I will come home in a few days, but must first put Cobden in touch with Rouher, and probably with Fould." On the 24th he continued: "I am still here in the midst of the whirlpool. M. Rouher has urged me to see the Emperor. He thinks the plan is useful. I have agreed to follow his advice, although I did not want to because it might keep me here a day or two longer, — I had other objections also. I have written to M. Mocquard [the Emperor's private secretary] and await the reply. I saw Cobden again today. He is to dine this evening with M. Feray, an ardent prohibitionist. One of them will eat the other, said M. Rouher, or else there will be nothing left but their tails. I am giving a private dinner to Rouher and Cobden only tomorrow." [28]

The decisive interviews of Chevalier and Cobden with the Emperor took place at St. Cloud on October 27.[29] Cobden has left us several long accounts of his audience in his journal and in letters to Lord Palmerston, Bright, and Chevalier. After discussing Anglo-French relations, which both Cobden and the Emperor agreed had reached a dangerous state of hostility, Cobden approached the subject of a commercial treaty. He wrote to Lord Palmerston:

---

[28] These letters of October 22, 23, and 24, 1859, are in the Renaudin Papers.
[29] Chevalier to Mme. Chevalier. Renaudin Papers.

" I then started to insist on the necessity of putting the two countries on a plane of mutual commercial dependence. We talked over an hour. I fear I talked too much, but Napoleon listened attentively and his comments made me believe he is well disposed towards free trade. I had heard he was before, even his enemies say so. But I find him badly informed; hence he fears the protectionists and exaggerates their number, power, and influence. He says they are a majority of the Senate and Législatif. He says the only means to effect the change is through a treaty with a foreign power which would be given the force of law by an imperial decree. He asked if England wanted a treaty. I said that England could not give France any exclusive advantage, but would agree to modify her tariff and incorporate the changes in a treaty, if this would help the Emperor to act. I said that probably next year Gladstone could reach an agreement with him for reciprocal reductions of tariffs. I announced as probable the free admission of ' Articles de Paris '! This made the Emperor smile and say that he had promised the manufacturers not to touch the protective system before 1861. I said that even if the treaty were signed next year some clauses need not take effect for two or three years; that the mere moral effect of a new commercial policy would be most important.

" Napoleon asked what I would do in his place. I said I would attack, as I had done in England, the article which was the keystone of the whole system; that is, French iron. I would admit pig iron free and possibly leave a small duty on bars and plates. I would silence the opposition of the iron masters through a Commission to grant an indemnity raised through a special loan. I could then deal with the other industries whose general complaint is that they cannot compete with England owing to the high price of iron and coal (I am told there will not be much difficulty in making coal free). The Emperor asked me for a list of the French articles imported into England on which we would reduce our duties. I gave this later through a note to Rouher. Napoleon asked if much land was left uncultivated after the abolition of the Corn Laws. I said that on the contrary agriculture had improved. He spoke of his veneration for the name of Peel. Napoleon cried: ' Je serais enchanté et flatté de l'idée d'accomplir la même œuvre en France; mais les difficultés sont bien grandes. Nous ne faisons pas de réformes en France; nous ne faisons que des révolutions.' Napoleon then alluded to the opposition of the Protectionists to several small reforms as the free admission of iron for ship building and the suppression of the sliding scale [on cereals]. I was struck by his fear of a small group of monopolists revealed by these allusions. Like all Frenchmen I know, except my friend Chevalier, the Emperor seems to lack moral courage. I got from this interview the impression that the Emperor, if let alone, would immediately adopt a free trade policy; but as he thinks there are many difficulties in the way I can't be sure what he will do. But Chevalier, who had an audience just before me, is most hopeful. I was careful to explain that I acted in my own name only and had no official powers. I am communicating all this to Lord Cowley [the British ambassador to France] from whom I have received great courtesy and kind-ness." [30]

It has been assumed by most writers that Cobden, in his audience on October 27, converted the Emperor to the idea of a commercial treaty with England; and as time passed and the negotiations proceeded toward their successful conclusion, Cobden began to believe that he had done so. Chevalier was gradually relegated to the position of a helpful adviser; the fact that he had been the first to propose the treaty and had actually had to convert Cobden himself was forgotten; and the document signed on January 23, 1860, became commonly known as the "Cobden Treaty." Three reasons may be given for this general failure to appreciate the part played by Chevalier. In the first place, Chevalier left no written account of his interview with the Emperor on October 27; and his letters describing the negotiations in general were chiefly private communications to friends, and the few that were published were printed in books on other subjects, and, therefore, attracted little attention. In the second place, Chevalier never took an important part officially in the negotiations. He never held the rank of pleni-potentiary and did not sign the treaty, and he attended the few formal meetings of the plenipotentiaries only as a technical adviser to the British negotiators. Finally, the Treaty of 1860 was signed for France through an act of autocratic power in violation of public opinion and in defiance of the well-known views of the majorities in both houses of the French Parliament. The Treaty was not, therefore, generally popular in France and even of the considerable body of people who had wanted a re-form of the French tariff, a large number disapproved of the manner in which the change was actually made. Thus, while Cobden became once more a national hero in England, Chevalier received little praise and much abuse in France.

[30] Cobden to Lord Palmerston, October 29, 1859. Cobden Papers. Cobden assumes that the Emperor's fear of the protectionists was excessive and due to lack of moral courage, yet the tariff history of the Second Empire shows how formidable their opposition was and also that Napoleon III was the first French ruler since 1815 who had really tried to meet that opposition.

It is important to note, in connection with the acceptance by
the Emperor on October 27 of the plan for negotiating a commercial treaty with England, that Cobden's audience did not
take place until three o'clock in the afternoon, whereas Chevalier
was received in the morning. Cobden states in his letters to
Lord Palmerston and Gladstone [31] written two days later that
Chevalier was the first to see the Emperor. On Chevalier's
side we have no letters written soon after the interview which
give any account of the conversation or name the time. Chevalier wrote to his wife merely that the interview had been successful and that he was leaving for home at once. But a few months
after the signature of the Treaty Chevalier met the English
economist Nassau Senior at a party in honor of the event. In
reply to Senior's request for an account of the history of the
treaty negotiations Chevalier said:

" Cobden and I had long been in correspondence as to the means of improving
the commercial relations of our countries. I always told him that it could be
effected only by a treaty as the Legislature is ultra-protectionist. He met me at
the railway terminus when I reached London last October to attend the Bradford meeting, told me that this was the time to make the attempt, that the
long annuities had just fallen in [32] and that he had seen Gladstone, who said that
he was resolved that the money thereby saved should not fall into the gulf
of a constantly increasing expenditure. He introduced me to Bright and to
Gladstone, both of whom I found earnest in the cause. On my return to Paris
I consulted Rouher, Fould, and Baroche. I found them ready to coöperate with
me. Cobden came to Paris, and it was agreed that on the 27th of October [33]
I should see the Emperor at eleven o'clock, and open the matter to him, and that
Cobden should see him at three the same day. I related to the Emperor the
substance of my conversation with Gladstone. I said that I had had no previous
communication on the subject with any of the ministers, that mine was a totally
unauthorized proceeding, and would fall to the ground without inconvenience
if His Majesty disapproved it. The Emperor received the proposal favorably,
and it was determined that, on this side of the water, no one should be admitted
to the secret except the Emperor, Rouher, Fould, Baroche, myself, Cobden, and
Lord Cowley. Walewski was peculiarly excluded from it. When we had settled

---

[31] Cobden to Gladstone, October 29, 1859. Gladstone Papers.

[32] These amounted to £2,000,000.

[33] Senior gives the date as October 24, which I assume to be a misprint,
since there are many in his book. Chevalier's letter to his wife, which was
written in his own hand immediately after his audience, proves that the correct
date is October 27.

the articles of the Treaty, of course it became necessary to tell Walewski, but it was then too late for him to interfere."

Senior asked: "It is not true then, as we have been told, that the Emperor proposed to us the treaty, in the hope of reconciling us to the annexation of Savoy?" Chevalier replied: "Utterly false. The Emperor never thought on the subject until Cobden and I suggested it to him. Perhaps he may have adopted our suggestion more readily because he thought it would please England. But I am sure that he also thinks it will be useful to France. Not having studied the subject he is naturally a free-trader, for free-trade is the obvious common-sense doctrine — protection is artificial." [34]

The statements of Chevalier show that he induced the Emperor to accept his plan for a commercial treaty before Cobden was admitted to his audience; and they also indicate that little argument was required to obtain the Emperor's consent and that, therefore, Napoleon III was not really converted at this time by anyone. Had the Emperor then been strongly protectionist it is not probable that Rouher would have urged Chevalier and Cobden to submit their plan to him, nor would he have been likely himself to express his approval. The whole course of the subsequent negotiations shows that the Emperor's ministers never dared to take the initiative in a matter of importance and there seems little question, therefore, that Rouher would either have discouraged the two economists or have declined to give them any assistance had he known his master to be opposed to any far-reaching reform of the French tariff. Rouher's conduct indicates that he believed Napoleon III to be in favor of such a reform, but that he did not know whether he would approve a proposal for making it by means of a treaty with England. This would explain his giving Chevalier and Cobden every encouragement and then waiting at the palace in obvious anxiety to learn what his master had said to them.

It is generally believed that the Emperor's motives in consenting to the commercial treaty were political, and there can be no

[34] Nassau Senior, *Conversations with M. Thiers, M. Guizot, and Other Distinguished Persons during the Second Empire* (2 vols. London, 1878), II, 314–315.

doubt that a desire for the English alliance was an important cause of his decision. It is clear that he desired England's sympathy, and, if possible, her active coöperation in his Italian policy. Austria had been defeated only a few months before at Solferino and negotiations for peace were then being conducted at Zurich. Prussia was opposed to the Italian war and to the unification of Italy, while England, under Palmerston, Russell, and Gladstone, was inclined to favor Italian aspirations; but she was suspicious of French intentions and strongly disapproved of the proposed annexation of Savoy. A commercial alliance between France and England would tend to draw the two countries together, moderate the mutual suspicion of their peoples, and make coöperation in Italy possible. Walewski, who was not in sympathy with the Emperor's Italian policy, had lost his master's confidence, as was shown by his exclusion from a knowledge of the secret commercial negotiations until the middle of December, 1859, when he could no longer offer effective opposition, and by his replacement two weeks later as Minister of Foreign Affairs by Baroche, who favored both the Italian and commercial policies of Napoleon. Finally, the Emperor had often said that his uncle was overthrown by the opposition of England, and that he favored replacing the policy of the First Empire by an English alliance.

But it does not seem to me to have been shown that the Emperor's motives in approving the plan for a commercial treaty with England were exclusively political. It has been said that before his advent to power he was strongly protectionist, but this assertion seems to be based wholly on a pamphlet on the sugar industry written when Louis Napoleon was a prisoner in the fortress of Ham and when anything he said or wrote was an appeal for popular sympathy. The writing of one such pamphlet is not positive evidence that the future emperor was strongly in favor of protection as a general policy. Ten years later, shortly before the proclamation of the Second Empire, Chevalier wrote to Cobden that Napoleon inclined towards protection, but was ready to adopt any policy that would promote the welfare of the masses in France. Within less than a year the new sovereign had issued the first of a series of decrees reducing tariff duties on foodstuffs and raw materials, and three years later his government introduced the bill to abolish prohibitions. These could hardly have been the acts of a ruler opposed to tariff reform, nor could they have been performed by his ministers without his knowledge and approval. On the other hand, Chevalier's statement to Senior in 1860 that "not having studied the subject he is naturally a free-trader" is open to criticism. The Emperor must have thought about the subject before consenting to a commercial policy which was so vigorously pursued, and Chevalier in 1852 stated that he had often talked with him about it. The truth would appear to be that Louis Napoleon had no economic principles and that his commercial policy was determined partly by considerations of foreign policy and partly by his well-known solicitude for the welfare of the working classes.

The acceptance by the Emperor of the idea of a commercial treaty with England did not commit his government to the negotiation of the treaty, nor did it insure the signature of the treaty if negotiations were begun. Napoleon III was as fearful of incurring political opposition on some occasions as he was recklessly defiant on others, and in the autumn of 1859 he was pursuing an Italian policy which had alienated many of his supporters in France and was certain to antagonize many more. It was impossible, therefore, to predict how often the Emperor would change his mind regarding the English treaty, and whether any such change would not prove fatal to the negotiations. But his acceptance of the idea enabled Cobden and Chevalier to begin unofficial conversations with the Emperor's ministers and through them to bring great pressure to bear on their master. Though similar conversations had been held before, this occasion offered a far greater chance of success than any previous one because the French Government now had the power to impose its will on a hostile parliament.

CHAPTER IV

THE UNOFFICIAL NEGOTIATIONS AT PARIS

THE acceptance of the idea of a treaty of commerce with England by the Emperor on October 27, 1859, gave Cobden and Chevalier the opportunity they sought of discussing their plan with those of the French ministers who were favorably disposed. It thus opened up great possibilities, but it did not give any assurance of success, for the Emperor had not committed himself in any way to the negotiation of a commercial treaty. His acceptance of the idea signified merely that, at the moment, he approved the plan that had been put before him. It did not show, either that he was determined that the plan should succeed in spite of the opposition, which was certain to be formidable, or that he would not change his mind before serious negotiations had begun.

Cobden felt keenly the uncertainty of the situation and believed that the Emperor's approval signified little or nothing. He showed this in a letter he wrote to Chevalier, who was then far away at Lodève.

" It seems to me," said Cobden, " that we have not yet taken the first step in the practical realization of your hopes. I don't think anybody is seriously occupied in even preparing the way for something being done. I saw Fould on Saturday (after I had written you) by an appointment made for me by Lord Cowley. He [Fould], who had been in the morning shooting with the Emperor, told me that he [the Emperor] had been satisfied with my audience with him, and had ' gained some courage ' — and that he [Fould] and I and Rouher were to talk over some details together on an early day.

" To-day,[1] I had occasion, by accident, to see Fould on another subject, and afterwards we talked again on the old topic — when he expressed his doubts whether a treaty was the right way of going to work, whether it would not be better to make it a legislative measure, in connection with which, among other

---

[1] Cobden to Chevalier. " Confidential," Monday, October 31, 1859. Flourens Papers.

64

things, he said, you could then speak and advocate reforms! (How I envy you your audience!) When I saw the Emperor he told me that the only way in which he could do anything was by ' decree ' through a treaty, and to hear, now, the opposite story from his first minister, is rather odd. Then again, to-day, he made difficulties about him and Rouher and myself meeting, fearing it could not be kept a secret. This, after it was, as I thought, understood on Saturday, that we three should talk it over, is certainly rather ' *léger* ' and ' *insouciant.*' I now draw into my shell. Any further initiative from me will only be misunderstood. I wish de Persigny could come across the channel — But I suppose he is kept in London by these endless diplomatic squabbles about comparative trifles — A determined, honest, earnest man is wanted among the ' *entourage* ' which does not much please me. I have often been thinking of Oxenstiern's saying — ' Go forth my son, and see with how little wisdom the world is governed.'

" What can I say to Gladstone? Here is an offer, which, if not embraced, can never be made again; — an opportunity for removing the whole duty off every article of French manufacture imported into England, $\frac{5}{6}$ of the wine duty, and brandy lowered to the excise on English spirits. If our tariff were handed over to you to do as you like, what could you do more? Am I to go back and say this offer is treated with indifference or suspicion? At least, you must come and let me know that it has been seriously considered, and let it be known that the initiative, which was so promptly responded to on our side, came from yourself. — There is more dependent on this than many wise people here are aware of. The political and commercial atmosphere is charged with dangerous elements — Nothing but a decisive change in the policy of your government will convince the world that it is in security — and a bold step in commercial reform is the only way. — Put this in the fire, I am writing to you as I would write to no one else."

A week later Chevalier was back in Paris, and almost immediately the situation changed. On November 7, he gave Cobden encouraging news regarding the attitude of the Emperor and Fould, and the next day Cobden wrote in his diary: [2]

" Saw Fould who said he had just come from the Emperor who desired him to tell me that he had not required to be convinced of the truth of my commercial principles; that he was satisfied of their soundness and, both on economic and political grounds, was anxious to carry out my views; that my proposal had received his most serious consideration, and he had ordered some documents to be prepared which would enable him to form an opinion of the effects which

---

[2] Cobden's Diary, Vol. I, November 7 and 8, 1859. Cobden Papers. The diary was begun October 18, 1859, the day Cobden left for Paris, and was continued until after the signature of the last Tariff Convention, November 16, 1860.

the changes proposed would have on the public interest in France. Fould expressed great anxiety to carry out a reform in their tariff; — and he stated his opinion that the only way to do this was by a commercial treaty with England."

Chevalier rendered further service to the cause by sending, on November 8 and 9, two long letters to the *Journal des débats*,[3] in which he said that his recent trip to England had convinced him that England's aims were only peaceful. It was necessary for England to have a fleet larger than that of any other power, or probable combination of powers, in order that she might protect her maritime trade, without which she could not live. But England, continued Chevalier, was now using her fleet purely for defense, as had been shown by her recognition of the rights of neutrals at the Congress of Paris, in 1856. Her recent increase of armaments should not, therefore, cause either alarm or impatience. England had no idea of attacking France, and her present Government had declared openly in favor of the French alliance as the best guarantee of peace.

Chevalier's letters produced an excellent impression in England, where their appearance was greeted by a chorus of approval from the liberal press. No one was better pleased than Cobden, who sent Chevalier his congratulations and his thanks for his labor in promoting the cause of international peace, which was the main object for which they both were working in their efforts to negotiate a treaty of commerce.[4] Cobden wrote from London, where he had returned on November 10,[5] to attend to private business arising from his unfortunate investment in the stock of the Illinois Central Railroad. He spent a week in England, and during that time, through letters and interviews, discussed fully with Gladstone the prospect for serious negotiations at Paris. Cobden urged Gladstone to abolish all the remaining duties on French manufactures, and to reduce the duty on wine to 1s. per gallon, and that on spirits to a rate

[3] See *Journal des débats*, November 8 and 9, 1859.
[4] Cobden to Chevalier, November 14, 1859. Flourens Papers.
[5] Cobden's diary shows that he left Paris November 9, and, after being delayed by a storm reached London on the evening of the tenth. See to the contrary John Morley, *The Life of Richard Cobden* (London, 1879), I, 717.

corresponding to the excise tax on home-made spirits. "If the Emperor is to do anything great you must supply him with this motive," said Cobden; "and, with this excuse to his own people, and with the sympathy and aid it would bring him from Paris, Lyons, and the wine region, he could do anything he liked in the way of the reduction of duties with safety to himself." [6] Gladstone replied that he was eager to coöperate fully with Cobden in the negotiation of a commercial treaty, but that he feared he could not grant a uniform duty on wine lower than 3*s.* per gallon. The only way to secure a lower duty, he thought, would be to establish a classification of wines on the basis of their alcoholic content, with a corresponding scale of duties ranging from 1*s.* 6*d.* per gallon on common wines to 3*s.* 6*d.* on wines containing 40 per cent alcohol. The duty on brandy probably could not be brought below 10*s.*, which was 2*s.* more than the British excise, but represented a reduction of 50 per cent.

Cobden was back in Paris on November 18, but was confined for many days to his bed and for three weeks to his house. His illness did not, however, prevent him from carrying on the commercial negotiations. A few hours after his arrival Chevalier called and told him that the Emperor was still anxious to negotiate, and that Rouher and Fould wanted to see Cobden before making a further report to their sovereign. On the 20th,[7] Cobden wrote in his Diary:

[6] Cobden to Gladstone, November 11, 1859. Cobden Papers. The diary shows that Cobden saw Gladstone on the tenth and twelfth in London. On the seventeenth he had a talk with de Persigny at Newhaven before taking the boat for Dieppe.

[7] There is a confusion of dates here. Cobden in his letter to Gladstone, dated November 21, speaks of having seen no one but Chevalier since his return, but of having agreed to receive Rouher and Fould in bed the next day (November 22). In a letter to Chevalier, dated November 22, Cobden speaks of this interview as occurring on the previous day (November 21). He thus gives three different dates for the same interview. The letter to Gladstone which I saw was a copy made at the direction of Mrs. Cobden after her husband's death; but the letter to Chevalier of November 22 is in Cobden's own hand. The diary also was copied. It is probable, therefore, that the interview took place November 21, as stated in Cobden's letter to Chevalier, the most authentic source.

" Received Rouher and Fould in bed. The former came with papers prepared to go through the items of the French tariff in order to get from me an opinion as to the changes our Government would expect to have made in the treaty. But, as I was not able to do so much, I explained in a general way the kind of reform I should advise. I urged the policy of bringing down all their duties gradually to the point which would prove most productive to the revenue — that I would recommend that all raw materials be admitted free — that articles partaking of the nature of raw materials, but on which some labor had been expended, such as cotton twist, pay 6–8%; commoner manufactures suited to consumption by the masses 10–15%; and that no article be liable to a higher rate than 20%. There did not seem to be any very great difference in our views. Fould thought 25% should be the maximum, whilst Rouher seemed inclined to join me in preferring 20 —."

Cobden went on to give the French ministers a list of the concessions they could expect from England if they agreed to a really liberal measure, such as the one he proposed. He said that Gladstone would admit all French manufactures into England free of duty, and for French wines he would fix a scale of duties based on alcoholic content, in such a way that wine containing less than 10 per cent alcohol would pay only 1*s.* instead of 5*s.* 9*d.*[8]

The reception of Cobden's proposal was followed by a month of secret negotiations, during which real progress was made, but every precaution was taken by the Emperor and his ministers against committing themselves to any action from which they could not easily withdraw. Under the Emperor's orders Rouher prepared a comprehensive plan for reforming the French tariff. In this great task he was aided by Chevalier, who worked

[8] Cobden wrote in his diary November 25: " Chevalier brought a written document prepared by himself, but which purported to be my original proposal for a basis for a commercial treaty. He had contrived, without any direct falsification, to leave the door open for Rouher to propose some alterations which might appear to give him an advantage in the negotiations. I gave my assent and the document was handed in." Cobden Papers, Diary, Vol. I.

In the Archives Nationales, F 12–2684, is a document entitled: " Propositions anglaises qui ont servi de bases au Traité," which is neither signed nor dated, but fits perfectly Cobden's description. In the Flourens Papers is the manuscript draft of this document in the hand of Chevalier's daughter, Mme. Leroy-Beaulieu, with copious corrections in Chevalier's own hand and at the top, the designation: " Première Note remise par Cobden à Rouher pour servir de base au traité."

with him continuously, and went back and forth between him and Cobden every day.

Rouher also received valuable information and advice from Jean Dollfus, an important manufacturer of printed cloths at Mulhouse and a staunch advocate of tariff reform whose views resembled closely those of Cobden and Chevalier. Every effort was made to have it appear that the French Government granted only a part of Cobden's demands, while wringing great concessions from him. In this way it was hoped that, when the negotiations were eventually made public, the French people would think that the Emperor had reformed the tariff of his own free will, and not at the instigation of England. In order to achieve this aim it was necessary to maintain absolute secrecy. Rouher locked himself in his office every morning and admitted no one except Chevalier, who obtained for him any documents or other information he needed. His notes were copied and revised by his wife; Cobden's notes were corrected and translated by Mme. Chevalier. These elaborate measures to insure secrecy were completely successful. Magne, the Minister of Finance, and Billault, the Minister of the Interior, who were both strong protectionists, remained in complete ignorance of what was going on, as did even the undersecretaries and clerks in the Ministry of Commerce.[9]

The attitude of the Emperor continued to give Cobden great anxiety. Lord Cowley told him on December 12, that while at Compiègne the Emperor had been eager for a commercial treaty, but that recently he had begun to talk of there being great difficulties in the way. Cobden confided this to the sympathetic Gladstone and added: "Entre nous — In the course of my conversation with Lord Cowley he said he had received a letter from Lord Palmerston, who said he was not anxious for a treaty unless we got as much as we gave!" Better news came from another quarter, however, for Chevalier reported that Rouher and Fould were now both ardent advocates of a treaty on

[9] See Cobden's letters to Gladstone of November 28 and December 2, 5, and 12, 1859, in Cobden Papers. Also for a description of the precautions to insure secrecy, see Chevalier's letter to Bonamy Price, January 8, 1869, in Flourens Papers, cahier No. 5, p. 170.

political grounds, since they considered it the only way to avert war with England.[10]

On the 16th Cobden wrote more hopefully:

" Another step has been taken in advance. I write this on the authority of Chevalier whose truthful exactness has never failed me. Tuesday (Dec. 13th) Rouher presented to the Emperor his plan for a commercial arrangement with England, with an ' exposé de motifs ' of over sixty pages, the whole of which was read to His Majesty who expressed his approval and declared his determination to carry it into effect. He agreed that Walewski and the rest of the Council of Ministers should be made acquainted with his intentions. The Emperor told Rouher he should publish his instructions to the world, and he actually produced a letter he had prepared to Fould and intended for the *Moniteur*, in which he made a declaration of his sentiments, announcing his determination to pursue a policy of peace and internal improvement, and stating that he should abolish the prohibitive system and enter upon a more liberal commercial policy, ' which he regretted France should be the last country to adopt! ' It seems that, partly at the suggestion of his ministers and partly because he found some arguments in Roucher's exposé he thought he could adopt, his letter is to be withheld for the present." [11]

Three days later the whole aspect of the negotiations was changed by Cobden's first interview with the French Minister of Foreign Affairs, Walewski, who told Cobden that he thought it desirable that, as soon as the terms of the treaty could be agreed upon, a diplomatic instrument should be prepared with as much speed and secrecy as possible. He added that he understood that, up to that time, nothing had been done officially. Cobden agreed entirely with this view of the situation and wrote to Gladstone: "Now that the matter has passed into the hands of the French Cabinet and Minister of Foreign Affairs, I feel that my irregular action as a prominent agent in this important negotiation must be superseded by some one having official authority to act for the British Government." [12]

Thus, two months after the Emperor's acceptance of the plan of Cobden and Chevalier for a treaty of commerce with England,

[10] Cobden to Gladstone, December 12, 1859. Cobden Papers. The letters to Gladstone in the Cobden Papers, which are copies, were compared by me with the originals in the Gladstone Papers and were found to be accurate in every case.

[11] Cobden to Gladstone, December 16, 1859. Cobden Papers.

[12] *Ibid.*, December 18, 1859.

the French Government signified its desire to begin formal negotiations. There was not yet any assurance that a treaty
would really be signed, for the Emperor had changed his mind
several times since the original proposal was put before him,
and the British Prime Minister was known to be indifferent,
while the Cabinet as a whole had taken no cognizance of the
unofficial conversations at Paris; but the French Government
had agreed to a serious discussion on the basis of Cobden's
proposal that England should abolish her duties on French
manufactures and greatly reduce her duties on wine and spirits,
and that, on her side, France should abolish prohibitions and
revise her entire tariff, so far as it affected British goods.

The semi-official negotiations asked for by the French Minister of Foreign Affairs could not be begun, however, with any
prospect of success, until Cobden knew more definitely what he
could expect from Napoleon III. For some time he had been
wanting to see the Emperor again, and, as early as December 12,
he had written to Chevalier:

"What I am most anxious about is that no decision in the negotiation should
be come to until at least after I have had another opportunity of seeing the
party most concerned. A peremptory and absolute refusal to do *any thing*, in
reply to my offer to do *every thing*, would, in the eyes of certain parties, be viewed
almost as tantamount to a declaration of war. *Any proposal, however small, nay,
however unreasonable, would be infinitely better than a refusal to do any thing.*
What Gladstone wants is an excuse for doing a great deal, but, if this offer be
absolutely rejected, you may take the power out of his hands. — As far as may
be absolutely necessary, you may let this be known in the proper quarter." [13]

Chevalier wrote to the Emperor's private secretary, and on
December 21 Cobden was received at the Tuileries. He explained to Napoleon that Gladstone was very anxious to know
as soon as possible whether the French Government had decided
to agree to a commercial treaty, so that he might make the
necessary arrangements for preparing his budget. The Emperor
replied that he had quite made up his mind, and that the only
question was as to the details of the arrangement. In discussing
these Cobden found that his imperial pupil had been considerably

[13] Cobden to Chevalier, December 12, 1859. Flourens Papers.

influenced by the arguments of his protectionist ministers, of whom the most outspoken was Magne, the Minister of Finance. Thus he learned that the French Government now proposed to omit from their plan all allusions to raw materials or agricultural products, and to deal only with manufactured goods, coal, and iron; and that the duties on these were to range from 10 to 30 per cent. Cobden stuck to his old figures of 7 or 8 per cent and 20 per cent, but found that Walewski, as well as the protectionists, had insisted on a maximum of 30 per cent, although Rouher appeared to favor 20 per cent. The French figures were, however, entirely satisfactory to Gladstone, who expressed his delight that France asked for nothing higher, and Cobden was eventually obliged to accept the French maximum of 30 per cent.[14]

In the meantime, Lord Cowley had written to Lord John Russell to ask for instructions regarding the commercial negotiations, since Walewski had sent for him to ask definitely what were the intentions of the British Government.[15] Lord John replied in a private letter, which Lord Cowley received on December 27, instructing him to proceed with the negotiations for a treaty, and expressing the wish that Cobden act as one of the plenipotentiaries.[16] This action, which made possible the commencement of semi-official negotiations, met with the cordial approval of Gladstone, who wrote to Cobden regarding instructions that "the simpler they are the better, provided they

[14] Morley, *op. cit.*, pp. 721–722. See, also, for details regarding the scope of the Treaty, Cobden, Diary, Vol. I, December 19, 1859, which gives a full account of his interview with Walewski, and Diary for December 23. It seems evident that de Persigny's influence had more to do with the Emperor's decision at this time to go on with the Treaty than any other single factor. The Diary shows that de Persigny was in Paris as early as December 22, and that he probably came even earlier. He left for England only on January 4.

[15] F. O., 27-1305. Cowley to Russell, Paris, December 23, 1859. No. 910. "Confidential." Cowley ends his despatch by saying: "I have only to add that if Her Majesty's Government decide upon pursuing the negotiation it can not be entrusted to better hands than those of Mr. Cobden. The merit of whatever is effected will rest solely with him, and it is but fair that he should have the satisfaction of putting his name to the final arrangement. I could feel no jealousy on such an occasion."

[16] Cobden, Diary, Vol. I, December 27, 1859.

give the needful credit and authority. For I apprehend that we have no points to fight with the French, and, if we go on at all, our decisions in detail won't depend on theirs, but we shall, for our own sake, go to the extremest point our material permits. On the other hand you, in your independent capacity, are likely to lead the French to the end of their tether, and official solicitations added where you fail, would, in all likelihood, only disincline them the more."

Gladstone went on to state what he thought should be the British concessions to France:

" 1. In your own words ' the removal of all duties on French manufactures,' and, in every material case, I think this might be immediate; that is to say, not later than April 1st, 1860. 2. Consideration of an immediate reduction on wine, and a further reduction after an interval to a scale the lowest point of which would certainly not be higher than a shilling. *This by law, not by Treaty.* 3. A reduction of the duty on brandy to nearly the same point with our own spirits. If we fix it at 9/, as against 8/, the difference would but faintly answer to the pressure of the excise and the great difference in the values of the articles. I should not expect to carry this change without a row.* * * As for time: when France is ready with the details of a plan, say in ten days or a fortnight, we too will be ready on this side. The judgment of the Cabinet can then be asked. If I feel myself too much pressed with difficulties in detail, I will endeavor to obtain help from my colleagues beforehand. But I can't anticipate any answer from the Cabinet other than assent. Parliament meets the 24th [January]. I earnestly hope nothing will go to the world before that. At any time after that we might conclude. And I have no doubt my colleagues would allow me to arrange for making financial statements at such a time as might best accord with this important operation that has so well prospered in your hands." [17]

Three days after Cobden's second interview with the Emperor on December 21, the question of the commercial treaty was brought before the French Council of Ministers, as a body, although the Emperor had already spoken to nearly all of them privately. Rouher told Cobden that the Council was very much divided and the majority protectionist. Magne, the Minister of Finance, who was the leader of the opposition to the proposed treaty, had sent the Emperor a long memorial begging him not to enter on a policy which would ruin his country. Billault, the Minister of the Interior, was also a protectionist, and even

[17] Gladstone to Cobden, December 23, 1859. Gladstone Papers.

Walewski seemed to be wavering. Rouher, however, according to his own account, supported the treaty strongly, and said that, if Walewski refused to do so, he would assume the responsibility of signing the treaty and if, as a result, a sacrifice must be offered to the protectionists, he was ready to be the victim.[18]

On January 3 a second meeting of the Council of Ministers was held to discuss the treaty policy. As before, Magne tried to deter the Emperor from going any further. He argued that the Emperor —

" . . . had promised the protectionists not to change the tariff; that it would not be putting the countries on equal terms if the Emperor were to be called on to reduce duties on British products by decree, whilst he would have to wait until the British Parliament lowered the duties on imports from France. He was answered by Rouher and his colleagues as well as by Persigny (who was present at the Emperor's invitation), who urged that the difference between the two countries made a different course of action necessary; that is, the English Government could not alter the tariff without the consent of Parliament, whereas the Emperor could, in the case of a treaty; besides it was well-known that a sufficient measure of commercial reform could not be passed through the legislative bodies of France, whilst any reduction of duties proposed by the Ministers in the British Parliament would be sure to be agreed to unanimously. Upon this latter point Persigny spoke strongly, declaring such a proposal as to make the treaty dependent on a vote of the French Chambers would be scouted by the English Ministry, which knew well that they would resist such a measure and delay it indefinitely, if they did not defeat it, and he added ' if such a proposal is made to Cobden he will immediately pack his portmanteau and return to England.' Persigny and Fould urged strongly the political motives for going on with the treaty. As a result, Magne, although not converted, was subdued, and it was understood that the negotiation for the treaty should go on." [19]

The opposition encountered in the Council of Ministers made the Emperor and Rouher anxious to settle the terms of the Treaty as quickly as possible. In fact, shortly after the first meeting of the Council, the Emperor sent word to Cobden that he would like to see the negotiations completed in three or four days. Such an attitude was startling indeed, in view of the fact that the Emperor's inability to reach a decision regarding the negoti-

[18] Cobden, Diary, Vol. I, December 26, 1859; Cobden to Gladstone, December 23, 1859. Gladstone Papers.
[19] Cobden, Diary, Vol. I, January 3, 1860.

ations, and stick to it, had been the chief reason why nothing definite had yet been accomplished. The real cause of his anxiety for quick action was the fear that, now that all his ministers had been taken into his confidence, the secret could not be kept much longer. The vision of protectionist propaganda throughout France, with deputations besieging the government offices in Paris, was most unpleasant to contemplate, and Napoleon and his advisers wanted at least to be able to defend themselves and their new policy through articles in the government's journals, for which preparations had already been made. It was hoped that in this way a strong and effective appeal could be made to the more logical elements in French public opinion.[20]

The eagerness of the French Government to hasten the conclusion of the negotiations resulted in frequent conferences between Cobden and the French ministers regarding the duties to be inserted in the treaty. Cobden was so eager for a low maximum rate on manufactured goods imported into France that he advised the French to take three years, or even more, to complete their reductions, in the hope that, by this concession, they could be induced to bring down the maximum by successive stages from 30 to 20 per cent. He wrote to Gladstone, therefore, that he might take as long a time as he liked for bringing the British reductions into operation. Before the end of December, Rouher reported that he had prepared a rough draft of the essential provisions of a treaty, which included the maximum rate on manufactures imported from England; and an immediate reduction of the French duty on British coal to the low rate then paid by Belgium, with the promise of a further reduction in the future to the still lower rate paid by Prussia.[21]

Cobden was greatly encouraged by the recent developments and, on January 5, he wrote to Lord Cowley, who was then in London:

" Baroche, the temporary successor of Walewski, has fixed to-morrow to meet

---

[20] *Ibid.*, December 26, 1859; Cobden to Gladstone, same date. Cobden Papers.
[21] Cobden to Gladstone, December 27 and 28, 1859. Also Cobden's Diary, Vol. I, December 28.

me with Rouher and Fould, when we ought to bring matters to a close. To-day I called on Fould where I found Magne. They treated the Treaty as almost a 'fait accompli.' The Emperor wants, for the sake of effect, and to strike all Europe with a sense of confidence and 'bon accord' between the two countries, that the Queen's speech and his to the Corps [Législatif] be delivered the same day. They are certain that they would be ready ten days after January 24th. 'Could Parliament be postponed to February 2nd or 4th?' Fould asks. I suggested that before anything like this could be done the treaty in all its details must be agreed to, and he said this might be done in two or three days." [22]

At this moment, when all seemed to be going well, Cobden was alarmed by a report that the Emperor had repudiated his promise to enter into a commercial treaty with England. Chevalier, who brought the news, said that the Emperor's reason was that he wished to enter into an alliance with England to settle the affairs of Italy, and that he would, therefore, prefer to postpone the commercial treaty, because it was feared there would be war with Austria. Chevalier's report was confirmed by the Chargé d'Affaires at the British Embassy, who added, confidentially, that Lord Cowley had taken to England a proposal from the French Government for an alliance on Italian affairs which, in certain contingencies, would involve the employment of force against Austria, or another Power, and said it was reported that the British Cabinet was divided on the subject, Palmerston, Russell, and Gladstone favoring the French proposal, while the other ministers opposed it. Cobden wrote at once to Gladstone to give him this report which, he said, he believed as confidently as if he had heard the Emperor talking to de Persigny about it; and he added: "Persigny recalled the Emperor to a sense of responsibility for his word in free language and, if I am correctly informed, said that the proposed conduct would be 'abominable.' I believe Persigny's protest prevented the Emperor from using similar language to his ministers. * * * Of course I am in no fear," he concluded, "that with these facts fully before the British Government they will now enter upon the discussion of another treaty which may be meant to be

[22] Cobden to Gladstone, January 5, 1860. Cobden Papers, inclosing copy of his letter to Lord Cowley.

either a substitute, or a rider, or a companion to the one in hand." [23]

The serious alarm felt by Cobden and Chevalier was, happily, groundless, as is shown by a letter from Lord John Russell to Gladstone. Lord John wrote: "What Persigny said to me was the reverse of what Cobden expected. He said that if England should determine to give no support to France in Italy, France might have an Austrian war on her hands, and then she could not afford to pay the compensations to the protected interests, which had been promised in case of the abolition of prohibitions and reductions of duty — But, if England and France should be united in the affairs of Italy, no war need be feared, and the Commercial Treaty might go on. . . . I see no harm in this conclusion, although perhaps policy is more apparent than logic in the reasoning." The day after receiving Lord John's letter Gladstone replied to Cobden: "If France were to be involved

---

[23] Cobden, Diary, Vol. I, January 5 and 7, 1860. Also Cobden to Gladstone, January 7. Gladstone Papers. The Emperor's plan to hold a congress on Italian affairs had just been given up. See F. O., 27–1331. Cowley-Russell, No. 2, January 1, 1860. Cobden does not say from whom Chevalier obtained his account of the interview between the Emperor and de Persigny. See also Morley, *op. cit.*, p. 725, for an account of Cobden's interesting conversation with Prince Napoleon, January 4, regarding the commercial treaty and possible alliance of England, France, and Sardinia for settlement of Italian affairs.

Lord Cowley in Memorandum of January 5, 1860 (F. O., 27–1331), reports a conversation with the Emperor, who asked what England would do if war between France and Austria were renewed, which would be a certain result of Austrian intervention to support the Pope. Cowley replied that England would disapprove such intervention and would endeavor to prevent it, but he declined further to commit England. He strongly recommended to the British Government an Anglo-French agreement regarding a common policy in Italy as the best guarantee of general peace in Europe. Cowley makes no mention, however, of any proposal by France for such an agreement.

De Persigny, in his despatch on January 8, 1860, does not refer to such a proposal, but says: "si j'avais à choisir entre un traité secret d'alliance défensive et offensive et un traité de commerce, je préférerais le second, car les effets politiques du premier pourraient être annulés par un changement de Cabinet et non pas, ceux du second." See de Persigny's Despatches, Archives du Min. Aff. Étr., 1860.

The evidence from all these sources indicates that France made no actual proposal for a political alliance with England based on a common policy in Italy, but that she intimated plainly her desire for English support in the Italian policy she had recently adopted.

in war with Austria, it would be difficult for her to pay compensations to the classes affected by the coming changes. In what manner and in what terms we were to help to keep her out of the risk of any such war I do not clearly know; but, in the meantime, I think there is, as yet, no apparent wish either to get rid of the Commercial Treaty, or to connect it in an illegitimate manner with any other subject." [24] This letter evidently satisfied Cobden and Chevalier that their project was not in the immediate danger they had feared, for there is no further allusion to the rumor of a political alliance in Cobden's diary or correspondence.

The negotiations for a treaty of commerce between France and England had now passed successfully through the stage of preliminary discussion. Both governments had signified clearly their desire to conclude such a treaty, and had stated broadly the terms they were prepared to offer. In one sense, it is true, the task of Cobden and Chevalier had only begun, for they had still to steer their bark through reefs and shoals that threatened disaster; but at least, after two months of incessant and laborious efforts to make the Emperor stick to his original approval of their proposal, they had brought the two governments together and put in operation the wheels of diplomacy. They had worked long and earnestly, as individuals, for the cause of international peace and friendship; now they must give up their independence and work as the accredited agents of their governments, in the official negotiations that were about to begin.

[24] Russell to Gladstone, January 8, 1860, and Gladstone to Cobden, January 9. Gladstone Papers.

CHAPTER V

OFFICIAL INTERVENTION AND SIGNATURE
OF THE TREATY

IN A little more than two months after the 27th of October, when the Emperor first said that he approved the plan of Cobden and Chevalier for a treaty of commerce between France and England, the most serious difficulties had, apparently, been overcome. The failure of the second great effort made by the protectionists, in the Council of Ministers at the beginning of the new year, to induce the Emperor to drop the commercial negotiations, seemed to show that the Emperor had at last reached a definite decision, and that he had acquired sufficient courage to stick to it. It appeared to be almost certain that some sort of treaty would be signed in the near future and the problem that remained was to secure an agreement on a few fundamental questions, such as the British wine duties and the French tariff on iron, and to defeat attempts by the protectionists to delay the progress of the negotiations and thus gain time to organize an opposition that might prove fatal. A successful solution was reached only through the insistence of Cobden, strongly supported by his Government, on prompt and decisive action by France; and by the ability with which Gladstone won the consent of his colleagues in the British Cabinet, not only to the terms of the treaty as already proposed, but also to new concessions on the vital question of the wine duties.

Almost immediately after their second failure in the Council of Ministers the protectionists tried to kill the treaty by delaying the negotiations. They had used similar tactics with complete success in 1856, when they had been suddenly confronted with the bill for repealing the prohibitions. On that occasion they had defeated the Government by the simple expedient of referring the obnoxious measure to a hostile committee, by whom it

was held until the prorogation of the Corps Législatif.   The
time thus gained was used to organize an opposition of such
strength that the Government withdrew its bill rather than see
it openly defeated.   The attempt to attack the Treaty in January, 1860, must have been made by some protectionists, or
group of protectionists, familiar with the negotiations and having
easy access to the Emperor.   Since only the ministers had, as
yet, been taken into the Emperor's confidence, it seems probable
that the chief author of this coup was the violently protectionist
Minister of Finance, Magne.   Just how the Emperor was approached and what was said to him is not known, but the result
of the maneuver was that on January 9,[1] Rouher asked Cobden,
on behalf of the Emperor, whether he would have any objection
to the Government's submitting the Treaty to the Chambers.
Cobden assumed that this meant giving the French parliament
an opportunity to discuss, and, therefore, to reject, all the clauses
of the Treaty.   Some comments made by Chevalier [2] indicate that
the Emperor's intention was rather to submit the Treaty as a
whole for ratification after its signature, in the same way that
decrees modifying the tariff were submitted.   In that case the
Chambers would have been confronted with a *fait accompli*,
and it is possible that they might have accepted it as such;
but they were so strongly protectionist that it seems more
probable that they would have exercised their right of refusing
to ratify the Treaty.   In that case the Emperor could have used
his constitutional power of promulgating the Treaty without the
consent of his parliament, but it would have been much more
difficult to do this than to promulgate it without having given
the Chambers any opportunity to express officially their opposition.   Cobden's refusal to consider submitting the Treaty to
the French parliament would seem, therefore, to have been

---

[1] Cobden, Diary, Vol. I, January 9, 1860.   Also Cobden to Gladstone, January
11, 1860.   Cobden Papers.

[2] Chevalier to Rouher, January 11, 1860.   Chevalier, in forwarding to Rouher
a translation of Cobden's letter of January 10, wrote: " Je lui ai expliqué hier
la chose dont il s'agissait ou s'était agie.   Il comprend l'énorme différence qu'il
y a entre ceci et le fait de soumettre aux Chambres françaises l'acceptation des
clauses du traité."   See Arch. Nat., F 12-2684.

amply justified, for that submission, no matter in what form it was made, would have meant the almost certain failure of the Treaty.

Cobden's letter to Rouher declining to consider his suggestion, or to transmit it for the consideration of the British Government, put the case so logically and clearly that it could result only in a rupture of the negotiations, or in the abandonment of the suggestion to which it was so effective a reply.

" My dear Mr. Rouher," he wrote, " I have, as you desired, taken until to-day to consider the proposal you made to me last evening, and am, I regret to say, only the more confirmed in my opinion that there are insuperable objections to making the Treaty dependent on a vote of your Legislative Bodies. Here are some of my reasons. — When I had first the honor of an audience with the Emperor at St. Cloud in October he expressed an opinion that he could not pass a substantial measure of commercial reform through his Chambers, and that his only way was by a ' Decree ' consequent on a treaty with a foreign power; and this opinion I have had confirmed by his ministers, and those statesmen with whom I have been in communication since I have been in Paris. It was in consequence of this difficulty, which I communicated to Mr. Gladstone and Lord Palmerston, that our subsequent negotiations were carried on. — England had, since 1846, renounced the principle of commercial treaties, and, with no other power than France, and, with no less a motive than to strengthen the alliance of the French and English nations, would such a policy have been revived. — In the face of these facts, it would, I fear, be impossible to inspire the English government with the conviction that the measures embraced in the Treaty would, beyond all doubt, pass your Legislative Bodies.

" Under the circumstances, I invite your friendly consideration of the disadvantages under which you are asking the British government to place themselves. On their side, the success of their measures in Parliament is quite certain. They will be passed unanimously and with very little discussion. This would be done on the responsibility which the British Ministry would assume for the success of the corresponding measures before the French Chambers. If they should fail our Ministers would assuredly be driven from power. But assuming even that your Legislative Bodies should ultimately pass these measures, it could not certainly be done until after long discussion and probably after a Committee of Inquiry had been appointed to investigate the matter. In the meantime what would be our position in England? It is the practice with the Chancellor of the Exchequer, in cases of the reduction of taxes or duties, to act upon the first resolution of the House of Commons, without waiting for the passage of a law through Parliament. Thus, within a few hours after the assembling of the legislature, the Ministry will be in a position to give effect to the terms of the Treaty. Before the end of April a large part of our plan for a reduction of the duties on imports from France will have been realized. In the meantime what would be our position if your Chambers were in the height of their discussions on the French portion of the Treaty! — I could enlarge on the subject, but I have probably said enough to show the insurmountable obstacles which prevent me from entertaining your proposal or communicating it to the British Government." [3]

Cobden succeeded, by this letter, in putting an end to the plan for submitting the Treaty to the Chambers; but within less than a week another attack was made in the Council of Ministers. The protectionist members of the Council, led by Magne and by Troplong, the First President of the Senate and the leader of the opposition to the Sénatus-Consulte of December, 1852, which confirmed the power of the new sovereign to sign commercial treaties without having to submit them to the Chambers for ratification, argued long and earnestly against the Emperor's attempt to ruin France by negotiating a treaty of commerce with England. When, at length, it seemed as if the Emperor could not be moved, they reminded him that when he had withdrawn the bill to abolish prohibitions in 1856, and had promised not to make another attempt to accomplish that reform for five years, he had also pledged himself not to take any action in that direction until after making a fresh investigation of the condition of French industry. Napoleon felt that he could not refuse to listen to this appeal to his honor, and, accordingly, he ordered an *enquête* to be begun.

The protectionist ministers may have thought that in obtaining an investigation they had won a substantial victory by seriously delaying the commercial negotiations. If they did cherish any such illusion they were soon undeceived. The Enquête was begun immediately, so that no opportunity was given for protectionist propaganda, and its duration was limited to two days. Furthermore, the Government summoned only a small number of manufacturers representing the iron, cotton, linen, woollen, and pottery industries, and among these was the staunch free trader Jean Dollfus, of Mulhouse, who had long been giving valuable assistance to Rouher and Chevalier in their task of revising the

---

[3] Cobden to Rouher, January 10, 1860. Arch. Nat., F 12–2684.

French tariff. The manufacturers were received privately by the Emperor and Rouher, and, to judge by the account of one of the most ardent protectionists among them, they were able to accomplish little.[4]

By the limited scope and duration of the Enquête the Emperor had in reality granted only the shadow, and not the substance, of what his protectionist ministers desired. Furthermore, he took this occasion to express his will with an emphasis that showed plainly enough the futility of further opposition. On January 15, the very day on which the Enquête began, the Emperor sent to the *Moniteur* his letter to Fould, the Minister of State, in which he announced a far-reaching program of economic reforms. By publishing this letter the Emperor wished to prepare public opinion for the announcement of the signature of the Treaty of Commerce with England by showing that he intended to subject French industry to the salutary stimulus of foreign competition, but that he intended also to give it the means of meeting that competition effectively.

"For a long time," said the Emperor, "the principle has been proclaimed that the multiplication of the means of exchange increases the prosperity of trade; that without competition industry remains stationary and prices continue high, which prevents an increase in consumption; that without the development of capital through industrial prosperity agriculture itself will remain primitive. It follows, therefore, that before developing our foreign trade through the exchange of goods, we must improve our agriculture and free our industry from all obstacles within the country which put it in a disadvantageous position. At the present time not only are our large enterprises hindered by a mass of restrictive regulations, but the prosperity of our laborers has not been developed nearly as far as in a neighboring country. Only a good general system of political economy, therefore, can, by creating wealth, make comfort widespread among the working classes."

He said further that "In order to encourage industrial production we must free from all duties those raw materials which are indispensable to industry, and as an exceptional measure

---

[4] Cobden, Diary, Vol. I, January 14, 1860; also Memorandum of de Clercq on the negotiation of the Treaty of 1860, p. 29, in the Archives of the Min. Aff. Étr., Série Angleterre, Vol. 94. Négociations commerciales. See also Ernest Feray, *Du traité de commerce de 1860 avec l'Angleterre* (Paris, 1881), pp. 11–12.

we must lend it at a low rate of interest capital to help it improve its equipment, as has already been done for agriculture with respect to drainage." After urging the necessity of developing as fast as possible the network of canals, roads, and railroads in France, in order to provide industry and agriculture with adequate means of transportation, the Emperor continued:

" The encouragement of trade through the multiplication of the means of exchange will follow as the natural consequence of these measures. The progressive decrease of the tax on foodstuffs of general consumption will, then, be a necessity, as will the substitution of protective duties for the system of prohibitions which restricts our commercial relations. Through these measures agriculture will find a market for its products; industry, freed from obstacles within the country, aided by the government, stimulated by competition, will fight successfully against foreign goods, and our commerce, instead of languishing, will have a new and vigorous growth."

The Emperor went on to say that these reforms could be made without creating any financial difficulties because the Government had available for drainage, loans to agriculture and industry, etc., the balance of 160,000,000 francs remaining in the treasury from the loan raised for the war in Italy. Furthermore, the amortization of the public debt could be suspended during the temporary period in which there would be a heavy loss of revenue from the abolition of the duties on raw materials, a loss for which the country could not immediately be compensated by an increase in trade. These would include the abolition of the duties on wool and cotton, the successive reduction of those on sugar and coffee, the energetic improvement of the means of transportation and the reduction of the rates charged, the granting of loans to agriculture and industry, the abolition of prohibitions and the signature of treaties of commerce with foreign powers.[5]

[5] Napoleon III to Fould, January 5, 1860. Arch. Nat., F 12–2514. The letter was published in the *Moniteur* of January 15. See Cobden, Diary, Vol. I, January 15, 1860. The letter was written, in large part, before the middle of December, 1859, and was submitted to Cobden for his consideration January 9, 1860. See Cobden to Gladstone, December 16, 1859, and January 11, 1860, and Cobden, Diary, Vol. I, January 9 and 15, 1860.

The importance of the letter to Fould is greatly increased by the existence in Arch. Nat., F 12–2684, of a document entitled: " Bases d'un Traité de

The publication of the Emperor's letter to Fould marked the end of the vacillation and indecision on the part of the French Government which had caused Cobden and Chevalier so much anxiety. At last they could say that the Emperor had committed himself to the signature of the commercial treaty with England. There remained only the difficulties incidental to securing the agreement of the French and British governments on the exact terms of the instrument they had both signified their intention of signing.

The vacillation of the Emperor in his attitude toward the proposed treaty of commerce with England was the dominant factor in the negotiations until it was definitely ended by the publication of his letter to Fould on January 15; but the views of the British Cabinet were also of the utmost importance and have received scant attention from writers on the Treaty of 1860. Gladstone, as we have seen, saw the great possibilities of Chevalier's plan even sooner than did Cobden, when the matter was first discussed between them at Hawarden, in September, 1859. On October 15 he received Chevalier at his official residence in Downing Street, and reached an agreement with him regarding the fundamental provisions of the prospective treaty. From that time until the treaty was actually signed Gladstone never failed to give sound advice and hearty encouragement whenever Cobden's letters disclosed complications or unexpected difficulties in the negotiations at Paris.

Lord Palmerston and Lord John Russell also were informed of the plan for beginning unofficial conversations before Cobden left London on October 16, 1859. The Prime Minister gave his consent, but took no real interest in the scheme, preferring to await developments and sanction the negotiations if they promised to be successful and advantageous to England, or disavow them if they did not. As late as the middle of Decem-

---

Commerce entre la France et l'Angleterre en 5 parties." This document is really a carefully prepared plan for a series of economic reforms in France of which the treaty with England was to be only the most important. Its terms and the question of its authorship are of such significance that their discussion has been reserved for the Conclusion of this book; the text of the document is given the Appendix, page 369.

ber he was reported by Lord Cowley as not anxious for a treaty unless England got quite as much out of it as France. On the 24th when Lord Cowley's dispatch conveying the request of the French Government for an expression of England's intentions regarding serious commercial negotiations was put before him, Palmerston grudgingly consented to the beginning of semi-official conversations, but remarked that he did not think it necessary for England to make all the changes she had agreed to unless the French made theirs before July, 1862.[6] Thus the attitude of the British Prime Minister was one of almost complete indifference. He was content to allow his colleagues and Cobden to negotiate the treaty, and he refrained alike from giving them support and from expressing opposition.

Lord John Russell, on the other hand, approved of the plan for a commercial treaty and gave it his active support. When Cobden saw him at the Foreign Office on October 15, he not only gave his consent to the proposed unofficial conversations with the French Government, but went on to offer Cobden the advice and assistance of the experienced British ambassador to France, Lord Cowley, and to write to his colleague Gladstone that the matter could be brought before the Cabinet whenever he wished. Lord John, it is true, attached far less importance to commercial than to political negotiations with foreign governments, but his letters to Gladstone show that he thought a commercial treaty with France would be a good thing. The feeling of Cobden, which has been echoed by his two principal biographers, that the treaty was negotiated by him alone, in the face of the complete indifference of both Palmerston and Russell, does not seem to be justified. The fact that Russell did nothing officially to help on the negotiations before the latter part of December, 1859, does not prove his indifference. Nothing could have been done officially, or even semi-officially, until Cobden and Chevalier had completed their task of screwing up the courage of the Emperor and his chief advisers. Gladstone himself felt that Cobden should continue his unofficial negotiations as long as any really serious difficulties remained to be over-

[6] Russell to Gladstone, December 24, 1859. Gladstone Papers.

come, as is shown by his letter of December 23, in which he said: "You in your independent capacity are likely to lead the French to the end of their tether, and official solicitations added where you fail would in all likelihood only disincline them the more." [7] The correspondence between Lord John and Gladstone testifies to the Foreign Secretary's active interest and assistance when Lord Cowley's request for instructions provided the necessary opportunity. The British ambassador wrote to the Foreign Office on December 23 and received on the 27th Russell's preliminary instructions, which gave the necessary authority for beginning semi-official negotiations. On January 7 Lord John gave orders for the preparation of full powers for Lord Cowley and Cobden to act as the Queen's plenipotentiaries, and ten days later these were sent to Paris, together with full instructions for the official negotiations. [8] Since the coöperation of Lord Palmerston and Gladstone and of several heads of departments, as well as the approval of the Queen, were necessary, it can hardly be said that there was undue delay on the part of Lord John Russell.

The Cabinet as a whole was not asked to give its formal approval of the commercial negotiations until after the beginning of the new year, but it had been informed some time before of the unofficial conversations at Paris. [9] The matter was brought up officially on January 10, when it seemed reasonably certain that the French Government was willing to sign a treaty of commerce. The Cabinet then gave the necessary authority for the continuance of the negotiations and approved the main provisions of the proposed treaty. Two days later Gladstone wrote to Cobden:

" I said that the Cabinet readily assented, but it was not the readiness of zeal, such as yours, except on the part of a few. Your objects are to cement the friendship with France, and, next to this, to increase trade and reduce the enormous establishments (military and naval). Of those objects the first is faintly appreciated at this moment and by way of a cold abstraction, the other

[7] Gladstone to Cobden, December 23, 1859. Gladstone Papers.
[8] F. O., 97–207.
[9] Gladstone to Russell, December 23, 1859. Gladstone Papers.

not at all. The idea in possession of the public is (that of a) French invasion.[10]
. . . A majority of the Cabinet is indifferent or averse. . . . It is no small thing
to get a Cabinet to give up £1,500,000 or £2,000,000 of revenue at a time when
all the public passion is for enormous expenditure, and the case is beset with
great difficulties. . . . There are four or five zealous, perhaps as many who would
rather be without the French treaty. It has required pressure, but we have got
sufficient power now, if the French will do what is reasonable. Lord John has
been excellent, Palmerston rather neutral. It is really a great European opera-
'tion! " [11]

The formal consent of the British Cabinet to the discussion
of the terms of the commercial treaty and the firm stand taken
by the Emperor when he published his letter to Fould now
made possible the beginning of official negotiations. Rough
drafts of a treaty had been prepared by both Cobden and
Rouher and the consideration of these showed the outstanding
importance of the question of the reduction of the British
duties on wine; the opinions expressed by the members of the
British Cabinet brought to the front another issue in the length
of time demanded by the French for the application of the
reductions in their tariff. The satisfactory settlement of these
two questions was to be the task of the plenipotentiaries in the
official negotiations which were opened at Paris on January 18.

The question of the reduction of the duties levied in England
on French wines had been the principal factor in former negotiations for commercial treaties, especially in those of 1840
and 1852. In 1856, when Chevalier proposed negotiations to
the British Government through Lord Clarendon, the one great
concession he asked from England as a means of inducing the
Emperor's government to consider a treaty of commerce was a
substantial reduction of the duties on French wines. The British
Government, on its side, also attached the greatest importance to
these duties. Peel had retained them chiefly as a means of
securing concessions from France, and for some years he had
continued to cherish the hope of negotiating a treaty of commerce. His successors showed no desire for a commercial treaty

[10] Gladstone to Cobden, January 10 and 12, 1860. Gladstone Papers.
[11] Gladstone to Mrs. Gladstone, January 11 and 13, 1860. See John Morley,
The Life of William Ewart Gladstone (3 vols. in 2, London, 1911), II, 22.

with France and looked upon the wine duties chiefly as a source of revenue. The problem that confronted Gladstone in 1859 was, therefore, difficult. A heavy reduction of the wine duties was the only way to get France to negotiate; yet the loss of revenue to the British treasury was likely to be considerable, for a number of years at least, because the English upper classes had become accustomed, since the Methuen Treaty, to the strong wines of Spain and Portugal, while the lower classes did not drink wine at all. It might not be possible to change these habits materially, and, if it should be accomplished, it would certainly take a long time; so that the increase in consumption following a reduction of the duties, would, in all probability, be slow and might never reach a point that would make the new duties an important source of revenue.

Gladstone was faced with another difficulty arising from the British wine duties which gave him even greater concern. He was willing to sacrifice the revenue that would be lost by a substantial reduction, for he believed that eventually there would be a considerable increase in consumption; and, furthermore, the gain to British industry from a general reduction of the prohibitive French tariff and the immense benefit to the entire country from a greater security of peace, would be ample compensation. The problem that seemed to him the most serious was that which might be termed the question of "vested rights." The Government of Sir Robert Peel had promised the dealers in imported wines not to reduce the British duties by treaty without paying them a drawback in compensation for the difference between the old duties under which they had imported their stocks and the new.[12] Gladstone felt that it would be extremely difficult to procure the consent of the Cabinet and Parliament to the payment of this indemnity in addition to the large loss of revenue to the customs service that would be the immediate result of a drastic reduction of the wine duties.

In October, 1859, Gladstone consented to a substantial reduction of the British duties on French wine when Chevalier asked it as the chief concession to be granted by England.

[12] Gladstone to Cobden, October 20, 1859. Gladstone Papers.

A few days later he wrote to Cobden of the difficulty that would have to be faced if wine were included in a treaty with France and said that there were serious objections to granting the drawback that the Government would have to pay to the British dealers.[13] In December, after Cobden had repeatedly spoken of a reduction of the British wine duties as one of the most important concessions he was offering the French, Gladstone wrote to him that he could not include wine in the Treaty, "as it would entail on us a heavy cost." [14] His purpose was to have a bill granting the desired reduction on wine introduced into Parliament immediately after the presentation of the Treaty for ratification and he urged Cobden to persuade the French to agree to trust the British Government to do this. In that way he could avoid paying the indemnity to the British wine dealers, because Peel's government had promised to make the payment only if a reduction were made through a treaty of commerce.

On January 5 Cobden reported that the French Government insisted that the reduction of the wine duties be made a part of the Treaty. He told Gladstone that many of the French ministers considered this one provision worth all the others in the Treaty combined, and that all of them, as well as the Emperor, felt that the inclusion of wine in the Treaty was absolutely essential in order partially to offset the opposition of the manufacturing districts by securing the support of the important wine-growing regions. Gladstone replied on the 7th that the peremptory French demand created a most difficult situation and he repeated all his old objections to making the reduction of the wine duties a part of the Treaty; but soon afterward he reconsidered his position, probably because he realized that unless he did so the French Government would refuse to sign the Treaty. On the 11th, after consulting his colleagues, he wrote to Cobden: "We have considered very largely the difficult questions about the drawback on wine and the general opinion seems to be that we may hold our ground upon them without any immoderate charge to the public and

[13] Gladstone to Cobden, October 20, 1859. Gladstone Papers.
[14] Gladstone to Cobden, December 17, 1859. Gladstone Papers.

yet put wine into the Treaty." [15] Thus Gladstone yielded when he saw it was necessary to save the Treaty and he never mentioned again the objections he had repeated against including the British wine duties.

The new scale of duties proposed by the British Government was based on alcoholic strength, because the British tariff provided for much higher duties on spirits than on wine.[16] It was stipulated, therefore, that liquor imported as wine could not contain more than 40 degrees of alcohol. Below that limit wines were divided into three classes according to their alcoholic strength, the duties ranging from 1*s*. on wine up to 12 degrees of alcohol to 2*s*. on wine containing 40 degrees. The French objected to this classification on three grounds: (1) that it was too complicated; (2) that alcoholic strength was to be tested by the Sykes hydrometer to which they were not accustomed; and (3) that nearly all French wines contained more than 12 degrees of alcohol, as measured by the Sykes hydrometer, and could not, therefore, be imported under the 1*s*. duty as they had expected. The French plenipotentiaries refused to accept the English wine schedule at the opening of the official negotiations on the 18th, and their determination was strengthened by the support of Cobden, who urged Gladstone to admit wine at 1*s*. up to 18 degrees of alcohol. Gladstone eventually agreed to 15 degrees as the maximum for the first class. This final concession was communicated to the French on January 28, and was inserted in the revised text of the Treaty which was signed on the 29th.[17] Thus the provision to which the French

[15] Cobden to Gladstone, January 5, 1860; and Gladstone to Cobden, January 7 and 11, 1860. Gladstone Papers.

[16] See the first and second drafts of the Treaty prepared by the British Government, January 12 and 17, 1860, the latter of these being sent to Paris. F. O., 97–207.

[17] See de Clercq, Memorandum on the Negotiation of the Treaty of 1860, pp. 46–51 and 76, in Archives Min. Aff. Étr., Série Angleterre, Vol. 94. Négociations commerciales. See also Cobden to Gladstone, January 18 and 20, 1860; and Gladstone to Cobden, January 19 and 21, 1860. Gladstone Papers. See also Min. Aff. Étr. à de Persigny à Londres. January 18, 1860. "à chiffrer." de Persigny Despatches. Archives Min. Aff. Étr. 1860. " Deux difficultés viennent d'être élevées par Cobden d'après les instructions qu'il a reçu

attached the greatest importance was finally included in the Treaty in a form that completely satisfied their demands, and the dispute which had wrecked so many attempts to negotiate treaties of commerce between France and England, and which nearly caused the failure of the negotiations of 1860, was settled at last by a French victory.

The second of the two great questions that came up for settlement in the official negotiations at Paris arose when the terms of the proposed commercial treaty with France were submitted to the British Cabinet on January 10.[18] Disappointment was expressed by the ministers at the almost complete absence of immediate concessions by France, and at the remoteness of the date set for the application of the minimum duties in the revised French tariff. In view of the great concessions to which the Cabinet had consented, such as the inclusion of the reduction on the wine duties in the Treaty, and the lowering of the British duties on foreign spirits, in case of need, to the level of the charge on spirits imported from the British colonies, Gladstone thought the French refusal to grant early reductions would make the Treaty appear ludicrous in the eyes of the British public, and he feared that the terms of the agreement might have to be revised when they came before Parliament, under pressure from a sullenly acquiescent government. He suggested to Cobden that this danger might be avoided by an offer from France to reduce at an early date her duties on linens, or yarns, or some other article whose importation into

---

de Gladstone: les droits sur les vins et sur les eaux de vie. On veut calculer le droit sur les vins de manière que nos vins paieraient tous 18*d.* au lieu de 1*s.*, sur lequel nous avions compté; pour les eaux de vie, on demande 2*d.* au delà des droits d'accise. Ces deux difficultés pourraient arrêter la convention. Il y a ici grande urgence à ce qu'elle soît signée. Voyez Palmerston, Russell, et Gladstone, et tâcher de les amener aux solutions que nous avons proposées."

De Persigny to Min. Aff. Étr., London, January 19. Telegram in cipher. "J'ai vu Russell et Palmerston, mais impossible de voir Gladstone. Je crains de ne pouvoir obtenir ce que vous demandez. Les deux ministres réunis sont convaincus que le chiffre proposé d'abord amènerait une autre perturbation grave dans le budget et forcerait à augmenter l'income tax, ce qui nuirait à la popularité de la mesure. Le Cabinet de Londres semble reculer devant le reproche de faire de trop grands sacrifices à l'amitié de la France."

[18] Gladstone to Cobden, January 10 and 12, 1860. Gladstone Papers.

France was not then prohibited and on which, therefore, the Emperor was not pledged to postpone any reduction until after July 1, 1861.

The same views were expressed in the official instructions to the British plenipotentiaries, which were not sent to them until January 17, but the drafting of which by Lord John Russell and Gladstone had been begun as early as the 11th.

"Her Majesty's Government," wrote the Foreign Secretary, "know that the Emperor is bound by pledges until some time after July 1, 1861, and that even after that he may want to reduce gradually. But such changes are less formidable in fact than in anticipation to those they immediately affect. And they [H. M. G.] feel justified in pressing that the time taken after prohibition ceases, for arriving at the standard duty to be fixed by the Tariff should not be prolonged beyond two years from the date, itself unhappily of necessity postponed, which may be fixed for the commencement of the change from a prohibitive system towards one of practically open trade.

"Her Majesty's Government want some French products not now prohibited selected for an early reduction of duty. Count Walewski's suggestion of British coal is not good, as the market for it here and abroad is such that no public interest would be aroused regarding the amount of the French duty on it. Indeed there still remains more or less of a disposition, which formerly was strong, to view this export with jealousy, or even subject it to fiscal restrictions. Her Majesty's Government hope you will find no difficulty in inducing the Government of the Emperor to enter into their views on the subject I am now treating. That Government cannot help feeling that, after every allowance has been made for the difference in the two points of departure respectively, it is necessary that there should be at least a partial correspondence in the times when the prospective arrangements are to take effect. The repeal of prohibitions will stand over in consequence of a pledge, the transition to low duties may require further time; but there are articles admitted on the list of the French Tariff which might be, or even are already, exported from this country, and with respect to which it is allowed, as Her Majesty's Government understand, that the duties are too high and ought to be reduced. In this class of cases there is no essential change of principle to be made, and I am at a loss to conceive any reason which could justify in itself, or could explain to the public in this country, the postponement for a lengthened time, of all reductions of duty to which any importance could be attached.

"The spontaneous offer I have authorized you to make with regard to the proceedings on the side of England places beyond doubt the value we attach to the principle. I repeat, you need not ask the Government of France to adopt a similar principle as its general rule of operation, but you will press with all your power for a reduction on some important articles of British Import as essential in order to realize in full the salutary effects which Her Majesty's Government anticipate from the contemplated Treaty." [19]

Cobden was much more interested in getting the French to reduce the maximum rate in their new tariff below 30 per cent and to fix a low minimum rate than he was in inducing them to put these changes into effect at an early date. The French had declined to name the minimum rate of the new tariff in the Treaty, because they were afraid of the effect such a concession would have on public opinion in France. Cobden was, therefore, eager to have them agree in writing that the minimum rate should not exceed 10 per cent, which was the percentage named by the Emperor when he received Cobden on December 21.[20] But, in compliance with Gladstone's request, he did try to get the French to advance the dates for their reductions, although he did not try as hard or succeed as well as Lord Cowley.

"I have your letter expressing the dissatisfaction of your colleagues at the limited extent of the measures to be taken on this side and the remoteness of the date when they are to come into effect," he wrote to Gladstone on January 11. He spoke of the Emperor's pledge not to remove prohibitions before 1861

---

[19] F. O., 97–207. Instructions to Earl Cowley and R. Cobden, Esq. pp. 8–12. Signed by Lord John Russell after thorough revision by Gladstone. The " spontaneous offer " refers to a proposal to be made in connection with the time for the change in tariffs to take effect, which in England was to be immediately on their approval by Parliament. " You will, however, propose on the part of Her Majesty's Government to retain under the Treaty a power of granting a time, not to exceed two years from April 1, 1860, upon special grounds and by way of exception from the rule to be generally observed." This was to apply to " any minor article, that is to say, to any article other than silk. But where such a delay is made for any article, the duty kept shall not exceed $\frac{1}{2}$ the present duty." There was to be one important exception only.

[20] Cobden to Baroche, January 13, 1860. Memorandum by de Clercq. Annexe 6. Min. Aff. Étr. Memoranda et Documents Angleterre, Vol. 94. A copy of this letter in English, dated January 12, is in the Gladstone Papers. It was probably translated by Chevalier and forwarded the next day, as was the case with Cobden's letter to Rouher of January 10. Baroche did not reply until January 22, the day before the Treaty was signed. He spoke of " un minimum qui n'a pu être précisément déterminé et qui variera suivant les conditions de fabrication de chaque produit, mais qu'on peut évaluer environ à 10%. Le Gouvernment de l'Empereur n'hésite pas d'ailleurs à penser que pour beaucoup des articles à l'égard desquels la prohibition sera levée, les tarifs à établir n'atteindront pas le maximum fixé par le traité."

and added: "But I agree with you that the drop to 25%
[of the maximum rate] ought not to be delayed so long. Backed
by your remonstrance I will try to fix it at January 1, 1863
[the date proposed by the French was October 1, 1864]. As
regards the absence of some articles, such as linens, from the
Treaty, on which the duties might be immediately reduced, I
have already pressed the point on Rouher. * * * I understand
that in fixing the specific rates, which must be done by a second
treaty before July, 1860, yarn will be about 10% and many
manufactures not above 15 or 20%, and I have calculated on
iron and machinery being low. In fact the rival interests which
must be let loose on each other as soon as the Treaty is known,
will force this policy on the Government. The Treaty will
look worse on our side than it really is. This is desirable to
ease off the French Government with its difficulties."

Two days later Cobden wrote again:

"I attach less importance than yourself to the *time* when the new tariff is
to come into operation, assuming that the time is fixed and does not extend
beyond 1861. Of course the delay will be made the most of by the inva-
sionist party [in England], but no measure would have satisfied them. . . .
The worst of it is that, until the second treaty has been executed, we can not
even have the benefit of its provisions, for to talk of the rates of duty we expect
to insert in that treaty would only put arms in the hands of the Protectionists
to embarrass the French Government. I shall be very much disappointed if
before next July the French tariff (which is to come into force in the autumn
of 1861) be not much more liberal than that of the Zollverein, Russia, or even
the United States. But I would not say as much to serve your government,
because it would endanger the success of the measure. It is our policy and interest to allow it to appear that we have the worst of the bargain. Still I will
use every effort to have linens inserted, and at least reduced to the level of the
Belgian duties. Woollen yarns are prohibited; also cotton yarns under
No. 160. I have looked through the tariff again and again to find something on
which there could be an appearance of something done. I had reckoned on
iron, but am satisfied that no measure could have been agreed to if the Emperor
had been pushed on that article at present. As soon as the spinners know that
yarns are to come in at a moderate duty they will insist on iron and machinery,
or rather machinery which will involve iron, being admitted at low duties.
The whole structure of the prohibitive system here is a house of cards and will
fall of itself as soon as it is rudely handled in any part. Rouher knows this
and hence his desire is to leave everything in the way of detail until the bomb-
shell explodes among the ' interests.'

" This sudden transition from a prohibitive system to a liberal tariff involves the necessity of previous preparation requiring time. Raw materials are heavily taxed and must . . . be set free, for which a fund has been provided. Besides the Emperor has a project for loaning money to the spinners for purchasing new machinery. . . . This all implies time.

" It is proposed, in a single measure," wrote Cobden again, " to effect far more than was accomplished in England in ten years by the united labors of two such men as Huskisson and Deacon Hume. There have been no preliminary measures — not a single step such as the repeal of the duties on raw materials has been taken to prepare for the complete revolution that is to be made in the tariff next year. Is it too much to allow eighteen months for the transition from a régime of prohibition to the most moderate revenue duties now levied in any large state excepting England, and not even excepting the United States? And by no other man (or body of men) but the Emperor could this great change be effected in France. His letter, published in yesterday's ' *Moniteur*,' has astonished all circles in Paris, and amidst the hubbub of criticism, there is from friends and foes a universal homage of admiration offered to his courage. Does it not become our duty under such circumstances to afford every facility in our power for surmounting the difficulties before him, even to the extent of allowing England to appear to be giving him far more than equal advantages in the terms of the Treaty? " [21]

Cobden was quite right in his appreciation of the vital importance of time to the French in the sweeping reform of their entire tariff. He analyzed the situation in France with keen insight, but he failed to understand the situation in England, which Gladstone, as a practical statesman and administrator, saw clearly. Gladstone, on his side, was quite as shrewd as Cobden, and his fear that the Treaty would be attacked in England, because of the striking lack of proportion between the concessions granted to the French and those given by them in return, was amply justified by the difficulties he encountered in steering the Treaty through the House of Commons. Lord

[21] Cobden to Gladstone, January 11, 13, and 16, 1860. Cobden Papers. See also Cobden's Diary, Vol. I, January 16, 1860, where he said: " Met by appointment Baroche, Rouher, and Chevalier. Explained great anxiety of Gladstone that some articles should be inserted in the Treaty for immediate reduction of duty. I proposed linen yarns and cloth, but found the Treaty with Belgium prevented these articles being dealt with before May, 1861, when they are willing to reduce the duties to the same level with those on articles coming from that country. We then turned to iron and agreed they should consult the Emperor on the propriety of admitting it to the tariff for immediate reduction. Further proceedings were deferred until the return of Lord Cowley from London."

Cowley was, happily, in a position to understand the situation in England as well as that in France, for he had spent the first two weeks of January in London and had returned to his post just in time to take part in the official negotiations. Through his intervention, aided by the efforts of Chevalier,[22] appearances were at least partially saved by concessions which he induced the French to grant at the last moment. Cobden summarized this achievement in his last long letter to Gladstone about the Commercial Treaty. "Lord Cowley," he wrote, "has bullied them into antedating their alterations in coal, iron, and machinery by three months, so that, with linen, they will altogether make a good exceptional list." [23]

The settlement of the two questions of the British wine duties and the time at which the French reductions were to take effect removed the last serious obstacle to the signature of the Treaty of Commerce. In the case of the former, the British had granted

[22] Chevalier, January 14, 1860. Probably to Rouher. As with many of Chevalier's letters, there is no form of address and no signature. This letter is, however, in his hand and is in the Flourens Papers.

"Je vous ai dit," he wrote, "que j'avais lu les lettres de Gladstone. Je les ai relues avec attention. Ce qui y est dit des dispositions du Cabinet est sérieux, pour ne pas dire grave. Non que le Cabinet recule devant ce que dans le langage accoutumé on appelle des *Concessions*. On est disposé à les faire immenses, inespérés, de ce côté ci du détroit, et à peu près immédiates (pour avril, mars, ou peut-être février). Mais on compare les stipulations du côté de la France à celles de l'autre côté, et on craint que la comparaison, faite dans le Parlement ne semble ridicule et n'attire les sarcasmes du public. Le mot de ridicule et d'autres plus forts ont été prononcés. On aimerait tout autant, si non davantage, faire au tarif anglais tous les changements dont il s'agit pour le simple amour du principe de la liberté du commerce, sans un traité, et nous laisser cuire dans le jus de la prohibition puisque nous trouvons que le régime protecteur est si bon. Cela ferait, dit-on, plus d'honneur à l'Angleterre, cela serait plus conforme à sa dignité qu'un traité où la prohibition est remplacée par des droits prohibitifs et où la substitution même est remise aux calendes grecques; et enfin cela profitèrait davantage au Cabinet.

"Si quelques arrangements dégageaient le traité de ce caractère d'inégalité et d'irréprocité trop flagrantes, cela aurait des avantages de plus d'une sorte. Les anglais auront toujours la plus grande peine à comprendre qu'un gouvernement fort, qu'ils regardent comme absolu, ne puisse faire quelque chose de plus considérable, et que, quand on vainc l'Empereur Nicolas et l'Empereur d'Autriche, on se croit obligé de compter à ce point avec M. Mimerel et M. Charles Dupin."

[23] Cobden to Gladstone, January 20, 1860. Cobden Papers.

the demand of the French that wine be included in the Treaty, and had signified, unofficially, their willingness that the first class of wines should be extended from those containing 12 degrees of alcohol to ·those containing 15 degrees. As regards the time for the application of the reductions in the French tariff, the British secured an advancement of the dates originally offered on coal, coke, iron, machinery, and linens. The concessions thus made by each side, though not in themselves of great importance, were significant because of the urgency with which they were demanded by the French and British governments; and unless they had been granted, the negotiations would almost certainly have been broken off. The Treaty was signed in great haste almost immediately after the agreement on these two outstanding questions had been reached, and without waiting for new official instructions from London regarding French wines, for the French Government was harassed by the protectionists, while the British Cabinet was eager to end the negotiations before the opening of Parliament. Accordingly, no formal ceremony marked the conclusion of the commercial entente between the two countries. There was merely a meeting at the Ministry of Foreign Affairs, on the afternoon of January 23, of the four plenipotentiaries, Baroche, Rouher, Lord Cowley, and Cobden, who listened to the reading of the text and then quietly signed the Treaty of Commerce.

The Cobden-Chevalier Treaty was a short instrument containing only twenty-two articles, but the provisions these embodied affected the most important of the industries of both countries. France agreed to abolish her prohibitions and admit British goods within two years at duties that were not to exceed 30 per cent, and within five years at a maximum rate of 25 per cent. The French Government named October 1, 1861, as the date when most of its reductions should take effect, because the Emperor had promised in 1856 not to remove prohibitions for five years, and in 1859 he had granted a further, but indefinite delay. In deference to Gladstone's urgent request, the reductions on a number of commodities were now to take effect before the end of the year 1860. Coal and coke were to be admitted at one half and one third respectively of the present duties on July 1; bar- and pig-iron in general, and certain kinds of steel, on October 1; and machines and tools, on December 31. Linens were to come in at the new rates on the expiration of the French treaty with Belgium on June 1, 1861.

England agreed to admit nearly all French goods free, in accordance with her general policy. The most important exception was French wine on which the old rate of 15*s.* a gallon was replaced by a scale of duties based on alcoholic content and ranging from 1*s.* per gallon on the weaker to 2*s.* on the stronger wines. French brandies and spirits were to pay 8*s.* 4*d.* per gallon instead of 15*s.*, a reduction of about 40 per cent. Other products subject to an excise tax in England were to be liable to a duty equal to that tax with the addition of a surtax equivalent to the expense caused the British producer by the system of excise. The Treaty was to go into effect on its approval by Parliament, with the exception of the article on wine, on which the full reduction was not to take effect until April 1, 1861, and with the reservation by the British Government of the right to retain upon special grounds half the duty on any article except silk for two years. Finally, it was stated in Article XX that the Treaty would not be binding on either country unless it was approved by the British Parliament.[24]

Both countries agreed neither to prohibit the exportation of

[24] De Clercq Memorandum, p. 73. Archives Min. Aff. Étr. New instructions on the points asked for, especially that of the upper limit of the first class of French wines, had not come from London and it was agreed to revise the clauses in question through additional articles or else through a new instrument in which the changes could be incorporated. After the signature on the twenty-third several verbal errors were discovered, which were due to the fact that the Treaty had been signed in great haste because of the harassing agitation to which the French Government was exposed. For this reason the British plenipotentiaries affixed their signatures before sending the full text of the Treaty home. But they secured the French promise to help effect such revision as was found necessary. See F. O., 97–207. Cowley to Russell, January 23, 1860. The verbal errors were corrected and the British concession changing the upper limit of the lowest class of French wines from 12 degrees of alcohol to 15 degrees was included in the new instrument signed January 29. The original date of the twenty-third was kept, but new seals and signatures were affixed. See de Clercq Memorandum, pp. 73–83.

coal nor to levy any duty on such exportation. In reality, of course, this was a concession by England alone, since France was a large importer of coal, and it aroused a storm of opposition in the House of Commons on the ground that England was submitting to French dictation and that she was restricting her freedom of action in time of war. In short, it was made to serve as the principal basis for the attacks on the Treaty, and it caused the Government more trouble than all the other twenty-one articles combined. France and England agreed further that any reductions or favors given by either of them to a third power should be granted to the other; and that no prohibition of imports or exports was to be enforced by one against the other unless it was also enforced against all other nations. Since both countries soon began the negotiation of similar commercial treaties with the other states of Europe, this article served as the basis for the progressive reduction of many of the duties retained in the Franco-British treaty. Finally, it was agreed that the Treaty should be valid for ten years, after which it should continue in force from year to year until twelve months after its denunciation by either of the signatory powers.[25]

In one respect the treaty signed on January 23, 1860, indicated only the basis on which the economic reforms it was intended to accomplish should be completed. By Article XIII it stipulated that the ad valorem duties mentioned in the earlier articles were to be converted into specific duties within six months, on the basis of the prices of the six months preceding the date of its signature.[26] The few British duties that were retained were already specific and this provision referred to the French duties,

[25] H. Reader Lack, *The French Treaty and the Tariff of 1860* (London, 1861), gives the full text of the Treaty and the subsequent tariff conventions. Lack was secretary to the British Tariff Commission. His book was published in February, 1861.

[26] Lack, *op. cit.*, pp. 32–34. Article XVII was made an exception to the general stipulation of Article XIII made by the direction of the Emperor on the insistence of the ironmasters. It provided that for the kinds of bar-iron then paying 12 francs (duty of 10 francs plus 2 décimes), the new rate should be 7 francs (including décimes) until October 1, 1864, and thereafter 6 francs per 100 kg.

nearly all of which remained unsettled save for the stipulation that for four years they might not exceed 30 per cent and after that 25 per cent. The strictly commercial benefits which England expected to derive from the Treaty were, therefore, made almost wholly dependent on the successful negotiation of this supplementary treaty, while an admirable opportunity was given the French protectionists to organize their forces and compel the Government to keep the duty on every article of interest to them at the maximum rate of 30 per cent. The reform of the French tariff, one of the main objects sought by Cobden and Chevalier, had scarcely been begun, and the treaty that had been signed was only the shadow of the measure that was needed to make free trade a reality in France.

But, in spite of this grave defect, the Treaty of January 23, 1860, was a document of decisive importance in Franco-British history. It was the long deferred fruition of a protracted series of attempts to end the state of hostility that had hitherto characterized the commercial relations of the two countries. A treaty had been signed in 1786, but it was concluded on a basis of strict reciprocity and was essentially a restrictive bargain from whose benefits other powers were excluded. Furthermore, it had dealt with a very few commodities, instead of with the general tariffs of France and England, and, finally, it was virtually still-born, since it was abrogated by the outbreak of the French Revolution of 1789. The attempts made to conclude another treaty, from the fall of the first French Empire to the foundation of the second, failed because neither the French nor the British Government was sincerely anxious for their success, and because the French Government throughout that period lacked the power to control the protectionist Chambers. But, even if in 1840 or 1852 a treaty had been signed, it would have accomplished little, for in each case there was no conception of anything greater than a restrictive bargain over a handful of commodities.

But, although the Treaty of 1860 was the result of the last of a series of negotiations which had been renewed at intervals for many years, and although it was concerned with many of the same commodities, it was conceived in a new and broader spirit. It aimed not at restriction, but at expansion, and instead of dealing with some half a dozen products it made stipulations which modified the general tariffs of both countries and transformed the whole economic organization of industry in France. It deliberately provided for the extension of its provisions to other countries, and it replaced the decadent system of prohibitions that was slowly choking all desire for progress out of French industries by a régime of moderate protection that brought to them the stimulus of foreign competition. Its principal authors were not professional diplomats intent on outwitting each other, but personal friends coöperating in an effort to secure, through a wholesome increase of trade and the promotion of industrial progress, an alliance which would unite the peoples of their countries in a common opposition to war. Their ideals were never fully realized, but they gave a vigorous and healthy character to the agreement which, in the opinion of the great English statesman whose support was so essential to its conclusion, probably prevented a war between England and France.[27]

The treaty planned by Cobden and Chevalier was signed after three short months of negotiation, but its birth was only the beginning of a new series of difficulties from which it did not emerge for nearly a year. Not only did it have to meet the onslaught of the many protectionists in France and the few in England, which everyone had expected, but it had to face also the attacks of the orthodox free traders in England, who fought against their own policy of tariff reform rather than aid in its victory by means of a treaty of commerce, and the denunciation of the British invasionists who feared anything that came from the heir of the great Napoleon.

[27] See Morley, *op. cit.*, II, 23. " 'It was and is my opinion, that the choice lay between the Cobden Treaty and not the certainty, but the high probability, of a war with France.' " Gladstone in an undated memorandum.

CHAPTER VI

APPROVAL OF THE TREATY BY PARLIAMENT

THE Cobden-Chevalier Treaty was signed on January 23, 1860, and was promptly ratified by both the French and British governments. Its principal authors had thus won a great victory in the success of the negotiations begun by them three months before, and the importance of their achievement was recognized by the press in England. Cobden was generally regarded as the real author of the Treaty by his countrymen and it was almost universally assumed that he had converted a not wholly unwilling emperor to the idea of signing a treaty of commerce with England. But Chevalier was not forgotten outside his own country and the first tribute to him came, most appropriately, from the organ of his friend:

" Cobden's task," said the *Morning Star* " has been most gloriously concluded, and he can leave the field in all confidence in the zeal and intelligence of the one faithful adherent to the great cause whom he leaves behind, Michel Chevalier — of whom the Emperor has often spoken laughingly as the only Frenchman besides himself who is really a partisan of Free Trade — has been, indeed the greatest and most indefatigable laborer in the cause, and to his help we are indebted for smoothing many of the difficulties which would otherwise have delayed success for some time to come. Throughout the whole of his career, while traversing the numerous governments which have dawned on France since the first appearance of Michel Chevalier as a public man, he has ever maintained the same dignified, disinterested attitude, and never lost sight of this, the main object of his public life. The principal reason of his adherence to the present Government consisted in the promise held forth by its imperial chief of some day or other aiding by his influence the progress of the free trade question in his dominions. The high character borne by Michel Chevalier, the immense reputation for science and learning, and the large independent fortune which he enjoys and which places his motives beyond suspicion, even on the part of the most bitter enemies of the cause, have all united in placing Michel Chevalier in the position of a man who has stormed successfully, although alone, a well armed fort, defended by hosts of the stoutest warriors, well provided with arms and ammunition. He could not take the fort — alone and unaided as he stood — but he has prevented the enemy from making the smallest attempt at a sally. They have captured no prisoners and have been compelled to live upon the stock of stale provisions, which is found to be considerably reduced in consequence. It was a lucky thing that Cobden came to the rescue of Chevalier; and it was an equally lucky thing for Cobden that he found the provisions and ammunition getting low in the fortress." [1]

Another tribute came from the *Economist* whose Paris correspondent wrote:

". . . Mr. Cobden signed the treaty on behalf of England. The honor of doing so was well earned by the great commercial reformer; and all will rejoice that the English Government had the good taste to confer that honor on him. But France also has her great commercial reformer, who has had far mightier odds to struggle against than Cobden had, and who has been at work for far more weary years than he was: I mean, of course, Michel Chevalier. Regret is felt that the French Emperor had not the tact to allow this distinguished personage to inscribe his name to the treaty by the side of that of his English confrère. The treaty, however, and the commercial reforms it inaugurates, are really his work; and, in addition to the glory of accomplishing so great a thing, he will have the satisfaction (of which Sir Robert Peel, for his part, was so proud) of knowing that he has secured plenty and comfort to millions of lowly households." [2]

Neither Chevalier, nor Cobden, however, felt that the great task had been completed. Cobden, indeed, went south to Cannes after the signature of the revised treaty on January 29, for his health had been greatly impaired by his hard labor during the negotiations in Paris; but Chevalier remained on guard. They both knew that there was still much work to be done, for the British Parliament must be induced to give its sanction to the reductions in the British tariff called for by the Treaty, and the French Government had still to negotiate with the British Government the conventions by which the ad valorem duties of the French tariff were to be made specific. The approval of the Parliament at Westminster was far from being as certain as Cobden had so confidently predicted in his letter to Rouher, for it depended on the ability of the Palmerston government to overcome the political opposition of the Tories led by Lord Derby and Disraeli, and the objections raised by the English

[1] *Morning Star*, January 21, 1860.
[2] *Economist*, January 28, 1860.

protectionists in the wine and silk trades, and by the orthodox free traders who would have opposed any treaty of commerce. These difficulties were far from insignificant, as subsequent events were to prove, and they were increased greatly by the rumors that spread almost immediately after the signature of the Treaty regarding the intention of Napoleon III to annex Savoy. Cobden could not join the fight in the House of Commons, as he wished, because his health forced him to spend the remainder of the winter in a milder climate, and Chevalier was a foreigner; but the British Chancellor of the Exchequer, who had already done so much to secure the success of the negotiations, was to prove himself not only a master of finance, in his great budget of which the Treaty became a part, but also a debater of consummate skill and power. Bright and de Persigny, the French ambassador, gave valuable assistance, but the lion's share in the credit for the victory that was won in Parliament belongs to Gladstone.

The commercial rapprochement with France was first revealed to the English people by the publication of the Emperor's letter to Fould on January 15, 1860. The credit for the inspiration of the letter was given by the British press to Cobden, but there was a general admiration of the Emperor's courage in thus openly defying the powerful protectionists in France, and the leading dailies declared the Emperor's act a most favorable indication of his peaceful intentions and called for reductions in the British tariff in reply.

"The letter of the Emperor to the Minister of State," reported de Persigny to his Government, "has produced an impression so great that it is hard to describe. It is a great event for this country. Everyone sees in it the evidence that an era of peace and prosperity is about to begin for Europe and especially for France and England. In the City everyone is talking about it and praising the Emperor with the greatest enthusiasm. This morning I saw Palmerston and Russell. Both considered that it will inevitably unite indissolubly the two peoples through the bonds of mutual prosperity and they think that the effect upon public opinion in England will exceed all that has been anticipated." [3]

---

[3] Min. Aff. Étr., 1860. De Persigny Dispatches, January 16, 1860. See also *Times*, January 21, 1860; *Morning Post*, January 16, 1860; *Morning Star*, January 17, 1860.

The news of the signature of the Treaty of Commerce was received in a very different spirit. De Persigny declared that the mass of public opinion was favorable,[4] but there was no outburst of enthusiasm in the press. Nearly everyone approved of closer commercial relations with France, but many thought that they need not necessarily have been secured by means of a treaty. The terms of the agreement, furthermore, were not announced until Gladstone presented his budget in the House more than two weeks later, and this lack of information together with the secrecy that had enshrouded the negotiations, aroused a certain amount of suspicion. The newspapers could do little to enlighten their readers, for the guesses they made at the provisions of the Treaty were often quite inaccurate, and they frequently assumed that England had made a bad bargain in addition to having violated the orthodox principles of free trade by making a bargain at all. The *Times* expressed this state of mind with some warmth:

"England pays ready money," it said, "and receives in exchange a bill at eighteen months without interest and without any extra benefit to England to compensate for the lack of interest. England merely loses duties imposed for revenue and, therefore, loses revenue, while France gains doubly by abolishing prohibitions through the source of revenue thus created and the decrease in the price of goods. England's loss of revenue must be made up by a tax on the necessaries of life. As for the principle, we had supposed England, being no longer a child had put away childish things. The conclusion of a commercial treaty is nothing less than a solemn declaration against those doctrines of political economy which have regulated the practice of this country since 1846. . . ."[5]

On January 24, Parliament was opened by the Queen's speech which informed the Houses that the Sovereign was "in communication with the Emperor of the French with a view to extend commercial intercourse between the two countries and thus to draw still closer the bonds of friendly alliance between them." Lord Derby and Disraeli replied by attacking the Treaty as representing a repudiation of the established principles of England's commercial policy, as involving reciprocity, and as causing

---

[4] Min. Aff. Étr., 1860. De Persigny Dispatches, January 26, 1860.

[5] *Times*, January 23, 1860. See also *Economist*, January 28, and *Morning Star*, January 21, 1860.

England a considerable loss of revenue without bringing her any signal advantage in compensation. The Duke of Newcastle and Lord Palmerston, on behalf of the Government, replied that the conclusion of the treaty with France was regarded by them as a wholly exceptional measure which would increase trade to the mutual profit of both countries and which would make less likely any interrupting of the political relations between them.[6] This exchange of opinions was, however, only a preliminary skirmish and the real battle between the supporters and the opponents of the Treaty was postponed until Gladstone should introduce his budget and submit, at the same time, the clauses of the Treaty which required legislative sanction. Before that could happen the whole aspect of Franco-British relations was changed by the publication of the report that the Emperor intended to annex Nice and Savoy.

On January 25, there had appeared an article in *La Patrie*, one of the semi-official organs of the French press, which declared that the doctrine of nationality would give Savoy and Nice to France, and that Savoy, at least, would become more and more a foreign element as Piedmont became the dominant power in Italy. France, furthermore, had held Savoy and Nice under the Treaty of 1814, and by recovering them, she would regain her natural frontier of the Alps. On February 5, another article on the subject was published by *Le Constitutionnel*, which, like *La Patrie*, was a semi-official organ. This spoke of the French sympathies of Nice and Savoy and of the widespread discussion of this in the French press because of the recent aggrandizement of Piedmont, but it insisted that the views of the press were in no way inspired. Copies of these articles were sent to the Foreign Office by Lord Cowley, who reported that at the time when France and Sardinia were considering coöperation against Austria, they discussed the cession of Savoy and Nice under certain contingencies. He added that Thouvenel, the French Minister of Foreign Affairs, had just informed him that the Emperor had not considered the acquisition of Lombardy by Piedmont as sufficient cause for asking the cession of Savoy

---

[6] Hansard's Parliamentary Debates, III Series, CLVI, 3–110.

and Nice; but that now, since there was no longer any chance of the creation of an Italian confederation, Sardinia might annex the states of Central Italy, and, in that case, France would have to look to the security of her frontier. Lord Cowley said that he thought France was then seriously considering annexing both Nice and Savoy and within a few weeks the Emperor's declaration proved the correctness of his opinion.[7]

The articles in the French press were copied by the English newspapers and the question of the annexation of Savoy and Nice to France became, for a time, an issue in British politics. Questions were asked in the House of Lords by the Marquess of Normanby and in the House of Commons by Disraeli; and the Marquess, supported by Lord Derby, moved an address to the Crown approving the objections made by Her Majesty's Government to the French plan of annexation and requesting the Government to do its best to prevent it.[8] The Cabinet was alarmed, for it could not openly support the Emperor without appearing to be subservient to France in a case where she was bent on territorial aggrandizement. On the other hand, it could not vigorously oppose the French intention without bringing on a crisis in Franco-British relations. Lord Russell, therefore, expressed in the House his disapproval of the Emperor's now evident intention, but discouraged inflammatory speeches against it.[9] The situation was serious for some time, however, as is shown by a letter sent by de Persigny to his friend Chevalier:

" But if the treaty, in my opinion, is not in any danger," wrote the ambassador, " the same cannot be said for the ministry which is overwhelmed by this unfortunate affair of Savoy. If the ministry is overthrown on some financial or other question, we shall be the real cause and for a second time we shall have overthrown Lord Palmerston, that worthy and noble friend of France and of the Emperor. The Savoy affair could have been settled easily and advantageously for us, but we apparently cannot refrain from proclaiming our greatness

[7] Cowley to Russell. F. O., 27–1331, No. 34; and 1332, Nos. 84 and 87. Also an unnumbered dispatch of Cowley to Russell, " Most Confidential," February 6, 1860, in F. O., 27–1332; F. O., 27–1334, No. 212, March 1, 1860, and 1335, No. 344, March 26, 1860; W. R. Thayer, *The Life and Times of Cavour* (2 vols., Boston, 1911), I, 530.

[8] Hansard, *op. cit.*, CLVI, 214, 445, 580–584.

[9] *Ibid.*, 1966, and 2166–2174.

and prestige with such precipitation that we run the risk of eating the fruit before it is ripe. I should like to see those wretched official or semi-official newspapers at the bottom of the sea bag and baggage, — for I cannot recall any service that they have ever rendered, while there is not a single affair that they have not spoiled, compromised, or ruined." [10]

The question of the annexation of Savoy was used by the Tories as a weapon with which they hoped to weaken the Palmerston government, but they did not want to turn them out immediately, because they knew that England was not in a position to oppose the Emperor's desire. Furthermore, they lacked a majority in Parliament, and they preferred to attack the reform bill which was to be introduced by Russell, rather than take office and find themselves obliged to present a bill of their own. Their opposition to the Treaty of Commerce was inspired by similar motives. The Treaty offered a convenient excuse for attacking the Government, but its rejection would strain Franco-British relations to a dangerous degree and would certainly not bring popular support to the party responsible for the creation of the crisis.

The political situation in England at the beginning of February, 1860, and the prospect it offered of securing the approval of the commercial treaty by Parliament were shrewdly analyzed by de Persigny, who adroitly cultivated friendly relations with both the Government and the leaders of the Opposition, although he took pains to secure full credit from his Government for everything that he accomplished.

" I hasten to say, besides," he reported on February 6, " that if the ministry is now in great peril, the treaty of commerce seems no longer to be endangered. I have learned as a result of long interviews with Lord Derby, M. Disraeli, and the principal leaders of the Tory party, that this party no longer seems disposed to fight the treaty of commerce, and will attack only the financial arrangements of the Cabinet. It will probably, therefore, accept the treaty as a more or less adequate expression of a political and commercial interest whose importance is understood by everyone here; and regulate its conduct in view of the fact that the rejection of the treaty would strain relations between the two countries and would touch the honor of the crown. But at the same time it will profit by the irritation caused by this wretched affair of Savoy to attack the Cabinet on all questions of detail connected with its financial arrangements; and if I can rely fully

---

[10] De Persigny to Chevalier, February 6, 1860. Flourens Papers.

upon the personal impression of Russell, who told me so this morning, the treaty will be accepted, but the ministry will pay with its life for the articles in the ' Patrie.' " [11]

The event that really assured the passage of the Treaty and gave strength and stability to the Palmerston Cabinet was Gladstone's great speech on the presentation of the budget. He rose from a bed of sickness, after the introduction of the budget had been postponed four days, and came into the House prepared to do the best he could. "Spoke 5 to 9 without great exhaustion; aided by a great stock of egg and wine," he wrote in his diary. "Thank God! Home at 11. This was the most arduous operation I have ever had in parliament." [12]   It was also the most successful. "He came forth and, 'consensu omnium,' achieved one of the greatest triumphs the House of Commons has ever witnessed. . . . It was a magnificent display, not to be surpassed in ability of execution, and . . . he carried the House completely with him. . . . For the moment opposition and criticism were silenced, and nothing was heard but the sound of praise and admiration." [13]

Gladstone incorporated the French treaty in his budget, so that the fate of that agreement was inseparable from that of the great reform which was to carry the free trade movement in England to its zenith. The budget provided for the reduction of the number of articles in the British tariff from 419 to 48, with a net loss of revenue of over £2,000,000, which was due chiefly to the Treaty. Gladstone proposed to make up the deficit by using the terminable annuities, which had just fallen in, and by increasing the income tax from 9*d*. to 10*d*. per pound sterling. The abolition of the duties which, in any event, would have brought gain, would thus be accompanied by an increase in taxation on the class most able to express its resentment in

[11] Min. Aff. Étr., 1860. De Persigny Dispatches. February 6 and 7, 1860.
[12] Gladstone in Diary, February 10, 1860. John Morley, *The Life of William Ewart Gladstone* (3 vols. in 2, London, 1911), II, 27.
[13] This was the testimony of Charles Greville, who approved neither of Gladstone nor of his policies. See his work, *The Greville Memoirs (third part); a journal of the reign of Queen Victoria, from 1852 to 1860* (2 vols., London, 1887), VIII, 296.

Parliament. For these reasons the plan was a bold one, but its success would mean the association of the Commercial Treaty with France with the final triumph of free trade in England. Further attacks on the Treaty as a violation of the established principles of England's commercial policy would, therefore, be futile, and the Opposition could criticize only the details by defending protection in individual cases; or else they must take the more dangerous ground of denouncing friendship with France.

" I know not what is meant by subserviency to France as regards the articles of a treaty like this," said Gladstone. " We have given to France, in the proper sense of the term, nothing by this treaty, if I except some very trifling fiscal sacrifice we are making with respect to a single article — brandy. . . . But, with that small and, I believe, solitary exception, we have given nothing to France by this treaty that we have not given with as liberal a hand to ourselves. And the changes here proposed are changes every one of which deserves the acceptance of this House on its own merits. But further, Sir, as respects the charge of subserviency to France, I know this treaty may be said to bear a political character. The commercial relations of England with France have always borne a political character. . . . The system of prohibitions during the French Revolution was built up on both sides as a political barrier and as such it was most effective. Now we must legislate by the reverse process in order to achieve not a base and servile union of the Governments, as under the late Stuarts, but a union of the nations beneficial to the world.

" This treaty is not an abandonment of the principles of Free Trade, because it involves no exclusive engagements or privileges. France is perfectly aware that our legislation makes no distinction between one nation and another and that what we enact for her we shall at the same time enact for all the world. . . . The only reason why we have not made bargains similar to the present one in former years is simply because we could not make them. It was not for want of trying. For four or five years this was almost the chief business of one or more departments of the State, and yet no progress could be made. Why? Because they set out upon a false principle — the principle that the concessions each party made to the other were not a benefit but an injury to itself. We have not proceeded upon that principle. We have never pretended to France that we were going to inflict an injury upon ourselves. We have offered France our best aid in breaking down her own vicious prohibitive system. In doing so, we may have given a greater benefit to France than to ourselves. I shall not attempt to measure it on one side or the other. What we have done is good — Nay, doubly good — good for ourselves if France had done nothing at all, doubly good because France has done a great deal. . . . The duties abolished are not really for revenue but are protective.[14] The protests by the interests concerned have never dwelt on the injury to the British exchequer. . . . There is, on the part of the most respectable classes, a desire for the protection of their own business. They show that, although they are without exception adherents of Free Trade, they are not adherents of Free Trade without exception. They make no secret of it, nor should there be any secret made of it here, that the duties in which they take an interest are not revenue duties, but are protective duties, and, therefore, ill adapted for purposes of revenue.

" Sir, I cannot pass from the subject of the French Treaty without paying a tribute of respect to two persons, at least, who have been the main authors of it. I am bound to bear this witness, at any rate, with regard to the Emperor of the French — that he has given the most unequivocal proofs of his sincerity and earnestness in the progress of this great work, a work which he has prosecuted with a clear-sighted resolution . . . with a view to commercial reforms at home and to the advancement and happiness of his own people. With regard to Cobden, speaking, as I do, at a time when every angry passion has passed away, I cannot help expressing our obligations to him for the labor he has, at no small personal sacrifice, bestowed upon a measure which he, not the least among the apostles of Free Trade, believes to be one of the greatest triumphs Free Trade has ever achieved. Rare is the privilege of any man who, having fourteen years ago rendered to his country one signal and splendid service, now again . . . has been permitted to perform a great and memorable service to his Sovereign and to his country." [15]

The great speech of Gladstone paralyzed the Opposition for the time being and prevented them definitively from effectively

[14] Gladstone gave as an example the British wine duties, the effect of which was to prohibit the importation of the cheaper wines and to levy on the more costly wines a tax that protected the home market of the British distillers of spirits and whiskey.

[15] Hansard, *op. cit.*, CLVI, 834–852. February 10, 1860. Gladstone told the House that the proposal to make the changes immediate on the English side, despite the postponement on the French side, did not come from France, but was made on the deliberate judgment of the English Government as being to the advantage of the English people.

In reply to an attack on Gladstone's speech in which it was alleged that the Treaty was forced on England as the price of continued friendly relations with France, Lord John Russell said: " The fact is, some months ago, when Cobden was going to Paris, he had a conversation with me, in which he informed me that he had several friends — one of them a person well known through Europe, Michel Chevalier — that he was anxious to converse with them in order to see whether there was any chance of a commercial treaty being entered into by France. I told him, on the part of the Government, that if he found there was such a disposition, I was sure Her Majesty's Government would be quite ready to empower their representatives to negotiate such a treaty." See Hansard, *op. cit.*, CLVI, 886.

attacking the Treaty as a whole. They resorted, therefore, to what Bright called a policy of pin pricks, in the hope that they might gradually weaken the Government and discredit the Treaty. The provision that was first selected for attack and that was opposed until the very end, was Article XI, which forbade any prohibition of the exportation of coal by either France or England, and declared that neither country would levy a duty on such exportation. It was argued that this article was an unconstitutional limitation of the prerogative of the Crown and an interference by a foreign state in the internal legislation of England. The Opposition asserted also that this article would enable France to accumulate stocks of British coal which she could later use in a war against England. Finally, they alleged that England was renouncing her right to tax exports of coal for revenue, whereas France was deliberately retaining her revenue duty.

To these attacks on Article XI, the Government replied by showing that neither the French nor the British Government attached any political importance to the prohibition regarding coal, and the Lord Chancellor gave it as his opinion that the prohibition "was not meant to work and can not work politically and has no effect upon belligerent or neutral rights." The Government argued further that, under Article XVII of the Treaty, England could not forbid the exportation of coal to France unless she applied the prohibition to all other countries, and that such an embargo would be the certain ruin of the British trade in coal and an indication of England's intention to open hostilities. In case of war with France the Treaty of Commerce, like all other treaties between the two countries, would be abrogated. Finally, it was explained that in the time of Sir Robert Peel, England had levied a duty on exports of coal, but had soon abolished it because of its harmful effects on British trade. For some time the Government had been uniformly opposed to the prohibition of exports on any article, and under the Derby administration a treaty in this sense had been concluded with Russia. Article XI, said Lord John Russell, had been framed for purely commercial reasons and its main object was to help the French manufacturers to obtain coal cheaply by an exportation that would be highly profitable to England. France had rich coal mines of her own and could also import heavily from Belgium, as she generally did, so that England could not prevent her from securing supplies sufficient for a war.[16]

The Opposition next attacked the Treaty through the budget of which it formed a part. On February 21, the second night of the great debate on the budget, Du Cane moved that "the House is opposed to adding to the existing deficit by diminishing the ordinary revenue; that it is opposed also to the reimposition of the income tax at an unnecessarily high rate." Gladstone remarked in rebuttal that this motion was not only an attack on the spirit and substance of the Treaty, but also a denunciation of the commercial policy of the British Government since the advent of Sir Robert Peel in 1842. The motion was defeated on the 24th by a vote of 339 to 223, which gave the Government a majority of 116. But in the meantime Lord Derby and his followers had pressed their attacks in other directions. The Treaty was denounced on the very ground which Gladstone had predicted in his letters to Cobden in January; namely, that by it England made immediate concessions in return for reductions by France in the more or less remote future. A motion embodying this criticism was, however, easily defeated by the Government, which secured a majority of 128.[17]

---

[16] Hansard, *op. cit.* The principal speeches against Article XI were delivered by Mr. Horsmann on February 13 and 17 and March 9, 1860, and by Lord Derby in the Upper House on February 20. On behalf of the Government the chief speakers in its defense were Lord John Russell on February 17 and 20 (giving the Lord Chancellor's opinion) and by Gladstone on March 8.

On February 27, Lord John informed the House that the French Government had offered to modify Article XI, but that the British Government had replied it desired no alteration. See Hansard, *op. cit.*, p. 1842; also Despatch Min. Aff. Étr. to de Persigny. February 16, 1860. Archives Min. Aff. Étr., 1860, de Persigny Dispatches. See also a letter of Chevalier to de Persigny giving facts in reference to French resources in coal, published in Galignani's *Messenger*, February 25, 1860. Copy in Flourens Papers.

[17] The principal debates on the Treaty and budget in the House of Commons

The final assault of the Tories on the Treaty and budget was made at the height of the excitement over the proposed annexation of Savoy and Nice to France. Long before, England had formally protested through diplomatic channels against the Emperor's intention. But that did not satisfy Parliament and a veritable wave of Francophobia swept over both houses. Motions were made and granted for the production of the official correspondence on the matter and angry speeches were made by excited members who asked whether the Emperor did not want the Rhine as well as the Alps. The excitement was increased by the Emperor's speech at the opening of the session of the French Chambers in which his intention to annex Savoy was made perfectly clear. The British Government had, happily, recovered from its panic on the subject and did what it could to calm the storm in Parliament, knowing that it could not prevent France from carrying out her design. Fortunately, also, the excitement of Parliament did not greatly alarm the country, and the Government was not forced to an aggressive attitude which would have been as futile as it would have been dangerous. But before the excitement died down the Opposition tried to have the vote on the address to the Crown approving the Treaty of Commerce deferred until the discussion of the proposed

---

were on February 20, 21, 23, and 24, 1860. The attacks were led by Disraeli and the defense by Gladstone and Bright. See Hansard, *op. cit.*

See also the letter of H. Benjamin Smith, M. P., to Chevalier, February 21, 1860, which is in the Flourens Papers. " You will have seen," he wrote, "that the struggle on the Treaty began last night. On the Speaker taking the Chair the House was crowded, both sides evidently being prepared for a sharp encounter. Disraeli opposed the Government's mode of procedure on the Treaty, and was very ably answered by Gladstone. The debate was sustained with great spirit on both sides and an unusual excitement existed until the close, when the Free Traders celebrated their triumph with loud and hearty cheers!

" This first move of the Tories was a pilot balloon to ascertain which way the wind blows. We must not flatter ourselves that the majority on the *mode of procedure* is evidence that we shall have no rocks ahead in the further discussions on the Treaty. The danger is that a combination of the anti-French party, Ribbon manufacturers, Distillers, Licensed Victuallers, Wine merchants, and those dissatisfied on particular points may defeat us by their union with the Tory party. We lost a few Liberals last night, but public feeling in favor of the Treaty is manifesting itself all over the country and I have no doubt we shall carry it."

annexation of Savoy had been completed to the satisfaction of the House.[18]   The Government granted a brief delay and then pressed for a vote on the address.   An amendment to omit Article XI of the Treaty was rejected and, by a vote of 282 to 56, the House of Commons agreed to an address approving the Treaty of Commerce with France.

The victory of the Government in the House of Commons on March 9 was completed by the approval of the Treaty by the House of Lords on the 15th.   Thus the consent of Parliament was finally given after a long struggle whose successful issue had been far from certain, although the speech of Gladstone in presenting his budget a month before would have assured final victory had it not been for the revival of the crisis regarding Savoy at the end of February.   It can be seen, sixty years later, that Gladstone's defense of the Treaty as a part of his budget on February 10, was in reality the decisive factor; but at the time the later debates seemed of considerable importance and the excitement over Savoy appeared to be a danger of the first magnitude.

" Russell and I have congratulated each other on the happy outcome of the debates on the treaty of commerce," reported de Persigny on March 10. " It

---

[18] The most important debates regarding Savoy were on February 28 and March 2, 5, 8, and 9, 1860. Bright denounced the discussion on March 2 with such violence that Russell felt obliged to express his dissent. See Hansard, *op. cit.*

Gladstone's views regarding Savoy are given in an undated memorandum published by Lord Morley in his work, *The Life of William Ewart Gladstone* (3 vols. in 2, London, 1911), II, 22. " The French Emperor had launched his project as to Savoy and Nice. It should have been plain to all who desired an united Italy, that such an Italy ought not to draw Savoy in its wake; a country severed from it by mountains, by language, by climate, and, I suppose by pursuits. But it does not follow that Savoy should have been tacked on to France, while for the annexation of Nice, it was difficult to find a word of apology. But it could scarcely be said to concern our interests, while there was not the shadow of a case of honor. The susceptibilities of England were, however, violently aroused. Even Lord Russell used imprudent language in parliament about looking for other allies. A French panic prevailed as strong as any of the other panics that have done so much discredit to this country. For this panic the treaty of commerce with France was the only sedative. It was, in fact, a counter-irritant and it aroused a sense of commercial interest to counteract the war passion. It was and is my opinion that the choice lay between the Cobden treaty and not the certainty, but the high probability of war with France."

is in fact a great and significant event destined to diminish greatly the deplorable disposition of the two countries to get annoyed over every difference of opinion. The question of Savoy has been an extremely inopportune incident which could have brought about the rejection of the treaty itself. Luckily good sense got the better of passion. These irritating, violent debates, so unworthy of a great assembly do not represent the real feelings of Parliament, and still less those of the English public. We have had in our chambers also some of those bizarre and violent characters, of those people so lacking in a sense of decency that they lower the tone of all debates; but the Kinglakes, Sir Robert Peels, and Horsmanns are really the exception in Parliament and carry with them only a small minority as is shown by the ridiculous number of 56 members who voted for the amendment of M. Horsmann. As you have doubtless understood, the numbers in yesterday's vote which I sent you from the House of Commons at the end of the session give only approximately the relative strength of the parties, because many conservatives did not vote in order to allow the treaty to pass without giving their support to the ministry.

"And now that the debates are over, it must be said in praise of Gladstone, that he conducted them on a high plane and with eloquence and a skill that do him the greatest honor. After having followed with care and interest all the incidents in the struggle, I believe that the good sense of the House of Commons would never have carried the day in this very stormy debate without the conspicuous ability of the Chancellor of the Exchequer." [19]

The attitude of Parliament toward the Treaty and Gladstone's budget represented fairly accurately the opinion of the country. Although at first opposition and suspicion were common, they gave way gradually to general approval, so that by the end of February both the Treaty and the budget were popular. During the month between Gladstone's great speech and the formal approval of the Treaty by Parliament, which was expressed in its address to the Crown, petitions poured in to both Houses and to the leading newspapers, and votes were passed by public meetings, municipal councils, and chambers of commerce. The great majority of these votes and petitions were in favor of the Treaty and the budget. The large manufacturing towns, such as Manchester, Birmingham, Leeds, and Bradford, supported the reforms, as did the ports of Liverpool, Southampton, and Newcastle, and the capital of Scotland, Edinburgh; and even the usually conservative town of Oxford sent in a favorable

[19] Min. Aff. Étr., 1860. De Persigny Dispatches. De Persigny to Min. Aff. Étr., March 10, 1860.

petition. Some industries were divided in opinion. Thus the *Shipping and Mercantile Gazette* and the *Liverpool Shipowners' Association*, representing the shipping industry, opposed the Treaty because of its retention of the French navigation dues and also, with strange inconsistency, because of its stipulation for the free exportation of coal; while the cities of Liverpool, Southampton, and Newcastle supported the Treaty. Similarly in the silk industry the manufacturers of Manchester petitioned Parliament to approve the Treaty, while those of Coventry and Spitalfields, London, declared that the free admission of French silks would be their ruin. But no important industry, and not one of the great cities of the country, expressed its strong and unanimous opposition to either the Treaty or the budget. This is good evidence of their general popularity in view of the great number of votes and petitions that were sent in to Parliament and the chief newspapers of London during the month preceding the final vote in the House of Commons.[20]

But the votes and petitions were not the only manifestation of public opinion at this time. The changes that took place in the views of the *Times* during the month of February, 1860, also, are of great interest as they illustrate what probably occurred in many of the best minds of the conservative classes in England. As Gladstone wrote to Cobden early in January, "invasionism" was then the dominant idea in the public mind. The volunteer movement was still popular in England and people knew that militarism must be dominating French policy because the ruler of France was a Bonaparte. Had not Napoleon III recently made war on Austria in the name of Italian nationality, but with the real object of recovering Savoy for France? Since France had thus proved herself militaristic, her ideas and plans were under suspicion and the Treaty of Commerce was regarded as being probably a means of promoting some unknown political aim. On the economic side the Treaty

---

[20] See *Morning Star*, February 13, 15, 16, 18, 23, and 24, 1860; *Times*, February 15, 20, 22, 23, and 29, 1860. The "United Towns' Association of Licensed Victuallers" met at Birmingham and passed a vote of protest against the Treaty and budget (see *Times*, February 15), while the wine dealers sent a deputation to lay their strong objections before Gladstone.

suffered from its combination with a budget which sought compensation not only in the retention of the income tax, but even in its increase. Thus, while the benefits of the proposed reforms would accrue to the mercantile and manufacturing classes, the burden of financing them would be borne chiefly by the conservative classes who owned the land and filled the government offices. The Treaty was, therefore, regarded for a time by many conservatives as undesirable both on political and on economic grounds, and this view was expressed by their organ in the press.

The *Times* began on February 11, by marvelling with withering awe at Gladstone's budget and at the eloquence with which it was presented. The Treaty, on the other hand, was declared to be not as bad as had been feared, although it was clear that France gained far more from it than did England. Two days later the *Times* had almost reached the point of believing that the Treaty was not bad at all. It declared that "the Treaty, whatever its merits or defects, has been concluded and ratified, and it seems to us perfectly clear that, all circumstances considered, Parliament can not take upon itself to annul the Treaty by refusing its aid towards the fulfilment of its conditions. The power is, no doubt, expressly reserved, but it would require a much stronger case than can be made out to induce the repudiation of an agreement involving such high political and social, as well as financial, considerations." This was certainly a favorable verdict and seemed to foreshadow support of the Treaty; but the *Times* suddenly remembered that, after all, France was militaristic and that, under Article XI of the Treaty, she could now easily get the coal she needed for making war, possibly for making war on England. In this state of mind the great daily, not unnaturally, remembered also that Napoleon III was really a despot and that, therefore, he was probably trying to impose his will on England through the Treaty of Commerce.

"The Treaty has come down to Parliament, it has been said, like a bill from the Upper House," remarked the *Times* on the 18th. "Louis Napoleon and Cobden, we hear it observed, have put their heads together and agreed on a treaty which answers both their purposes, and they now expect the British Parliament to ratify it as complacently and as much without exception as their shadowy imitation at Paris. Supposing there to be just a foundation, although not a justification for this charge, and that the British Parliament is treated without due regard to its freedom of character and its deliberative function, how is the insult, intended or not intended, to be met? The most natural way of repelling the implied slight would be to take the Budget, with the involved Treaty, into free and unfettered consideration. Amend it; strike out this; insert that; alter figures and dates if need be; and so teach Emperors, Chancellors of the Exchequer; and even the great unadorned and undecorated, that they must respect and abide by the wisdom of Legislatures."

In its next editorial on the Treaty, the *Times* suddenly recollected that, although it might sometimes roar like the British lion, it was really the oracle of the nation. It even ate some of the words it had so recently uttered, and from that time until a new war panic clouded its vision in the following summer, it advised the English people about the Treaty with wisdom and moderation.

"Gladstone may spare himself," it said on the 22d. "He need not convince any of his antagonists of what they are anxious to proclaim. They have proved abundantly the lamentable state of feeling between England and her nearest neighbors, and an extraordinary crisis in these feelings, driving both sides to a ruinous expenditure. Here, then, is a crisis for an exceptional budget, and for the interposition of an income-tax, if that will meet the emergency. It is just such a crisis as Sir Robert Peel himself had laid down for the use of this great weapon of finance. We use it in the confidence that, by enabling us to lower the tariff, it will also enable us to win the confidence of our neighbors, induce them to contract their armaments, and so allow us to contract ours also, and reduce our expenditure."

The last important editorial of the *Times* on the Treaty showed that the great daily had now decided to give it its undivided support. It could even be called the best reasoned and most effective editorial in favor of the Treaty that appeared in any of the influential newspapers of London during the debates in Parliament. As a summary of the case for the defendant and an irresistible attack on the Opposition it was admirable.

"The majority of 116 in a very full house against Du Cane's motion," declared the *Times* on February 25, "is just what might be expected from the rather remarkable fact that no one of its supporters, however ingenious or eloquent, has produced one real objection to the Treaty with France and the financial measures of the Government. There have been objections without number, and they have been stated with effect; but they have all been such as, rightly reasoned upon, told the other way. As a matter of sentiment, for example, we may all deplore that a treaty has been signed, and that the two Governments do not spontaneously vie with one another in doing what is even more beneficial to their own people than to their neighbors. But, if our side of the Treaty is itself a national benefit, the French side is so much in addition. The objection that France has not conceded more, admits that any concession is a gain and surrenders the whole objection to a treaty as such. The objection that French wine is a luxury is really an objection to the tariff which made it a luxury, not to the Treaty, which will cheapen and extend its use. . . . The objection that our manufacturers will gain little might be strong if urged by themselves, but not when urged against them by politicians who also believe the Treaty to be too much in the interest of trade. The objection that France is hostile and warlike points to any fair and ordinary means for diverting her high intelligence and vast resources to the pursuits of peace. The objection that on the French side the bargain, if such it is to be considered, is not so complete and expeditious as ours, concedes that what is to be done is so good when it comes that we may complain of a single day's delay. . . .

" An opposition of this nature could not be real or sincere. . . . From Dizzy downwards there is not one of the Conservative body who has not dreamt long ago of a Commercial Treaty with France as the best thing that could happen to either of these countries." [21]

A treaty that could thus win the support of the habitual champion of the invasionists and the accredited organ of the conservative classes might justly claim to have great intrinsic merits. It had won also the favor of the great majority of English free traders, despite the fact that, as a treaty of commerce, it was in apparent contradiction to the orthodox principles of their faith. But the approval of the French Treaty by the British Parliament, as well as by the great majority of the English people, was not due solely to its own merits. The adherents of Lord Derby had shown themselves ready to attack the Treaty, regardless of the great aims it was intended to achieve, because it was introduced by their political opponents. They had even raised anew the old cry that England was threatened by the militarism of France, when the plan for the annexation of Savoy gave them the opportunity. The Treaty

[21] See *Times*, February 11, 13, 15, 18, 22, and 25, 1860. Its editorials on Savoy were published March 6 and 8.

survived these attacks partly because those who were not inspired by purely political motives believed that it deserved to, but also because its defense was made on such lofty ground that the Opposition could not attack it directly with any real hope of success. Gladstone had incorporated it in a budget that was one of the greatest measures for the promotion of free trade that had ever been proposed. He showed that the manufacturers who opposed it because it abolished the duties on products competing with their own, were really protectionists and as such could not pose as guardians of the national revenue. And finally he proved not only that the Treaty was the sole means by which the French and British tariffs could simultaneously be reduced, to the mutual benefit of the two countries and the promotion of the principles of free trade, but also that it was the most effective instrument then available for preserving peace and securing international friendship. The idea of the Anglo-French Treaty of Commerce came from Chevalier; its embodiment in a form that was acceptable to the Emperor of the French and the British Cabinet was the work chiefly of Chevalier and Cobden, but the acceptance of the completed Treaty by the British Parliament and people was the achievement of Gladstone.

CHAPTER VII

THE ENQUÊTE AT PARIS AND THE TARIFF CONVENTIONS

THE negotiations that ended successfully in the signature of the Anglo-French Treaty of Commerce on January 23, 1860, were rendered difficult, and, at times, critical by the reluctance of the Emperor to commit himself irrevocably to a radical reform of the French tariff. Cobden said that Napoleon III lacked moral courage, as did all his subjects, with the single exception of Michel Chevalier,[1] and this opinion was apparently confirmed by the remark of Prince Napoleon to one of Cobden's French friends that his cousin was slow in reaching decisions.[2] Cobden also expressed the opinion that the Emperor showed a wholly unreasonable fear of the protectionists in France, whom he could put to rout by the mere exercise of his power to reform his tariff through a commercial treaty with another country. But the great English free trader, whose power of persuasion had won him the nickname of "Unabashed Eloquence,"[3] failed to realize the difficulty of the problem which confronted the Emperor in France. Napoleon had no powerful organization, such as the Anti-Corn Law League, to support him in his attack on the French protective tariff, and he knew that he must expect, not the support, but the organized and determined opposition of the French manufacturers. He remembered well that none of his predecessors on the throne of France had been able to effect a substantial reform of the tariff, and that four years before he himself had been defeated in his first attempt. If he used the power given him by the constitution which he had

[1] Cobden to Lord Palmerston, October 29, 1859. Cobden Papers.
[2] Prince Napoleon to Arlès-Dufour, January 16, 1860. Arsenal. Fonds Enfantin. No. 7762.
[3] Lord John Russell to Gladstone, December 24, 1859. Gladstone Papers.

forced upon his country to destroy the system of high protection in France, could he be sure that the opposition aroused would be confined to petitions and remonstrances respectfully addressed to the Sovereign? Had he not said to Cobden at their first interview in October, 1859: "Nous ne faisons pas des réformes en France, nous ne faisons que des révolutions"? [4]

The Emperor was sincere in his desire to free French industry and agriculture from the shackles of the prohibitive system, but he was also a shrewd politician. The letter which he addressed to his Minister of State on January 15, 1860, even if its main provisions were not framed by him, was prepared as early as the middle of the preceding month to be used as a means of securing popular support for a program of widespread economic reforms of which the Treaty, whose negotiation was still concealed from the public, would be the central feature. By combining an obnoxious attack on the protective tariff with long desired aid in reforestation, drainage, and the construction of railroads, as well as by government loans to industry, the Emperor wisely thought that he could confine within safe limits the opposition that would be aroused against the commercial treaty. The reception of the letter to Fould soon proved the correctness of his calculation. From nearly all parts of France, whether industrial or agricultural, came petitions thanking the Sovereign and urging him to meet quickly the needs of the country for new railroads and canals, while many districts expressed pleasure also at the prospect of free raw materials and the abolition of prohibitions. [5] There can be no question but that the program of economic improvements laid down in the letter of January 15 greatly softened the blow that came a week later in the announcement that a treaty of commerce had been signed with England.

The organized opposition of the great manufacturers, however, was not averted. The only argument that could appeal to them was force, and until the Government had shown that it had determined to use it, if necessary, they intended to exert their power in an attempt to terrorize the Emperor and his ministers.

[4] Cobden to Lord Palmerston, October 29, 1859. Cobden Papers.
[5] The collection of these petitions is in Arch. Nat., F 12–2685.

They had done so successfully in 1856, and it never occurred to them that they could fail in 1860. On January 19, the *Moniteur industriel*, in its first issue after the publication of the letter to Fould, printed the full text of that document and immediately after it the note inserted in the *Moniteur universel* on October 17, 1856, postponing until 1861 the abolition of prohibitions, and the letter of Rouher to the Chamber of Commerce of Lille of May 11, 1859, declaring that, because of the war in Italy, the Government would defer indefinitely the opening of the Enquête that was to precede the repeal of prohibitions. This was a significant hint to the Government that the protectionists would fight against any attempt to reform the tariff. The *Moniteur industriel* declared itself disturbed by the letter, but approved of the plan for internal improvements and, particularly, of the fact that the different features of the plan would be submitted to the Chamber for legislative sanction. The organ of the protectionists concluded by saying that the persistent rumors in the French and English press of the signature of a treaty of commerce had spread consternation among French manufacturers, but that they could not be accurate because treaties of commerce were given as the last of the items in the Emperor's program.

Despite the declaration of the *Moniteur industriel*, the manufacturers did not really believe that the rumors of a commercial treaty were without foundation. Had not several of their number just been summoned to the Tuileries by the Emperor and his Minister of Commerce? The leading manufacturers of Rouen, from which town Pouyer-Quertier had been called to the palace, were so alarmed that they chartered a special train and rushed to Paris in a body. At the same time one hundred and twenty spinners and other manufacturers from Lille and Roubaix appeared in the capital in a state of consternation and demanded audiences with the Emperor and Rouher. By the 20th the crowd of manufacturers in Paris had grown to over four hundred, but still the Emperor refused to see them and the negotiations for the Treaty went on. The manufacturers, therefore, resorted to their last weapon of attack and drew up a petition in which they reminded the Emperor of his declaration in October, 1856, and of that of his Minister of Commerce in May, 1859, postponing the abolition of prohibitions. Now, they said, he was planning to change not only prohibitions, but simple duties that would affect all French industries at once, and, worst of all, this action was to be taken without giving them a hearing.

" We ask you, Sire, what then becomes of that promise of an *enquête* in which we were obliged to put our trust," said the petitioners. " For the industries of France could not accept as an adequate *enquête* the brief words exchanged with the Minister of Commerce and the reception by Your Majesty of certain manufacturers who represent only an infinitesimal part of the branches of our national production. We were unable to gain permission to argue in defense of our interests and now we are going to be condemned without having been heard. . . . And under what circumstances is Your Majesty eliminating that debate which should have preceded the removal of prohibitions and which was promised to us in so solemn a manner? At the very moment when it is essential to have the benefit of all the knowledge and experience of the special boards and councils as well as all competent individuals. It is a very serious matter to bind us to England by a treaty of commerce."

The petitioners reminded the Emperor of the disastrous results of the Treaty of 1786 which they attributed to the Government's failure to consult the manufacturers.

" We shall add only a word," they concluded. " The measures Your Majesty is about to take constitute nothing less than an economic and social revolution. It seems impossible to us that in dealing with so many matters without the advice of the representatives of our manufacturing centers, the Administration should not commit many and important mistakes. The existence of a more or less considerable number of our industries is threatened. What will be the remedy when we are bound by a treaty? We must choose between two alternatives. Either we must submit to the disastrous consequences, or we must go to war and destroy the treaty by cannon fire. It is between these two terrible alternatives that you have placed us." [6]

This petition was signed by one hundred and sixty-six manufacturers then in Paris, but during the following three weeks over a thousand additional signatures were secured, so that the total was nearly fourteen hundred. The great majority of the signers were textile manufacturers from Lille, Roubaix, and Tourcoing in the north; Amiens, in Picardy; Rouen, Elbeuf,

[6] *Moniteur industriel,* January 19 and 20, 1860. The text of this petition is given in an Appendix (pp. 372–375).

Lizieux, and other centers in Normandy; and Mulhouse and other towns in the Vosges. A fair number were ironmasters, and a few judges or municipal officials. The audacity of the petitioners in thus addressing a despotic government was amazing, and shows clearly how confident they were that they could frighten the Emperor into abandoning or again postponing the proposed reforms. But Napoleon remained unmoved even by this threat of a war, the first step towards which would, almost certainly, have been an attack on his government. The boldness of the manufacturers was, as the Government undoubtedly realized, an attempt to conceal their serious alarm, and the ironmasters, who profited most by the existing prohibitions, were too greatly concerned by the prospect of British competition to confine their protests to threats. The petition of their leader, Léon Talabot, president of the Comité des Forges, shows that they were really in a plaintive mood verging on despair.

" I have the greatest respect for the Emperor," said Talabot. " I am one of those who believe that he has done the greatest things that a man could achieve. But I do not carry my respect to such a point that I must admit that in industrial matters the Emperor knows every one of the many factors which enter into the conditions of existence of French industry. If I had had the honor of being admitted to discuss before His Majesty the very serious measures which are being prepared, I should have felt under obligation not to publish anything I had said or written on that occasion. But the fate, the very existence of the iron industry in France is in question. His Majesty is not fully informed; I am sure of it. . . . The Emperor had begun an *enquête*, but no one can say that it was adequate. It seems to be closed. . . . Under these circumstances I am fulfiling a duty in writing what I should have said to the Emperor; and, if it is necessary to make public this paper, I should not feel that I was lacking in that respect which I deem it an honor to hold. . . . It is impossible not to recognize in the sad details of the real condition of our iron industry, which I shall now describe resolutely, the characteristics of a death-bed confession. It is the gravity, the solemnity of these circumstances which leads me to say publicly what I should have submitted, perhaps usefully, to the enlightened appreciation of the Emperor. As for myself, I shall not have failed in my duties as president of the Ironmasters Association."

Talabot sent with his petition a long memorandum on the comparative cost of transportation and of coal to the French and English foundries, by which he intended to show that the

French ironmaster could not possibly compete with his rival across the Channel. In view of his threat to publish these figures, together with his petition, the Emperor, to whom the matter had been referred, ordered Rouher to investigate and prepare a refutation for publication in one of the Government journals. The investigation, made by the Inspector General of Mines, Combes, disclosed that Talabot was the managing director of the Denain and Anzin foundry in the north of France, where he procured his coal from the near-by mines of the Anzin Company, but had to get ore from a considerable distance. Talabot had not made any arrangement with the Anzin Company for special rates, so that he was obliged to pay the usual monopoly prices. In short, largely through his own fault, his foundry was most disadvantageously placed. He compared it, however, with a Welsh foundry whose situation was exceptionally favorable, and he used the figures given in a year when prices in Wales were unusually low. As if this were not enough, he falsified the figures he used, diminishing Welsh prices and increasing French by from 20 to 50 per cent.[7] Well might Rouher urge Cobden, when the negotiations for the tariff convention began, to procure his own figures from English sources, because the French ironmasters were consistent liars.[8] The petitions in the Government archives show that his accusation was amply justified, and that the case of Talabot was only one example of the slight importance attached to veracity by the great majority of the French protectionists.

[7] Arch. Nat., F 12–2514. At the end of Talabot's petition is a note from Mocquard, the Emperor's private secretary, dated January 22, 1860: " Mon cher Rouher," he writes, " Je vous envoie le mémoire que l'Empereur recoit a l'instant, de M. Talabot. Comme il en annonce la publication, S. M. désire une étude *immédiate* de la missive et une réfutation toute prête pour les journaux." Combes gave his conclusion in an undated memorandum supplemented by a letter to Rouher dated January 31, 1860. Both are in Série F 12–2514.

[8] Cobden wrote in his diary April 26, 1860 (Vol. III): " Called on Rouher who is very anxious that the English producers should appear before the Commission to state their facts in opposition to the French protectionists. He is so anxious for a fair statement of the case that he is willing to pay the expenses of the English deputation to ensure their coming to Paris. The French manufacturers have lied wholesale to the Emperor and the members of the Commission."

The chief textile centers of the north, and Rouen in Normandy, were not satisfied with the share of their manufacturers in the great petition of January 20, and, accordingly, each of them sent in a petition of its own. They begged the Emperor to reconsider his hasty decision, or, at least, to delay for several months the ratification of the Treaty.[9] It is interesting to note that these great textile industries, together with the iron industry, were the ones which enjoyed a practical monopoly of the French market through the prohibitions then in force. Thanks to their favored position, they had been able to use antiquated machinery, or sometimes to depend to a great extent upon hand labor by workers in households, such as had been prevalent in England at the beginning of her industrial revolution, sixty or seventy-five years before. Many of the iron foundries were situated in mountain districts, far from both railroads and markets because, under existing prices, they could still afford to burn wood instead of coal. The increasing pressure of competition by the more favorably situated foundries which smelted with coal was never mentioned as a reason for their difficulties, because it was much easier to blame everything on the Treaty so obviously concluded at the instigation of perfidious Albion. All joined in one chorus of despair, and announced their impending ruin on the application of the new tariff reductions. Two of the towns in the north of France, which were particularly loud in their complaints, were visited in October, 1860, by a manufacturer from Reims who reported their condition to his friend Chevalier:

" I send you a few words hastily," he wrote, " to let you know that there is the greatest activity in the mills of Roubaix and Tourcoing. We are doing active and important business in both cities; we often have to go to them and in fact we have just spent several days in them. I repeat, then, that these two industrial centers are working at full speed and I have rarely seen, even in the best seasons, as great an activity as they now display. What can we think then when people so busily engaged complain with bitterness and violence that the measures about to be enacted will complete their destruction? " [10]

---

[9] *Moniteur industriel*, January 26 and February 2, 1860.
[10] J. Warnier to Chevalier. Reims, October 29, 1860. Flourens Papers.

In the face of the clamor of the protectionist manufacturers the Government remained calm and immovable. A certain number of deputations were received by the Emperor and Rouher, and some of the features of the recently completed Treaty were explained to them, but no favors were granted. The *Moniteur industriel* was seized for publishing the bold and threatening petition of the manufacturers at Paris on January 20, and when the prohibitionists in the great textile centers not only threatened to close their factories, and thus drive their men to revolt through unemployment, but actually began to put their threat into execution, the Government sent word that, if the workmen were incited to revolt, the manufacturers who had incited them, and not the workmen, would go to jail. The Government's threat was sufficient, for it showed the manufacturers that they could not succeed in their object of intimidating the Emperor and his ministers. The agitation in the industrial centers soon died down,[11] and the victorious Government began the necessary preparation for the completion of the commercial negotiations, which called for the conversion of the existing ad valorem duties into specific duties of 30 per cent, or less, based on English and French prices during the six months preceding the signature of the Treaty of January 23, 1860.

The excitement in the manufacturing districts caused by the publication of the Emperor's letter to Fould on January 15, followed closely by the news of the signature of the Treaty with England, never constituted a serious menace to public order, or the authority of the Government, owing to the firmness shown by the Emperor and his advisers. It was aroused by the protectionist manufacturers because there seemed a chance that they could succeed in bringing sufficient pressure to bear on the Gov-

---

[11] See *Morning Star*, January 26, and *Economist*, February 4, 1860. See also *Moniteur industriel*, January 29, 1860, in which is printed a letter from the Committee of the Association for the Protection of National Labor. "Nous venons protester, auprès de votre Excellence, avec énergie contre le reproche que vous avez fait à l'un de nous, de vouloir semer l'agitation dans le pays, et de chercher à exciter les ouvriers. . . . Nous persistons à affirmer, M. le Ministre, que la pétition [that of January 20] remise à Sa Majesté, en exprimant l'opinion et les vœux de l'immense majorité de l'industrie nationale, était restée dans les limites d'une discussion permise et d'une modération respectueuse."

ernment to modify or postpone its intended reform of the French tariff. After the complete failure of the agitation, the protectionists had no further opportunity to protest until they could bring the matter up in the Chambers, whose sessions were opened on March 1, 1860. Even then they could do nothing effective, in view of the fact that the Treaty was not brought directly before the Chambers, because of the power granted by the Constitution of 1852 to the Emperor to sign and promulgate treaties of commerce without submitting them for legislative sanction. It was hoped, however, that the eloquence of protectionist deputies and senators might have some influence on the negotiations for the tariff conventions that were to be held during the coming summer.

The opportunity sought by the protectionists to express their views in the Chambers came when, on April 24, the Committee of the Corps législatif reported out the Government's bill for the free admission in French ships of raw wool and cotton. Few, even among the opponents of tariff reform, disapproved of the bill, because it was generally recognized that free wool and cotton would be of great value to the chief textile industries of the country. The passage of the bill was, therefore, never in doubt and its presentation was important only because of the opportunity it gave to criticize the Treaty of Commerce with England. Pouyer-Quertier, one of the leaders of the protectionists, and an important cotton manufacturer of Rouen, who was chosen to report the bill to the Chamber, devoted himself almost exclusively to the defense of the threatened protective system of France. He dwelt eloquently on the great development of French industry since the close of the great revolution, and attributed it wholly to the security given by a high protective tariff. He then reminded the Government of the words of the Minister of State, Fould, who, as Minister of Finance in 1851, had denounced the tariff bill of Sainte-Beuve, declaring that the Government rejected absolutely the principle of free trade. He was convinced, he said, that the rates of 30 per cent and 25 per cent stipulated by the Government in the Treaty with England showed that it still intended to maintain the protective system.

" France," said Pouyer-Quertier, " has fixed a maximum; but, up to that, she is free to regulate her tariff as she pleases, and, in the last resort, even if she formally fixed the duties on all articles at 30 per cent, she would have fulfilled her promises to England. It is France then and France alone who should settle the decrease in the tariff below 30 per cent which it may be convenient to effect. The English Government has no concern in the matter." [12]

The report of Pouyer-Quertier showed that the object of the protectionists was to make the maximum rate of 30 per cent, which was to be reduced to 25 per cent in 1864, the general level of the new specific duties, and that this could be accomplished by the fixation of the duties by the French Government, aided by the Chambers. They contended that, under the terms of the Treaty, France could arrange her new tariff without any further negotiations with England, and that she was not bound to agree to rates below 30 per cent. A strict interpretation of the written engagements embodied in the Treaty would have made such action a legal fulfilment of French obligations. The French Government had purposely made the provisions general, in order to disarm opposition in France, and the British negotiators had agreed to take the risk involved because of their confidence in the integrity of the motives of their French colleagues. The French Minister of Foreign Affairs, Baroche, had written to Cobden that the rates of 30 and 25 per cent named in the Treaty were maxima which would be attained only exceptionally, and that the majority of the new duties would range between those rates and a minimum of approximately 10 per cent.[13] Furthermore, it had been understood on both sides that the conversion of ad valorem to specific duties in the French tariff would be made by further negotiations between the two countries on the basis of the prices of the six months preceding the signature of the Treaty on January 23, 1860. The French Government was not, however, legally bound to reduce below 30 per cent any duties other than those on coal and iron named in Articles XI and XVII, because

[12] *Moniteur*, April 24, 1860.
[13] Baroche to Cobden. January 22, 1860. Min. Aff. Étr. Mémoires et Documents anglaises, Vol. 94. Memoranda of de Clercq on the Treaty of 1860, Annexe 7.

no such obligation was mentioned in the text of the Treaty. It could have evaded its agreement to negotiate the specific duties with England, because Article XIII of the Treaty, which provided for such negotiations, stipulated in addition that the ad valorem duties in the French tariff should be retained if a supplementary convention was not signed before July 1, 1860; and also in the case of any articles upon which no specific duties should have been settled by common consent.

Baroche replied, in the name of the Government, to the attack of Pouyer-Quertier.[14] He said, first, that the Government had not abandoned the policy laid down by Fould in 1851; that it was still opposed to free trade on the one hand, and to prohibitions on the other. It believed now, as then, that only infant industries should be strongly protected, and that adult industries should receive just enough protection to enable them to compete on equal terms with the industries of other countries. The Government believed also, however, that the need of protection should be determined, not by the condition of the worst firms, but by that of the best. As for the Treaty of 1860, the specific duties of the new French tariff were the real objective of the negotiators, and they were not settled before the signature only because French industry had become so greatly alarmed by rumors regarding the negotiations with England that the Treaty was signed in haste. Baroche explained that the Treaty did not provide for a mixed commission to agree upon the specific duties, but that such a commission would have to be named for the investigation which must determine the prices on which the new duties would be based.[15] He made it perfectly clear to the protectionists that the Government had no intention of sacrificing its honor, as they demanded when they called for a general rate of 30 per cent to be imposed arbitrarily by France; and that it would negotiate with England

[14] *Moniteur*, April 30, 1860.
[15] Article XIII of the Treaty reads: "The ad valorem duties established within the limits fixed by the preceding articles shall be converted into specific duties by a Supplementary Convention which shall be concluded before July 1, 1860. The medium prices during the six months preceding the date of the present treaty shall be taken as bases for this conversion. . . ."

regarding the new duties according to the understanding reached by the negotiators. In closing, Baroche said that he would put "beside the treaty the report of the honorable M. Pouyer-Quertier in order to show how difficult it is to perform an act of real utility."

The speech of Baroche in the Corps législatif marked the failure of the second attempt made by the protectionists to intimidate the Government. The Emperor and his ministers had remained firm in the face of the agitation in the manufacturing centers aroused by the publication of the letter to Fould and the news of the signature of the Treaty with England. They were unmoved again when the protectionists demanded in the Chamber that the Government abide by the strictly legal terms of the Treaty and, by refusing to complete the negotiations, secure the retention of 30 per cent as the general level of duties in the French tariff. The speech of Baroche in the Chamber had its effect on the Senate, for there was no debate of importance on the bill admitting wool and cotton in French ships free of duty, while the discussion on a group of petitions from protectionist manufacturers showed that the Senate, though undoubtedly protectionist at heart, was so eager to please both the petitioners and the Government that it simply could not make a decision. Baroche and Rouher had only to intimate that the Government desired the rejection of the petitions, and the victory was won.[16] Thus, despite the great outbursts of oratory, the protectionist attack on the Treaty in the Chambers was a complete failure.

The final negotiations for the settlement of the duties in the new French tariff, whose determination was a necessary complement to the Treaty signed on January 23, 1860, raised problems of such difficulty that prompt action was impossible. Article XIII of the Treaty required the specific duties established to be based on the average prices of the preceding six months, so that

---

[16] See *Moniteur*. The most important speeches in the Senate were delivered on May 12, 21, 22, and 23, 1860. The "Talabot Petition" referred to in the *Moniteur* was sent to the Senate March 15, 1860. It was signed by Léon Talabot and by fifteen other heads of industrial concerns, chiefly those in textile industries. See Arch. Nat., F 12–2684.

an investigation of price conditions in France and England had to be made before discussions regarding the tariff could be begun. In March, therefore, Rouher informed Lord Cowley that he would be glad to receive deputations of British producers, and that it might be useful to have them discuss rates and prices with French delegates in the presence of the French and British commissioners appointed to negotiate the tariff convention.[17] The result of this suggestion, which met with the hearty approval of Cobden, was the holding of a series of conferences at the office of the Board of Trade in London, to which representatives from the principal manufacturing centers of Great Britain were invited. On their conclusion, arrangements were made to send to Paris deputations from British chambers of commerce to give evidence concerning British prices of goods likely to be exported to France. Cobden, on his return from the Riviera late in March, was urged by both Rouher and Lord Cowley to undertake the negotiation of the tariff convention. Accordingly, while in London, he helped to organize the discussions at the office of the Board of Trade, and secured from the Foreign Office his appointment as Chief Commissioner for the coming negotiations, with the powers of a plenipotentiary to sign the ensuing treaty. It was arranged that he would be assisted by Mr. (later Sir Louis) Mallett of the Board of Trade and Mr. Ogilvie of the Customs Department, who would follow him to Paris as soon as the French were ready to begin the collection of information on French and British prices.[18]

In the meantime the French Government had completed its arrangements. Herbet, the former Consul General at London and a man of conspicuously liberal views on the tariff, was appointed Chief Commissioner for France; and a number of special agents were appointed to assist him in the collection of evidence, among them the well-known free trader Amé, the author of a recently published history of the French tariff,

---

[17] F. O., 27-1334. Cowley to Russell. No. 281. March 12, 1860.
[18] See Cobden, Diary, Vol. II, April 4 to 17, 1860. Cobden Papers. Cobden reached England on April 3 and returned to Paris on the 20th. On his return from the Riviera he had stayed only ten days in Paris (March 24 to April 3).

and Guillaume Petit, an editor of the *Journal des débats*. On April 11, the Government issued a decree directing the Conseil Supérieur du Commerce, after hearing the evidence presented by interested parties: (1) to determine the average price of British goods during the six months preceding the signature of the Treaty; (2) to find from this the means to fix the equivalent of the maximum ad valorem rate of 30 per cent; and (3) to collect the information necessary to ascertain the degree of protection needed by the different French industries.[19] The composition of the Conseil Supérieur, which was to conduct this important investigation showed that the Government intended to effect a radical reduction of the French tariff. The president was Rouher, whose liberal views were well known. Among the other members were the Comte de Morny, the Emperor's brother, who had advocated tariff reforms as early as 1853, and the newly appointed senator, Michel Chevalier. Since eight of the other members either held liberal views on commercial questions, or were government officials under the orders of Rouher and Baroche, the Government could rely upon the support of eleven out of the twenty members of the council.

The Conseil Supérieur du Commerce began its hearings on May 7 and met several times a week until the latter part of August. As each industry was considered, the French and British manufacturers interested were called upon to testify before the Council regarding prices and conditions of production in the two countries. The British manufacturers were sent for and instructed by Cobden and his two assistants, and were aided by the advice and sympathy of Chevalier, who not only fulfilled regularly his duties as a member of the Council, but also kept in constant communication with Cobden. The evidence given by the witnesses was taken down by shorthand, but the printed reports were shown only to members of the Council and other government officials. This meant that the French manufacturers knew nothing regarding the testimony of witnesses unless they were themselves present at the session in which the evidence

[19] See *Moniteur*. Session of the Senate, May 12, 1860. Speech of Dumas, a member of the Conseil Supérieur du Commerce.

was given. Hence they could not readily combine to influence public opinion through the press, or to start an agitation in opposition to the policy of the Government. Neither could they again accuse the Government of reforming the tariff without giving them a hearing.

After taking the testimony of witnesses for three months, the Conseil Supérieur du Commerce adjourned late in August in order to allow its members to attend the sessions of the Conseils Généraux of the various departments in which they resided. The next official session was not held until September 28, three days before the date when the decree giving the new duties on iron and steel was to be issued. Rouher read the new tariff, but did not call for a vote, or ask any member of the Council to express his opinions. Similar tactics were adopted at the later sessions, when the reports of the Government's special agents on the chief industries affected were read, but no discussion was allowed. The Government, in short, filed for its own use the information obtained from the witnesses at the hearings, but allowed no deliberation on it by the members of the Council. It had technically fulfilled its obligation to ascertain French and British prices and to give French manufacturers a hearing. In its eyes the Conseil Supérieur had accomplished all that had been expected of it, for the Government had decided upon the policy it intended to pursue before the Council had been directed to begin its investigation, and advice from individual councillors, therefore, was not desired. No one was in a position to make an effective protest, and the Enquête, so often demanded by the protectionists, which had been opened publicly with great ceremony, was closed in an obscure office of the Ministry of Commerce.[20]

[20] For accounts of the work of the Conseil Supérieur du Commerce see the anonymous *Historique du traité de commerce de 1860 et des conventions complémentaires* (Paris, 1861), pp. 107–143. Much of the author's information was derived from the *Economist*.

See also Ernest Feray, *Du traité de commerce de 1860 avec l'Angleterre* (Paris, 1881), pp. 13–18. The testimony taken at the hearings was published in six volumes by the Government in its *Enquête de 1860 sur l'état de l'industrie en France*. Five of the reports by the Government's special agents on the ability of French industries to meet foreign competition are in the Archives Nationales.

The prolonged Enquête conducted by the Conseil Supérieur du Commerce had made necessary the postponement of the official negotiations for the convention embodying the new specific duties of the French tariff. Accordingly, on June 27, 1860, a second additional article to the Treaty of January 23 was signed by which the date for he conclusion of the negotiations was extended from July 1 to November 1, 1860. It was agreed, further, that instead of one convention, there should be three conventions, of which the first should deal with iron, steel, and machinery; the second with the yarns and manufactures of flax and hemp; and the last with all other British products specified in Article I of the Treaty of January 23. This agreement was subsequently modified by a protocol signed on November 5, by which the number of conventions· to be signed was reduced to two, and the date for the conclusion of the last convention was extended to December 15, 1860.

The official meetings of the French and British commissioners began on August 20, after the close of the hearings held by the Conseil Supérieur. The chief negotiators were Cobden and Rouher, but the sessions were attended also by Cobden's two assistants, and by four officials of the French Government, of whom the most important were de Forcade La Roquette, the new Director General of Customs, and Herbet, the former Consul General at London. Experts were frequently called in by both sides to give evidence regarding prices and conditions of production, for the British commissioners disputed nearly all the facts and figures presented by the French. Rouher, on his side, kept with perfect loyalty the informal agreement that 30 per cent was to be a maximum attained in but few cases, and, in accordance with his statement to Lord Cowley of the intentions of the French Government, made no attempt to raise to 30 per cent any duties in the existing tariff that were below that figure. He denied, however, that the French Government was com-

In the Série F 12–2514 are the report of Legentil on linen and of Guillaume Petit on wool; and in the Série F 12–2696 the reports of Natalis Rondot on silk, and of Ernest Baroche on wool and cotton. See also the invaluable Chapter XIV in the first volume of Leon Amé's *Étude économique sur les tarifs de douanes* (2 vols., Paris, 1876).

mitted, through the correspondence between Baroche and Cobden, to duties not exceeding 10 per cent on raw materials; and, eventually, Cobden accepted the French contention that the Emperor's ministers had agreed only that the maximum rate was to be 30 per cent and the minimum approximately 10 per cent. Rouher generally opened the discussion on each article of the tariff by offering higher duties than he expected to obtain, but, like all Frenchmen and most negotiators, he wished to leave room for concessions. His official utterances at the formal meetings and his private remarks to Cobden both show that he intended to make substantial reductions in the French tariff, and that great pressure was not needed to induce him to abandon the system of high duties that frequently amounted to prohibitions.

The Conventions that were signed on October 12 and November 16 show that, in nearly every case, the French Government granted reductions in its tariff that greatly exceeded what England had expected and more than fulfilled the obligations incurred in the Treaty of January 23. In the first Convention, which comprised iron, steel, other metals, and machinery, the French agreed to admit British cast iron at 25 francs per 100 kg.; machinery at a rate of approximately 15 francs, a reduction of 75 per cent; and cutlery at an ad valorem duty of 20 per cent. In each case there was to be a further reduction in 1864. In the second Convention, signed on November 16, which comprised all the other articles named in the Treaty, similar reductions were made on textiles, so that most British cloths could be imported on payment of a duty of 15 francs per 100 kg., with a further decrease in 1864 to 10 francs.[21] Thus the last im-

---

[21] See the Procès Verbaux of the fifty-one sessions of the Tariff Commission. Min. Aff. Étr. Mémoires et Documents anglaises, Vol. 95. These were written out after each conference by Alexis de Clercq and were signed by the Commissioners. A duplicate set, without the signatures, is in the F. O., 97–207. Various letters and memoranda of interest are in the Min. Aff. Étr. Négociations Commerciales, Série C, Carton 22ᵈ and 22ᵉ. For the correspondence between Baroche and Rouher regarding the maximum and minimum rates in the French tariff, see Min. Aff. Étr. Mémoires et Documents anglaises, Vol. 94. Memoranda of de Clercq. Annexes 6 and 7. Cobden to Baroche, January 13, and Baroche to Cobden, January 22, 1860.

portant questions in the tariff negotiations were settled to the satisfaction of both governments a month before the date set by the protocol of November 5, and the obligations incurred under the Cobden-Chevalier Treaty were fully carried out in accordance with the informal agreements of the negotiators and the assurances given to Cobden by the Emperor.

The signature of the Tariff Convention of November 16, 1860, marked the successful termination of the negotiations begun in London thirteen months before by Chevalier. The Treaty signed on January 23 had embodied the reductions in the British tariff, but, on the side of France, it had merely assured the abolition of prohibitions and provided the basis for a subsequent measure which was to complete the reform of the French tariff. After ten months of delays and difficult negotiations that measure had now been enacted and all the stipulations of the Treaty had been carried out. The French Emperor had ignored the outspoken opposition of his parliament and of a large part of his subjects, and, through his Minister of Commerce, had honorably and generously fulfilled his agreement with Cobden and the British Government. He and Rouher, even more than Cobden, are the men to whom full credit should be given for the completion of the Anglo-French Treaty of 1860.

The political aims of the Emperor in the negotiations for the commercial agreement were also achieved. Even if a cordial friendship between the French and British peoples was not established, a basis for closer and freer commercial relations was secured, and the "nation of shopkeepers" across the Channel was not slow to appreciate the fact. The Treaty was, furthermore, an indication that Napoleon III was not wholly intent on projects for military conquests, and its conclusion undoubtedly made it easier for both countries to pass through the dangerous crisis created by the annexation of Savoy. The economic entente facilitated also a political rapprochement of the two governments, which rendered possible the maintenance for some time of a common policy on the Italian question. But the political results of the Treaty, though valuable temporarily, were not permanent. Essentially they were all embodied in the relief of the tension aroused by the Orsini plot in France and the volunteer movement in England, which meant the removal of the danger of war between England and France.

The economic results of the Treaty were far more important than its diplomatic or political effects. The Emperor hoped through its conclusion greatly to increase the prosperity of French industry and to improve the living conditions of the working classes, and his desires were largely fulfilled. The great industries, which had declared loudly that their immediate destruction would be the first result of a radical reform of the French tariff, survived and prospered exceedingly, despite both the Treaty with England and the Civil War in America. The stimulus of foreign competition forced them to enlarge their factories and improve both their machinery and their methods of production. The great development of French railroads in the later years of the Second Empire was, to a very considerable degree, the result of English competition, which brought down the price of French iron, and both increased the supply and improved the quality by compelling the small ironmasters to abandon their inaccessible forges in the mountains and establish themselves in favorable situations where they could smelt with coal. The use of wood for smelting was declining before 1860, but the change to the burning of coal was completed with rapidity after the conclusion of the Commercial Treaty.

The Anglo-French Treaty of 1860 was most important, however, as an example. The change from a prohibitive to a moderately protective tariff in France, and the complete adoption of free trade in England, which had been so eagerly desired by Chevalier and Cobden, as well as by Gladstone, were reforms of great significance and value. The increase of the direct trade between France and England was also a great benefit to both countries. But the Treaty of 1860 did even more than secure these reforms and benefits to its two signatories. It set an example that, within the next ten years, was followed by all the great states of western Europe. Both France and England began at once to negotiate commercial treaties with other countries, and, in each case, they insisted on a provision extending the concessions made in the new treaty to the other powers with whom the signatories had already made similar treaties, because such an extension was stipulated for by Article XIX of the Cobden-Chevalier Treaty between England and France.

In this way the Treaty of 1860 served as the first link in an ever lengthening chain of commercial agreements that for twenty years helped to increase trade and break down tariff barriers throughout Europe. And all these new treaties of commerce were not, like the treaties of earlier periods, restrictive bargains dealing with a mere handful of commodities, but were broad agreements dealing with the general tariffs of the countries concerned. The international trade of Europe owes much to Napoleon III who announced the new commercial policy in his letter to Fould on January 15, 1860; it owes much also to Richard Cobden, the champion of free trade and the principal negotiator of the Anglo-French Treaty; and to Gladstone, through whose statesmanship both free trade and the French Treaty were carried to victory in England; but it owes still more to the man who conceived the idea and began the negotiation of the Treaty of 1860, Michel Chevalier.

CHAPTER VIII

THE IMPERIAL LOAN TO THE MANUFACTURERS

BEFORE attempting to study the effects upon some of the more important industries in France of the Anglo-French Treaty of 1860 and of the series of agreements with other European states which followed it, it is desirable to consider the merits and effects of a law by which the French Government hoped to assist the manufacturers in making the change in their methods and equipment that would enable them to meet foreign competition more readily. This law set aside a considerable sum to be granted in loans to manufacturers. Its enactment was first recommended in an anonymous plan prepared in the summer of 1859 [1] for a series of economic reforms in France, of which the commercial treaty with England was to be only the most important. Together with several other features of this plan the idea of such a loan to French manufacturers was incorporated by the Emperor in his letter to Fould published on January 15, 1860. The proposal was criticized severely by French economists, not only by the small group of orthodox free traders who followed the Manchester school in their opposition to all treaties of commerce, but even by the partisans of such treaties. Chevalier's advocacy of the loan is thus one of the important links in the chain of evidence which proves him to have been the author of the anonymous plan of 1859, because no other French economist of that period would have recommended such a loan, the common view being that French industry had suffered for years from regulation and protection by the Government, and that what it needed was to stand on its own feet. Chevalier approved of the regulation of industry by the Government, although he was the leader of the free

---

[1] For the evidence of the authorship of the plan see the Conclusion.

trade school in France. He felt that the economic life of the nation needed not less, but more, control, for he was the disciple of that social reformer who wanted to reorganize the state on the basis of industry and trade — Henri de Saint Simon.

What reasons did Chevalier give for recommending a large loan to manufacturers in 1860? His plan of 1859 gives a fairly satisfactory answer, for in it he puts such a loan, together with free raw materials and the establishment of training schools for skilled workmen, as among the ways and means of securing the general acceptance of the Treaty of Commerce with England, and the drastic reduction of the French tariff which that treaty would involve. Even if the loan did not induce manufacturers to accept cheerfully the prospect of British competition, it would give the Government some justification for saying that it had done what it could to enable them to meet that competition. This was certainly the reason why the Emperor accepted the idea so readily. He sanctioned the economic reforms of 1860 because he hoped the Treaty would promote more cordial relations with England, and because he felt it would cheapen for the poor the price of food, clothing, and other necessities of life; but in promoting these desirable objects he did not wish to arouse the open hostility of the industrial leaders of France. Perhaps an offer of money, together with a duty of 30 per cent on iron, the assurance of free raw materials, and the promise of a formal investigation by the Government of the condition of French industry would suffice to placate the manufacturers; if not, these measures would surely deprive them of the support of public opinion which they had secured so successfully in 1856, and on other occasions when they had prevented the reduction of the tariff.

Chevalier saw clearly the political advantages of having the Government lend money to the manufacturers. He felt that there were also economic reasons for taking this step. French manufacturers must be forced by foreign competition to improve their methods and lower their prices, but the changes to be made would be difficult and costly. Much had to be done, and the time allowed the manufacturers was short. It was true that they had only themselves to blame for this, for it was their obstructive policy and blind opposition to all reform that had forced the Government to negotiate secretly the Treaty of Commerce with England and confront the French public with a *fait accompli*. But if the manufacturers were pressed too hard industrial depression might follow and undo the work of reform. French manufacturers had enjoyed almost complete protection against foreign competition since the beginning of the revolutionary wars in 1792. As a result they had had complete control of the home market, and such a monopoly has never promoted progress in industry. Among the more startling examples of industrial backwardness that could be cited as prevalent in France in 1860 are hand weaving and smelting iron with wood. The manufacturers must, then, enlarge their plants and instal machinery, or improve the old machinery they had, and they must do this within a year. There seems to be reason, therefore, for saying that Government aid to industry could be justified on economic grounds.

Action on the proposed loan to manufacturers was taken promptly. The draft of a bill to give the necessary legislative sanction was approved by the Council of State on March 5, 1860, and Chevalier's last act as a member of that body before his promotion to the Senate, in recognition of his share in negotiating the treaty with England, was the preparation of the report recommending the bill to the Corps Législatif. Chevalier states in this report that the object of the proposed loan was to facilitate the renewal of industrial equipment. He admits the general principle that public funds should be used for public, and not private, purposes, but claims that exceptions should be made temporarily in certain cases under unusual circumstances. It has been admitted several times, he says, that the state can give bounties to encourage industry. The French Government was then paying 4,000,000 francs a year in bounties to encourage deep sea fishing, although this might be justified on the ground that this industry helped to train sailors for the navy. There are other cases, he continues, where the interests aided by the use of state funds are essentially private in character. After the Revolution of 1848 bounties were given for the exportation of certain goods solely to relieve the congestion of private warehouses. At the same time the Government advanced funds to organize workmen's associations. After the Revolution of 1830 the sum of 30,000,000 francs was lent to commerce and industry.[2] A precedent of even greater importance is to be found in British legislation, when Sir Robert Peel, in 1846, had Parliament lend to British agriculture the sum of 75,000,000 francs, which was subsequently doubled, to enable landowners to make the adjustments forced by the repeal of the Corn Laws. There is no country, says Chevalier, where it is more the rule to leave industry to its own devices without help from the Government, yet experience amply justified the exception made in this case.[3]

"Now that France is modifying her economic régime in the general interest and that, in this connection, a decisive step has been taken by means of a treaty of commerce with the leading industrial power in the world, the Government of the Emperor, with the solicitude which it has always felt for the country's industries, has sought for the best means of making easier the period of transition and of eliminating from it shock and suffering. Hence, in addition to permanent measures destined to lower the cost of raw materials as well as of transportation and to increase general consumption, the Government has deemed it expedient, as a temporary and exceptional measure, to set aside the sum of 40,000,000 francs for loans to industry for the renewal and improvement of its equipment.[4]

"It is true that our national industries have not remained stationary in the midst of the general progress noted throughout Europe. They have greatly improved their products and their equipment so as to come nearer that low cost of production which is in the public interest. It must be said, however, that in

---

[2] *Moniteur*, October 19, 1830. Louis Philippe signed on October 17 the decree which promulgated the law voted by the Chambers.

[3] British Statutes at Large, 9 and 10 Victoria, c. CI, Act of August 28, 1846. The statute authorizes loans for drainage in England up to £2,000,000 and in Ireland up to £1,000,000. No particular reason is given for the enactment of the statute at that time, and a number of the earlier statutes granting similar loans are cited.

[4] The records of the Commission on Loans to Industry established by the Act of August 1, 1860, are in Arch. Nat., F 12, Nos. 4640-4645. Chevalier's report to the Corps Législatif, the correspondence between the Ministers of Commerce and Finance, where not covering a loan to an individual firm, and the first report of the Commission to the Emperor, April 25, 1861, are in No. 4640. The papers regarding individual loans are in the other folios, classified alphabetically according to the names of the manufacturers, without regard to industries.

spite of the warnings which the Government has given freely, the renewal of machinery and equipment in general has not everywhere progressed as rapidly as could have been desired, and there is reason to believe that certain coal mines, iron foundries and general industrial establishments could still make very serious efforts towards improvement.

" Among the leaders of industry who are thus backward to their own injury as well as to that of the consuming public, there are none who do not feel keenly the need of putting themselves in a position where foreign competition can do them no harm. The Government, besides, has tried to mitigate the effects of this competition by duties which may be as high as 30%. But among these honorable manufacturers there are certainly some who can not obtain in the time allowed and in the ordinary financial markets the sums they need for the renewal of their equipment, especially if the loans they obtain are to be repaid in short term annuities."

Chevalier goes on to assure the Corps Législatif that the proposed loan is not likely to bring loss to the Government. His optimism was probably justified, although the records available at present do not enable us to say exactly how many of the loans to individuals were completely repaid. The distinguished reporter seems to have failed, however, to foresee the eagerness with which the manufacturers would seek to fish in the well-stocked pond of the Government. He assures the Corps Législatif that the number of manufacturers who will be unable to secure the necessary funds from private sources will be small. This was probably the case, but the records show that many, even of the great captains of industry, thought it would be cheaper and easier to get the money they wanted from the Government than to make the effort to raise it themselves; and that the real object for which they wished to use the money was the increase of their ordinary capital, or the enlargement of their profits. If they could get funds for this on easy terms from the imperial treasury, why should they take the trouble to enlarge their mills or buy new and costly machinery? Great care had to be taken by the officials who passed on applications for loans to insure the use of the money for the purpose intended by the Government. The only positive recommendation of Chevalier on this point was that the rate of interest charged by the Government should be not less than 5 per cent, the usual rate for commercial loans then being 6 per cent; and that annual reports regarding the loans granted should be made to the Emperor and the Corps Législatif.

Chevalier concluded his report by saying:

" Such, gentlemen, are the arrangements of the bill. Without claiming to state in advance under exactly what conditions individuals will secure the loans mentioned, we believe we can state that its principal influence is intended to be moral. It will show that special class of leaders of industry who, while honest, industrious and intelligent, have yet been unable to accumulate sufficient capital, that the solicitude with which the Government regards them is as benevolent as that shown the captains of industry who are more powerful or who have been more fortunate. It will strengthen in the working classes the conviction which is so salutary and patriotic, that the Government has at heart the maintenance of employment throughout the country by means of the effective support it knows how to give the industrial leaders in the accomplishment of that transformation which it was impossible to postpone further and by which alone the country could be assured of the benefits of production at a low cost so favorable to the interests of all and to the increase in the power of the state."

The law authorizing a loan to industry of 40,000,000 francs was promulgated by the Emperor August 1, 1860. The text of the statute itself is of little interest. It merely authorizes the loan and fixes the rate of interest at 5 per cent. The Government is left free to issue its own regulations regarding the conditions under which it will lend money to the individual manufacturers. These regulations were published in the imperial decree of October 24, 1860, which announced that a commission would be appointed to examine the applications for loans; that it would have power to decide the order in which these applications would be considered, and to determine the amount to be granted in each case, and the nature of the guarantee the borrower must furnish. The decisions of the commission were to be approved in every case by the Ministers of Commerce and Finance. Finally, on December 5, 1860,[5] a second decree announced the names of the commissioners. M. Boinvilliers, head of one of the sections of the Council of State, was appointed president; M. Julien, director of Internal Commerce, secretary; and three Maîtres de Requêtes attached

[5] The three decrees of August 1, October 24, and December 5, 1860 are all published in the *Bulletin des lois.*

to the Council of State (MM. Bosredon, Marbeau, and Aucoc) were designated to write the reports on the individual applications for loans. The other members of the commission were M. Germiny, governor of the Bank of France; de Boureuil and Lavernay of the Council of State; Guillemot, director-general of the Caisse des Dépôts; Denière, president of the Tribunal of the Seine; and Chouré, directeur du Contentieux in the Ministry of Finance. It was, in short, what we should call a commission of financial and legal government experts.

At its first meeting on December 24, 1860, the Commission on Loans to Industry voted to receive applications for loans up to January 20, 1861, but we find from the correspondence between the Ministers of Commerce and Finance that this limitation was not observed, for the latter (then Achille Fould, who, in 1860, was Minister of State) wrote to his colleague in February, 1864, that he felt the manufacturers should be notified that no applications for loans would be received after July 1 of that year. The printed forms sent out to applicants by the commission show that the loans were to be made in three instalments to be paid (1) on the official signing of the contract by the applicant and the representative of the Minister of Finance; (2) when the use made by the recipient of the first instalment had been approved by the Government; and (3) when the same had been done for the second instalment. The loans were to be repaid with interest during the twelve years following the signature of the contract. During the first two years interest only was to be paid; then for ten years the principal was to be repaid in equal annual instalments together with interest on the balance still unpaid. The law left the Government free to ask such guarantees of repayment from applicants as it deemed proper, and in most cases a first mortgage on the factory or manufacturing equipment of the applicant for the full amount of the loan was requested, and if this could not be furnished the loan was refused; but in a few cases, when the applicants were important manufacturers with a national reputation, no such guarantee was demanded.

At the same meeting the Commission appointed a committee

of the three reporters, the director of Internal Commerce, and the president of the Commission, to obtain information regarding the applicants for loans. They were to make the necessary inquiries through the prefects, the chambers of commerce, the engineer of the department in which the applicant had his factory, and the Bank of France and its branches. The prefects, who evidently furnished a great part of the information desired, were instructed to treat it as strictly confidential; but they could ask for the assistance of the local director of registration who would attend to financial details.

The Commission submitted its first report to the Emperor April 25, 1861. This stated that over 500 applications for loans had been received, and that the total amount asked for was 80,000,000 francs, or twice the sum authorized by the law of August 1, 1860. The Commission rejected 272 applications, approved 200, and at the time of reporting was still considering the remainder. The loans granted were distributed among the following industries: metallurgy, 27 loans for a total of 9,100,000 francs; textiles, 88 loans for 15,060,000; transportation, 5 loans for 1,200,000; mines, 11 loans for 3,800,000; machinery, 18 loans for 1,417,000; sugar, 6 loans for 3,250,000 francs; and paper and other industries, 45 loans for 4,583,000. The total amount thus granted in loans was reported as 38,440,000 francs. This amount varied somewhat in the following years, since loans were cancelled or applications for loans withdrawn and new loans granted, but it was always kept within the legal limit of 40,000,000 francs.

The records of the Commission show that great solicitude was felt for coal mining and iron manufacturing firms, probably because of the fundamental importance of these two industries and the dependence of other industries upon them. In many cases the loans to such firms were very large, and there are examples of loans to firms whose difficulties were chiefly the result of unwise financial operations. In the case of the Compagnie des Houillères de Béthune, in the Pas de Calais basin, the reporter writes that the company really sought a loan in order to pay more cheaply for improvements that it had been able to finance from its own funds, and the Commission reduced the loan to be granted from the 1,200,000 francs asked to 200,000 francs; but when the Thivencelles coal company, which was suffering from financial troubles in former years, asked for 1,000,000 francs, they received the full amount, although the reporter wrote that they were in no danger from foreign competition. An even more serious example is that of the Decazeville iron company, run by the Duc Decazes, the heir of the well-known minister of Louis XVIII. In 1861 the firm received the full 1,500,000 francs it asked, of which 900,000 francs was to be spent in taking the top off a mountain so that coal could be mined in the open air; 200,000 francs was to be used for new coke ovens; 120,000 francs for a workshop for naval construction; and 200,000 francs to build an aqueduct to bring pure water. The company said that in the past they had mined coal for their own use exclusively, but that now, thanks to the new railroad being built to Bordeaux by way of Perigueux, they could develop the selling of coal and drive the English from the Bordeaux market. These grandiose plans would seem to have deserved investigation, but the reporter stated merely that the credit of the firm was excellent and that its reputation was world-wide. In the spring of 1865 the Duc Decazes applied to Béhic, the Minister of Commerce, and an important iron manufacturer of Marseilles, to give his firm an extension of time for the repayment of the loan granted in 1861. Béhic was anxious to help him, but before anything could be done the Decazeville company was declared bankrupt by the courts. The duke ascribed his troubles to insufficient circulating capital, of which practically all manufacturers of that period complained, and to the steadily falling price of iron; but the indications are that the real cause of the failure of the firm was the excessive issue of securities.

Other loans to metallurgical firms were made more wisely. James Jackson & Company, of St. Seurin sur l'Isle, Gironde, received 1,200,000 francs instead of the 2,000,000 francs asked, for the repair of several blast furnaces and the purchase of various machines for the production of steel on a large scale.

The reporter to the Commission wrote that it was important to encourage the production of Bessemer steel, since the future of the whole iron industry using wood as fuel depended on it; and that the manufacture of rails, ships, cannon, and agricultural machinery soon would depend on it. The wisdom of attempting to retard by Government action the substitution of coal for wood in the smelting of iron may be doubted; but the encouragement of the Jackson firm was wise, for its directors were among the leaders of that period in the increase of production and the improvement of methods. Another firm that deserved encouragement was the Langlois company of Nantes, described as an important furnisher of the navy and the merchant marine, which received the full amount asked, 400,000 francs, in March, 1861. They stated in their application that English competition had forced down the price of iron, and that they proposed to meet it by increasing their production 40 per cent, which would decrease the cost by about two francs per ton. To do this they needed a railroad in their yards, one new puddling and one reheating oven, a saw to cut iron, a steam engine of twenty horsepower for puddling, a steam boiler of twenty-five horsepower, a steam hammer of two tons, and equipment for rivets and armor plating of ships.

Of the eighteen loans granted to constructors of machinery, totaling 1,417,000 francs, that given Mercier of Louviers in Normandy is of unusual interest, as the reporter said. We know from the posthumous book of Charles Ballot on the introduction of machinery into France, and from other sources, that Mercier was one of the great leaders of the industrial revolution in France, a man of real vision and remarkable energy. Mercier had printed at the time of making his application, March 14, 1861, the following letter, which was evidently sent to all the members of the Commission on loans. After speaking of the services he could render French manufacturers in supplying them with better equipment, which was the main object of the law of August 1, 1860, he said:

"In the last ten years I have sold machines worth 8,000,000 francs with the defective equipment of my shops, although with high protection, far higher than that which machines will have under the Treaty. When my shops are reorganized to meet the new needs I shall be able to produce machines to the value of 2,400,000 francs a year which would otherwise be imported. Even then my shops will be inferior in organization and equipment to English workshops which are able to specialize as I cannot, and which have all the industrial centers of the world as markets. In view of this competition I must lower my prices 20 per cent compared with last year. To do this and still get a legitimate profit of 10 per cent my enlarged shops must have all the economical methods and machine tools used in England. I plan to spend 550,000 francs of the loan [he asked for 700,000 and received 600,000 francs] on this and to use the rest to meet the increase in the volume of trade and to increase my circulating capital. The latter is necessary as I have always had to give customers long credit. This the English will not do. They deliver for cash down and often ask payment in advance. Only through these credits have many manufacturers been able to complete their equipment.

" In the last six years I have spent over 150,000 francs to make looms running up to seven shuttles, so as to make even the most varied novelties. I have also worked on the replacement of the mule-jenny by the water-frame, which makes finer yarn and takes less room; and finally, on machines for making felt recently invented by Vouillan, who received a medal at the Exposition of Rouen. My shops as now equipped could not properly develop these new discoveries, and would force me to maintain high prices on the machines I alone sell. As guarantee I offer my shops, which will be worth 1,000,000 francs when enlarged and producing on an increased basis, and in the presence of the new foreign competition, which will be further increased by the application of the new treaties planned with Belgium and Germany."

According to the first report submitted in April, 1861, the Commission granted eighty-eight loans to textile manufacturers for the sum of 15,060,000 francs. The greater part of this went to the cotton industry, which was the most deserving of help because of the colossal development of the rival industry in England. But before considering any of the loans to manufacturers of cotton we may stop to notice a few of the small number of loans to manufacturers of woollens and silks. The case of Granier, a maker of blankets at Montpellier, is curious and might deserve serious criticism if the sum loaned had been large. He ingeniously claimed that the treaty with England had injured him through causing the abolition of the bounty paid for exports; that the abolition of the duty on raw wool was no compensation, because the price of wool had risen. Granier, therefore, asked for 83,000 francs to enable him to renew his equipment and fight England in the markets of North and South America, and he received 40,000 francs. The price of wool did rise temporarily because of the rapidly increasing demand for woollens in view of the expected shortage of cotton owing to the crisis in America, but it was soon brought down by a flood of imports from South America and Australia. Another loan for 200,000 francs granted Hurstel, in the Department of Aisne, is interesting because the reporter describes it as coming within the spirit if not the letter of the law in that it would promote a decrease in prices, and thus permit a fight against foreign competition. Hurstel was a comber of wool, but he asked for help in order to add spinning and weaving mills to his plant for combing by machinery. He wrote that foreign and home competition forced him to do this because his rivals, the spinners and weavers, had taken to combing in order to save the profits paid to middlemen like himself. In short, the boom in woollens caused by the cotton crisis was forcing the integration of the industry.

In the silk industry there is only one loan that should be noted. The Vignat firm of St. Étienne, printers and weavers of plain ribbons, asked for a loan of 1,200,000 francs in July, 1861, and finally received 500,000 francs in January, 1862. The case was a difficult one to decide, for the Vignats had been obliged to suspend payments on the death of their father, the former head of the firm, shortly before they applied for the loan. They were, therefore, practically bankrupt. The money obtained from the Government would be used to satisfy creditors, and not for the purchase of new equipment. On the other hand, the Vignat application was indorsed by the mayor of St. Étienne, the prefect of the Department of Loire, and the Minister of the Interior, de Persigny, a personal friend of the Emperor. The Vignats had a valuable plant, employed many workers, and had rendered great services to the silk industry. They had been the first to break away from the prevailing organization of the mills in the district about St. Étienne, where the yarn was handed out to the girls of the countryside who wove the ribbons in their own houses. They had built a large mill in which were set up over one hundred mechanical looms. They had taken this step in order to meet Swiss competition and the crisis which had depressed the silk industry since 1857, because of the change in fashions followed by the virtual loss of the American market. The initiative taken by the Vignats had been somewhat timidly followed by others, but mechanical weaving in mills had not yet been firmly established at St. Étienne. The prefect wrote that if the Vignats were allowed definitely to fail, all progress in the silk industry of that district would cease. This appears to have been the reason which induced the Commission to overcome its natural scruples and grant the loan. It shows that in a deserving case the letter of the law could be broken in order to abide by its spirit.

A study of the loans granted to manufacturers of cotton is difficult because of the crisis brought on by the American Civil War and the attendant cotton famine. Virtually every mill owner who received a loan asked within two or three years, or even less, either to have it increased, or else to be granted exemption from repayment in whole or in part. In practically every case the cotton manufacturer had either to change his machinery in order to make woollen or linen cloth or yarn, or else had to adapt it to the use of Indian cotton instead of American, which was difficult because Indian cotton had a shorter staple, was full of impurities, and gave yarn whose threads broke more easily. Yet, despite the complications caused by the American crisis, we can learn something regarding the use made of the loans granted to cotton manufacturers. A few examples will show what happened in most cases.

Baril of Amiens, a manufacturer of Utrecht velvet for furniture, asked for a loan of 150,000 francs in March, 1860, renewed his request in August, and received 100,000 francs in March, 1861, when the first payments were authorized by the Commission. Baril was the first manufacturer in France to weave Utrecht velvet on mechanical looms. Since the market for his product was not sufficient, he made also ordinary velvet, the manufacture of which was an important industry at Amiens. The reporter informed the Commission that Baril was an able manufacturer and safe from competition in his own specialty, but that in cotton velvet he would encounter difficulties, since the whole industry was likely to have a hard fight against English competition. In March, 1862, Baril had satisfied the Commission that he had made good use of the first two instalments of his loan, and in April he received the third instalment. Meantime, in August, 1861, he had asked that his loan be increased to the original amount asked, 150,000 francs, on the ground that the low prices of his English competitors were possible only through large scale production, and that he could not produce on a larger scale without more funds. This request was refused by the Government in April, 1862. Then Baril began to feel the effects of the American cotton famine. In December, 1862, he asked for a new loan to enable him to change his looms and buy preparatory machines for the weaving of linen. His application was indorsed by the prefect of the Somme, who wrote that the other manufacturers of cotton velvet were making the same change, and that they all deserved the utmost assistance the Government could give. Baril's application was rejected in January, 1863, on the ground that there were no funds available, and a second request made in July was refused in August for the same reason. Finally, in June, 1865, Baril put his case in the hands of the Chamber of Commerce of Amiens and asked for the cancellation of half his debt to the Government. The chamber wrote earnestly to the Minister of Commerce indorsing Baril's request and stating that the existence of the whole industry of Utrecht velvet was at stake. The Minister of Commerce sent the papers to the Minister of Finance in August with a favorable recommendation, but the records of the Commission do not show what action was taken.

Baril's letter to the Chamber of Commerce is of great interest because it shows us what his difficulties were and what use he made of the loan. He writes that he organized his company in February, 1857, with a capital of 300,000 francs, to buy and exploit Anglo-French patents for the mechanical weaving of Utrecht velvet. In May of that year he signed an agreement with J. Crossley & Son of Halifax regarding the patents, and in

March, 1858, the French Government granted permission to import the desired machines from England. The looms came in June, but the preparatory machines had practically to be invented, because the usual ones were not suited to the manufacture of Utrecht velvet. Another difficulty was the finding of a French constructor of machines who could make looms from the English models. This was finally solved in December, 1858, when fourteen looms were set up in Baril's mill, but an English foreman and workmen had to be brought over to show how they should be run. At first the cloth produced was inferior to that made by hand, and the general costs were too high; then the price of mohair yarn rose 30 per cent until Baril found that his cost of production exceeded that of hand-made velvet. After long investigation of possible improvements it was discovered that one of the chief causes of the inferior quality of the cloth was the inferior wooden rings for the looms brought from England. After many failures Baril finally succeeded in making perfect rings at Amiens and, finding that his mechanical looms could now meet the competition of hand-made velvet, he secured French patents in June and July, 1860.

At the beginning of 1860 Baril had fifty-eight looms running; thirty-eight making Utrecht velvet and twenty cotton velvet. Since his general costs were too high he secured the promise of funds with which to buy one hundred more looms for cotton velvet. Then came the announcement of the abolition of prohibitions, (that is, of the Treaty of Commerce with England) which frightened the capitalists.

" I was sure their fears were exaggerated," wrote Baril; " I was well informed regarding the English market, and certain that Amiens could compete. I therefore asked for a loan of 150,000 francs in August, 1860, and received 100,000 in March, 1861, and January and April, 1862. I used this to erect a new building and to buy and set up 108 looms for cotton velvet, and I already had 82 of these when the crisis of the American war came. The result was the quick rise of cotton with which the cloth could not keep up, loss on the goods, stagnation of trade, lack of credit, and the closing of one of the chief markets for Utrecht velvet.

" I had to stop the manufacture of both forms of velvet," continued Baril. " I studied linen and got orders from Amiens merchants and an agreement from the Pont Remy mill to supply yarn. But my funds were sufficient to change only 30 looms and this was not enough to pay. Then the medal awarded me at the Exposition of London [1862] attracted the attention of French manufacturers to the mechanical weaving of Utrecht velvet. Payen, and later others, gave me enough orders to resume work with 38 looms. I had great difficulty in training workmen in mechanical weaving, and these difficulties kept cropping up and still do. Meantime wages and excessive general costs due to an insufficient number of looms, interest on capital, the cost of all these investigations, the change of looms; all these meant continued loss. My net loss is now 331,-429 francs. My average annual sales since 1858 have been 280,000 francs. With my equipment I should sell for 1,000,000 francs. My present plight is due wholly to insufficient production."

The cases of other cotton manufacturers who received loans show, that, as in the case of Baril, the money was used to purchase better equipment and thus to increase production and decrease costs. One spinner in the Department of Somme wrote that with his loan of 300,000 francs he was able to buy and set up new machines, and to spin yarn of better quality than the English, and that he could have sold it at the same price under normal conditions. A weaver of muslin in the Department of Rhône, who received a loan of 300,000 francs in March, 1861, wrote that he had used hand looms scattered widely through the country, but that the prospect of English competition had brought down wages 30 per cent and the price of goods 25 per cent, which would force him to build a mill and set up mechanical looms. A third case is that of a spinner named Leyherr at Laval, in southern Normandy, who asked for a loan of 600,000 francs and received 400,000 in March, 1861. He wrote that he had run his mill seven years and had renewed his equipment once; but that the reform of the French tariff would now force him to renew it again. He had 12,000 mule-jenny spindles and 3,000 spindles for twisting yarn, and he also printed and dyed cloth. He wished to replace his spindles by an equal number of self-actings and by the latest model of spindles for twisting yarn which, with the necessary accessories, would cost 550,000 francs. In addition Leyherr planned to erect a mill for mechanical weaving at a cost of 200,000 francs to replace the hand weaving which was universal in southern Normandy. The

Commission replied that his resources were not sufficient to justify so ambitious a program and that he must revise his plans if he wished a loan. As a result Leyherr renewed only his ordinary spindles, one half water-frames and one half automatics. He estimated that this would increase his production by 600 kilograms of yarn a day and decrease his costs 20 per cent. These improvements had cost him 650,000 francs. Finally, we should note the case of the Wibaux-Florin firm, makers of the famous mixed goods of Roubaix near the frontier of Belgium. This was clearly a firm in the forefront of industrial progress with a reputation of which it was exceedingly proud. The owners actually wrote to the Government that they would not accept a loan unless their personal note was regarded as sufficient guarantee of repayment, and the Commission agreed to grant a loan of 500,000 francs on this condition in March, 1861! The firm was organized in 1811 and claimed to be the first in Roubaix to make mixed goods. They had built a spinning mill in 1821, and in 1846 had replaced its machines by 400 self-actings of 500 spindles each. In 1844 they had set up the first mechanical looms in Roubaix for weaving fancy cloth. In 1860 they had ordered 33,000 new spindles, and they planned to use the loan to complete this equipment. They wrote that they had two steam engines of 200 horse-power with which they could run 51,000 self-acting spindles. The correspondence with the Government shows that the Wibaux firm spent the whole of their loan before the end of the year 1861.

The records of the Commission on Loans to Industry are so incomplete that it is almost impossible to draw general conclusions regarding its operations and the results they produced. We have available only the first report of the Commission to the Emperor issued in April, 1861. None of the correspondence covering grants to individual applicants goes beyond the year 1865, when repayments of capital had barely begun. We can say nothing, therefore, regarding the repayment of the loans. A few inferences only can be made from the existing records. It seems evident that the total sum authorized by the Act of August 1, 1860, was never exceeded, and it seems probable that

CHAPTER IX

THE IRON INDUSTRY

AMONG the industries which had profited most from the monopoly of the home market none was more important than that of iron and none had protested more vigorously against the reform of the tariff or assured the Government more earnestly of its impending ruin. The ironmasters, through their national committee, even told the Emperor [1] that their industry would be completely destroyed if British iron were allowed to compete with theirs in the French market, and that the unemployment created would be so great that France would have to declare war in order to put an end to the iniquitous treaty of commerce! Their language was quite different, however, in the book prepared in 1914 by the Comité des Forges [2] to celebrate the fiftieth anniversary of its organization, and intended to be read only by the faithful. This valuable work, together with the documents from the Ministry of Commerce in the Archives Nationales, throws much light upon the effects of the new commercial policy of France on the iron industry.

The development of the French iron industry before 1860 had been very slow. This was due in great part to the monopoly of the home market enjoyed by the producers, but there were other causes that should be noted. France was then working many small deposits of iron scattered widely through the country, but few rich mines of great depth. As a result, the industry could not concentrate easily and iron was mined, smelted, and refined in a large number of very small establishments. Another

---

[1] *Moniteur industriel,* January 19 and 20, 1860. See also Petition of Léon Talabot to the Emperor, January 20, 1860, in Arch. Nat., F 12-2514.

[2] Comité des Forges, *La Sidérurgie française 1864–1914.* Privately printed in 1920 for the Ironmasters' Association. A copy was seen through the courtesy of the Secretary of the Comité des Forges, M. Desportes de la Fosse.

cause of retarded development was the inadequate system of transportation which made it so costly to move the ore, and even the pig-iron, that most of the manufacturing of iron had to be done close to the mines. The same lack of sufficient means of transportation forced the ironmasters to use such fuel as they could find close to their furnaces and foundries. In most cases that fuel was wood. France had abundant forests, owned in part by the national and local governments which were, therefore, interested in selling wood to the ironmasters, and in part by the masters themselves. Owing to this abundance of wood the French manufacturers were not obliged to develop the smelting and refining of iron with coal, unless deposits of coal were so near their foundries that their use would be notably cheaper than that of wood. One of the greatest stimulants to the improvement of the methods of smelting and refining iron in England, the scarcity of wood, was thus lacking in France. A few French establishments which were near coal deposits, or owned coal mines themselves, as did the great firm of the Schneiders at Le Creusot, improved their methods and increased their production through the use of coal and coke, but the great majority of the French firms continued to use wood. Some of them could not get coal in sufficient quantity, or at a moderate price, but many knew nothing of the economies that the use of coal offered. Only as the establishments using coal grew in size and in the amount of iron they produced did they gradually bring pressure to bear on the smaller firms using wood. The change of fuel in France made slow progress, partly because coal was neither abundant nor cheap in most places, and partly because the prohibitive tariff enabled all manufacturers to charge such high prices that iron could be produced at a profit by the most antiquated and costly methods.

The greatest stimulant to the development of the French iron industry before the invention of the Thomas-Gilchrist process for the manufacture of steel in 1878 was undoubtedly the construction of the railroads. A drastic reduction in the cost of transportation resulted which brought down the price of iron. This made itself felt with increasing force when order had been restored after the Revolution of 1848; that is, in the decade preceding the Treaty of 1860, when most of the main railroad lines were built. The construction of the railroads stimulated the iron industry also through the demand for rails, which became so great after 1850 that the metallurgical establishments of France could not meet it and large importations had to be authorized by the Government.[3] As a result of these developments the manufacture of pig-iron was largely transformed; three quarters of it was made with coke in 1864, the amount being 876,000 tons as compared with 224,000 made with wood, and 113,000 with coke and wood mixed. Only two French furnaces used coke in 1819, of which one was Le Creusot; in 1830 there were 29 out of 408 furnaces making pig-iron with coke; in 1840, 41 out of 462; in 1856, 120 out of 591; in 1865, 147 out of 413. The use of wood as fuel showed no increase after 1824, but there was no marked decrease until 1860. Meantime, however, the use of coal and coke increased steadily, the production of pig-iron with this fuel being only 1000 tons in 1819 and 706,025 in 1865, out of a total output with all forms of fuel

[3] The length of the railroads in France increased between 1850 and 1860 from 3008 kilometers to 9,442; by 1870 the total was 17,476. See Alfred de Foville, *De la transformation des moyens de transport et ses conséquences économiques et sociales* (Paris, 1880), p. 18.

For authorizations to import rails see Enquête, March, 1854, of the Ministry of Commerce (Arch. Nat., F 12–6408). Beginning with the Decree of November 18, 1854, permits were granted in urgent cases until 1858. The Government usually levied a duty equal to the difference in cost of production in England and France. This was usually between 60 and 80 francs per ton, whereas the normal duty was 120 francs.

The French producers do not seem to have been entirely to blame for the delays in furnishing rails. They complained that the railroad companies gave large orders suddenly for quick delivery and then waited for months or years before giving new orders, so that there was no regularity in the demand that would justify a permanent increase in production. On the other hand, the evidence of railroad directors like P. Talabot and Émile Péreire (see Enquête, 1860. *Traité avec l'Angleterre*, I, 197–224) shows that the ironmasters combined to charge monopoly prices. If rails were wanted for a line in the south a contract was signed with a firm in the north and the railroad company paid for the transportation of the rails to the south; but the rails were really made by a foundry in the south and the profits were divided. The railroad companies had to submit to this arrangement and take what quality of rails the ironmasters chose to supply, in the hope of getting the rails quickly.

of 792,058 tons. In short, long before there was an absolute decrease in the use of wood there was a relative decrease as compared with coal and coke.[4]

A study of the principal regions where iron was manufactured in France will show even more clearly the degree of development attained by the industry when, in 1860, it was called upon to meet British competition. The most important region in France is now the east which, for convenience, we might refer to as Lorraine. Here the Department of Meurthe and Moselle alone in 1912 produced 2,200,000 tons of steel, which was 50 per cent of the national production of that year. In pig-iron the dominance of this district was even more pronounced, for it made 3,400,000 tons out of 4,900,000, or 69 per cent of the national production. The same department again produced more than 90 per cent of the iron ore mined in France. The overwhelming importance of Lorraine was, however, the result of the invention of the Thomas-Gilchrist process for making steel in 1878, which made available the phosphoric ore of that region. Before that date, although the mining and manufacture of iron in Lorraine can be traced back to 1320, this region was one of the least important in France. Its iron industry in 1850 produced only 9.1 per cent of French pig-iron, and in 1860 only 11.7 per cent. These figures, furthermore, represent the production of the entire province of Lorraine, whereas the figures of 1912 represent only the production of the part of the province that had remained French after the war of 1870.[5]

In the north of France, where the chief departments manufacturing iron were those of the Nord and Pas de Calais, the industry was older than in Lorraine, but was of even less importance until about 1820, when the French producers claim that their prosperity began through the high tariff which then gave protection against the very strong Belgian industry in the district of Liège. We may question this statement that the tariff was the cause of the development of their industry after 1820. The ironmasters themselves mention three other factors

[4] Comité des Forges, *op. cit.*, p. 120.
[5] *Ibid.*, pp. 167–190.

that must have been fundamental causes of that development, namely, the adoption about 1820 of the process of puddling iron with coal, the discovery about 1832 of important iron deposits near Boulogne, and the great development, at about the same time, of the coal beds of the Nord and Pas de Calais, which soon proved to be the richest in France. The region of the north enjoyed other advantages in its large industrial population which gave abundant labor, and in the ease of transportation by both rail and water. The iron industry of the north grew rapidly and prospered until about 1860, and it developed some of the most important establishments in France, such as those of Denain-Anzin (connected with the chief coal mining company in the country), Montataire, Outreau, and Marquise.

Beginning with 1860 there came a period of hard times which the manufacturers of the north publicly attributed wholly to the new tariff and British competition. They admitted privately, however, that the iron beds of the Nord were exhausted by 1868 and those of the Boulonnais by 1875–78, and it is clear that all through the decade from 1860 to 1870 the iron industry of the north was suffering from an increasing scarcity of ore produced within its borders.[6] In short, its cost of production was increasing rapidly and without relation to the new tariff. It seems probable, therefore, that the difficulty of getting sufficient ore cheaply was an important cause of the crisis through which the iron industry of the north passed during the 'sixties, and that only a part of the blame, if any, can be attributed to the treaty with England. It is true that the north was the part of France most exposed to the competition of British iron and, after 1861, of Belgian iron also; but, on the other hand, much pig-iron was imported from both England and Belgium for refining in the north of France, and those countries sent also considerable quantities of coal and coke. The reduction of the duties on coal and on pig-iron was, therefore, helpful to the industry of the north of France, and there is no evidence that that region was flooded with pig- or bar-iron from England or

[6] *Ibid.*, pp. 191–223.

Belgium. The statistics which were compiled subsequently by the British Iron Trade Association indicate that exports of pig- and bar-iron to France increased considerably from 1860 until 1865 and then decreased again to approximately the former amount; and they indicate also that at no time were these British exports large enough to threaten seriously the French iron industry even in the north.[7] The duty of 30 per cent on pig-iron imposed by the treaty of 1860, and reduced to 25 per cent in 1864, as the treaty required, though representing a decrease of about 40 per cent from previous rates, gave real protection to the French ironmasters.

The region of central France, including the departments of Allier, Cher, Indre, Nièvre, Rhône, Saône-et-Loire, and Loire, was the most important until about 1875. Here the real large scale industry was first developed and the foundations laid for the great progress of the later nineteenth century. Even during the period when wood was used as the only fuel and iron was smelted and refined in small and widely scattered establishments, the production of this region was important, for it had good forests and several rich beds of ore, such as those of the province of Berry, which were easy to mine. The center did not, however, become the dominant region until coke replaced wood as the principal fuel, for other regions had supplies of wood that were even more plentiful; then its real superiority came because it possessed the richest coal mines in France until the full development of the Pas de Calais and Nord basin toward the middle of the nineteenth century.

The center had the great iron-manufacturing firm of Le Creusot, the most important in France down to 1878, the workshops of Petin and Gaudet at Rive de Gier on the Rhone, and other important establishments such as Terrenoire. It was the first region in France to develop the smelting of iron with coke in the blast furnace, Wilkinson being brought over from England to Le Creusot at the beginning of the nineteenth century to demonstrate his successful method. It had also the first puddling furnace in France in 1820 and the first French steam hammer in

[7] Comité des Forges, *op. cit.* pp. 191–223.

1841. The center was the first region also to develop the manufacture of steel by the Bessemer and the Martin processes. Its ironmasters were leaders in improving both methods of manufacture and equipment and in combining to form associations that would have sufficient capital for manufacturing on a large scale. Like the north, however, the center began in time to suffer from the exhaustion of its beds of iron ore, so that before the Thomas-Gilchrist process made Lorraine the dominant metallurgical region of France the center had lost its supremacy. In 1860, however, the center was still the dominant region, so that from it came far less opposition to the treaty of commerce with England than from the north, and far fewer complaints of the competition of British iron.[8]

In sharp contrast with the center of France, with its large firms and improved methods, was the much smaller district of the upper Marne, a part of the ancient province of Champagne. From this district came the loudest protests against the new tariff policy of France begun in 1860. These protests were caused by a severe crisis through which that district passed. The local iron industry of the upper Marne had very serious problems to solve, so serious, indeed, that we can say that their solution proved that the influence of the Treaty of 1860, and that of the other treaties that followed it, were not disastrous to the iron industry of France. The upper Marne was not very far from the great market of Paris and it was near the important iron mining departments of Meurthe and Moselle. It had other advantages in abundant forests, excellent and plentiful water power, and a considerable supply of good ore, although this was scattered through a large number of small beds. Before the advent of the railroads and the extensive development of smelting and refining with coal and coke, the upper Marne produced considerable quantities of iron of excellent quality which was highly valued in Paris and other markets, although its price was very high because the cost of production was great and the cost of transporting the finished product to the market was greater still. As long as the price of iron remained high in most French

[8] *Ibid.*, pp. 115–116.

markets the upper Marne prospered without making any painful efforts to improve its methods and reduce its cost of production.

With the development of the railroads and of the use of coal and coke as fuel the situation of the iron industry in the upper Marne changed, and a difficult period of transition began. The price of wood, the mainstay of the local producers, rose steadily because of the continued increase in the number of furnaces and foundries using it, which enabled the owners of the forests, who were often ironmasters themselves, to make a handsome profit. The manufacturers who did not own forests, however, suffered from the increasing cost of their fuel, and all the ironmasters in common began to feel the competition in the markets of Paris, Rouen, and the northwest of districts such as the Moselle, the north, and the Pas de Calais. In these districts the cost of production was much less because of their use of coal and coke, with the improved methods that this change in fuel made possible, and because the cost of transportation had decreased until it was possible for nearly all districts in France to send their products to distant markets. The upper Marne began to suffer from the high cost of transportation owing to its mountain barriers and the scarcity of railroads within its area. It suffered also from its high cost of production. Iron in the Moselle cost only half as much as in the upper Marne and coal was much cheaper, so that, although the quality of Moselle iron sold was distinctly inferior, it was able to compete with the unusually good iron of the upper Marne.

In their complaints to the Government, which were loud and frequent between 1860 and 1870, the ironmasters of the upper Marne said, first, that they would be ruined by British and Belgian competition, and next, that they had been ruined. Their letters and petitions in 1860 were sent to the Inspector General of Mines, M. Combes, who made a report to the Minister of Commerce which is in the Government archives.[9] Combes

[9] See Petition of the Chambre Consultative de Joinville to the Minister of Commerce January 30, 1860, in Arch. Nat., F 12-2525; also their memorandum of March 10, 1860, in F 12-6222. Petition of the Chamber of Commerce of St. Dizier, January 23, 1860 in F 12-2525 and its letter to the Emperor January 29, 1860, in F 12-6222. Combes' report to the Minister of Commerce in reply to

pointed out that when the producers of the upper Marne complained of the high price of wood they were themselves responsible for it in great part, for many of them owned forests; furthermore, he showed that at the same time they expressed their fear that the price of wood would fall sharply as soon as British and Belgian competition was felt, and that this would be a disaster to the iron industry. Combes remarked shrewdly that on the basis of this reasoning the discovery of the prolongation of the Sarre coal basin into French territory was a national calamity! Even if these mines were so new that the amount of their production was still uncertain, the new coal fields of the north and the Pas de Calais were very effective realities. It would seem obvious to anyone not an interested party that the competition of coal had to be met, and that the only way to do it was to lower the price of wood. Such a decrease would not be the result of the new commercial policy of the French Government, said Combes, but of the revolution in the manufacture of iron caused by the use of coal as fuel.

There is ample evidence to support the correctness of Combes' conclusion. We have seen that the change in fuel had made considerable progress before 1860 and that ironmasters using wood, such as those of the upper Marne, were feeling the pressure before the new commercial policy had been thought of by the Government. They could not have kept up the price of wood much longer even if there had been no foreign competition to meet, for, owing to the development of the railroads, the cheaper French iron smelted or refined with coke was steadily gaining the ascendancy in the principal French markets. The manufacturers of the upper Marne were themselves getting coal from the Sarre, Belgium, and northern France by both rail and water, and were using it generally for refining pig-iron, and were even mixing it with charcoal in smelting pig-iron itself. The real difficulty was that many of the furnaces and foundries in this region were in the mountains and far from good means of

the foregoing communications is in F 12–2525. See also letters from Joinville to the Minister of Commerce April 17, 1862, F 12–4476D, and April 3, 1868, F 12–6220.

transportation. The ironmasters of the upper Marne hoped that they could make the Government believe that the critical situation of some of their establishments was a general condition characteristic of all.

The criticism that Combes made of the cutlery industry of the upper Marne, one of the chief markets for the ironmasters of the region, shows what was probably going on in the iron industry in general there and that the real desire of the producers was to keep up both the price of wood and the tariff, so that their badly placed establishments could continue to manufacture iron by the old methods without loss, and their more efficient or more favorably placed foundries and furnaces at an enormous profit. The Consultative Chamber of Joinville (the town was too small to have a real chamber of commerce) asked, on the signature of the treaty with England in 1860, that the prohibition of the importation of cutlery be kept in the new tariff, but the request was based only on the personal opinion of four manufacturers of Nogent, the chief center of the widely scattered cutlery industry of the upper Marne, who had visited Sheffield in 1856 when the French Government introduced a bill in the Corps Législatif to remove the principal prohibitions from the tariff.

Combes remarked that the Joinville petition, based on the report of these manufacturers from Nogent, carefully refrained from giving any information of comparative methods of production in England and France. The Government, however, had such information, and Combes stated that the lower prices in England were due to the use of machinery, good tools, a wise division of labor, and the lower cost of fuel and steel. He said, rightly, that the manufacturers of the upper Marne should have introduced in their factories the better methods they had seen in England. Other disadvantages that could not be removed could be compensated for by a protective duty of about 30 per cent, which Combes thought high enough for common cutlery for general consumption, since the price of labor was the chief factor in the cost of production and this was lower in France than in England. The opinion of Combes that the cutlery industry

Marne suffered from the competition of iron made with coke in France, and from that of imported pig-iron which was able to penetrate that district and was mixed with local pig-iron to the extent of 20 to 25 per cent. This was stated in a memorandum of the ironmasters of Joinville to the Minister of Commerce in April, 1862, and there seems no reason to doubt the accuracy of the statement. On the news of the conclusion of the treaty with England the price of iron fell from 300 francs to 230 francs in extreme cases; but, as Combes had predicted, it rose again and by the beginning of 1862 reached 255 francs. One of the chief difficulties was the scarcity of a cheap means of transportation. The manufacturers complained that the rates charged by the Est railroad on coal, ore, and iron goods were high and that the promised waterways were not being completed quickly. The Government, on announcing the treaty with England, had promised to carry out promptly a great development in the means of transportation in France and a general reduction of rates both on the railroads and on the canals. It did encourage the construction of new railroads and canals and it did reduce the rates, but it made haste so slowly that complaints seem to have been justified. On the other hand, even the ironmasters of Joinville admitted in their memorandum of April, 1862, that the crisis through which their industry was passing was not due wholly to the Treaty, and they told the minister that the cutlery manufacturers of Nogent, who had been in great difficulties for eight months, had themselves to thank for most of their troubles because they had not improved their methods of production.

When we examine the iron industry of the upper Marne some sixty years later we find it flourishing with greater vigor than ever and with good prospects for the future. The valuable account of the industry given in the book by the Comité des Forges shows us how the transformation of the industry was brought about. The combination of the reduced tariff on iron in 1860 and the competition of the iron industries of the Meurthe and Moselle departments which used coke virtually put an end to iron mining in the upper Marne and killed the charcoal industry, and only one establishment making pig-iron survived through erecting modern furnaces using coke, and through using local ore only for mixture with the cheaper ore from eastern France and Luxemburg. But those establishments that were situated near the railroads or the canals, or were placed close to the river, survived and increased their output greatly after changing their equipment and improving their methods. Many learned to specialize in making cast-iron, and the manufacture of wrought- or weld-iron prospered. Rolling-mills were modernized and produced large quantities of fine iron and steel in the form of wire, sheets, nails, switches, chains, axles, locks, tubes, wheels, boilers, and agricultural tools. The manufacturers, in short, brought their equipment up to date and specialized in the production of goods of superior quality, especially in that of finished parts for machinery of all sorts and sizes.

The ironmasters of the upper Marne found that they had three great resources in: (1) their position between the Department of Meurthe and Moselle,[11] producing raw materials and fuel, and the great market of Paris; (2) their abundant water power, which increased steadily in value; and (3) their large supply of skilled labor. Their industry in 1912 had a far larger number of workers than in 1860 and had greatly increased the volume and improved the quality of its output. Save for the period of transition, which was inevitable, the industry was not injured by the new commercial policy of the Second Empire; in fact, there are many grounds for saying that the reforms so bitterly opposed in 1860 were of great and lasting benefit to the manufacturers of the upper Marne.[12]

Let us see now what effect the new commercial policy begun in 1860 had on the iron industry of the country as a whole. Information coming from other parts of France was not as abundant as was that from the upper Marne, but sources such as the books of the Comité des Forges and of Amé, director general of Customs, tell us much; and in addition we have a memorandum of the British Iron Trade Association sent to the

[11] After the cession of Lorraine to Germany in 1871 the remnants of the Departments of Meurthe and Moselle were combined into one department.
[12] Comité des Forges, *op. cit.*, pp. 119–121.

Board of Trade in 1876, when the renewal of the Treaty of 1860 was being considered. There were also discussions in 1868 in the French Senate and the Corps Législatif that brought out facts and figures of great interest. The report of the British Iron Trade Association shows how British exports to France were affected by the Treaty. The duties on ordinary castings in the new tariff averaged 30 per cent, as they did on most wrought-iron. These proved protective, and often prohibitive. On pig-iron the average duty was 35 per cent; on rails, 38 per cent; on bars, 29 per cent; and on plates, 35 per cent. These duties were modified somewhat by the French system of admitting partly manufactured iron under bond, provided an equivalent amount of finished goods was exported. This was a help to British pig-iron. The figures of the Board of Trade show that exports of British pig-iron to France for the five years ending in 1860 averaged 74,247 tons; to 1865, 138,116 tons; to 1870, 104,687 tons; and to 1875, 82,400 tons. The statistics of the exports of wrought-iron and material for railroads show that in those goods there was not even the temporary increase found for pig-iron. There was, in fact, no important change before 1865, and after that there was a steady decline. These figures in tons per year were as follows:

ARTICLE	Averages for five-year periods			
	1856–60	1861–65	1866–70	1871–75
Bar-iron	10,063	13,607	5,175	88
Rails, chains, etc.......	18,240	13,848	1,864	23
Wire.................	99	486	291	324
Sheets and plates......	4,956	2,064	1,745	2,321
Cast and wrought-iron wares..............	2,788	7,208	4,262	5,009

The failure to increase British exports of iron goods to France was attributed by the British ironmasters partly to the French tariff which, in many cases, remained in effect prohibitive, and to the great development of the French iron industry. French ironmasters had made use of scientific discoveries and had so greatly improved their methods of production that they exported large quantities of iron goods to foreign markets outside Great Britain, especially locomotives and other machinery.[13]

French importations of iron, nearly all of which came from Great Britain or Belgium, are given by Amé in tons as follows: [14]

Period	Pig-iron	Bar-iron	Steel	Total
1827–36	10,126	5,935	791	16,852
1837–46	36,279	3,763	446	40,488
1847–56	67,975	17,105	550	85,630
1857	95,459	29,373	1,270	126,102
1858	63,186	15,706	1,172	80,064
1859	43,023	1,736	1,110	45,869
1860	28,941	661	742	30,344
1861	117,604	12,980	1,892	132,476
1862	199,994	80,887	2,282	283,163
1863	160,058	12,104	1,809	173,971
1864	36,374	2,112	1,058	39,544
1865	65,526	3,263	691	69,480
1866	72,323	9,326	1,598	83,247
1867	80,377	5,789	2,835	89,001
1868	18,513	14,038	3,067	35,618
1869	6,871	11,910	3,447	22,228

These statistics, though not giving as many details as could be desired, show that there was a considerable increase in the

[13] F. O., 27–2222.

[14] Léon Amé, *Étude économique sur les tarifs de douanes* (2 vol. ed., Paris, 1876), II, 400. Amé in 1860 was Director of Customs at Paris. His figures are the official statistics of the Customs service. They are difficult to compare with the figures of the British Iron Trade Association, because they cover imports from all sources and not from Great Britain alone, although the only other important source was Belgium.

In 1862 the French Government by decree authorized the importation under bond of partly manufactured iron, provided an equivalent amount was exported in finished goods. Before 1862 the law required that exactly the same pieces of iron imported under bond be thus exported in the form of finished goods. We do not know how much pig-iron was sent into France in bond, and this amount may have been large beginning with 1862. We do know that there were loud complaints from many ironmasters in France of an extensive trade in the sale of permits to import such iron.

imports of iron between 1850 and 1858 due, in great part, to the needs of the French railroads and merchant marine. These importations were favored by decrees reducing the duties in general, and stating the willingness of the Government to reduce them still further in urgent cases. The most important of these decrees was that of October 10, 1855, which authorized for three years the importation free of duty of iron for shipbuilding. The imports under this decree were as follows: for 1856, 23,885 tons; for 1857, 13,766 tons; for 1858, 10,010 tons. Considerable quantities of rails during the later 'fifties were admitted on payment of 60 francs per ton, which was one half of the normal duty at that time. These imports amounted to 39,948 tons in 1856; 7,841 in 1857, and 1,260 in 1858.[15] These figures indicate that in 1856 a large part of the imports of iron came in either free for shipbuilding, or at a reduced duty in the form of rails. For 1857 and 1858 the imports of iron that came in free or at a reduced duty amounted to only a small part of the total. For the imports between 1860 and 1870 we lack such detailed information; but the figures of the French customs service indicate that the duty on bar-iron of 70 francs per ton in 1860 (effective 1861) and 60 francs in 1864 proved almost prohibitive, and this is confirmed, as we have seen, by the statements of the British ironmasters. For pig-iron the imports were unusually large for three years only, that is, in 1861, 1862, and 1863. If we can say that these imports were due to the reorganization of the French iron industry and the efforts of the French manufacturers to adjust themselves to British and Belgian competition, the period of transition was not long. After 1863 the duty on pig-iron imposed by the Treaty of 1860 seems to have given effective protection.

Though the statistics of imports show that France was not flooded by iron from Great Britain after the signature of the Anglo-French Treaty of 1860, her iron industry had to prepare to meet some competition, especially in the manufacture of pig-iron, and her manufacturers could not continue to enjoy the enormous

[15] L. F. R. Wolowski, "La Réforme douanière," *J. des écon.*, Series II, XXV (January, 1860), 435.

profits they had collected when they had the complete monopoly of the home market. The Treaty was certainly beneficial in that, through forcing French manufacturers to meet a moderate amount of competition, it stimulated them to develop production on a larger scale and with improved equipment and methods. In this way it helped to bring down the price of iron. When the ironmasters complained bitterly of the Treaty they referred particularly to the drop in the price of iron which reduced their profits, but which was an inestimable boon to the industries using iron, especially to the textile industries which needed more and better machinery. Another cause of the difficulties that the ironmasters had to meet was the failure of the demand for iron in France to increase immediately, as had been expected. This increase came in time, but not at the moment when the manufacturers of iron needed it most. The result was that the French market was flooded, not with British, but with French iron. One of the first results of the reorganization of the French iron industry was, in short, overproduction from which the industry suffered severely for some time after 1860.[16]

In attempting to determine the results of the Chevalier-Cobden Treaty of 1860 on the French iron industry we must not regard the treaty as the sole, or even the principal, cause of the reorganization of that industry. It would be easy to give figures proving that the smelting of iron with wood decreased notably after 1860; that a large number of furnaces, foundries, and forges that were badly situated, or that produced on a very small scale, succumbed; that the surviving establishments using coal and producing on a large scale grew larger and more important. But if we did this we should neglect two causes that were more important and whose influence was felt before 1860; the increasing use of coal in the smelting and refining of iron, and the building of the railroads. Both the difficulties from which the iron industry suffered after 1860 and the benefits felt

---

[16] Wolowski, *op. cit.*, p. 424; also Amé, *op. cit.*, II, 397 and Comité des Forges, *op. cit.*, pp. 115–116. See also *Moniteur* for speeches before the Corps Législatif of Deputy Liegeard of the Moselle, May 13; Forcade, Minister of Commerce, May 15; and Rouher, Minister of State and one of the negotiators of the treaty with England, May 20, 1868.

by French industry as a whole, as well as by French trade and agriculture, were due far more to the increasing use of coal and improved means of transportation, than to the very important change in the commercial policy of France inaugurated by the Emperor in 1860 on the advice of Michel Chevalier.

The Anglo-French Treaty of 1860 was not, then, the principal cause of the reorganization of the iron industry in France, because that reorganization began long before 1860. The difficulties of the manufacturers were due largely to the fact that the Treaty caught them in the midst of that reorganization, and that it caught them suddenly like a bolt from the blue. They were loud in their denunciations of it because they hoped that they could influence the Government to keep the maximum duties that the terms of the Treaty permitted, in which they were largely successful; and because they hoped to conceal their own shortcomings and greed. Their real aims were clearly understood by the Government and not even the Emperor was deceived when the ironmasters spoke feelingly of the protection of national labor, an old argument that had proved effective under the Restoration and the July monarchy, and which was to prove effective again under the Third Republic. Combes wrote to the Minister of Commerce, in 1860, that the real object of the Comité des Forges, under the presidency of Léon Talabot of the Denain company, was to keep up the price of iron by whatever arguments or threats seemed to them most likely to be effective.[17]

What, then, were the positive effects of the Treaty of 1860 on the iron industry of France? We have studied the negative effects and can state that it did not ruin or even injure seriously the iron industry; but did it really accomplish anything? Can we say that it did more than merely prevent matters in France from getting worse? Let us attempt to answer these questions by considering the aims of the principal author of the Anglo-French Treaty, Michel Chevalier. We know from his private papers and from an important document in the national archives written by him [18] that he did not regard the treaty as an end in

[17] Arch. Nat., F 12–2514.
[18] See the Conclusion.

itself, but as part of a plan for the reform of the entire economic system of France which should include a great increase in the means of transportation and a notable reduction in their cost. He wished to lower the tariff in order to stimulate French industries to improve their methods and increase their production so that they could lower their prices; and of all the industries in France he considered that of iron the most important and the most backward. We should remember that he was not merely an economist, but also a skilled engineer with professional knowledge of the condition of the iron industry in France, England, and the United States.

Chevalier put the greatest emphasis on cheap iron because he wished iron to be used freely in all industries and agriculture, so that the great mass of the French people, through efficient production on a large scale, could have cheaply and abundantly the necessities of life. This was his object in submitting to the Emperor, in the autumn of 1859, his plan for the reform of the economic system of France of which the treaty with England was to be the principal feature, and we can say that his object was achieved. The Treaty did help to bring down the price of iron and, in time, of machines of all sorts for industry, agriculture, and transportation; and it gave a guarantee that as long as it lasted the price would never rise again to the old heights of monopoly. The Treaty only helped to do these things, it is true, but is not that exactly what legislation should do in matters like the tariff? Is it not dangerous for the legislator to attempt to create or destroy industries in defiance of economic laws? Is not his real field, rather, to aid the operation of those laws in order to insure their best results for the people of his country? Should he not try to increase the good effects of such laws and mitigate those that bring suffering or disaster? If we admit that these are the proper aims of the legislator we can say that, because in this case they were achieved, the Treaty of Commerce of 1860 between England and France was successful, for it helped to bring about the full development of the industrial revolution in France.

CHAPTER X

THE DEVELOPMENT OF THE COTTON INDUSTRY IN FRANCE

THE industrial revolution, which grew to importance in the late eighteenth century, seemed at the time to give England a power in industry and trade that was almost irresistible. Not only did most of the great inventions occur in England, but every effort was made to see that the new machines and the men who could run them should be kept at home, so that England exclusively might profit from them, and force other nations to buy from her the goods that she alone could produce cheaply and in large quantities. The danger to the industries of other countries was well understood by them, and the blockade decreed by Napoleon to ruin English trade was kept after Waterloo in the form of a prohibitive tariff to save French industry from what its leaders felt to be certain destruction. Great was their consternation when, in January, 1860, they were suddenly informed that a treaty had been signed with England; that after more than fifty years of prohibition British goods would be admitted under moderate duties and British competition would become a reality.

What was the real condition of the French cotton industry when faced with what it called the supreme crisis in its history? Impartial evidence is scanty, for almost without exception the manufacturers tried to convince the Government of the folly of its course in suddenly adopting the system of free trade with England, and they arranged, and even falsified evidence to prove their point. But the manufacturers by overemphasizing some facts and suppressing others reveal interesting truths to the investigator. We can interpret their misstatements also in the light of evidence collected by the Government of the Second Empire and of studies by economic historians, such as the late Charles Ballot's *L'Introduction du machinisme dans l'industrie française.* By observing the growth of the cotton industry in the three great regions of Normandy, Alsace, and the Nord, we can learn much about its real strength and weakness when it was called upon to compete with England in 1860.

Our best evidence on the early years of the French cotton industry comes from Normandy. We find that toward the end of the seventeenth century Rouen imported cotton yarn from the Levant for the wicks of candles and for gloves.[1] Then the merchant Delame[2] found it cheaper to bring in the raw cotton and spin the yarn himself. This yarn was first used for Siamoises, cloths of which the warp was of silk and the weft of cotton. Rouen soon succeeded in imitating most of the cloths made in England and Holland, whether of cotton mixed with wool, linen, or silk, or of pure cotton. By 1759, after the fall of the French East India Company, Norman spinners were able to produce yarn fine enough for muslins, and the weavers began making painted cloths and *indiennes* which soon proved a great success. An abundant supply of labor was found among the workers trained in the older textile industries of wool and linen, both of considerable importance in Normandy. Spinning was done in their country homes by the peasants after their work in the fields, or in the seasons when work on the farms was less exacting. The system grew until before the Revolution Arthur Young found the whole region of Caux, between Rouen and Havre, industrial.[3] Thanks to this supply of labor provided by the older industries, the abundance of water power on the small but swift streams, and the facilities for trade furnished by the ports of Rouen and Havre, the cotton industry grew rapidly.

As in England, the industrial revolution transformed first the cotton industry, so in France we find machinery first used to spin cotton. England, as we have seen, did her best to keep the

---

[1] J. Levainville, *Rouen, étude d'une agglomération urbaine* (Paris, 1913), p. 194.

[2] Charles Ballot, *L'Introduction du machinisme dans l'industrie française* (Lille, Paris, etc., 1923), p. 41.

[3] Levainville, *op. cit.*, p. 204.

monopoly of her new inventions by forbidding the exportation of machines and the emigration of skilled workmen, but the rewards offered in France were great and smuggling was, therefore, successful. Before the outbreak of the French Revolution the three principal spinning machines invented in England were in actual operation in France and one of them was widely known. The spinning jenny, invented by Hargreaves in 1765, was set up at Rouen and Sens in 1771, in the factories of Jean Holker, a government inspector, with financial aid from the French Government and the active assistance of twenty-five English workmen.[4] Jennies continued to be manufactured at both centers and were distributed through France with women to teach their use. Although it was difficult to procure and set up English carding machines to prepare the cotton for the jenny, and although the quality of the yarn spun by it left much to be desired, the new spinning machine met little opposition because it was admirably suited to the needs of domestic industry. We find the jenny firmly established in Normandy before the beginning of the Revolution, and its hold greatly strengthened by the need of meeting British competition under the Treaty of 1786.

The next machine brought over from England was the water-frame invented by Arkwright in 1769 and set up near Lyons by the Milne family in 1782.[5] This machine, unlike the jenny, spread very slowly, and encountered active opposition because it could not be used at all in the homes of the peasants and because it produced a much larger quantity of yarn and thus threatened to cause great unemployment among hand spinners. Much capital was necessary to build mills for the large and heavy water-frame, and capital was hard to find in those days because of the bad economic and financial condition of France. Hence the first mills nearly all failed soon after the outbreak of the Revolution and for a time the water-frame made little progress.

The last of the three spinning machines of England, Crompton's mule, invented in 1779, was brought to France in an

[4] Ballot, *op. cit.*, p. 46.
[5] *Ibid.*, p. 65.

effort to meet British competition and was set up in Amiens in 1788 by Spenser and Massey, with the financial assistance of the Société d'Encouragement d'Industrie of that city.[6] Like the water-frame it gained ground slowly because it had to be used in mills, and therefore suffered from the scarcity of capital and the conservatism of labor. But it possessed many advantages over the frame. It could carry 200 spindles instead of 80, and its yarn was good for both warp and weft, not merely the warp, as had been that of Arkwright's machine, because the new yarn combined the strength of that spun by the frame with the softness of that made by the jenny. The struggle between the two machines was long. The number of mule spindles surpassed that of the water-frames only in the later years of the First Empire and the mule's victory was not won unaided, for in 1810 Napoleon had imposed a much higher duty on American cotton [7] than on that from the Levant, which the mule alone could spin finely enough for calicoes.

We may now inquire what progress was made by the French cotton industry in the period of the Revolution and the First Empire, when spinning machinery first came into general use. The period opened with the Anglo-French Treaty of Commerce of 1786, which confronted the young French industry with British competition before there had been any substantial development of the use of machinery in France. Although the records of the period are so incomplete that few conclusions can be drawn, it is clear that the great increase of British imports did not kill the French cotton industry, and that it greatly stimulated the use of the jenny and, to a lesser extent, of the water-frame. The return of high protection and prohibitions at the beginning of the long period of war in 1793 seems to have had little effect on the French cotton industry because the weak republican Government was unable to enforce its laws and keep out British goods. But with the foundation of the Empire we find the industry greatly stimulated through the isolation of France under the Continental blockade. The use of machinery

[6] *Ibid.*, p. 86.
[7] *Ibid.*, p. 116 (tariff of Trianon, August 5, 1810).

increased notably and the quality of the yarn improved until by 1806 the spinning of No. 100 was common, while Paris was able to spin up to No. 150 and St. Quentin, only two years later, up to No. 180.[8]

There was, however, practically no use of power other than that of water, which became almost universal in Normandy and Alsace. There were few large mills because of the high cost of machinery, equipment, and English foremen and mechanics, for which the cheapness of building material and ordinary labor was not sufficient compensation. Spinning in Normandy left the huts of the peasants on the plateaux and came down to the valleys where it was concentrated in small mills on the banks of the many streams. A similar development came in Alsace, though that region, except in printing, was then far behind Normandy. In the Nord, where the industry was even younger, the crisis under the Empire caused a great and rapid growth of cotton spinning with a concentration that apparently exceeded that of Normandy and Alsace. In short, the use of machinery for spinning was firmly established in France during the Revolution and the First Empire, and time alone was needed to destroy spinning by hand. Weaving by hand was, of course, still universal in France, and became one of the great resources of the peasants because the enormous increase in the production of yarn caused an equivalent increase in the demand for cloth. But despite the great progress made in spinning the French cotton industry was weak because of the crises of 1809, 1811, and 1813, the last of which endangered its very existence.[9] Its development had been too rapid and had been made in time of war and abnormal conditions of trade.

On their return to France in 1814 the Bourbons promptly showed a desire to abandon the prohibitive tariff established during the Revolution and Empire as a war measure against England. The Comte d'Artois, as Lieutenant General of France ordered the replacement of the high duty on raw cotton by a mere charge for registration. In 1816 the Government wished to admit raw cotton free and levy a duty of 15 to 18 per cent on

[8] Ballot, *op. cit.*, p. 127.   [9] *Ibid.*, p. 120.

cotton cloth.[10] This would have meant the abandonment of the prohibitions directed against England and a refusal to extend the prohibitive system by law in time of peace to the goods of all countries. It had been so extended in practice during the years of war because there was no other way of striking at British trade, and because manufactured goods, whatever their nominal country of origin, were nearly all the products of British industry. The government of the Restoration also took the view that, though French industry had progressed under the prohibitive system, it would have developed far more under the stimulus of foreign competition. M. de Saint Cricq, director general of Customs, in introducing the Bill of 1816, said:[11] "We should have less progress to make if too long an interruption, in our commercial relations had not constituted a prohibition, under the shelter of which it was possible to neglect with impunity means of improvement which a beneficent competition would not have failed to develop."

Unfortunately Louis XVIII and his advisers lacked the political power to impose their economic views on the nation. After the Hundred Days they had no illusions concerning the popularity of the Bourbon dynasty. Nor were they left in any doubt of the wishes of the manufacturers. The order of the Comte d'Artois abolishing the high duty on raw cotton met with a roar of protest. The manufacturers demanded an indemnity of 30,000,000 francs and the maintenance of the prohibitions on manufactured goods. The Chamber of Commerce of Rouen wrote to the King on May 27, 1814:[12] "Prohibitions constitute a social and political right. From the manufacturer who has used all his financial resources to build up his factory to the workman who finds in it the means to support himself and his family, all claim, and with reason, the right to supply all that is consumed in the country they inhabit."

The Government did not dare to oppose the organized manu-

---

[10] Léon Amé, *Étude économique sur les tarifs de douanes* (2 vols., Paris, 1876), I, 84.

[11] *Ibid.*, I, 82.

[12] Gaston du Boscq de Beaumont, *Industrie cotonnière en Normandie* (Paris 1901), p. 39.

facturers, and granted their demands promptly. By the Act of April 28, 1816,[13] a duty of 15 to 30 francs per 100 kilograms was charged on short staple cotton, and of 30 to 50 francs on long staple; the prohibition of the import of cotton cloth of British origin was kept and extended to the goods of all countries. In 1836 the tariff on cotton was modified to admit yarn finer than No. 142,[14] but there was no important change until the Treaty of 1860 with England.

Let us now see what progress the cotton industry made under the system of prohibitions in time of peace. Much information is given about the development of spinning, especially in Alsace and the Nord, but there is a general silence regarding weaving, except in Alsace, that is most significant. The least important of the great cotton manufacturing regions of France in 1814 was Alsace, yet it was there that the greatest progress was made in the improvement of the methods of spinning. Mechanical spinning was introduced in the late eighteenth century, but in 1806 Alsace had only three mills using machinery.[15] Then began a steady increase in its employment until by 1820 hand spinning had nearly disappeared. The number of mills using machinery increased from three to eleven by 1812, and they had between one half and one third of the total number of spindles in Alsace, which Chaptal gives as 70,336 in the year 1818. By 1828 Alsace had 500,000 spindles, by 1846, 859,000, and by 1860 the total number had reached 1,600,000.[16] The mills were growing steadily larger, as is shown by the average number of spindles in each, which increased from 9,517 in 1828 to 17,967 in 1856; several mills were very large indeed, Nicholas Schlumberger

---

[13] Auguste Arnauné, *Le Commerce extérieur et les tarifs de douane* (Paris, 1911), p. 155.

[14] *Ibid.*, p. 158. The reform was promised in the Act of May 24, 1834, but not formally made until the Act of July 2, 1836.

[15] Louis Reybaud, *Le Coton; son régime — ses problèmes — son influence en Europe* (Paris, 1863), p. 419. The author quotes the report of October, 1862, by Charles Thierry-Mieg, secretary of the Société Industrielle de Mulhouse, on the cotton industry in the Department of Haut Rhin.

[16] Robert Lévy, *Histoire économique de l'industrie cotonnière en Alsace; étude de sociologie descriptive* (Paris, 1912), p. 86. This probably includes the Vosges, Bar le Duc, and Troyes. Alsace probably had about 1,150,000.

having 55,000 spindles in 1834, Jacques Hartman 50,000, and Charles Naegley 84,000.[17] Finally, we should note not only that Alsace came to use machinery for all her spinning long before 1860, but that she was constantly improving that machinery and developing the construction of machines at home, instead of importing them from England at enormous expense. In 1850 the best type of mule-jenny, known as the *renvideur* or "self-acting," because it performed all the operations of spinning itself, was introduced from England; and before 1860 fully half the spindles of Alsace were on self-acting machines.[18] The explanation of the rapid spread of this new type of spinning machine lies in the fact that the cotton industry of France as a whole enjoyed great prosperity between 1850 and 1857, the boom following the long depression begun by the industrial crisis of 1847 and intensified by the Revolution of 1848. It is true that the expense of installing the self-acting mule was very great and labor was cheap in Alsace and the neighboring region of the Vosges. On the other hand, the economy from the use of the self-acting mule was greatest in fine yarn, and we know that the manufacture of fine yarn in Alsace was started by Nicholas Schlumberger[19] in 1819 and was an industry of considerable importance by 1826. Evidently a further stimulus was needed to bring in the newest machines, and this was supplied by the manufacture of cotton sewing thread which began in Alsace in 1849. The following table prepared by Charles Thierry-Mieg for the Société Industrielle de Mulhouse shows the increasing use of the self-acting mule:[19]

Year	No. of Mills	Mule-jennies	Self-acting	Total
1828	49	466,363		466,363
1846	45	779,300		779,300
1851	52	819,006		819,006
1856	67	866,122	108,179	974,298
1857	72	715,232	256,956	1,072,188
1859	80	710,520	382,260	1,092,780
1861	86	547,174	680,208	1,227,382
1862	88	543,054	694,260	1,237,314

[17] *Ibid.*, I, 168. [18] Reybaud, *op. cit.*, p. 419.
[19] Lévy, *op. cit.*, p. 168.

The region of the Nord, the youngest of the three, prospered greatly between 1814 and 1860, and the cotton spinning industry grew rapidly. The Lille district in 1808–10 claimed 22 spinning mills with 207 mule-jennies and 20 water-frames, the former having 39,570 spindles and the latter 1,700. There was also a large number of hand-jennies.[20] Roubaix had 13 spinning mills and Tourcoing 8. In 1859 the Lille district had 703,791 spindles in 57 mills; Roubaix had 12 mills with 217,640 spindles, and Tourcoing, whose number of mills is not given, had 157,634 spindles. To these should be added the spindles of small centers like Armentières, and 400,000 for the Province of Picardy, making a total of approximately 1,500,000 for the whole region of the north,[21] which is about the same as the total for the group of the East, including the provinces of Alsace, Lorraine, and Champagne. Most of the spindles in the Nord in 1859 were undoubtedly run by steam, since that region lacked the great resources in water-power of Normandy and Alsace, but had cheap coal from the rich basins of the Nord and Pas de Calais. The first steam engine for a spinning mill was set up in Lille by Auguste Mille in 1820, when most of the factories ran their machines by hand or horse-power. In 1832, we are told, 17 of Lille's 50 spinning machines used steam engines and 7 more were installing them.[22] It seems safe to assume, therefore, that steam was the principal source of power for spinning in the Nord in 1859, and not chiefly an auxiliary source, as in Alsace and largely in Normandy.

For Normandy we have practically no figures that show the development of cotton spinning between 1814 and 1860. Levainville[23] tells us that the Rouen district in 1837 had 317,000 spindles, but he mentions none of the other districts. Beaumont[24] says that in 1859 there were 1,817,328 in the Depart-

[20] Jules Houdoy, in his *La Filature du coton dans le nord de la France* (Paris, 1903), p. 41, almost the only source for the region, gives the number of hand-jennies in the Lille district as 10,000 with 60 spindles each, or a total of 600,000 spindles.

[21] *Ibid.*, pp. 59–60.

[22] *Ibid.*, p. 58.

[23] Levainville, *op. cit.*, p. 215.

[24] Du Boscq de Beaumont, *op. cit.*, p. 45.

ments of Seine Inférieure and Eure. If we make due allowance for lower Normandy, where there were many small cotton-spinning establishments in the Departments of Orne and Calvados, and for southern Normandy, where there were many other small centers, we shall reach a total number of spindles close to 2,500,000, which is the figure given for 1860 in the series of volumes edited by Michel Chevalier [25] on the International Exposition of 1862 at London.

On the development of weaving in the cotton industry of France before 1860 we have little information. The use of the power-loom, even in England, came much later than the use of machinery in spinning, for although the first power-loom was invented by Cartwright in 1785, it was not a practical success, and the first one able to compete successfully with hand weaving was that invented by Sharp and Roberts in 1822.[26] In Alsace, the only region where we can trace the progress of cotton weaving in any detail, the power-loom was introduced in 1822, and by 1826 Issac Koechlin alone had 240 of these machines.[27] The growth of mechanical weaving is shown by the following table of Charles Thierry-Mieg of Mulhouse: [28]

Year	No. of mills	Hand-looms	Power-looms	Total
1828	17	20,000	2,123	22,123
1846	—	12,000	10,000	22,000
1851	34	10,000	12,128	22,128
1856	56	8,657	14,920	23,577
1858	65	7,000	19,932	26,932
1859	72	7,000	21,772	28,772
1861	75	5,000	24,320	29,320
1862	84	4,000	25,153	29,153

In Alsace, mechanical weaving was supreme by 1860; and only very fine or fancy cloths, or those of unusual width, were woven by hand. The weaving industry, however, showed far less concentration than the spinning. Of 56 weaving mills

[25] Carcenac, *Exposition universelle de 1862*, IV, 356.
[26] A. P. Usher, *The Industrial History of England* (Boston, 1920), p. 302.
[27] Lévy, *op. cit.*, p. 144.
[28] Reybaud, *op. cit.*, p. 422.

operating in 1856 only 13 had between 200 and 300 looms and 12 had less than 100.[29] The survival of the small mill in Alsace was due to two important factors, water power and cheap labor. The mills tended to stay in the mountain valleys on the banks of the swift streams, where water-power was sufficient for most of their needs, and the farming population could work in the mills without complete neglect of their agriculture. Steam was used only as an auxiliary to water-power in most places, chiefly in the summer, so that the high price of coal was not a great handicap. But for printing and for the spinning and weaving of fine cloths, where skilled labor was a factor of great importance, the mills found it more economical to move to the cities like Mulhouse, where such labor could be obtained more easily and steam power could be economically used on a large scale because of the relative cheapness of coal.

The other regions of France that manufactured cotton were far behind Alsace in the development of mechanical weaving. Normandy alone had a considerable number of power-looms, used chiefly for making raw cloth for bleaching and printing. The mills using these looms were almost all in the Departments of Seine Inférieure and Eure. It is clear that the amount of mechanical weaving in the rest of Normandy was insignificant in 1860, because labor was still so cheap that there was little economy in the use of machinery, most of which had to be imported at great expense and run with coal which was also imported and was costly if used far from the coast or the navigable Seine. Many of the small manufacturing centers in central and southern Normandy were not even on railroads. In the Nord there was only a slight use of power-looms, although French coal was available at reasonable prices, and the large cotton centers were on railroads. Lille, Roubaix, and St. Quentin had only a few power-looms, and Amiens, the chief center for the manufacture of cotton velvet, was preparing to instal them. We know that the famous mixed cloths of Roubaix were woven entirely by hand, as were the gauzes and muslins of

[29] Lévy, *op. cit.*, p. 170.

St. Quentin. The Government's investigators in 1860 [30] found the same absence of power-looms at Tarare, where a great variety of plain and fancy gauzes, fine muslins, tarlatans, and figured gowns were made. Both coal and water-power were available there, Tarare being in the mountains behind the Loire and the Rhone and close to the coal mines of St. Étienne. Hand weaving was universal also in the cotton hosiery industry of France. The Government felt that this was not unreasonable in the case of fine hosiery, which was woven by hand even in England, but for coarse hosiery Nottingham had both rotating rectilinear looms and great circular looms all run by steam, while French centers like Troyes and Moreuil had no machinery at all for weaving.

In our study of the growth of the French cotton industry up to the conclusion of the Treaty with England we have considered chiefly the introduction of machinery in spinning and weaving. We have seen that in the manufacture of yarn machinery was dominant, and that most of the work was done in mills, even if few of the mills were of great size. It seems clear, however, that the machinery used was of an antiquated type, and that the French spinners did not as a rule adopt improvements as they were made in England. It is true that transportation facilities were inadequate and too costly; that, largely because of this, fuel for power was expensive and hard to get; and that, on the whole, French manufacturers were unduly conservative. It was generally admitted in France that the price of yarn was very high and that the amount produced was often inadequate. Was there any remedy for this, or were the manufacturers justified in saying that natural conditions necessarily made the cost of production much higher in France?

We have the opinions of a few captains of industry who were able to see beyond their own financial interests, such as Jean Dolfus of Alsace and Fernand Raoul Duval of Normandy; of government officials who made a special study of the question,

---

[30] *Enquête: Traité de commerce avec l'Angleterre* (7 vols., Paris, 1860). Six volumes only are in the Bibliothèque Nationale. The seventh, which contains the reports of the Government's agents, was found for me at the Ministère du Commerce by M. Charles Schmidt of the Archives Nationales. See pp. xliv–l.

such as Ozenne of the Ministry of Commerce,[31] Ernest Baroche,[32] an investigator for the Conseil Supérieur du Commerce and Amé, a high official in the customs service and later director-general of customs; and finally of Michel Chevalier, engineer and economist, member of the Conseil d'État, and author of the Anglo-French Treaty of 1860. These men felt that the natural difficulties confronting the French cotton industry were not insuperable, that France was not doomed to permanent inferiority as compared with England. They asserted that France had shown that she could spin yarn of as high numbers and as good quality as England, and that she could weave this yarn successfully into the finest cloths as well as her rival across the Channel, while in beauty of design she was frequently superior. They felt that the real cause of the backwardness of the French industry was the prohibitive tariff, which gave French spinners and weavers a monopoly of the home market and relieved them of the troublesome necessity of studying British improvements and modifying their own manufacturing methods. The deadening influence of a prohibitive tariff on industrial progress is well known and needs no demonstration. There is no reason to believe that this influence was less deadening in France between 1810 and 1860 than it has been elsewhere and at other times. Let us see what happened when France abandoned her prohibitive tariff and prepared to meet British competition. Her cotton-spinning industry used machinery, though it was rarely of the newest and most efficient type, but her weaving was done chiefly by hand, with all the expense and waste of the old domestic or putting-out system. Could the cotton industry under these conditions compete successfully with the British giant?

The Anglo-French Treaty of Commerce of January, 1860, provided that the tariff on cotton should take effect only in October 1861,[33] in order to give the French cotton industry time

---

[31] Secretary of the Conseil Supérieur du Commerce which directed the Enquête of 1860. In 1868–69 he visited most of the industrial regions of France and reported on their condition and on their wishes regarding changes in the tariff.

[32] An agent in the Enquête of 1860, son of Jules Baroche, the minister of Napoleon III.

[33] Clause 5 of Article XVI.

to prepare to meet British competition, and because the French Government had promised in 1856 not to remove the prohibitions in the tariff for five years. What little evidence we have indicates that the French manufacturers did order a fair number of improved spinning machines and some power-looms and that they tried to reorganize their mills with a view to greater efficiency in production. But before they could complete their preparations to fight their British rivals the cotton industries of both countries were overwhelmed by the most serious crisis in their history with the outbreak of the American Civil War. Within a few days after the attack on Fort Sumter President Lincoln declared a blockade of the ports of the Confederacy, and before the end of the year 1861 the world's chief supply of raw cotton had been almost entirely cut off. The following tables show the effect of the Federal blockade on the importation of cotton into France:

TOTAL IMPORTS OF BALES OF COTTON INTO FRANCE, WITH STOCKS AT THE END OF EACH YEAR (from U. S. Consular Reports)

Year	Import	Stock at end of year
1855	467,470	59,526
1856	509,164	51,840
1857	481,101	92,795
1858	573,170	141,510
1859	432,631	46,750
1860	684,594	112,425
1861	624,600	140,345
1862	271,570	59,193
1863	381,539	32,852
1864	460,880	61,630
1865	509,805	40,239
1866	689,890	119,450
1867	605,440	63,050
1868	762,593	84,890

FRENCH IMPORTS OF BALES OF COTTON FROM VARIOUS
SOURCES (from U. S. Consular Reports)

Year	From U. S. A.	From Brazil	From Egypt	From other countries
1857	392,734	7,615	21,018	59,734
1858	499,760	6,535	24,781	42,094
1859	376,760	2,374	25,812	27,685
1860	609,030	1,654	21,650	52,260
1861	520,730	922	39,760	63,188
1862	31,420	4,653	32,643	202,852
1863	4,169	9,642	50,058	317,670
1864	4,740	29,501	82,521	344,118
1865	26,361	31,222	65,063	387,159
1866	217,539	63,711	39,491	369,149

The outbreak of the Civil War found the French cotton industry
in a weakened condition.   A considerable amount of capital
had been sunk in the improvement of mills and the purchase of
machinery to meet British competition in the autumn of 1861.
Furthermore, the industry had been unusually active in the
previous three years and it seems clear that France, like England,
would have suffered a severe crisis from overproduction if the
American war had not come.   English mills in 1861 had stocks
of cotton goods in their warehouses that were more than double
the normal amounts, and French warehouses had stocks that
would more than meet the needs of the country for an entire
year.   In addition to this large supply of cloth France, like
England, had abnormally large stocks of raw cotton because the
American crop of 1860 had been remarkably large and most of
it had been exported before the proclamation of the blockade.
Finally, France had recently experienced a commercial revolution
through the growth of her industries in the early years of the
Second Empire, and even more through the development of her
railroads.   The trade in cloth, which had formerly operated
within narrow limits, with the purchases of dealers based generally
on the demands of a single season, suddenly expanded.   Owing
to the development of banking, long-term operations became
possible with the increased facilities, and the keen competition
which the railroads aroused between the different manufacturing

regions of France made it necessary to tempt the buyer with a greater variety of goods and longer credit.[34]

We have scanty information on the prolonged crisis produced in the French cotton industry by the Civil War in the United States. It seems clear, however, that the first effect was a fall in the price of cloth in the autumn of 1861. England, as we have seen, had enormous stocks of cloth which she could not sell at home, and she had lost the valuable American market. When in October, 1861, the moderate tariff on English yarn and cloth became effective in France, it seemed to open a new market in which part of the surplus English goods could be sold. Cordier, who wrote a little book on the cotton crisis in the Department of Seine Inférieure, tells us that English cloth was poured into France for three months, until French prices were brought down and the flood was checked. Since Cordier, like most cotton manufacturers, was a rabid protectionist, we can accept his statement that the flood of British goods was checked within three months. His estimate that these goods did not exceed 10 per cent of the production of Normandy seems reasonable. The difficulty was that the British excelled in just the coarse goods Normandy produced, while the Normans had no chance of finding a new market and could not reap in time the reward of their efforts to improve their machinery and methods of manufacture. The result of the imports from England, combined with the rising price and decreasing supply of raw cotton, was to precipitate a panic in Normandy with a hardening of credit at Rouen and Havre, where the future appeared dark for the small firms. The crisis was clearly worse in Normandy than elsewhere because her manufacturing centers were nearer England than any others in France, except a few in the North, and goods could reach Rouen by the cheap means of direct water transportation. Furthermore, Normandy was bound to suffer from the rising price of cotton more than any other region because the price of cotton forms a much larger part of the

[34] See Alphonse Cordier, *La Crise cotonnière dans la Seine Inférieure* (Rouen, 1864), pp. 52–55; E. D. Adams, *Great Britain and the American Civil War* (2 vols., New York, 1925), especially Chapters VIII and X.

cost of producing coarse than fine cloth. Many of the small mills failed, and a number of them could not be sold for several years, when they were sometimes finally disposed of for one quarter of their value. They failed because they lacked sufficient capital to sell their goods at a loss for a time, or to hold them until the price of cloth recovered. It is probable also that they lacked proper machinery and equipment, and so could not compete with the larger mills that enjoyed those advantages.

The crisis in the cotton industry was both long and severe. The General Council of the Department of Seine Inférieure wrote to the Government in September, 1862, that there was widespread suffering because of the scarcity and high price of cotton; that complete or partial unemployment was very common; and that much public relief was necessary.[35] It is interesting to note that the English cotton workers had begun to suffer in the autumn of 1861 and that the height of the crisis in Lancashire was reached in November, 1862, when approximately 80 per cent of the operatives were receiving public relief or private charity.[36] In January, 1863, the Prefect of Seine Inférieure reported that the spinning and weaving of *indiennes* and *rouenneries* were only 40 per cent of the normal amount.[37] From lower Normandy the Chambre Consultatif of Flers, in the Department of Orne, reported in February, 1862, that part-time work was general and several mills had closed.[38] Although a few years later this same Chamber blamed the treaty with England for all its troubles, in this report of 1862 it named five causes for the crisis: (1) bad crops in France in 1861; (2) the American war with the doubling of the price of cotton and the loss of the American market; (3) the scarcity of indigo and its rise in price; (4) the financial crisis with the restriction of credit; (5) the Treaty of Commerce with England. In January, 1863, Flers reported that all its spinning mills had closed and two thirds of its looms were idle.

In Alsace the cotton crisis was less severe. The Prefect of the

[35] Arch. Nat., F 12–4476D.
[36] T. Ellison, *The Cotton Trade of Great Britain* (London, 1886), p. 95.
[37] Arch. Nat., F 12–4476D, letter of January 18, 1863.
[38] *Ibid.*, letter of February 6, 1862.

Upper Rhine,[39] the Department in which was the bulk of the cotton manufacturing, reported in July, 1862, that there was little suffering or unemployment in the big center of Mulhouse, where there was plenty of cotton and where long-term contracts had been made for yarn and cloth. The printing industry was suffering and had partial unemployment, but the fashions had deserted its product and preferred plain white cloths or light woollens and silks. Fortunately for the workers, printing employed only a small number. The prefect wrote that the smaller centers were much worse off than Mulhouse and had great unemployment. Among these he named the towns of the Belfort and Colmar districts and Sainte Marie aux Mines, where there was an important industry of weaving fancy cloths by hand. He wrote that the unanimous desire of these centers was for European intervention to end the American war. This observation is interesting because it was in July, 1862, that the Emperor Napoleon III received the Confederate commissioner Slidell and asked the British Government whether it would consider joint intervention.[40] In general we can say that Alsace suffered less than Normandy [41] because she had a large supply of raw cotton, her distance from the sea having made it necessary for her to keep large stocks in her warehouses. It is true that the price of cloth rose there as elsewhere, because of the increasing cost of cotton, and that many mills were sold, but few were closed for lack of buyers, as in Normandy. Alsace, on the average, made rather fine yarn in which the cost of cotton was a much smaller factor than in the case of Normandy.

Much light is thrown upon the progress of the cotton crisis in France by the following table prepared by the Société Industrielle of Mulhouse: [42]

[39] Arch. Nat., F 12–4476D, letter of July 19, 1862.

[40] Adams, *op. cit.*, pp. 19, 24.

[41] Although the stock of cotton in France early in 1861 was large, little of it seems to have been held in Normandy probably, because in normal times it had been easy to get cotton as needed from Liverpool.

[42] Lévy, *op. cit.*, p. 306.

Year	Prices (average, in francs per kilogram)			Prices, work on order	
	Cotton	Yarn	Calico	Spinning	Weaving
1860	1.78	3.27	4.59	1.49	1.32
1861	2.39	3.33	4.44	0.49	1.11
1862	4.64	4.91	5.38	0.27	0.47
1863	6.07	6.40	7.07	0.33	0.67
1864	6.46	7.13	7.77	0.67	0.64
1865	4.66	5.34	6.41	0.68	1.07
1866	3.93	5.13	6.54	1.20	1.41
1867	2.82	3.83	4.59	1.01	0.76
1868	2.76	3.48	4.23	0.72	0.75
1869	3.10	3.70	4.45	0.60	0.75

These figures show that the hardest year for the spinners and weavers was 1862, and that in the next year, when the spinners were almost as badly off, the weavers cut their losses considerably. This fits in with our information from Normandy that the height of the crisis at Rouen was reached in the autumn of 1862. From there it evidently spread slowly, for the French Government states in the *Exposé de la situation de l'Empire* [43] that in France as a whole the extremity of the crisis was in May, 1863, when even the district of the Vosges was badly affected. After that there appear to have been some improvement and a decrease in unemployment. One of the principal causes of this improvement was the importation of cotton on a large scale from India, which began in France in 1862 and gave substantial relief in the following year. (See table of imports, p. 194.) There were several reasons why such large importations were not made earlier. In the first place the manufacturers in both France and England believed the American Civil War would be short. Secondly, the production of India had to

[43] November, 1863. The writer has found only four numbers of this bulletin, dated November, 1863, February, 1865, January, 1866 and November, 1867. Though clearly written to impress the public, they contain items of information of some value.

be increased, and a year's delay was necessary to accomplish that. Thirdly, Indian cotton had a shorter staple than American and a fiber that broke much more easily. Fourthly, it was necessary for the manufacturers to adapt their machines to use Indian cotton, which took time and a large amount of capital. Hence, while the change to the use of Indian cotton brought relief to the French cotton industry in general, it caused the failure of many small mills that lacked the necessary capital.

In February, 1865, the French Government [44] reported the situation as still difficult because there were great and sudden fluctuations in the price of cotton, and because the cotton from India and the Levant was hard to use. The crisis of unemployment in Normandy had ended in 1864 when those formerly employed in mills then closed had been absorbed by other industries or by agriculture. The difficult task of improving machinery had been completed and there was great manufacturing activity in Alsace and the Nord. The end of the American Civil War came suddenly in April, 1865, and inevitably caused a sharp decline in prices, which brought a brief crisis in Normandy and the Vosges. This was followed by renewed activity, and the news that the American crop was small caused prices to rise until the difficulty of selling cotton goods in competition with other textile fabrics brought them down again. The situation was still difficult, but at least the industry was active and there was no unemployment. The year 1866 was a good one for the cotton industry in France, and 1867 began well with a brisk trade at Havre and full employment in all manufacturing centers. But the American crop of 1866 had been larger, and this brought down the price of cotton, which fluctuated so greatly that it was difficult to adjust the price of cloth to it. The inevitable result of using better machinery was now felt through a short and mild crisis, due to overproduction, which caused a certain amount of unemployment in the Department of Eure in Normandy, in the Vosges, and in Alsace.

The difficulties confronting the manufacturer of cotton in the years between the end of the American Civil War and the begin-

[44] *Exposé de la situation de l'Empire présenté au Sénat* (Paris, 1861–69).

ning of the War between France and Germany are illustrated
by the testimony of M. Raoul Duval before the Committee of
the French Parliament investigating the economic régime of
France in 1870. M. Duval [45] in 1865 had joined a cotton manufacturer in Normandy in starting to make yarn for cotton hosiery. The firm was ready to begin operations in December,
1866. In their first year of manufacturing, 1867, during which
they bought cotton only as they needed it, they lost heavily
because the price of both cotton and yarn fell all through that
year. Then M. Duval gave his manager authority to buy cotton
freely as conditions justified, and in the next two years he made
large profits through the fluctuations in price. He estimated
that the margin between the highest and lowest prices of cotton
per kilogram was 1.46 francs in 1867, 1.20 francs in 1868, and
0.86 francs in 1869. He said in explanation: "De semblables
écarts, si on devrait intégralment les subir, emporterait les
économies possibles de quelques centimes de revient; ils empor-
teraient toute protection, faible ou forte, que l'on voudrait établir."

If a man had bought cotton at the lowest, and sold at the
highest price in 1867, he would thus have made a profit of
526,000 francs on the 217,000 kilograms of yarn produced by
the Duval mill. Buying at the highest and selling at the lowest
price he would have lost 233,000 francs. In 1868 this specula-
tor's profit would have been 460,285 francs and his loss 182,876
francs; in 1869, 298,930 and 97,572 francs profit and loss, respectively. In each case the profit or loss would have been far
greater than any possible economy in manufacturing. In each
case also, said M. Duval, the chance of a big profit was far
greater than that of a big loss. This was no mere lottery, for
with the telegraph and cable a trader could keep track of price
changes in France, England, America, and India, and buy and
sell accordingly. If his judgment was sound he could have made
money in any one of those years, but if he lived in a remote
mountain valley, as in the Vosges, without telegraph and cable,

[45] *Enquête parlementaire* [1870] *sur le régime économique en France* (Paris 1872),
Session of May 23.

he would have been sure to lose. The fundamental importance of speculation in the late 'sixties cannot be overemphasized. The losses among the mills in the small centers, and especially among those in the Vosges mountains, were heavy. Without bearing in mind this period of feverish speculation, we cannot study the formidable crises of 1869 in the cotton industries of France and England.

The Enquête of 1870 on the economic régime of France was held at the demand of the French manufacturers, a large number of whom hoped that through it they could bring pressure on the Government to denounce the Treaty [46] of Commerce with England. They did their best to convince the Government that the French industry was suffering chiefly because of large imports of British yarn and cloth after the end of the American Civil War. The British witnesses at the Enquête, whose testimony was listened to by the French manufacturers present with impatience and scant courtesy, claimed that their industry had been in no condition to make such shipments. We have also, as corroborative evidence, a letter from Messrs. Ashworth of Manchester to the firm of Dolfus, Mieg of Mulhouse, written April 20, 1870:

"We hasten to offer evidence to prove," say Messrs. Ashworth, "not only that our manufacturing industry has suffered disasters sufficient, if continued, to assail even its existence, but also that the Anglo-French treaty has not in any appreciable degree mitigated our sufferings. Many influences have co-operated in bringing about the present state of trade. . . .

"The greatly increased price of American cotton during and after the war not only rendered the production of goods too costly for profitable shipment, but also compelled spinners to invest large sums in adapting their machinery to other staples. Trade has never been sufficiently good to recoup this outlay, and the disbursements thus made proved in many cases the first step on the road

---

[46] Houdoy, *op. cit.*, pp. 118–121. The manufacturers of the Nord sent a Manifesto to the Government on December 4, 1869, when they realized from Ozenne's visit that the Government had no intention of denouncing the Treaty. They demanded its denunciation and reminded the Government of the Sénatus Consulte of September 11, 1869, giving the Corps Législatif the power to regulate the tariff. They insisted on an *enquête* run by the Corps Législatif and not by the Conseil Supérieur du Commerce named by the Government. Ollivier agreed to this.

to ruin. The high price of cotton had also the effect of diverting the custom of the world to linen, woollen, and mixed fabrics. Through emigration and destitution the labour market became disorganised, and to the frequent scarcity of operatives has been added the complication of Trade Union influence.

"We would not, however, attribute the greatest share of our disasters to the direct influence of the American war on the price of cotton. Before that event the industry had been unduly, extended, and facilities of credit stretched to improper limits. Thus the cotton trade was in no condition to withstand so severe a trial, and the shock found the mill-owners weakened by over-extension and the consequent want of working capital.

"It will be unnecessary to trace the various steps which led to the present condition of the cotton trade, and it is unimportant to describe those occasional gleams of improvement which, having no solid basis, ended only in disappointed hopes. Suffice it to say that in the year 1869 the extreme badness of trade resulted in an extent of disaster which, both in the amount of property involved, and in respect to the hardships and ruin entailed on the manufacturers, is almost without parallel in the history of our commerce. In that year alone upwards of 80 spinners and manufacturers in this district failed, independently of those who compounded with their creditors unknown to the general public; while those whose wealth enabled them to avoid absolute ruin were left with crippled means and greatly depreciated property. . . . The destitution among the operatives in some localities caused an enormous advance in the poor-rates, and in order to avoid liability to taxation on unworked factories the machinery of many was cleared out and even sold for old metal.

"Such is the condition of the industry your protectionists consider has suffered less than that of France." [47]

The crisis of 1869 in France was not felt with equal intensity in all the cotton manufacturing regions. It was comparatively mild in Alsace, where only 4 per cent of the power-looms and one half of 1 per cent of the spindles stopped running.[48] On the other hand it was not yet over when war broke out with Germany in the summer of 1870. The testimony of the witnesses at the Enquête of that year indicates that the crisis had been more severe in the Nord and that it had been very severe indeed in the Vosges and in Normandy. The causes of the crisis were many. Among the more important was the competition with cotton of the linen and woollen industries. While the cotton industry, during the American war, was struggling with the

---

[47] F. O., 146–1486. Printed as a pamphlet by the Manchester Chamber of Commerce under the title: *Condition of Cotton Trade of Lancashire and the Operation of the Anglo-French Treaty of Commerce.*

[48] Lévy, *op. cit.*, p. 309.

difficulties of an insufficient supply of raw material and high prices, its rival, the woollen industry, was aided by large importations from Australia and the Argentine, made possible partly by the recent development of sheep-raising for wool in those countries, and partly by the free admission of wool into France by the Law of May 5, 1860,[49] as a part of the economic reforms of that year. As the price of cotton cloth rose its consumption fell, while that of woollens increased and, under the stimulus of British competition, the methods of manufacture were improved and the costs of production in the French woollen industry were lowered. Thus one of the chief causes of the sufferings of Rouen in 1869 was the competition with her *indiennes* of the cheap woollens of Reims. Another cause was the superior efficiency of the cotton industry in Alsace, which used more and better machinery than Rouen and could thus undersell her hand-woven *rouenneries* by putting on the French market similar cloths made by machinery.

Other causes of the crisis of 1869 in France were the period of feverish speculation in cotton beginning during the American Civil War, and the overproduction of cotton goods, which was the inevitable result of the effort to recover some of the ground lost to the woollen and linen industries, and was furthered by the improvement of machinery for both the spinning and weaving of cotton. This had begun in the prosperous period of the 'fifties and had been greatly stimulated by the Treaty of 1860 with England, which was followed by similar treaties with Belgium and the Zollverein.[50] French manufacturers were also feeling very uneasy for many months before the outbreak of the War of 1870 over the series of diplomatic defeats suffered by the Second Empire, which demonstrated the decline of French prestige in Europe. Then the expedition to Mexico and the maintenance of a large army were expensive, as was also the support of the Imperial Government with a luxurious court.

[49] Amé, *op. cit.*, II, 37.
[50] The treaty with Belgium was signed May 1, 1861, and that with the Zollverein August 2, 1862, but it was not ratified by all the member states until July 1, 1865, when it went into force.

In short, the financial burden of the Second Empire, coupled with its obvious decline both at home and abroad, aroused a general feeling of insecurity and anxiety that was a depressing influence on industry.

We must end our study of the French cotton industry with the crisis of 1869, because little material is as yet available in the government archives after 1870, and because the loss of Alsace, as a result of the war with Germany, so changed the situation of the cotton manufacturers in France that the influence of the Treaty of 1860 becomes too difficult to trace. For the decade ending in 1870 our principle source of evidence is the Enquête conducted by the Corps Législatif in the spring of that year, the testimony on cotton being taken between the middle of March and the middle of June. Unfortunately this Enquête was not held for the purpose of making an impartial study of the condition of French industries. It was called in the hope of forcing the Emperor to denounce the treaty with England, and thus deal a death-blow to the whole system of tariff reductions of which it was the foundation. As we know, the French cotton industry had been suffering from severe depression for many months and had enjoyed little prosperity for more than a decade. Like suffering children the majority of its leaders struck at the obstacle that seemed most nearly within reach, and declared the English treaty to be the cause of all their troubles. One manufacturer in Lille wrote a pamphlet entitled *The Death-Rattle of French Industry*[51], and his colleagues did their best to persuade the Government that it must choose between the death of that industry and the destruction of the iniquitous treaty.

In their testimony at the Enquête the French cotton manufacturers had little to say about the American Civil War. It was the Treaty, they claimed, that had closed so many of the mills of Normandy. It was the Treaty, again, that caused the crisis of 1869 because it allowed the English to flood the French

[51] Houdoy, *op. cit.*, p. 105. The author was du Mesnil Marigny and the full title of his pamphlet, evidently written in 1868 for the Chamber of Commerce of Lille, is *Le Râle de l'industrie française et les interpellations qu'il a provoqués*. The interpellations referred to were questions asked the Government in the Corps Législatif in May, 1868, regarding the effects of the Treaty of 1860.

market, and thus made it impossible for the French to sell their own products at home. Overproduction in France was not mentioned as a cause of the crisis by the majority of witnesses, nor did they speak of the great increase in French exports, which, in many cases, notably exceeded the increase in imports, as for example in the case of mixed woollens made at both Roubaix and Bradford. Then they attempted to prove that French manufacturers could never compete with England on equal terms because everything cost more in France, and they analyzed their payments for cotton, fuel, machinery, building materials, and nearly everything else. In no case was a comparison made between a specific mill in France and a mill similarly situated in England. The witnesses simply gave the cost per spindle of each item in their budget and compared it with the cost of the same item in England. One weaver from Normandy, a member of the well-known family of Waddington,[52] even testified that the French could not compete since they had to pay their workmen higher wages than in England, partly because of the far greater cost of food. Yet France was then shipping to England every year large quantities of meat, vegetables, eggs, and fruit, and it was common knowledge, testified to by most of the other witnesses, that wages were distinctly lower in France despite the increase in recent years.

The higher price of cotton in France was claimed as one of the great disadvantages of the French manufacturer in his effort to compete with his English rival. This was emphasized particularly by the witnesses from Normandy at the Enquête. One of their spokesmen, Lamer,[53] testified that the difference in the price of cotton between the markets of Havre and Liverpool was always in favor of the English port and that the difference was usually 11 francs per 100 kilograms. His figures were analyzed by a broker from Havre, Le Cesne,[54] who testified that the average difference was much less. He found that Lamer had compared the prices in the two markets, not of the same grades

---

[52] Session of April 11.
[53] Session of April 8.
[54] Session of May 30.

of cotton, but of different grades. For the years 1868 to 1869 Le Cesne found the price of cotton at Havre higher than the figure at Liverpool by an amount almost exactly equal to the freight rate on cotton between the two ports. He also disproved the statement made by many Norman witnesses, that, as Frenchmen, they had to pay commissions amounting to 2 or $2\frac{1}{2}$ per cent in buying cotton at Liverpool. He showed that such a sum was paid only if the purchaser lacked English currency or accepted credit at Liverpool; that for properly accredited buyers the price was the same regardless of nationality.

The higher price of coal in France was claimed as a disadvantage by virtually every protectionist witness at the Enquête. It was even claimed that at Rouen the price of coal was between four and five times the price in England. This question was taken up by Raoul Duval,[55] one of the few reliable witnesses present. He explained that there were many different qualities of coal and that it paid to give a good price for English coal of excellent quality that had been screened before shipment. When French coal was used a poorer quality was generally accepted. If French manufacturers took a good grade of French coal, such as they would import from England, they would find that the difference in price would represent only the cost of transportation. This cost of transportation, added M. Duval, would decrease in the future with the increased use of steam in the coastal trade.

The exaggeration of difficulties by the protectionist witnesses at the Enquête and the minimizing or omission of advantages of the French cotton industry as compared with the English could be noted in further detail and evidence given to correct such errors. But we should gain little knowledge of importance regarding the development of the industry in France between 1860 and 1870. Nor was substantial evidence given for the claim made by many manufacturers that France, after the close of the American Civil War, was flooded with British cotton yarn and cloth. The English witnesses who testified in June,[56]

---

[55] Session of May 23.
[56] Session of June 17.,

after all the French witnesses had been heard, stated repeatedly that, though the Board of Trade did not keep a record of British exports to France for French consumption, they knew from their own experience that no great increase in trade with France had resulted from the Treaty of 1860. The French tariff with its specific duties was sufficiently high to exclude almost completely coarse yarn from England. This is shown clearly by French evidence as well as by British. On fine yarn the duty was much lower in relation to the value of the product, and here there seems to have been effective competition, one result of which was to increase greatly the production of coarse yarn in France and the mutual competition of different French centers. A muslin manufacturer from Tarare,[57] where in 1870 there were forty-one mills making fine muslins for dresses, testified that Tarare had never been able to get French fine yarn spun with sufficient care. Until 1836 the manufacturers relied on smuggling for their supply of yarn, and after that year, when yarn finer than No. 142 could be legally imported, they continued to get their yarn from England, although at a lower cost. Even down to No. 90, said this witness, French yarn was still inferior to English. On the other hand a witness from St. Quentin said that he got his best fine yarn from Lille, although he also imported a considerable amount from Switzerland and England. Since at St. Quentin, however, muslins were used for curtains instead of dresses, the manufacturers could probably afford to be less exacting regarding the quality of their yarn. It seems clear that the production of very fine yarn in France did not increase after 1860 and that it may have decreased. But it does not appear that this involved any great change, since the finest yarn had long come largely from England.

The difficulties confronting the French manufacturers of cotton in 1870 were great. Their error lay in attributing most of them to the Treaty with England. They did so because they hoped to get help from the Government through the restoration of high protection, which seemed to them a much less painful remedy than helping themselves through an increased use of

[57] M. Godde. Session of May 30.

machinery, or the improvement of their methods of marketing, which Raoul Duval described [58] as the greatest need of France in 1870, as it was one of the greatest assets of England. There were at least two factors which, apart from the causes of the crisis of 1869, were responsible for many of their difficulties: first, changes in the fashions, and, second, the industrial revolution, which made necessary the increased use of machinery and the change to large-scale production with the inevitable tendency to the concentration of industry. We have seen an example of the first factor in the declining demand for printed cloths and *rouenneries* in France; of the second, in the failure of many small mills and the survival or even prosperity of many large ones during the American Civil War. The existence of both these factors was an indication that under the influence of competition, both internal and foreign, the French cotton industry was maturing, and that it was suffering, not from an iniquitous treaty of commerce, but from growing pains.

There were two main changes of fashion that affected the cotton industry between 1860 and 1870, one the preference for goods made from other textiles than cotton, and the other the new liking for fancy rather than plain cloths. In addition the public demanded cloths at the lowest possible price, even if of inferior quality. The growing distaste for pure, cotton goods was largely due to their scarcity and high price after the beginning of the Civil War. The increased demand for other cloths was the cause of great progress in the linen and woollen industries, so that they were able to offer attractive cloths at very moderate prices. We have mentioned also the fall in the price of wool due to the removal of the duty in 1860 and to the large importations from La Plata and Australia. As a result,

---

[58] Session of May 23. "Que resulte-t-il de ma déposition et de l'étude très consciencieuse à laquelle je me suis livré sur les faits qui se sont passés dans la période que j'ai signalée, c'est à dire depuis le traité de commerce? C'est que le traité de commerce n'a été pour rien dans les résultats de l'industrie du coton. . . . La seule condition vitale et dominant toutes les autres a été la question commerciale. . . . Si tous nos industriels étaient bon commerçants nous aurions une grande force; cette force l'Angleterre la possède. Je désire que sous prétexte de protection nous ne dispensions pas nos industriels de l'acquérir."

printed calicoes were abandoned and the French public turned to the cheap woollens of Reims or the mixed goods of Roubaix. The tulle industry was also affected by the change, for plain cotton tulle was no longer in demand for the bonnets of working women, nor for dresses. Instead bonnets were now made of wool and dresses of silk tulle, as being lighter and cheaper.[59] The demand for cheaper cloths was increased by English competition, for England excelled in producing such goods with a fine finish which made them attractive and easy to sell,[60] even if they were not durable. The manufacturers of Roubaix had to learn to copy the cheap cloths from England and this took time, so that wholesale merchants in Paris complained that the inferior finish of Roubaix cloths caused them to run and fade and made them hard to sell.[61] As a result of these changes there were loud complaints against the treaty with England from most of the manufacturers of pure cottons in France, from the printers of Rouen, who do not seem to have built up the large foreign trade that was the salvation of their rivals in Alsace, from the makers of plain cotton tulle in Lille and the region about Calais, and finally from the manufacturers of mixed woollens and cottons of Roubaix. Yet it was unquestionably those changes that were largely responsible for the closing of twelve of the thirty-two printing mills in the region about Rouen, and for the desperate condition of the plain cotton tulle industry both in the north of France and in England. Finally, these changes formed one of the factors causing overproduction in France because the same machine could produce far more goods if it made coarse yarn or cloth.

The increased use of machinery forced by the Treaty affected both the spinning and weaving of cotton. Most spinning was done by machinery before this time, though not by the best machinery, that is, the commonest machine for spinning was the old mule-jenny rather than the self-acting. We have abundant evidence that British competition caused the introduction of

[59] The session of May 27 was devoted entirely to the tulle industry.
[60] Testimony of M. Esnault-Pelterie, draper, Paris, June 13.
[61] Testimony of M. Larivière, draper, Paris, June 3.

large numbers of self-actings. Alsace had them already, but Rouen, Lille, and Roubaix among the large centers appear to have had few in 1860, and smaller centers such as the towns of lower Normandy and St. Quentin in Picardy had scarcely any. The change was expensive and had to be made during the American war or in the almost equally difficult period between it and the war with Germany in 1870. A few examples will show how backward many French manufacturing centers were. In lower Normandy the cotton district of Condé-sur-Noireau, Flers, and Falaise [62] in the Departments of Calvados and Orne had in 1870 some 183,000 spindles in thirty-seven mills, of which 73,000 spindles were self-actings on machines of 800 spindles each, all imported from England since 1860. Of the remainder 40,000 were water-frames (we are not told whether they were the old frames or the improved throstle) and 70,000 mules. In the hosiery industry the centers of the Department of Aube had in 1860 a total of 62,800 spindles, of which only 2,800 were self-actings; in 1870 the total was 81,416, of which 37,400 were self-actings. [63]

Even more important than the improvement of machinery for spinning was the increase in the use of the power-loom in France. In 1860, with the exception of Alsace and of centers like Rouen, Lille, and Roubaix where there were some power-looms, it would not be far from the truth to say that all weaving was done by hand. Thus in 1859 Rouen had 6,420 power-looms and Havre 3,324; in 1869, 68,510 and 4,512. [64] In the group of centers in lower Normandy there were in 1870 only five mills with a total of 600 power-looms, all erected after 1864, while 80 per cent of the weaving was still done by hand. [65] We are told, however, that the number of hand-looms had decreased from 5,850 to 3,500. At Amiens, the great center of cotton velvet manufacture, there was in 1860 only one mill equipped with power-looms; in October, 1869, it had 683 power-looms and hand weaving in the

[62] Session of May 13.
[63] Sessions of May 13 and 25.
[64] Beaumont, *op. cit.*, p. 93.
[65] Session of May 13.

surrounding country had disappeared.[66] In the hosiery industry the centers of Troyes in Champagne, Moreuil in Picardy, and Falaise in lower Normandy had in 1860 only 50 power-looms, all set up after 1856. In 1870 they had over 2,000.[63] On the other hand there were centers where no progress was made. Thus at Lavalle and Mayenne in southern Normandy there were no power-looms even in 1870.[67] The same thing was true of the more important centers of Roanne and Tarare in central France. In the North, although there were power-looms in the larger towns, there was still much weaving by hand in the country about even such important centers as Roubaix and St. Quentin. The worst case is that of the plain cotton tulle industry in the neighborhood of Calais,[68] where no power-looms had been set up and the number of hand-looms had decreased from 900 in 1860 to 238 in 1870. This, however, was clearly the case of a dying industry, and there are indications that the cotton industry of Lavalle and Mayenne was declining, certainly as regards weaving. In centers like Roanne and Tarare hand weaving survived partly because of the exclusive production of very fine or fancy cloths, and partly because of the cheapness of labor in the mountains.[69]

We have scanty information regarding the concentration of industry in the manufacturing of cotton. In Alsace, which in so many respects was the most progressive region in France, there was a considerable concentration at a fairly early date in spinning. As early as 1834 there were several large spinning mills, as we have seen, and the number of spindles per mill doubled between 1828 and 1846. It is clear also that the factory system was well established by the time of the Revolution of 1848.[70] In Rouen we know that there were a number of large spinning mills in 1860. After that date the few figures given by different writers conflict, but they show that the number of mills decreased while the number of spindles and power-looms in-

[66] Session of May 18. Testimony of M. Vulfran-Mollet, president of the Chamber of Commerce of Amiens.

[67] Session of May 13.   [68] Session of May 27.

[69] Sessions of May 11 and 30.

[70] Lévy, *op. cit.*, p. 159.

creased. This seems to justify the opinion that there was considerable concentration in both spinning and weaving. It is obvious that large mills having more capital must have been better able to weather the stormy years beginning with the American Civil War, and that the majority of the failures occurred among the small mills, resulting in a further increase of concentration. In Lille and Roubaix there were many large mills. We know that between 1860 and 1870 Lille added 110,000 new spindles, and that 20,000 of these were in one mill,[71] but the indications are that there was much less concentration in weaving. In Roubaix weaving was more important and there was at least one mill with 500 looms. A considerable degree of concentration there is indicated by the notable increase of production between 1860 and 1870. We know that weavers were moving from the country to the town in large numbers. The same manufacturer who had 500 looms,[72] which were run by power, succeeded after a brief strike in getting each weaver to look after two looms, although the workers tried to defeat his scheme for a time by running one loom in the morning and the other in the afternoon! His colleagues, when they attempted the same improvement, appear to have failed. It would seem that the factory system in Rouen was well established in both spinning and weaving, in Lille in spinning, and in Roubaix in weaving.

Outside the large cities, however, the resistance to the tendency toward concentration seems to have been successful. In Roanne and Tarare, where hand-looms were universal, there could not have been many large mills. In the mountain valleys of the Vosges we know that the mills remained small, and this was true in lower Normandy. The reason was that coal was expensive and water power and labor were comparatively cheap; the fact that the streams were generally small and often ran dry in the summer made large mills impossible because a great amount of water could not be depended upon. In northern

---

[71] Jules Simon, Le Libre échange (1870), p. 202. From his speech January 20, 1870, before the Corps Législatif.

[72] *Enquête of 1870.* Session of May 28. Testimony of M. Delfosse, president of the Chambre Consultative of Roubaix.

Normandy, outside the Rouen district, and in many parts of Picardy and the Nord, there was evidently no appreciable concentration. It is clear that in all these districts, which successfully resisted concentration, the old domestic or putting-out system retained a strong foothold, and that the workers who spun or wove cotton devoted a large part of their time to agriculture. The persistence of rural industry is one of the most striking characteristics of the development of cotton manufacturing in France.

In conclusion we may ask what influence the Anglo-French Treaty of Commerce of 1860 had on the development of the cotton industry in France. This question is difficult to answer because other factors, such as the American Civil War and the construction of railroads, were far more significant. The negative side of the picture is fairly clear. We can say that the Treaty was not the principal cause of the troubles through which the French cotton industry passed in the 'sixties; that the industry was not ruined by it, as the protectionists in 1860 had predicted it would be and in 1870 claimed it had been; and that at no time was France flooded with British goods, with the possible exception of the last quarter of 1861, immediately after the new tariff on cotton became effective. There is no evidence to support the protectionist thesis that the crisis of 1869 was caused by British competition. Such a crisis was inevitable while the price of cotton was falling to its normal level; and the overproduction which intensified it was due quite as much to the French as to the British manufacturers.

On the positive side we can credit the Treaty with one important achievement. It destroyed the system of prohibitions and thus made possible a limited amount of British competition. A certain amount of internal competition would have come in any event with the railroads, but the competition of the most progressive nation of the day in cotton manufacturing was needed to awaken completely the French manufacturers from their profitable slumbers. There was great improvement in spinning machinery throughout France and considerable progress was made in mechanical weaving. Most of the new machinery came from England; without the lowering of the French tariff it could not have been imported on a large scale, nor would it have been ordered without the stimulus of British competition. The evils that came with the rapid growth of the suddenly stimulated cotton industry in France cannot be charged to the Treaty because they were the inevitable concomitants of the industrial revolution of which that industry now felt the full force. England had suffered first from the social evils of the factory system and from the periods of overproduction followed by industrial crises; France in her turn was bound to feel these unpleasant results of the use of machinery, large-scale production, and the widening of markets. The principal benefit from the use of machinery, the gradual fall in the price of manufactured goods, was not realized in the case of cotton cloth in France for some time because of the American Civil War, but a considerable decrease had taken place by 1870, as was stated by the wholesale merchants of Paris in the Enpuête of that year. The Anglo-French Treaty of Commerce of 1860, then, was not a disaster but a benefit to the cotton industry of France, because it put an end to a deadening monopoly and opened the door to progress.

CHAPTER XI

THE WOOLLEN AND WORSTED INDUSTRIES

THE cotton industry in France had, as we have seen, a rapid development, and felt the full effects of the industrial revolution more quickly than any other textile industry. By 1860 mechanical spinning was general and the power-loom was well known. The comparatively rapid progress of this industry was largely due, as in England, to its youth, which made changes less difficult, and to the comparative ease with which cotton could be spun and woven by machinery. But when the French cotton industry was faced with British competition it had to fight hard for a time because of the far greater size of its British rival and the far greater development in England of the use of machinery. In addition to this difficulty it went through a severe crisis at the beginning of the struggle with England because the chief supply of the raw material was cut off by the American Civil War.

The French woollen and worsted industries, on the other hand, developed more slowly, as had the same industries in England. By 1860 mechanical spinning was well known, but not universal, and the power-loom was used in only a few important manufacturing centers. The retarded progress of the industrial revolution in these industries in France, as in other countries, can be attributed to well-established methods of manufacture which were hard to change and to the considerable difficulties to be overcome in the application of machinery, because wool required far more preparation than cotton and was harder to spin and weave. The same difficulties had been encountered in England, so that, when the tariff of 1860 made it possible for her to compete in the French market, England was not unduly in advance of her in the use of machinery and had no notable superiority in size. She had, however, a more fully developed organization for foreign trade. The crisis experienced by the woollen and worsted industries of France because of the American Civil War was brief and was followed by several years of extraordinary prosperity, resulting in great expansion both in production and in the organization of foreign trade. Instead of a dearth of raw material the French woollen and worsted industries enjoyed abundant and rapidly increasing supplies brought from Australia and Argentina which greatly facilitated their rapid development during the period of great prosperity. The woollen and worsted industries of France were strong in 1860 and well able to meet British competition, and, in consequence, we find only mild protests made by the manufacturers against the reform of the French tariff.

One of the chief elements of strength in the French woollen and worsted industries in 1860 was an adequate supply of wool. This had not always been the case. In the eighteenth century, when France was already famous for some of her cloths, she produced only wool of inferior quality and imported small amounts of merino wool from Spain. Not until 1776 did Louis XVI succeed in importing two hundred merino sheep from Leon and Segovia. In 1786 he brought three hundred and sixty-seven more, with which he formed the first French flock at Rambouillet.[1] Large numbers were brought into France during the Revolution, so that under the Restoration merino sheep were well known and made possible the great development of the manufacture of merino cloths at Reims, an industry which had become so strong by 1860 that it asked for free trade. But the cost of raising merino sheep was high, so that the amount of wool produced was necessarily somewhat restricted. The great landowners who raised nearly all the merino sheep suffered from the expense and from the competition of cheaper wool in France, and therefore asked the government of the Restoration for protection. The result was a series of acts from 1816 to 1826 by which duties equivalent to 30 per cent were imposed on the importation of

---

[1] *Enquête parlementaire* [1870] *sur le régime économique en France* (Paris, 1872). Testimony of M. Roger of the Amiens Chamber of Commerce. Session of June 22. See also J. H. Clapham, *The Economic Development of France and Germany, 1815–1914* (Cambridge, 1921), pp. 25–26.

raw wool. There is no evidence that this high protection, which was maintained [2] until after the establishment of the Second Empire in 1852, stimulated to any marked extent the production of wool in France. Sheep raising was a declining industry throughout western Europe even if the decline was slow before 1860. "Continental cultivators," says Dr. Clapham, "have never succeeded in fitting sheep into the system of mixed arable farming as practiced in England. . . . The reasons are many and can only be suggested here. Chief among them are the smallness of holdings, their dispersion, and the lack of inclosures. As commons and open grazing land have declined sheep have declined with them." [3]

The supply of home-grown wool, then, would not have made possible the great expansion of the woollen and worsted industries which became noticeable about the time of the foundation of the Second Empire. Though our information is meager, we know that the importation of wool was increasing slowly, despite the high protective duty and the surtaxes imposed on cargoes of wool brought into French ports in foreign ships, and on those not coming directly from the country of origin. It seems probable that, as in the case of England, Spain and Germany had ceased to be important sources of supply for French manufacturers before the middle of the nineteenth century and that their places were gradually taken by Australia and Argentina, the former being apparently preferred by worsted manufacturers and the latter by those making woollens. After 1850 these importations grew with the improvement of marine transportation and the construction of railroads in France, together with the heavy reduction of the duty on wool in the French tariff in 1856 [4] and the admission of wool free under the act of May 5, 1860,[5] a part of the economic reforms of that year of which the principal feature was the commercial treaty with England.

---

   [2] The duty on wool was decreased one third by the Act of July 2, 1836, which left an average protection of 20 per cent.

   [3] Clapham, *op. cit.*, p. 176.

   [4] Amé, *Étude économique sur les tarifs de douanes* (2 vols., Paris, 1876), I, 278.

   [5] *Ibid.*, p. 306.

We must turn now to the methods of manufacturing woollens and worsteds in France, and, in order to estimate the strength of these industries in 1860, we must study their development after the late eighteenth century, as far as this is possible from the evidence available. We find in the years preceding the French Revolution two tendencies clearly marked, the one toward concentration, and the other toward dispersion of manufacturing. Both tendencies had their roots in widespread economic conditions and both maintained themselves after the introduction of machinery. We find first that weaving, long concentrated in the towns, began to spread to the neighboring villages after the middle of the eighteenth century, and in a few places it spread far into the country. In Picardy the scattering of weaving through the countryside from centers like Amiens, Abbeville, and Beauvais was rapid. Thus in 1785 Amiens had 4,740 looms and in 1788 only 3,030; for Abbeville the figures were 1022 and 638; Beauvais in 1789 had only one fifth of its looms in the town.[6] Nearly every village in Picardy worked up wool, often to the exclusion of agriculture. The same tendency toward dispersion was at work in other parts of France. Thus at Elbeuf, in Normandy, one of the oldest and most important centers for the manufacture of woollens, most of the spinning was done in outlying villages, as was a large part of the weaving also, even as late as 1860.[7] An even more striking case is that of Reims where the concentration of industry had developed farther than almost anywhere else in France, yet in 1860 a large part of the yarn used there was spun in the Ardennes and a considerable amount of cloth was woven there.[8] The dispersion of the woollen and worsted industries was strengthened by the jenny, which was adapted to the spinning of wool just before the beginning of the French Revolution and was still in general use in 1847.[9] At that date the combing of wool by machinery

[6] Charles Ballot, *L'Introduction du machinisme dans l'industrie française* (Lille, Paris, etc., 1923), p. 164.

[7] Louis Reybaud, *La Laine. Nouvelle série des études sur le régime des manufactures* (Paris, 1867), p. 306. Also Enquête, *op. cit.*, Session of June 15. Testimony of M. Flavigny, member of the Chamber of Commerce of Elbeuf.

[8] Ballot, *op. cit.*, p. 217.   [9] *Ibid.*, p. 223.

had barely begun. The dispersion of the industry, which became important in the late eighteenth century, was accompanied by the acquisition of the control of most of the manufacturing processes by merchant-manufacturers who bought, washed, and cleaned the wool in the towns and had it dyed, after which they sent it into the country to be spun and woven into cloth which they generally fulled and finished in their own mills.

The tendency to concentration in industry, which was also conspicuous in the late eighteenth century, was marked at centers such as Reims, where a small number of big merchants manufactured cloth chiefly for foreign markets. There was much concentration also at Sedan, where in 1775 half the looms were in big mills, four of which were royal establishments, as were some of those at Abbeville in Picardy, and Carcassonne and Mazamet in the Midi.[10] At Louviers, not far from Elbeuf in Normandy, there were in the same year fifteen big entrepreneurs, of whom one had five large mills. The tendency to concentration was greatly strengthened by the introduction of machinery. This began in the late eighteenth century with the growth of the cotton industry, which drew labor away from other industries and created a demand for machinery, especially in spinning, which was the operation requiring the most labor. It was found also that machines like the jenny and water-frame, invented for spinning cotton, could be adapted to wool. By 1787 Louviers had eight of these jennies and Elbeuf six. The Van Robais mill at Abbeville, which had been established by Colbert, took them up and found that they saved one third of the labor cost of spinning, despite the necessary preparation of the wool and the spinning of it into coarse yarn to make it ready for the jenny. In the same year the jenny was in use also at Vienne, in the lower valley of the Rhone, and gradually it spread throughout France.[11] The water-frame, on the other hand, did not become popular in France in the woollen and worsted industries. Although it was well known in Yorkshire as early as 1790 and we know of one mill with small frames at

[10] Ballot, *op. cit.*, p. 168.
[11] *Ibid.*, p. 175.

Orléans in 1799,[12] the most popular machine in France remained the jenny until it was slowly replaced by the mule. Unfortunately the distinction between the jenny and the mule or mulejenny is rarely made in the reports and records on the woollen and worsted industries in France, so that we cannot say with precision when, or how rapidly, the change to the mule was made.

The introduction of machines for preparing wool for spinning was necessary before any great extension of mechanical spinning could be made. The first important step forward was taken by the woollen industry with the adaptation of machines used in the cotton industry to the carding of wool. Several such machines were in use in France as early as 1783 and by 1797 Martin had a machine in his mill at Orléans able to card as much wool as four or five workers.[13] Here and at Louviers at the same period wool was carded by machinery sufficiently well to make it available for the spinning of fine yarn. In the worsted industry progress was far less rapid. The problem of combing wool by machinery had long occupied the attention of inventors in England beginning with Cartwright, who made a combing machine as early as 1790,[14] and a long series of machines appeared that were used in both England and France, but they were expensive and inefficient. Wool-combing by machinery did not effectively displace hand combing until the invention of a new machine by Josué Heilman of Mulhouse in 1845.[15] It is true that two English inventors, Donesthorpe and Lister, had worked out the problem independently, but their machine was not so good as that of the Alsatian inventor.[16] It was Heilman's combing machine that, between 1850 and 1855, by enormously increasing the quantity of wool combed, by improving the quality, and by cutting the cost in half, revolutionized the worsted industry in France.

---

[12] Ballot, *op. cit.*, p. 178.

[13] *Ibid.*, p. 179.

[14] Michel Alcan, *Fabrication des étoffes. Traité du travail de la laine cardée: notions historiques — progrès techniques — développement commercial* (2 vols., Paris, 1866), I, 91.

[15] *Ibid.*, p. 121, and Ballot, *op. cit.*, p. 206.

[16] James Burnley, *History of Wool and Woolcombing* (London, 1889), p. 222.

When we come to consider the growth of the French woollen and worsted industries up to 1860, we find that there was notable progress and that the system of prohibitions did not have the deadening effect that was so marked a feature of the history of the cotton industry. It is possible, and even probable, that the French industries manufacturing wool would have grown faster and developed farther their foreign markets under the stimulus of competition from foreign countries and of cheaper wool at home, but we cannot say that their growth was seriously checked by protection. We find that the woollen and worsted industries in France were greatly stimulated by the treaty with England in 1786 and that they profited from the crises through which the cotton industry passed under the First Empire. Verviers was then French and through the presence there of the Cockerill firm was the most important center on the continent for the construction of machinery for the manufacture of wool.[17] At the very end of the Empire we find carded wool being spun in mills with machinery in the regions about Rouen and Reims and in Paris, although this machinery was most commonly run by horses or oxen, or less frequently by water power, as at Reims, where the city authorities had to intervene to protect their supply of water from the river Vesle. During the cotton crisis of 1828–29 the spinning of carded wool by machinery began definitely to drive out hand spinning.[18] There was also considerable progress made in the development of new types of cloth. This was to be expected in the case of merinos because of the large supplies of merino wool produced in France under the Restoration. The manufacture of these cloths was improved rapidly until it became one of the principal industries of Reims and exported its products on a large scale, even to England. Another important specialty was that of imitation Cashmir shawls, stimulated by the demand for oriental shawls arising from Napoleon's expedition to Egypt. Ternaux, the great inventor and captain of industry, failed to acclimatize the Khergiz goat in France, but with Jaubert he did establish the spinning

[17] Ballot, *op. cit.*, p. 192.
[18] *Ibid.*, p. 218, and Alcan, *op. cit.*, p. 101.

of its wool and the manufacture of shawls from the yarn at Paris and at other centers such as Reims.[19]   Then in 1833–34 Bonjean at Sedan created the fancy cloths of mixed shades known as "Draps de Fantaisie," [20] which became one of the most brilliant of French specialties and which were further developed through the mixture of wool with silk, cotton, and flax in Alsace, Normandy, and the Nord.   We find that by 1860 these fancy woollens formed 80 per cent of the production of Elbeuf.[21]   But perhaps even more important than the development of these various specialties in fine woollens and worsteds, which we should rather have expected in any case, was the manufacture of cheap and coarse woollen and worsted cloths, with a weft of wool and a warp of cotton, and of shoddy cloth for the use of the working classes.   By 1860 this industry was of great importance in Normandy at centers such as Louviers, Lisieux, and Evreux, and it was firmly established also at towns in the south such as Vienne on the Rhone, Mazamet, an ancient center of the woollen industry founded in the mountains north of Carcassonne by Huguenot refugees, and at Lodève in the Cévennes.   The rise of this manufacture of cheap and coarse "Unions" and shoddy was not, as has sometimes been indicated, one of the results of the Treaty of 1860 with England, but was due to imitation of English goods between 1820 and 1840.[22]

With the signature of the Anglo-French Treaty of Commerce of 1860 the French woollen and worsted industries were faced for the first time with British competition.   The manufacturers did not threaten the Government with organized strikes, as had the cotton manufacturers and the ironmasters, nor were there any other signs of general panic.   There was no widespread expression of anxiety, for both industries were conscious of their strength.   The amount of wool used in France in 1860 was nearly as large as that used in England and the British in-

---

[19] Alcan, *op. cit.*, pp. 97–99.

[20] Amé, *op. cit.*, I, 370.

[21] *Enquête of 1870.*   Session of June 15.   Testimony of M. Flavigny.

[22] Clapham, *op. cit.*, p. 67.   See also *Enquête of 1870.*   Reports of the Chambre Consultative of Louviers and the Chambre des Manufactures of Lisieux, Session of June 29.

dustries did not enjoy any decisive advantage from greater concentration. They did have more large mills than the French and they used machinery more extensively, power-looms being almost universal in England and little used in France. England specialized in the production and manufacture of long wool, and she was, therefore, superior in such cloths as serges, ascots, poplins, and damasks, all of which were made on a large scale in the Bradford district of Yorkshire. She was clearly superior also in the manufacture of certain mixed worsteds and alpacas, partly because of the long wool used, and partly because of the other materials such as cotton and mohair. England had another advantage in the greater extent of her foreign markets, although there is no reason to believe that this advantage was great enough to enable her to check seriously the expansion of French exports in woollens and worsteds. France had distinct advantages on her side, such as a large supply of cheap rural labor, which went far to explain the smaller size of many French mills and the slower progress in the use of machinery. She specialized in the production and manufacture of short wool and undoubtedly had as great an advantage here as England enjoyed in long wool. France was as clearly superior in the manufacture of merino cloths as England in that of alpacas. She was noted also for her flannels, manufactured on a considerable scale in the district of Reims and exported in great quantities. Finally, the pure worsteds of France were probably the best in Europe as regards the quality of the cloth, the variety of fashions, and the brilliance and stability of the dyes. There was every indication, in short, that the woollen and worsted industries of England and France were evenly matched; that there was no danger of serious injury to the industries of either country from competition by the other; but that in all probability, such competition would stimulate the industries of both countries to their mutual benefit.

The history of the French woollen and worsted industries during the decade following the treaty with England can be traced more easily than that of cotton because neither the crisis from the American Civil War nor the struggle against British competition was as severe. The evidence given by the manu-facturers in the Enquête of 1870 was, therefore, much more reliable since, having suffered little, they were not greatly tempted to exaggerate their difficulties in order to justify re-quests for help from the Government. The majority of the witnesses favored the continuance of the commercial treaties, the most important of which were those with England, Belgium, and the Zollverein, and a few asked for a further reduction of the tariff. But if the manufacturers were satisfied with the tariff the farmers who raised sheep in France were not. Several of them testified at the Enquête, and others wrote to the prefects of their departments or directly to the Minister of Commerce, complaining that they were being ruined by the disastrous decline in the price of wool and holding the treaties responsible.[23] A study of the fluctuations in the price of wool between 1860 and 1870 shows that the troubles of the farmers were not imagi-nary, but indicates clearly that the cause of these troubles was not the tariff. Wool had been admitted free by the Act of May 5, 1860, and importations had increased greatly, but there was no appreciable decline of prices. After the crisis of 1861–62 caused by the American Civil War, the price of wool in France, as else-where, rose to heights hitherto undreamt of because of the great expansion of the woollen and worsted industries due to the scarcity of cotton. After the end of the Civil War the cotton industry began to recover some of the ground lost to the other textile industries, and a fierce struggle between all these industries arose, resulting in general overproduction and a serious crisis. Prices of woollens and worsteds declined, slowly at first, but rapidly in 1868, when the crisis was at its height, and the price of wool followed, reaching its lowest point in 1869. The French farmers suffered severely, but so did the farmers raising sheep in other countries. Great as was the fall in the price of wool, it was shown that the lowest level reached in 1869 was not as low as the prices during some of the crises before 1860, such as that of 1848; it seemed an unprecedented calamity chiefly

[23] See the series of petitions and letters from agricultural organizations in Arch. Nat., F 12–6223.

because it came immediately after a series of years of abnormal profits, and because the manufacturers who suffered from the overproduction of cloth could not use the whole of the French clip and absorb all the imports, as they had during the period of expansion. The troubles of the French sheep farmers in 1869, from which they had not yet recovered when they gave their evidence at the Enquête of 1870, were due primarily to the world crisis brought on by the overproduction of cloth, and consequently of the wool from which the cloth was made. Another cause was the deterioration in quality of French wool, of which nearly all manufacturers complained. The reasons for this deterioration lay partly in the growing manufacture of coarse cloth which, as we have seen, became noticeable long before 1860, partly also in the increasing demand from the growing cities for mutton, which caused farmers to breed larger sheep yielding more meat but poorer wool, and, finally, in the general decline of sheep raising throughout western Europe, which became a factor of ever increasing importance after 1860.

In the spinning of woollens and worsteds considerable progress in the use of machinery was made in France between 1860 and 1870. Carded wool was spun by machinery long before 1860, but the use of machines for spinning combed wool was not general before the invention of Heilman's comber in 1845. We lack evidence for a study of the progress made in spinning during the 'fifties, but in 1870 the statements of witnesses at the Enquête and such reports as are available from other sources indicate that practically all wool in France, whether carded or combed, was spun by machinery, and that the machine most commonly used was the mule-jenny, which had evidently driven out the once popular hand-jenny. Reims in 1870 had 21 spinning mills, 13 for carded wool with 64,450 spindles, and 8 mills for combed wool with 70,000 spindles, or a total for the city of 134,960 spindles. Most of the machines were mules, self-actings being little used. It is interesting to note that the mills spinning combed yarn had, on the average, 8,000 spindles each; those making carded yarn had an average of only 5,000.[24] Much of

[24] *Enquête of 1870.* Session of June 24. Testimony of M. Dauphinot, manufacturer and mayor of Reims, and M. Lelarge, spinner and weaver of carded wool.

the yarn used for the cloths of Reims was spun in 1870, as earlier, in the Ardennes where the Enquête indicates that there were 106,360 spindles, almost as many as in the city of Reims. The machines used in the Ardennes also were mules constructed by the Schlumberger firm of Mulhouse in Alsace, and they made yarn chiefly for merino cloths, flannels, and novelties or fancy cloths.[25]   At Amiens great progress was made after 1860; the number of mills decreased from 15 to 9, while the number of spindles increased from less than 5,000 to 80,000, and self-actings were introduced cutting in half the number of spinners needed.   Our informant from Amiens tells us that even greater progress was made in the Nord,[26] especially in the Fourmies district, where the worsted industry was started only in 1825, and a competition had arisen between the rapidly growing centers of the North and old centers such as Reims and Amiens, and the smaller towns in the valley of the Oise.   Only one of the witnesses from Fourmies[27] spoke of spinning, but he made the significant statement that the number of spindles there between 1860 and 1870 increased from 120,000 to 320,000.   At Roubaix, also, there was evidently a large increase in the amount of spinning, for the wages of spinners rose 30 per cent and self-actings were introduced, enabling each worker to care for between 1700 and 1800 spindles instead of the 600 customary when mules were used.[28]   On the other districts of France we have little information.   In Normandy we know only that the use of self-actings was just beginning at Elbeuf in 1870, whereas they were used more extensively at Lisieux where the number of spindles had increased 20 per cent since 1860 and wages had increased 15 to 20 per cent.   Elbeuf was then making chiefly fancy cloths which required fine yarn, whereas Lisieux manufactured chiefly coarse cloths for the peasants and was, therefore,

[25] *Enquête of 1870.*   Session of June 24.   Testimony of M. Tranchard of Neuville near Rethel, Department of Ardennes.

[26] *Ibid.*, Testimony of M. Burgeat of Amiens, spinner of combed wool.

[27] *Ibid.*, Session of June 27.   Testimony of M. Legrand, comber, spinner and weaver.

[28] *Ibid.*, Testimony of Flipo, a member of the Commission Ouvrière, sent to give evidence on behalf of the workers in the worsted industry.

in a position to gain far more from the use of machinery. It seems evident that in the woollen and worsted industries of France as a whole the amount of spinning increased considerably between 1860 and 1870, that the use of machinery was practically universal, and that the type of machines used was slowly improving under the influence of rising wages and internal and foreign competition.

The weaving of woollens and worsteds in France was done almost entirely by hand in 1860, but in that year, under the threat of British competition before the end of 1861, most of the important manufacturing centers began to instal power-looms, although some of them took this step reluctantly on the ground that it was a great expense and did not promise to be successful. The most reluctant town in the woollen industry was probably Elbeuf, where in 1870, ten years after the introduction of the power-loom, there were only 268 of these machines, with the addition of 102 more in near-by valleys. Less than half of Elbeuf's fancy cloths, which represented three fourths of her production, were woven on power-looms, the machines being used chiefly for the plain cloths of a single color. The manufacturers admitted that for these plain cloths the power-loom was cheaper than the hand-loom because it wove more rapidly and evenly, but they contended that for most of them the expense of buying these looms would be almost prohibitive, since their mills were small and lacked power, and that the moving of the weavers into the town would result in strikes and a decline of their morality. At Lisieux, on the other hand, where the principal industry of ready-made clothing was feeling keenly British competition, there were 400 power-looms in 1870, all of them introduced after the signature of the treaty with England, but the number of hand-looms had decreased from 2,500 to 1,200, and the industry showed a strong tendency to concentrate in the town.

Reims was clearly progressive in weaving, as in the other processes used in manufacturing woollens and worsteds. Her mayor reported that in 1870 she had 3,173 power-looms of which 2,193 wove worsteds and 980 woollens and he stated that there were only 2,000 hand-looms in the city, but that the bulk of the cloth sold in Reims was woven by hand, often as far away as the Ardennes. Reports from the Ardennes indicate, however, that, though power-looms had not been introduced until 1860, they had increased so rapidly that by 1870 they numbered over 1,000 as compared with some 400 hand-looms. At Sedan, on the other hand, where in 1870 there were nearly 5,000 looms, only 100 were run by power, the reason given being that French looms were very expensive and took so long to instal that it was necessary to import looms from England, Germany, or Belgium. Yet the pressure from the scarcity of labor was slowly forcing the use of power-looms despite the expense.[29] In the neighboring region of the Nord considerable progress had been made by 1870 in the introduction of the power-loom. We are not told the number of these machines in Roubaix, but from the great increase in the amount of cloth woven and in the size of the mills it is clear that it was large. A further indication of mechanical progress is the extremely rapid increase in population, a thing unusual in the history of French industrial centers, as well as the fact that the weavers' wages rose considerably. At Fourmies there were 650 power-looms in 1870, while there were between 3,500 and 4,000 hand-looms in the country homes of the weavers. Wages for both classes of weavers had risen, but those using power-looms were paid at a higher rate. Though the power-looms at Fourmies represented only one fifth of the total number they were slowly driving out hand weaving, especially in the manufacture of merino cloths.[30] This situation at Fourmies illustrates the general tendency in the weaving of woollens and worsteds in France. Hand-looms were still in the majority even in the manufacture of plain cloths, but they were steadily losing ground. By 1870 the ultimate victory of the power-loom for the weaving of all but the fanciest cloths was assured, and the progress on which that assurance rested was

[29] *Enquête of 1870.* Session of June 24. Testimony of Messrs. Varinet and Cunin-Gridaine, manufacturers.

[30] *Ibid.* Session of June 27. Testimony of M. Legrand, comber, spinner and weaver.

made wholly during the decade following the signature of the commercial treaty with England.

The French woollen and worsted industries had prepared themselves for the struggle with England in October, 1861, when the treaty tariff on their products went into effect, by renewing their equipment so as to increase their use of machinery in general and to secure the newest and best machines. It would be interesting to study in detail the efforts of British manufacturers to capture French markets while insisting to the Board of Trade that they could barely keep up an insignificant trade with France, and of the French industrialists to increase their exports to England while complaining to their government that, unless they received effective protection, their industries would be destroyed. Unfortunately we lack an adequate body of information for such a study and instead find ourselves confronted with sharply conflicting statements from industries, such as those manufacturing worsteds in Bradford and Roubaix, which bewailed their sufferings, yet continued to grow and prosper exceedingly. On the British side it must be remembered that England was admittedly superior in the production of long and shiny wool, that she controlled the importation of mohair and alpaca wool and had acquired exceptional skill in spinning them into yarn, and that she had a distinct advantage in the manufacture of worsteds mixed with cotton because of the greater size of her cotton industry, which made possible large-scale production at lower cost and with greater skill because of increased specialization. Furthermore, it is only human to long for things of which one has been deprived and it is, therefore, not surprising that when the system of prohibitions was abolished in France by the Treaty of 1860 British cloths became fashionable. On her side France was admittedly superior in the production of short wool and her merino cloths, flannels, and pure worsteds had long been in demand in England, as in other countries. In the manufacture of cheap and coarse woollens she had learned her lesson from England so well that centers like Elbeuf and Lisieux and some of those in the North had built up a big trade in France itself; and Sedan had established the manufacture of a new cloth made of pure woollen warp and shoddy weft and was selling the product on a considerable scale in England.

When the struggle began in 1861 Roubaix was famous chiefly for her fancy mixed worsteds woven by hand. She had also made alpacas on the demand of the Paris merchants, but the cloth was full of defects and was sold only because the importation of English alpacas was forbidden. As soon as this prohibition was removed by the Treaty, Roubaix stopped making alpacas, although the merchants asked for them and sent English samples; the manufacturers replied that such goods could be woven only from yarn spun by the throstle which they could not do at Roubaix.[31] In other respects, however, Roubaix seems to have made every effort to fight her rival in Yorkshire. The Bradford Chamber of Commerce reported in 1870 that Roubaix had increased the number of her power-looms from approximately 1,000 in 1855–56 to 10,000 in 1867 and that because of these new looms, as good as the best possessed by Bradford, Roubaix had been able to increase her exports of mixed worsteds to England from 10,766,000 francs in 1861 to 37,549,000 francs in 1866. Though, as we know, weavers had been moving from the country into Roubaix and wages had been rising, Bradford contended that her French rival had many hand-looms, which was correct, and that with these she could manufacture many kinds of reps, furniture stuffs, and pure worsteds, which the Yorkshire manufacturers could no longer afford to make. Roubaix, on her side, claimed that Bradford increased so greatly her exports of mixed worsteds to France that Roubaix had to give up making them, although they had been one of her most important products. The evidence available shows that there was a considerable decrease in the manufacture of mixed worsteds at Roubaix, but it does not justify the assertion that this was due primarily to a large increase in importations from Bradford. It would appear, rather, that the bulk of the imports of mixed goods was not strictly mixed worsteds, but alpacas of various kinds; that in the earlier years of the decade between 1860 and

---

[31] There are indications that before 1870 Roubaix was beginning to produce alpacas again that she could sell in France in the face of British competition.

1870 the price of cotton was so high that mixed goods, whether of British or French manufacture, were difficult to sell anywhere; and that in the latter part of the decade, when the price of cotton was falling again, the prevailing fashions did not favor that kind of mixed worsteds. Furthermore, after 1867, all the western European countries were suffering increasingly from overproduction, so that Bradford in 1870 complained bitterly of the duty of 15 per cent in the French tariff on mixed cloths, in which cotton predominated, because it was probably becoming impossible to sell worsteds at a profit in England.[32]

The decade between 1860 and 1870 was clearly one of rapidly changing fashions and in the struggle between British and French manufacturers these changes favored sometimes one side and sometimes the other. Much light is thrown on these changes and the effect they had on the worsted industry of Roubaix by the manager of the Magazins du Louvre, which is still one of the most important department stores in Paris. He testified at the Enquête of 1870 that during the first year after the Treaty tariff went into effect there was a rush for English goods, but that for most cloths it did not last. British goods of shiny wool for summer wear remained popular, but at the end of the decade Roubaix was manufacturing similar cloths that were more advantageous to buy, presumably because of the duty on imported English cloths. Roubaix, as we have seen, was improving her machinery and methods under the stimulus of competition, and the result was a decrease in the price and marked improvement in the quality of her cloths. Black goods such as reps, cretons, and Orleans continued to be made at Roubaix despite British competition and were found

---

[32] On the struggle between Roubaix and Bradford see the Memorials of the Council of the Bradford Chamber of Commerce to the Board of Trade, February 7, 1870, in F. O., 146–1485, and December 30, 1871, in F. O., 146–1611; of the Yorkshire Chamber of Commerce meeting at Bradford April 4, 1876, in F. O., 27–2221.

See also Amé, *op. cit.*, I, 377, and II, 410; and Louis Reybaud, *La Laine. Nouvelle série des études sur le régime des manufactures* (Paris, 1867), pp. 383–384. Also the speech of Rouher, Minister of State, in *Moniteur*, May 21, 1868, and the testimony of Planche, merchant of Paris, in the *Enquête of 1870*, Session of June 22.

stronger than similar goods made in England and better suited for country wear, and their price had decreased 15 per cent. Fancy goods, such as striped and checked cloths, evidently continued to be made well and sold cheaply at Roubaix, since that city in 1870 furnished the Magazins du Louvre with all they needed. Though, as we have seen, fashions favored English fancy goods for summer wear, they continued to favor French goods for the winter season. The manager of the Magazins du Louvre concluded that France need not fear British competition because England's superiority was clear in the case of only a few goods, such as milled Orleans cloths made of shiny wool, and alpacas.[33]

Roubaix is the only French manufacturing center in the woollen and worsted industries of which it can be said, on the basis of a considerable body of evidence, that it had to fight hard against British competition between 1860 and 1870. Elbeuf, in 1870, complained of its troubles with some bitterness, but their principal cause appears to have been a rigid conservatism expressed in resentment of all competition, whether internal or foreign, as if it were a personal injury suffered by the local manufacturers for which they could hold the national government responsible. It was claimed at Elbeuf that French cloths were neglected after 1860 because English cheviots became the ruling fashion in France. These cloths were described as an imitation of real cheviots made of poor wool and exported chiefly from Huddersfield.[34] There are indications that such cloths were imported into France, possibly on a large scale, and that the customers of Paris tailors demanded them, but there is no evidence that their importation ruined any French merchants, or that it caused any real trouble in Elbeuf itself. We know that Elbeuf suffered from the financial crisis of 1864, from the loss of the American market due to the Civil War and to the high American tariff on woollens and worsteds, from rising wages, and

[33] *Enquête of 1870.* Session of June 27. Testimony of M. Chauchard.

[34] *Enquête of 1870.* Session of June 15. Testimony of M. Flavigny, manufacturer of Elbeuf. Also Session of June 27. Testimony of M. Chauchard, manager, Magazins du Louvre, Paris.

from the increasing intensity of competition among French manufacturers. Her production increased greatly in the decade of the 'sixties, chiefly in common cloth sold to the poorer classes in the French provinces and exported to Chili and Peru. At Elbeuf there was no important change made in the methods of manufacturing and no notable progress in the introduction of machinery, despite the increase in wages. It seems clear, therefore, that the woollen industry at Elbeuf prospered between 1860 and 1870, because, otherwise it would have been forced to change its methods and use machinery on a considerable scale. What the manufacturers really resented was the fall in prices and the decline in the rate of profits; that is, they had to change from large profits on a small production to small profits on a large production, and this change called for increased exertion on their part.

Reims offers an example of a manufacturing center which prospered largely through an increase in foreign rather than domestic trade. The two most notable cloths made there were the merinos, which are usually classed as worsteds, and the flannels, which are generally included among woollens. There was a decline in the exportation of merinos from Reims for several years after 1860, largely because of the loss of the American market through the high tariff, these cloths having been sent there on a considerable scale by way of England; but before 1870 this industry had recovered completely. The loss incurred was evidently small or was made up by an increased production, because there were no complaints made to the Government. The general prosperity of the woollen and worsted industries of Reims is shown by the increase in the number of mills and in the size of the individual mill. The local combing industry, for example, doubled in size between 1860 and 1870.[35]

As in the case of the iron and cotton industries, we cannot attribute all the progress made in the development of the manufacture of woollens and worsteds between 1860 and 1870 to the treaty with England and the other economic reforms that

[35] *Enquête of 1870.* Session of June 22. Testimony of M. Merle, former mayor of Reims. Also the testimony of M. Dauphinot, the mayor, June 24.

accompanied it. Some of the causes of this development appeared before 1860, such as the manufacture of cheap woollens in imitation of English goods, which began between 1820 and 1840, and the invention of Heilman's comber, which revolutionized the worsted industry between 1850 and 1855. Another cause of the utmost importance was the immense development of transportation. The construction of railroads in France in the 'fifties created a truly national market for the products of most industries and started internal competition that greatly stimulated manufacturing. Similarly, the development of marine transportation was opening up new foreign markets, while in the case of the woollen and worsted industries it had an even more important influence in bringing to France large supplies of cheap wool from Australia and Argentina, without which the truly remarkable growth of those industries would have been impossible. Finally, there was the scarcity of cotton created by the American Civil War, which raised the price of cotton goods to such a height that people could not afford to buy them and turned to woollens and worsteds.

But if some of the causes of the great development of the woollen and worsted industries in France were not directly connected with the economic reforms of 1860, other causes did bear a direct relation to those reforms. Thus, while the development of ocean transportation made possible the importation of cheap wool on a large scale, the Act of May 5, 1860, by admitting wool free of duty did much to increase such importations by diminishing the cost still further, and this statute was a part of Chevalier's plan for the reform of the economic system of France, of which the treaties with England and other countries formed the principal feature. Even more important, however, was the stimulus of foreign competition, whose effects were seen, on the one hand, in the improvement of methods of manufacturing resulting in the production of goods of better quality at lower prices; and, on the other hand, in the growth of exports. We have seen how greatly Roubaix increased her use of machinery under the influence of British competition and how she improved the quality and lowered the price of her goods until she was able not only to compete with England in the French market on equal terms, but even to drive out many British cloths that had apparently secured a firm foothold in France. We have seen also how bitter were the complaints from Bradford of the growing competition there from the sale of worsteds made at Roubaix and, in this case, we have evidence that the exportation of French worsteds continued to increase after 1870. Reims, on the other hand, never felt to any great extent the competition of British worsteds or woollens because England did not attempt to compete with her in the principal cloths she produced, such as merinos and flannels, for the reason that the supremacy of Reims in those specialties had long been firmly established. Reims felt only the benefits of the reforms of 1860 in the expansion of her foreign markets. Her case shows us that there was room for a considerable importation of British woollens and worsteds into France without any decrease in the production of French cloths because, in the main, the two countries produced different articles.

CHAPTER XII

THE LINEN INDUSTRY

THE history of the French linen industry resembles that of the woollen and worsted industries rather than that of cotton. Like the woollen industry the manufacture of linen in France is very old, so that its origins cannot be described, as is possible in the case of cotton. It was also an industry found in nearly all parts of the country and carried on chiefly in the houses of the peasants during the winters or at other times when work in the fields was light. As with woollens and worsteds, such as merinos and flannels, France made certain fine linens with notable skill and was able to export them on a considerable scale. Cambrics take their name from the town of Cambrai in the north, where they are supposed to have been woven first in early modern times. Lawns and damasks also have been manufactured in France since long before the age of machinery. Coarse linens, such as sail cloth and sacking, were also woven extensively by large numbers of peasants, particularly in Normandy and Brittany. Unlike the woollen and worsted industries, however, we hear of no great establishments created by the Crown, such as those of Sedan or the Van Robais at Abbeville, or arising independently as at Reims. Partly for this reason we have practically no detailed information regarding the linen industry before the time of the industrial revolution in France, and even in the nineteenth century it is rarely possible to trace the growth or decline of the industry satisfactorily. We can speak only of the introduction of machinery for spinning and weaving in France, of the effect of British, Irish, and Belgian competition in several cases, and of the boom caused by the American Civil War and the crisis from the extensive over-production that followed. The effects of the Anglo-French Treaty of 1860 on the French linen industry, however, cannot be traced in any detail for any region in France, as was possible in several cases in the cotton and woollen and worsted industries. It is clear, however, that international competition, chiefly Irish and Belgian, greatly stimulated the development of mechanical spinning and weaving and with them, to a limited extent, the concentration of manufacturing in certain towns, although hand spinning and weaving of linen survived to a considerable extent and the domestic or putting-out system remained of real importance. Finally, it is clear that in France, as in most countries except northern Ireland, the linen industry, unlike the woollen and worsted industries and the manufacture of silk, never recovered fully from the blow it received at the hands of the infant cotton industry in the eighteenth century; and that in the mechanical age linen never won a permanent place as one of the major textile industries.

Flax was grown extensively in many parts of France, although in 1860 the principal regions were the north, including the departments of Nord, Pas de Calais, Somme, and Aisne; Normandy, including the departments of Eure and Seine Inférieure; and Brittany. Feray,[1] the great manufacturer of linen of Essonnes, near Paris, and one of the most valuable of the witnesses at the Enquête of 1870, when he was not discussing tariff duties, lists some forty departments as growing flax, but it seems clear that the most important regions were producing a steadily increasing proportion of the total crop in France. The best flax grown in France in the 1860's came from the north;[2] that produced in Normandy seems to have been less good and the flax of Brittany was distinctly inferior.

In other parts of France it seems safe to assume that the cultivation of flax was declining. It is doubtful whether the tariff had any appreciable influence on this decline in production. Though our sources of information are wofully meager, it seems clear that the protection of flax through duties on its importation, which was established by the Law of March 27, 1817,

---

[1] *Enquête of 1870.* Session of July 4.
[2] Report, Raoul Duval, chairman of the Textile Commission, to Conseil Supérieur; *Économiste français*, July 22, 1876.

increased in 1836, and abolished only in 1861,[3] was not an important influence, for the duties were insignificant in amount save on scutched flax after 1836. The decisive factors were rather the steadily increasing production of Russia, whose flax, though rarely of fine quality, was good enough for ordinary linens and very cheap; the competition of cottons and woollens with linens which checked the expansion of the linen industry and eventually caused its decline in France as in England and Scotland; and the competition with flax of other crops, such as beet sugar. Though all these factors played a part, the importation of flax from Russia was of overwhelming importance.

There was a large increase in the acreage devoted to the cultivation of flax during the cotton famine caused by the American Civil War, but it was short-lived, as in Ireland, and caused overproduction, as did the enormous increase in the number of spindles and looms manufacturing linen. The resulting crisis was intensified by a series of bad crops in France in the late 'sixties and in 1870. M. Robert, the secretary of the Linen Committee of the Department of Seine Inférieure, testified at the Enquête of 1870 that up to 1865 the production of flax of his department and that of Eure had been sufficient to meet the needs of the manufacturers of linen in Normandy. After that date the crop failed each year, owing to frosts after sowings in the spring, plant lice, and droughts later on. He does not include the equally important factor of the severe depression of the linen industry with the recovery of the dreaded rival cotton, which must have caused a great decrease in the demand for flax. He denounces the poor methods of cultivating flax in Normandy, particularly the insufficient use of fertilizer and the equally poor methods of harvesting, retting, and scutching in the region known as the Pays de Caux, where most of the flax of Normandy was grown. He tells us that, as the result of such poor cultivation and preparation, the flax of Normandy, despite unusually favorable soil and climate, was invariably coarse and that consequently it could not compete with the

---

[3] Léon Amé, *Étude économique sur les tarifs de douanes* (2 vols., Paris, 1876), I, 163–168, 260.

coarse but much cheaper flax of Russia.[4] It seems doubtful, however, whether the flax grown in Normandy had ever been fine, for in the seventeenth and eighteenth centuries, as in the nineteenth, the linens of Normandy were chiefly coarse and occasionally medium, but never fine. The flax growers of Normandy were clearly succumbing in 1870 to Russian competition, as were those of Brittany, Maine, and Anjou. There was only one brilliant exception to the general decline of flax growing and that was in the north, which had long produced flax of excellent quality that was used locally for the fine linens of Cambrai, Lille, and other centers. Favored alike by the climate, the soil, and the waters of the Lys, which had exceptional qualities for retting, the north held its own easily against the competition of cheap Russian flax, as did Belgium and Holland, the quality of flax produced being so good that it was exported on a considerable scale to northern Ireland where it was used for the manufacture of the finest linens.

The preparation of flax for spinning in France appears to have been in an interesting stage of transition at the time of the Enquête of 1870. M. Robert, secretary of the Linen Committee of Seine Inférieure, testified that labor in Normandy was deserting the country for the towns. He begged the Government to encourage the cultivation of flax through bounties and prizes, and to help his committee in financing the organization of agricultural societies to teach better methods of growing flax and of scutching it after it had been harvested and retted.[4] His statement that twenty-one scutching mills in Normandy were idle in 1870 because of the decrease in the cultivation of flax indicates that there was a fair number of such mills in that region, although there is no indication that they used machinery. An important manufacturer from the Department of Finisterre in Brittany[5] testified that his firm had been trying for some years to help the local spinning industry by introducing mechanical scutching mills run by water power, with the exception of one that used steam, although the fact that most of the streams of

---

[4] *Enquête of 1870.* Session of July 4.
[5] *Ibid.*, Testimony of M. Hormou of Morlaix.

that region were mere brooks made this difficult. It seemed to be the only remedy, however, for the decreasing production of flax and the growing scarcity of labor. The witness stated that mechanical scutching was quicker and cheaper, but that it did not leave the flax fiber in as good condition as scutching by hand. In the north the secretary of the Linen Committee of Lille, M. Agache,[6] tells us that mechanical scutching was only just beginning and that the whole of France had only between 30 and 40 such mills in 1870 as compared with 1,200 in Ireland. He claimed that nearly all the mechanical scutching mills were in the Department of Nord. This would have been natural because that department had an abundant supply of cheap coal and steam was extensively used in 1870 in both the cotton and woollen mills of Lille, Roubaix, and Tourcoing.[7]

Flax was spun entirely by hand in France until the invention of a machine by Philippe de Girard in 1810, although attempts to solve the problem of mechanical spinning had been made as early as 1782. Ballot tells us that the first machine for spinning flax was brought from England to France by the Milnes, who introduced Arkwright's frame for cotton spinning in that same year, 1782.[8] He gives no details and no other dates, however, and dismisses the subject by saying that various machines, both French and English, were tried in France and that all failed. In the meantime the problem had been solved in England, where the competition of cotton with linen threatened the existence of the older industry by the rapid development of mechanical inventions for spinning. The result of the struggle for survival by the linen industry was the invention of a machine for spinning flax by Kindrew, an optician, and Porthouse, a cloth manu-

[6] *Enquête of 1870.* Session of July 4.

[7] More light on the progress of mechanical scutching comes from the testimony of another witness at the Enquête of 1870, M. Colombier, a merchant of Lille, who also had spinning and weaving mills at various places in the Nord. See Session of July 6. He tells of the beginning of a sort of domestic or putting-out system of retting and scutching. Men went about to buy flax from the farmers, of many of whom they took advantage. It would appear that interest in the cultivation of good flax was declining in the north.

[8] Charles Ballot, *L'Introduction du machinisme dans l'industrie française* (Lille, Paris, etc., 1923), pp. 232–233.

facturer, at Darlington in Yorkshire in 1787. This machine appears to have been used first in 1788 by John Marshall, who became the founder of a large and successful mechanical spinning mill at Leeds, which was the principal center of the new industry for the next thirty years. Marshall used first a Savery engine for power, but in 1792 he bought a real steam engine from Boulton and Watt and improved his machine until it would carry 200 spindles. Mechanical spinning spread quickly into Lancashire where it increased, although more slowly than in Yorkshire, because of the greater competition of cotton in the west; and it spread also into Scotland, where the principal center was Dundee, although its development on a large scale was checked there by the cheapness of labor.[9]

The English machines succeeded in spinning yarn well, but they could not be used for medium or fine yarns. The flax fibers being very short and also viscous were hard to pull out through the process known as "roving," which was necessary before they could be spun. Through a gentle movement of the fingers the hand spinner could perform this operation more efficiently than the early machines. The machine invented by Philippe de Girard in 1810 was of real assistance in this respect because it made possible the spinning of finer yarn by passing the flax fibers through a bath of hot alkaline solution. De Girard failed to secure the general acceptance of his machine in France, partly from lack of business ability,[10] and partly from the bad economic and financial condition of the country. One of his partners, Hall, went to England about 1815, where the machine proved successful almost immediately. In 1825 Kay found that by soaking the flax fibers in cold water for several

[9] Conrad Gill, *The Rise of the Irish Linen Industry* (Oxford, 1925), p. 264; also A. J. Warden, *The Linen Trade, Ancient and Modern* (London, 1864), p. 382.

[10] Ballot, *op. cit.*, p. 244. Ballot describes de Girard shrewdly in the following sentence: "Philippe de Girard fut le véritable type de l'inventeur et là fut la cause de son infortune. Jaloux de ses inventions il les produit avant qu'elles fussent à point; inquiet de leur perfection, cependant, il cherchait ensuite à les améliorer, et annihilait par ses recherches le bénéfice même de leur exploitation; très mauvais administrateur, commerçant incapable, il était toujours talonné par les besoins d'argent et disperçait ses efforts, se croyant toujours sur la voie de la découverte qui lui assurerait la richesse."

hours they could be made slippery without being injured by dissolving out the gum. De Girard claimed that Kay's process was a violation of his own patent, but this was denied in England, where it was held that Kay's method of soaking the flax six hours before beginning to spin it was a different and a more important discovery.[11]   Kay's invention, which made possible the spinning of really fine yarn by machinery, explains the notable development of the spinning industry in England which resulted in the beginning of the exportation of yarn to France on a considerable scale about 1830.

The development of mechanical spinning in England had been due primarily to the competition of the cotton industry which, although much younger than the linen, began the use of machinery first.   In France mechanical spinning gained ground slowly, even in the cotton industry, because of the cheapness of labor and the relatively high cost of fuel for power and of iron for the construction of machines.   The cause of the development of mechanical spinning in the French linen industry is not, therefore, to be found, as in England, in the competition of cotton, but in the shipments of mechanically spun yarn from England which, as we have seen, began on a considerable scale about 1830. This yarn proved to be well made and about 30 per cent cheaper than that produced by hand in France, so that French spinners soon began to suffer from its importation.   One of their leaders who testified at the Enquête of 1870, M. Feray of Essonnes,[12] near Paris, described the introduction of English machines into France in the decade between 1830 and 1840.   England then forbade the exportation of any of her new machines, as well as any designs of them, and the emigration of skilled workmen who might be able to set them up in foreign countries.   She was unable to enforce these prohibitions effectively, although she did make their violation difficult and dangerous.   French manufacturers had gone to England and had been unable even to enter

---

[11] Ballot, *op. cit.*, pp. 240–241; Gill, *op. cit.*, pp. 316–317.   This is Gill's contention.   Ballot insists de Girard's invention was pirated and says Kay did not attempt to defend his patent when de Girard denounced it.   Both Gill and Ballot are reliable authors accustomed to the critical use of sources.

[12] Session of July 4.

the spinning mills when Feray made several trips in the year 1834. He does not tell us how he succeeded in getting into the mills, although he says he and his friend Scrive, one of the most important spinners of Lille, who evidently went with him, ran the risk of heavy fines and imprisonment. After long efforts and the expenditure of 96,000 francs he and Scrive succeeded in their purpose. They could not get out whole machines, but did secure various parts which they shipped separately. Even so, many shipments were seized and confiscated and the missing parts had to be replaced by designs obtained from English constructors. Finally, it was necessary to bring over English foremen to set up the machines and to show the French spinners how to use them. All this was expensive and it was several years before the French spinners made financial profits from their machines, but there were glory and honor at least for M. Feray, who states that he sent the first sample of French mechanically spun yarn to the Minister of Commerce, M. Duchâtel, on October 1, 1835, and received by return mail the cross of the Legion of Honor. By 1838 there was a well-established factory near Paris for the construction of machines for spinning flax run by a Frenchman named Decoster; and we are told that in 1839 these machines were used in fourteen mills in France.[13]

We lack detailed evidence on the competition of mechanical with hand spinning in France, but the private investigation conducted by agents of the Conseil Supérieur du Commerce in the summer of 1860 showed that the mechanical spinning of flax yarn was then universal in France up to No. 250, and that the hand spinners had been driven out even more rapidly than in Belgium and were then rare. Some branches of the linen industry used very fine yarn up to No. 800 and this was imported, chiefly from Germany.[14] The following table throws additional light on the increase in the number of mechanical spindles in France as compared with the progress made in England.[15]

[13] Charles Coquelin in *Revue des deux mondes* (July 15, 1839), p. 198.
[14] Arch. Nat., F 12–2514. Report of Legentil to the Minister of Commerce, August 28, 1860.
[15] *Enquête of 1870*. Session of July 4. Testimony of Agache; also Gill, *op. cit.*, p. 319, and Warden, *op. cit.*, p. 382.

Year	France	England	Scotland	Ireland	Total, Great Britain and Ireland
1836	6,000				200,000
1840	25,000				350,000
1844				155,000 Belfast only	
1845	120,000				
1850		266,000	303,000	396,000	965,000
1851	330,000				
1853				581,000	
1854		300,000	350,000		
1856	468,000				
1857		442,000			
1860	502,690				1,200,000
1862		344,000	312,000	593,000	1,249,000
1866	705,350				1,700,000
1868		474,000	264,000	905,000	1,643,000
1869	525,000				1,600,000

When in 1830 England began to export yarn to France on a large scale France had only a very moderate tariff on flax yarn, so that she was quite unable to keep out the British product. By 1840 the situation of the French spinning industry struggling to develop the use of its newly acquired machinery was very difficult. The manufacturers of linen had not built up a strong organization for bringing pressure to bear on the Government in favor of high protection as had the cotton and, to a less extent, the woollen industry, and the Government accordingly seemed disposed to do very little for them. It was felt also that it would be undesirable to stop the importation of yarn until the French spinners could satisfy the demands of the weavers who, for this reason, opposed strongly the demands of the spinners for protection. Further opposition came from the spinners of Belgium, who had been in the habit of sending considerable quantities of yarn to France and who were afraid of losing this valuable market. The July monarchy was anxious not to antagonize Belgium for political reasons and because it hoped to secure a more favorable tariff for French silks and wines. If Belgium could not be brought under the political domination of France it might be subjected to economic control through a favorable tariff, or even through a customs union, a project that was actively discussed in official circles for more than a decade after Belgium acquired her independence in 1830.[16]

The French Government finally yielded to the demands of the spinners and by the Act of May 6, 1841, gave them protective duties averaging 11 per cent. The Government was also given power to raise the duties by decree if the difficulties of the French spinners increased. This proved to be the case, for English exports to France had grown in 1840, and still more in 1841, with the prospect of an even greater increase in 1842. In consequence French prices of yarn fell so greatly that the spinners could sell only at a loss and the growers of flax and hemp also began to suffer from the decreasing demands of the spinners. The Government declared it had received complaints from sixty-five of the French departments and determined, therefore, to make use of its discretionary powers. In the Decree of June 26, 1842, the Government gave the spinners protective duties that excluded almost completely yarn up to No. 100. Belgium alone was exempted from the full force of the decree through a treaty signed July 16, 1842, which allowed her to export to France under the duties of the Act of May 6, 1841, yarn not exceeding 2,000,000 kilograms.[17] Provision was made for the admission of greater quantities of Belgian yarn at higher duties that were still below the new tariff applied to the yarn of other countries; but these rates were never applied, since Belgian exports up to 1860 never reached even the total of 1,000,000 kilograms. The increase in the French tariff on flax yarn, directed so plainly against England, accomplished its object. English exports to France declined rapidly until all danger to the

[16] Arch. Nat., F 12-2485. Chambre des Députés, Document 185, Session of 1843. Speech of the Minister of Agriculture and Commerce, June 5, 1843, presenting the tariff bill. Also Chambre des Pairs, Document 64, Session of 1846. Report of M. Fevrier on the government bill to ratify the Belgian treaty of December 13, 1845.

[17] Amé, *op. cit.*, I, 238–241, 414. Gives the tariff rates and much information on Franco-Belgian commercial relations. See also Arch. Nat., F 12-2514, Report of Legentil to the Minister of Commerce, August 28, 1860.

young French industry of mechanical spinning was entirely removed. No effective foreign competition, therefore, was felt by French spinners until after the Anglo-French Treaty of 1860. The effect of this protection was to shut off imports of coarse yarn to whose manufacture the French spinners devoted themselves almost exclusively. As the duties did not increase in proportion to the increasing fineness of the yarn above No. 160, the French weavers continued to import fine yarn from England in order to meet Belgian competition in linens.

The following table gives the official figures of the French customs service for the importation of flax yarn from England and Belgium in kilograms between 1830 and 1860. Though the absolute accuracy of these figures in detail cannot be relied upon, they do show the general movement of imports, and confirm our information from other sources that neither British nor Belgian competition was a serious factor for the French spinners after 1842.[18]

The cotton famine resulting from the American Civil War caused a sudden and dangerous expansion in the French linen industry. Its effects were particularly serious in mechanical spinning because of its great development before 1860. We have seen that the number of mechanical spindles in France grew from 502,690 in 1860 to 705,350 in 1866, the highest point ever reached. But in the meantime the American war had ended and the French cotton industry had begun to recover, so that the mechanical spinners of linen were unable to sell their large stocks of yarns with the result that, by 1869, the number of spindles run by power in France had fallen to 525,000, a loss from which the linen industry never recovered.

The boom of the early 'sixties affected the mechanical weaving of linen in France less seriously because that industry was in its infancy. There is little evidence regarding it before 1860, so that it can be stated only that practically all weaving was done by hand at the time of the signature of the commercial treaty

[18] For figures through 1845, see Arch. Nat., F 12–2485. Annex to Document 15, Chambre des Députés, Session of 1846. For figures of 1846–59 see the Report of Legentil, August 28, 1860.

Year	England	Belgium	Other countries	Total importations
1830	3,049	831,243	184,107	1,018,399
1831	14,532	676,655	104,030	795,217
1832	56,378	688,125	115,995	860,498
1833	418,483	824,782	180,159	1,423,324
1834	826,439	714,289	190,987	1,731,715
1835	1,295,593	654,751	176,308	2,126,652
1836	1,901,074	635,690	210,103	2,746,867
1837	3,199,917	541,251	177,871	3,919,039
1838	5,245,742	405,880	153,416	5,804,038
1839	6,167,731	498,904	150,593	6,817,228
1840	6,161,529	585,671	98,223	6,845,423
1841	9,185,934	645,258	83,849	9,915,041
1842	10,695,082	547,326	71,127	11,313,525
1843	6,483,847	11,077,788	68,345	7,629,980
1844	6,356,983	1,731,979	11,607	8,100,569
1845	4,661,631	2,281,656	27,482	6,970,769
1846	3,115,691	1,775,898		
1847	772,201	1,170,008		
1848	144,237	243,821		
1849	139,697	715,487		
1850	237,454	816,661		
1851	421,387	621,949		
1852	317,118	706,762		
1853	150,131	911,331		
1854	94,591	520,770		
1855	102,390	679,027		
1856	145,838	830,401		
1857	218,957	981,474		
1858	134,842	565,610		
1859	152,836	531,127		

with England. The total number of power-looms in France could hardly have exceeded 1,000 in 1860 [19] and may have been as low as 600; but in 1864 Amé reports that the Department of Nord alone had 2,270; and in 1866 it had 4,300.[20] After that date the number of power-looms continued to increase for at least a decade, instead of declining rapidly, as had the number of mechanical spindles. Thus the whole of France had

[19] *Enquête of 1870.* ﹒Session of July 4. Testimony of Agache and Feray.
[20] *Op. cit.*, II, 424.

between 9,000 and 10,000 in 1870;[21] 17,000 in 1873, and 20,-000 in 1876.[21]   The explanation of the continued development of mechanical weaving during the period of acute depression in the linen industry between 1867 and 1871 is that so little linen had been woven on power-looms that overproduction could not result.   The increase in the production of cloth woven by machinery continued, therefore, until a new point of equilibrium with mechanical spinning had been reached, about 1876, after which it shared in the general decline of the linen industry in France, as in most of the other states of western Europe. The weaving of linen, however, did not become wholly mechanical, as had the spinning.   It is true that power-looms were improved sufficiently to make their use for even very fine linens economical.   There are also indications that in many places weaving was concentrating in larger towns like Lille and Tourcoing in the north and Lisieux in upper Normandy, and that in such towns the size of the individual mill was increasing. But the general decrease in the use of linen and the well-known tendency toward the maintenance of rural and small-scale industry which has been so strong in France checked the progress of the power-loom in time and saved the hand-loom from extinction.

We may now inquire what the effect of British competition was on the French linen industry.   There can be no doubt that together with the factors we have noted, such as the expansion of the linen industry caused by the American Civil War, such competition stimulated the use of the power-loom.   Was British competition, however, responsible for the crisis of 1868-70 in France, as the French manufacturers of linen have claimed? There is little evidence available from French sources, yet the information we have indicates that French manufacturers of linen differed widely in their opinions.   When the revision of the French tariff was being discussed in 1876, and even at the Enquête of 1870, it was shown that French exports of linens had increased greatly and fairly continuously since 1860.   It

[21] F. O., 27–2224.   Report of Messrs. Barbour and Jaffe to the Chamber of Commerce of Belfast, October 12, 1876.

was shown, further, that the interests of spinners and weavers often conflicted; that the former eagerly demanded increased protection while the latter displayed only a mild interest in the question and occasionally stated that they did not need an increase in protection. The investigation of the condition of the French linen industry in 1876 was ably conducted for the Conseil Supérieur du Commerce by a commission under the direction of Raoul Duval, whose shrewd and accurate observations threw so much light on the condition of the cotton industry in 1870. In his report Duval said: [22]

" Our spinners of coarse numbers not only do not fear foreign competition, but even compete advantageously with the Belgians and English in their home markets. Except, perhaps, for the question of climate, against which no effective protection would be possible, the supremacy of Belfast over Dundee, as well as Lille, with respect to the manufacture of fine yarn depends essentially on the skill of its workers and on the remarkably intelligent and careful management of its mills. It depends far more on these than on special conditions of a material nature. We believe, therefore, that raising the duties on fine yarns would have no effect in modifying such a situation. On the contrary such an increase might have disastrous results for our weaving industry which . . . exports large amounts of cloth that is far superior to the cloth which is imported. The weavers of the Department du Nord have protested vigorously against any increase in the tariff. . . ."

In conclusion M. Duval stated that his commission recommended the retention in the new general tariff of the classification and duties established by the convention signed under the provision of the Anglo-French Treaty of 1860.

On the British side we have as evidence correspondence of the Chambers of Commerce of Dundee and Belfast with the Foreign Office in London, chiefly in the year 1876 when the British Government asked for the opinions of manufacturers regarding the proposed revision of the Anglo-French Treaty of Commerce of 1860.[23] Dundee, the principal center of the linen and jute

---

[22] *Économiste français*, July 22, 1876, p. 121.

[23] Reports of the Chamber of Commerce of Dundee, April 12, 1876 in F. O., 27–2222; November 17, 1876 in F. O., 27–2224; and Memorandum of the Chamber to the Foreign Office, June 8, 1880 in Parliamentary Paper, Commercial, No. 38, 1881. Also reports of the Chamber of Commerce of Belfast, June 9, 1876 in F. O., 27–2224; and that of October 12, 1876 in F. O., 27–2224.

industries of Scotland, replied that the treaty had been found of little service. Her yarns and cloth, most of which were very coarse and intended for kitchen cloths or sacking, were not imported into France, but the French were able to sell their yarn in Dundee itself, despite the cost of transportation and commissions, and to sell their linens in competition with Scotch merchants in the markets of northern Europe and the Orient. It was the opinion of Dundee that the French duties which were moderate in 1860 had since become prohibitive because of the great progress made by the French linen industry.

The reply of the Chamber of Commerce at Belfast to the British Foreign Office resembles in its conclusions that of Dundee, but is of greater interest because it consists chiefly of the observations of two delegates, Messrs. Barbour and Jaffe, sent to inspect French linen centers in the summer of 1876. They wrote:

" We believe the French flax trade needs no protection against British competition. Up to No. 30 (yarn) the French spinners are better than we and sell these (yarns) in Ireland when we cannot in France. The French are quite as good up to No. 70. In the fine numbers their workers, both in spinning and preparation, are probably less skilled; but we have to get flax from Belgium or France and send back the cloth. This compensates for any slight advantage of Irish spinners. Even this [advantage] is likely to go with the spread of fine machinery through France as shown by the great progress of the last fifteen years in low and middle numbers. There is no reason, therefore, for a [French] duty on yarn. The present duties on cloth are practically prohibitive. Our exports to France are limited to a few specialties which are largely made up into goods to be reëxported. Our products practically don't enter into French home consumption at all. The French are very skilled in the manufacture of all classes of linens and give us no chance to compete with them in France, even selling goods partly made of British yarns in Great Britain. We therefore urge the free admission of British linens into France. The statistics shew a steady increase in French exports, and that her imports are very irregular and tend to decrease." [24]

The paucity of evidence on the French linen industry makes it very difficult to give general conclusions regarding the influence on its development of the Anglo-French Treaty of Commerce. The boom of the early and middle 'sixties was due

[24] F. O., 27–2224. As cited in Note 22.

primarily to the cotton famine caused by the American Civil War, which resulted in the rapid increase in the use of the power-loom in France. British competition undoubtedly strengthened this tendency by making the adoption of machinery more necessary. Further than this we cannot go in tracing the positive influence of the treaty negotiated by Chevalier and Cobden. On the negative side it can be said that there is no evidence to show that the French market was ever flooded by British goods for any length of time, or that the French linen industry was injured in other ways by British competition. It would appear rather that British competition acted as a stimulant. The subsequent decline of the French linen industry was clearly not the result of British competition, at least during the validity of the Anglo-French Treaty of Commerce. The dominant factor in causing that decline, which came in England as well as in France, was the irresistible competition of the cotton industry.[25]

[25] The competition of the rising jute industry was a factor of increasing importance after 1860, although no body of evidence sufficient to justify its discussion was found by the writer. Jute affected the consumption of very coarse linens only, being used chiefly for sacking.

CHAPTER XIII

THE SILK INDUSTRY

WHEN the majority of the textile industries of France were confronted in 1860 with the prospect of British competition they were filled with anxiety because of their more limited use of machinery, and their inferiority in the development of large-scale organization in manufacturing. They were also very far behind England in their selling methods, especially in the penetration of foreign markets, although they did not fully realize their backwardness in those respects. While they generally met England on equal terms and often surpassed her in the production of textiles of very fine quality, those goods usually formed only a small part of their total production. In view of all these difficulties and of the natural pessimism of men who had scarcely ever been called upon to meet foreign competition, the great majority of the textile manufacturers of France strongly favored protection, and regarded the tariff reforms of 1860 as unwise and dangerous.

The silk industry presented a marked contrast to the other textile industries. The development of the use of machinery driven by power was not yet a major problem in the manufacture of silk because the delicacy of the material made the use of such machines difficult and often inadvisable. In organization for both the manufacture and the sale of pure silks the great firms of Lyons were more than a match for their foreign rivals. The artistic gifts of the French were a priceless advantage in the silk industry where color, finish and design were of vital importance in the production of nearly all kinds of cloth and ribbons. The majority of silk manufacturers of France realized their strength, understood the advantage of expanding their foreign markets, and strongly supported the lowering of tariff barriers begun by the commercial treaty with England.

The protectionist minority was not large and caused little trouble. It was composed, first, of the ribbon industry of St. Étienne, which dreaded the competition of Switzerland and Rhenish Prussia and felt rightly that tariff favors granted to England would soon be extended to other countries. It included also the manufacturers of plain tulle who were aroused from their profitable slumbers by the threat of British competition, because they knew that in their specialty England had achieved notable success through the extensive use of machinery of the most approved type, whereas French machines, while commonly used, were so antiquated that the free entry of British tulle would force their immediate replacement.[1]

The most serious problem, however, that confronted the French silk industry in 1860 was neither that of machinery nor that of fighting protectionist propaganda, but was the struggle with England for control of the trade in raw silk. With the improvement in marine transportation and the opening of China and Japan, London had replaced Lyons as the greatest market for raw silk and the importance of this was being understood more clearly every year through the steady increase in the ravages of disease among the silkworms in France, which made French manufacturers more and more dependent on the supply of silk from the Orient.

The raising of silkworms was an old industry in France, but did not become really important until it was systematically encouraged by Colbert. Further progress was made in the late eighteenth century through the inventions of Vaucanson that brought notable improvements in growing silk and in other preparatory processes. These inventions were due partly to the steadily increasing demand for silk from the merchants and manufacturers of Lyons, and partly to careful encouragement by the French Government, which subsidized the construction of large throwing mills with good machinery.[2] Soon afterward,

---

[1] Arch. Nat., F 12–2696. Report of Natalis Rondot on Silk, October 8, 1860.
[2] Charles Ballot, *L'Introduction du machinisme dans l'industrie française* (Lille, Paris, etc., 1923), p. 332.

in 1804, the weaving of silk was revolutionized by the loom invented by Jacquard,[3] who began his experiments with an old and discarded loom constructed by Vaucanson many years before. The Jacquard loom made possible the mechanical weaving of all sorts of fancy silks and increased the demand of the Lyons manufacturers for thrown silk. It was soon adapted to the weaving of other textiles and thus started the great development of novelties and of mixed goods which became a great resource for silk manufacturers in their time of need.[4] Further improvements were made in preparatory processes in the early nineteenth century, as a result of which the French silk-growing industry showed a vigorous growth, the production within the country increasing from 11,500,000 kilograms in 1831 to 25,000,000[5] kilograms in 1853, which was the maximum attained in France.[6] Even with this increasing production France was sometimes obliged to import half of the silk she consumed from Italy which, like France, produced an excellent quality, and from Spain, the Levant, and India by way of England.[7]

The rearing of silkworms in France began now to suffer from a series of diseases which soon reached the proportions of an epidemic. The silkworm had always been delicate and subject to disease or death from changes in temperature or in the quality or the condition of the mulberry leaves on which it fed, and the liability to disease increased with the distance from its original home in China.[8] The worst of these diseases, *pébrine*, was first noted in France in 1820. It reached the Cévennes mountains by 1843 and thereafter spread rapidly through all the regions of France were the silkworm was raised. Efforts to

---

[3] Charles Ballot, *op. cit.*, p. 334.

[4] *Ibid.*, p. 378.

[5] E. Pariset, *Histoire de la fabrique lyonnaise. Étude sur le régime social et économique de la soie à Lyon depuis le XVI⁰ siècle* (Lyon, 1901), p. 337.

[6] Louis Reybaud, *Études sur le régime des manufactures. Condition des ouvriers en soie* (Paris, 1859), I, 7.

[7] E. Pariset, *Les Industries de la soie* (Lyon, 1890), p. 174.

[8] Louis Gueneau, *Lyon et le commerce de la soie* (Lyon, 1923).

fight the disease and to improve the degenerated races of French silkworms proved vain until, after several futile investigations, the work was taken up by Pasteur in 1865.[9] He discovered the germ of *pébrine* and found that the worms could be protected from it by selective breeding under hygienic conditions.[10] After several years Pasteur's recommendation began to be generally followed and the silk production of France increased; but it never again reached even 20,000,000 kilograms a year and was generally considerably below that figure.[11] Other factors contributed to prevent the complete recovery of the silk industry. Improvements in transportation had made the importation of raw silk from China and Japan cheap and easy, so that the French growers with high labor costs and the expense of the selective breeding of worms and the microscopic examination of eggs found this competition difficult to meet. Finally fashions had changed by 1860 and favored cheaper silks or mixed fabrics instead of the pure silks of fine quality, for which French growers had been providing the raw material. Not only did the raising of silkworms in France never fully recover from this combination of disasters, but the reeling and throwing industries which had depended upon it also were permanently crippled. Although in 1850 France had over 600 establishments for reeling silk with 30,000 pans and a production of 2,000,000 kilograms of raw silk, in 1855 she had only 400 establishments with 20,000 pans and a production of 750,000 kilograms.[12] The throwing industry in France might perhaps have recovered by adapting its machinery to the use of the inferior silks imported from the Orient, but it never did so.

The manufacture of silk cloth and ribbons in France began some time before the raising of silkworms. It was a natural outgrowth of the trade in silks with Italy which began to attract attention late in the fourteenth century during the

[9] Natalis Rondot, *L'Art de la soie. Les soies* (2d edition, 2 vols., Paris, 1885–87), p. 95.
[10] Frank Warner, president of the Silk Association in Great Britain, in the *Encyclopaedia Britannica* (11th edition), XXV, 104.
[11] *Ibid.*, p. 104.
[12] Gueneau, *op. cit.*, p. 109.

captivity of the popes at Avignon.[13]   At that time important
fairs were held several times a year at Lyons, which was on
one of the main trade routes between Italy and Flanders.
Because of its strategic position Lyons soon became the center
of the trade in silks with Italy, the first country in western
Europe to begin the manufacture of this textile.   The Italian
traders quite naturally wished to have all maufacturing done in
Italy, but in the reign of Louis XI the industry was started at
Lyons, in Franche Comté, at Nîmes, and at Tours.[13]   Looms
were introduced from Italy in the reign of Francis I and Lyons
learned to weave velvets and taffetas, but continued to import
her finer silks from Italy.   Meantime the manufacture of ribbons and braid, greatly in demand for the decoration of uniforms,
had been started at St. Chamond near the present great center
of that branch of silk manufacture, St. Étienne.   Gayotti, a
native of Bologna, left that city in 1515 at the risk of his life
because of the knowledge of the processes of silk manufacturing
he could reveal to foreigners, and came to St. Chamond where
he set up his machines for throwing silk, building a mill in one
of the suburbs.[14]   The small hand-loom then in use at Lyons was
brought to St. Chamond later in the sixteenth century, but was
superseded there in the seventeenth century by a better type
that had been perfected at Zurich, in which, by the use of a
long crossbar moved by a man, some six to eight looms could be
run at the same time.[14]

The rise of St. Étienne as the principal center of the ribbon
and braid industries must have begun late in the sixteenth century,
for a guild of ribbon-makers existed there in 1605.[15]   The industry
grew rapidly and by the time of the revocation of the Edict of
Nantes in 1685 it employed between 4,000 and 4,500 workers.[15]
There followed a period of decline, caused presumably by the
emigration of Protestant weavers and the wars of Louis XIV,
which was ended by the introduction of another and better kind

[13] Gueneau, *op. cit.*, p. 109.

[14] *Enquête of 1870.* Session of July 15. Testimony of M. Richard, vice-
president of the Chamber of Commerce of St. Étienne.

[15] Pariset, *op. cit.*, p. 361.

of loom, again brought from Zurich in 1760, which made it possible to weave several ribbons at once on the same loom. At the outbreak of the French Revolution St. Etienne and the surrounding district — for most of the weavers worked at home in the country — had 6,000 looms weaving ribbons. In the nineteenth century the silk industry of St. Étienne grew rapidly and the goods manufactured included all sorts of ribbons, whether of fine silk or velvet, neckties, elastic goods, cloth for trimming hats and various kinds of braid. The height of its prosperity was reached in 1855 when St. Étienne had 123 active establishments with 350 manufacturers, 30,000 workmen and 15,000 looms and a production worth between 90,000,000 and 100,000,000 francs.[16]

Lyons, like St. Étienne and other centers of silk manufacturing, suffered from the emigration of Protestant workers to Switzerland, Prussia, and England after 1685, and it was injured again by the disastrous wars of France, an acute crisis occurring in 1701 and 1702. Then followed a long period of growth and prosperity during which Lyons began to export silks on a considerable scale to Leipzig and Spain. At the outbreak of the Revolution she produced silks worth 60,000,000 francs, of which France consumed only one sixth. The Revolution was a disaster to the industry and trade of Lyons, and the opposition of that city to the government of the Convention was so serious that it had to be put down by troops. The number of silk looms fell sharply and the depression continued during the government of the First Republic because of the loss of the principal consumers of silk goods, the privileged classes. With the advent of the Consulate there was a return to luxury and, although fashions favored plain rather than fancy silks, Lyons had 5,000 looms in 1801. Its industry grew rapidly from that time, with only brief crises during the Revolutions of 1830 and 1848. In 1810 Lyons had 12,000 looms and produced silks worth 53,000,000 francs; in 1824 the number of looms was 20,000 and the production was valued at 100,000,000 francs; and in 1853 Lyons had 60,000 looms and sold silks worth 250,000,000 francs of which three

[16] L. J. Gras, *Histoire de la rubanerie et des industrie de la soie à St. Étienne et dans la région stephanoise* (St. Étienne, 1906), p. 609.

quarters were exported.   During these years the weaving of silk was being radically transformed by the adoption of the Jacquard loom which, although invented in 1804, was not in general use at Lyons before 1850.[17]

One of the smaller branches of the silk industry, the manufacture of silk tulle, deserves our attention because of its opposition to English competition in 1860.   Tulle had been made at Lyons for some time before the nineteenth century, when St. Pierre-les-Calais, a suburb of the well-known port on the English Channel, rose into prominence as the most important center of manufacture.   An improved loom was smuggled over from England by British workmen in 1816.   After this the industry grew rapidly there just as it did at Nottingham.   A circular loom was introduced at St. Pierre in 1824, evidently, as before, from England, and in 1836 began the manufacture of fancy silk tulle which became the great specialty of the town.   By 1846 there were 900 looms making silk tulle at St. Pierre and Calais, and the industry enjoyed many prosperous years.   The only difficulty was the frequent changing of fashions, which often forced the tulle manufacturers to use cotton or wool instead of silk, a change that was very unwelcome to them because of the high tariff duties on cotton and woollen yarn.[18]   Lyons was then making both plain and fancy tulle.   The process of making the plain tulle, known as 'bobin de soie', had been invented in France and in the nineteenth century this tulle was exported on a considerable scale, chiefly to England.   Under the system of prohibitive tariff duties, however, the French manufacturers, like so many of their colleagues in other industries, made such large profits that they saw no need of improving their methods or machinery.   Their looms were generally old and poorly constructed, having been bought from manufacturers of cotton tulle in northern France and adapted to the weaving of silk tulle at great cost.   They were run by hand, but England had installed looms run by steam power and had improved her methods so that she was driving the French from the markets of

[17] Pariset, *op. cit.*, p. 363.
[18] *Ibid.*, p. 359.

the United States, Spain, Germany, and Italy. The French manufacturers were not willing to replace their antiquated looms quickly when threatened with British competition in their home market in 1860 because of the cost, and also because of the labor difficulties that would be created by the ownership of the looms by a large number of master workmen in small establishments.[19]

Lyons began its career as the center for the manufacture of silk in France in the reign of Louis XI, as we have seen, because of its position on the main trade route between Italy and Flanders which had made its fairs of great importance. It soon became the chief market of the silk trade in France and one of the most important in Europe. Its supremacy in France was assured by an edict of Francis I in 1542 which imposed a small duty on imported silk and directed that all such silks be taken to Lyons, where alone the duty might be paid.[20] This monopoly was broken late in the seventeenth century, but not before southern French centers like Nîmes, which might have imported their silk directly from Italy, had grown accustomed to obtaining it from Lyons. In the seventeenth century, also, the geographical position of Lyons had become less advantageous because the Mediterranean trade routes to the Orient, which were short, but required transhipment of goods that was expensive, were replaced by the Atlantic routes by which cargoes were brought directly to Europe. This disadvantage was neutralized for a long time by the development of silk growing in Europe itself. As we have seen, this had begun in Italy and from there spread to France. As late as 1850 it could still be said that Europe supplied most of the silk it needed for manufacturing and that the silk grown in France was the best that could be had. Lyons was well situated with regard to the silk-producing regions of France and, therefore, was in a stronger position as a market for raw silk in the early nineteenth century than ever before. But in the middle of that century, when Lyons seemed to be at the height of its power, new factors arose which gave the mer-

[19] Arch. Nat., F 12–2696. Report of Natalis Rondot on Silk, October 8, 1860, p. 24.
[20] Gueneau, *op. cit.*, p. 65.

cantile supremacy to London. The disease of the silkworms cut the French silk crop to less than half its normal size soon after 1850, so that once more Lyons became almost wholly dependent upon the importation of silk from the Orient. The great French center began now to feel the full effects of its disadvantage in not being on the trade routes through the Atlantic while London was profiting by its fortunate position on those routes. Even more important was the large volume of trade with the Orient developed by England through the control of India, and greatly increased by the opening of direct commercial relations on a considerable scale with China in 1842 and with Japan about 1853.[21] London was now the market from which Lyons had to obtain most of its silk, while at the same time the important British silk industry was stimulated to new efforts to compete with its rival across the Channel.

In England the manufacture of silk is probably an industry as old as in France. A law of 1454 forbidding the importation of ribbons or bonnets of silk would indicate that there was some manufacturing in England. It is known that a guild of silk-workers existed in London early in the seventeenth century, and that these workers had come chiefly from Flanders in the great immigration of 1585 caused by the sack of Antwerp by the Spaniards. There was a much larger emigration of silk-workers from France to England after the revocation of the Edict of Nantes in 1685,[22] which established firmly the silk-manufacturing industry in Great Britain. Soon afterward an Englishman named Lombe went to Leghorn and succeeded in mastering the technical processes used in Piedmont for silk throwing.[23] Lombe started the machine-throwing industry in England which grew slowly but steadily through the eighteenth century. The British Government gave its silk industry protection in every possible form. The importation of both thrown silk and cloth was forbidden from 1765 to 1824; bounties were given for the

[21] Gueneau, *op. cit.*, p. 66.

[22] Pariset, *op. cit.*, p. 375; Sir Frank Warner, *The Silk Industry of the United Kingdom. Its Origin and Development* (London, 1921), pp. 23-43.

[23] Warner, *op. cit.*, p. 199.

exportation of cloth, and the British colonies were reserved as a market for the manufacturers of the mother country. When the industrial revolution began later in the eighteenth century the British silk industry was eclipsed by the greater development of cotton and wool, but it was able to profit from many of the machines invented in England, and still more from the loom invented by Jacquard in France. While Lyons continued to devote itself almost entirely to pure silks, England learned to throw silk well, to manufacture silks of good quality, and to make strong black crêpe for mourning that was so popular both in Great Britain and America that the French could not compete with it in foreign markets.[24] The British industry was stimulated by the repeal of the prohibition of all imports in 1825 and the substitution of duties of 25 per cent to 35 per cent ad valorem on silks,[25] and it profited again by the repeal of the Navigation Acts in 1849. The height of prosperity was reached in 1861, when there were 75,000 looms in England using 1,870,000 kilograms of silk out of a total importation of over 4,000,000 kilograms. All sorts of silks were manufactured. Nottingham specialized in tulle and lace, competing successfully in foreign markets with Lyons and Calais; Coventry, and, to a lesser extent, Congleton and Derby, in ribbons, competing with St. Étienne; Norwich in crêpes such as Lyons could not produce; and Spitalfields in London, Manchester, Middleton and Macclesfield in plain and fancy silks.[26] Such was the great industry, supported by the most important silk market in Europe, with which the French industry found itself in open competition both at home and abroad after the signature of the Treaty of Commerce of 1860.

The only other country able to compete seriously with France in 1860 was Switzerland. A few silkworms were raised in some of the cantons, but most of the raw material was imported from Italy. Throwing became an industry of some importance, as did the spinning of waste silk brought from Italy, which can

---

[24] Arch. Nat., F 12–2696. Rondot Report, p. 19.
[25] Pariset, *op. cit.*, p. 375.
[26] *Ibid.*, p. 377; Warner, *op. cit.*, pp. 107–198.

be traced back to the sixteenth century. Swiss superiority in the preparation of this spun silk was maintained in the earlier nineteenth century by the invention of machines for both spinning and combing. At the same period Zurich developed with considerable success the manufacture of taffeta and when, after the middle of the century, the change of fashion favored mixed silks, Zurich turned to them and weathered the crisis caused by the transformation. It was not these branches of the Swiss industry that the French feared, however. France was glad to take much of the spun silk made in Switzerland and she was late in developing on a considerable scale the manufacture of mixed silks. French alarm was aroused only by the development of the Swiss ribbon industry at Bâle.

This industry appears to have started as early in Switzerland as in France and to have developed more rapidly, for at St. Chamond in the seventeenth century and at St. Étienne in the eighteenth century the French greatly improved the weaving of ribbons by importing Swiss looms. In the period between 1850 and 1860 the Swiss made both plain and fancy ribbons well, although they manufactured them on a much smaller scale than the French, their production in 1859 being valued at 45,000,000 francs,[27] whereas that of St. Étienne in 1855 was worth between 90,000,000 and 100,000,000 francs. The French manufacturers, therefore, could not reasonably have been concerned over the size of the Swiss industry. What they feared was rather that the Swiss would sell a larger proportion of their production in certain other foreign markets, of which the most important was that of the United States. They were moved also by resentment at the promptness with which the Swiss copied French designs and they claimed that, while they gave legal protection to Swiss designs in France, the Swiss gave no such protection to French designs in their country. The truth appears to be that for very little reason the manufacturers of St. Étienne had been afraid of Swiss competition for many years.

Natalis Rondot, a well-known silk merchant of Lyons, who investigated the whole French silk industry for the Conseil Supérieur

[27] Pariset, *op. cit.*, p. 386.

du Commerce in 1860, with a view to recommending the duties that should be inserted in the Tariff Convention with England, estimated that the Swiss had been selling in Paris for some years ribbons worth 4,000,000 francs annually. This represented only 10 per cent of the total Swiss production which, as we have seen, was less than half that of St. Étienne. Furthermore, these ribbons from Bâle were generally of very fine quality and did not compete with the ribbons of St. Étienne, which were generally cheap and of inferior quality. The manufacturers of St. Étienne were accustomed to selling only 20 per cent of their production in France, so that they were quite unable to meet the demands of their own home market which consumed annually 7,000,000 francs' worth of foreign ribbons, including the 4,000,000 francs' worth imported from Switzerland.[28] The merchants of Paris protested strongly against the increase in duty demanded by St. Étienne on the ground that many of the ribbons they needed were not made in France at all. They pointed out also that the manufacturers of ribbons in Alsace, who were starting a new industry close to the well-established industries of Switzerland and Rhenish Prussia, and who in 1860 had only 500 looms, showed no fear of foreign competition. Natalis Rondot concluded his report on the ribbon industry by remarking that at the very moment when St. Étienne was asking increased protection against Switzerland she was flooding England with her own ribbons and causing acute distress to the British industry at Coventry.

In comparing the ribbon industries of France and Switzerland it must be understood that both industries in 1860 were going through a period of marked depression which had begun in 1856.[29] The disease of the silkworm was causing an alarming decrease in the production of silk in France, which affected both the Swiss and French ribbon manufacturers through a sharp rise in the price of their raw material. A second cause of the depression lay in the fact that the American market, in which both countries sold large quantities of ribbons, was over-

---

[28] Arch. Nat., F 12–2696. Rondot Report, p. 386.
[29] Gras, *op. cit.*, p. 490.

supplied. A third cause was the financial panic of 1857 in the United States, which was felt within a few weeks in Europe. Finally, the ribbon industries of both France and Switzerland suffered from the abandonment of their product by the new fashions. The depression of the ribbon industries resulting from the combination of all these factors was long and severe, and explains the acute anxiety over Swiss competition of the manufacturers of St. Étienne, who felt rightly that the negotiation of a commercial treaty with England might be followed by similar negotiations with Switzerland. In their anxiety to prevent this they naturally stressed their own sufferings and made no mention of the equally severe hardships endured by their Swiss competitors.

The strongly protectionist policy of the ribbon manufacturers of St. Étienne was shared by only one or two other branches of the silk industry whose conditions were exceptional, such as the manufacture of plain silk tulle, or crêpe, of yarn spun from waste silk, and of sewing thread. The manufacturers of plain tulle, as we have seen, had neglected to improve their methods of production or their looms, because the prohibitive tariff gave them the monopoly of the French market without any exertion on their part. Free competition with England would have compelled the manufacturers of Lyons to renew all their looms immediately at great expense. Their chamber of commerce, therefore, recommended the replacement of the existing prohibition of importation by a duty of 20 per cent for three years, then a duty of 10 per cent for two years, and after that free admission. The Government approved these recommendations, but provided that, instead of admitting tulle free in 1866 as the Lyons chamber had proposed, a duty of 5 per cent should be imposed for five years more.[30] The same rates were granted the manufacturers of crêpe who asked for a continuation of the old duty of 30 per cent in the tariff convention. Natalis Rondot, the Government's investigator, felt that the request of the crêpe manufacturers was unreasonable. He reported that France did not make the same kind of crêpe as England, whose cloth was

[30] Arch. Nat., F 12-2696. Rondot Report, p. 25.

stiff and strong and was used chiefly for mourning in England and America; whereas the French crêpe was delicate and in bright colors. The real reason for the request of the French manufacturers for a high duty was the cost of the researches in which they were then engaged with a view to discovering the process by which the English produced their crêpe, so that they could compete with them in the American market. This was a laudable enterprise, but did not justify a government subsidy in the form of a duty of 30 per cent, because there was no danger of a destructive competition by England in the French market.[31]

The manufacturing of cloth from waste silk represented what could almost have been called an infant industry. We hear of it first in 1824 when France had only three weaving mills and the spinners, fearing an increase of competition with Switzerland, asked that the duty on yarn be increased from the existing 90 centimes per kilogram to 7 or 8 francs, a request which the Government refused. In 1860 Switzerland had only 36,000 spindles and France 90,000.[32] The dangerous competition was not in the Alps but across the Channel, where England had 180,000 spindles producing 550,000 kilograms of yarn a year.[33] France produced chiefly the finer qualities of yarn, probably because of the fine quality of her own raw silk, while the poorer qualities, on which the duty bore more heavily, had to be imported, so that the manufacturers of cloth that used spun silk yarn, especially those producing foulards, found it hard to get it at a reasonable price and were, therefore, in favor of free trade. The Government settled the dispute by imposing a very moderate duty of 4 per cent on both the yarn and cloth made from waste silk.[34] In the case of sewing silk, produced chiefly at Paris, the demands of the manufacturers seem to have been quite unreasonable. They asked for protection on the ground that Swiss and German labor was much cheaper than French, and they did not

---

[31] *Ibid.* Rondot Report, p. 19.

[32] *Ibid.*, p. 10.

[33] *Enquête: Traité de commerce avec l'Angleterre* (7 vols., Paris, 1860), Vol. 7. Section on Silk.

[34] Arch. Nat., F 12–2696, Rondot report, p. 6.

mention the fact that French labor was more skilful and that the importation of sewing silk was insignificant while the exportation was considerable, as was shown by the fact that in 1859 France had imported 230 kilograms and exported 29,000.[35]

The silk industries of England and Switzerland, and to a lesser extent those of Rhenish Prussia, were strong and active and able to compete with France in cheap silks or in mixed goods containing cotton, wool, flax, or mohair. England, in particular, was strong in the manufacture of mixed silks, but France had important centers in various parts of the country. The French Government in 1860 felt that in competition the French manufacturers of mixed silks, would enjoy the same advantage as those of pure silks, through their unusual ingenuity and good taste and their skill in the use of colors and designs. The fact that Lyons still took pride in producing almost exclusively pure silks of the finest quality was no evidence that she could not succeed also in the manufacture of mixed silks. All that was needed was the spur of competition. The mixed silks of Manchester were not remarkable for their cheapness, nor were they notable because of their quality, skill, or design. The soundness of the Government's judgment was proved by the great development of the manufacture of mixed silks in France after 1860 under a duty of only 8 per cent,[36] as compared with the previous prohibition of the importation of all such goods except those containing only flax or hemp yarn mixed with silk. The French manufacturers of mixed silks made no request for protection. They asked only that all textile yarns be admitted free and that the duties on coal and machinery be made as low as possible. Finally, the manufacturers of pure silks in France were almost unanimous in their demand for free trade. The Conseil Supérieur heard witnesses from nearly every center in France and was so impressed by their unanimity that it abandoned its plan of levying a duty of 5 per cent on all pure silks as a convenient source of revenue and advised the Government to admit all pure silks from England free.[37] The manufacturers realized the strength of

[35] Arch. Nat., F 12–2696, Rondot report, p. 7.   [36] *Ibid.*, p. 6.
[37] *Ibid.*, p. 2.

their position in international trade through the incontestable superiority of their finer goods. They expected to profit considerably from the opening of the English market and they knew that their reputation would suffer if they did not admit free the goods of their weaker rival. They knew also that they had been becoming increasingly dependent on oriental silks imported through England and that this dependence could be diminished most effectively, not by attempting to check the trade of England, but by developing in every way the trade of France.

The effects of the Anglo-French treaty of 1860 on the silk industry of both countries are as difficult to isolate from other factors that influenced them as is the case with the other textile industries. In general, we can say confidently that the expectations of the great merchants and manufacturers of Lyons that the silk industry of France would only gain from free competition were justified. The gain is very clear when we study the effects of the Treaty on the ribbon industry of England, whose chief center was Coventry. In this case the French had a distinct advantage. The industry of St. Étienne was large and strong and protected by a duty of 8 francs per kilogram from 1860 to 1864 [38] when, through the treaty with Switzerland it was brought down to 4 francs. For four years, therefore, St. Étienne enjoyed the same protection against British competition that she had had before the Treaty was concluded, whereas Coventry after 1860 received no protection at all, although before that, with duties of 15 per cent to 30 per cent, she had had some difficulty in meeting French competition. The bitterness that was doubtless felt by all the ribbon manufacturers of Coventry and their workmen was expressed by one weaver, Jabez Cramp, who wrote directly to the Foreign Secretary, Lord Derby, in 1876, as follows: [39]

" Seeing by the Public Press that the Present Republican Government of France wish for a renewal of a Fresh Commercial Treaty of Commerce with the Present, I am pleased to say Strong Conservative Government and long may it continue I do hope that you will try to get Justice done to the Ribben and Silk Weavers of this Country and use your utmost endeavours to get us at least Reciprocity

---

[38] Gras, *op. cit.*, p. 499.
[39] F. O., 27–2221, April 24, 1876.

if not any Protection — because we do expect a deal more Justice under a Conservative Government than we ever expected to get under the Political Scool of Gladstone, Bright and Co. I do not think any trade has suffered more from the effects of the last unequal Treaty of Commerce than the Ribben Trade of this Country has . . . there was one place Coventry that it greatly affected which I for one know to well — then having had to sell Machinery that cost me a working man £200 — sold it for £40.

"The Weavers now in Coventry are having to work for 28% less than in 1860 and Provisions the Principal ones in the Household 75% dearer than in 1860 before the French Treaty takes place so that we are now placed in a worse position as far as our purchasing powers are concerned by 100% and only half employment at that. . . ."

The statements of Jabez Cramp, while clothed in rather picturesque language, are confirmed by a formal and grammatically correct petition from the ribbon trade of Coventry to Lord Derby, and by other sources of information.[40] In the two years following the signature of the Treaty there were 1,400 empty houses in Coventry and the poverty of the weavers was so great that looms costing £40 or more were often sold for £5 while many, from the lack of money for buying fuel, were broken up for firewood. During those years 10,000 persons lived on a great national fund raised by the British public and 4,000 more received parochial relief. Much of this suffering in Coventry seems to have been the result of lack of consideration of the needs and wishes of the silk industry by the British Government when the Treaty was signed with France in the month of January, 1860. The silk industry was classed among the "small manufactures" of Great Britain and the fact that it still used relatively little machinery driven by power was considered a sign of backwardness. It was felt, in short, that the silk manufacturers of England were largely responsible for the relatively weak condition of their industry as compared with that of France and that, therefore, they needed to be roused to activity by unrestricted competition. Coventry suffered severely because of the suddenness of the announcement that a commercial treaty had been signed with France, and because of the time of the year at which the announcement was made.

[40] F. O., 27–2222, May 16, 1876. See also dispatch of the Foreign Office to Mr. Adams of the Paris Embassy, May 29, 1876.

" Before the passing of the Treaty," writes Sir Frederick Warner, " the trade [in ribbons] was to a great extent speculative. Goods were very largely prepared in anticipation of customers' wants, and a rough census taken at the time showed that something like £1,000,000 worth of ribbons was ready for the Spring trade. With the prospect of foreign ribbons entering untaxed, no buyer would operate freely, small purchases only were made to cover immediate needs and a few weeks' delay in selling articles for fashionable wear may mean goods reduced to half their prices. If the wider interests of the nation demanded that the silk trade should be sacrificed, common justice should have delayed the free entry until the commencement of the Autumn season. . . . Only the houses with considerable capital could stand the losses that ensued. Stock after stock was tendered, failure after failure was announced, until thirty to forty firms had succumbed in the terrible depression that followed." [41]

For three years the ribbon industry of Coventry suffered acutely, but gradually it revived and recovered much of the ground that had been lost. New branches of the silk industry arose, such as the weaving of elastic webbing, while the old ribbon industry adjusted itself to the new conditions of trade. Colored goods were no longer made in advance, as they had been before the signature of the Anglo-French Treaty, but were manufactured only on the receipt of definite orders giving sufficient time for delivery. Coventry had had a good organization for manufacturing and selling her ribbons and she could deliver them to London merchants more quickly and at a lower cost of transportation than her continental competitors. It was not until after 1876, therefore, that the permanent decline of the ribbon industry of Coventry began, so that the French Treaty cannot be held responsible for much more than the severe crisis of 1860–63.

The effects of French competition upon the silk industry of Spitalfields,[42] London, resembled somewhat those on the ribbon industry of Coventry, but there was one difference of real significance. The industry in Coventry was highly prosperous at the opening of the year 1860, but the industry in London had been declining for many years. The energy of the manufacturers and the artistic ability of the weavers had suffered from the

---

[41] Warner, *op. cit.*, p. 119.
[42] *Ibid.*, pp. 78–90.

many years of prohibition and restricted foreign competition. When the signature of the treaty with France was announced the Spitalfields industry was plunged into a crisis from which it never recovered. Yet the Treaty was merely the final blow, and not the sole cause of the ruin of this industry. There is every reason to believe that even if no treaty had been signed with France the decline of silk manufacturing in Spitalfields, which had begun long before 1860, would have continued.

The British silk industry as a whole suffered less than either Coventry or Spitalfields. The superiority of the French silks had been recognized by British manufacturers at the Exposition of 1851, and, although they made every effort to acquire greater skill in color and design, they admitted in 1860, after sending a deputation to the chief silk manufacturing centers on the continent, that they could not compete with the French in those respects, or even with the Swiss and Germans. In the throwing of silk the British found they could not keep up with the improvements made in Italy and their exports of thrown silk decreased greatly, although they continued to supply the home market in part. The spinning of waste silk from the Orient was developed in England [43] and became an important industry before 1880, but in general the manufacturing of silk declined in importance. The English manufacturers could not meet readily the constant changes in fashions and the endless variations in design and in texture brought by the increasing use of inferior qualities of silk, which made dyeing and finishing of far greater importance, and the equally great variations in the mixture of silk with other textiles to form the mixed goods that grew steadily in popularity. In addition to these factors England after 1860 lost her supremacy as a market for raw silk and Lyons recovered her former position for a brief period, after which it was challenged with considerable success by Milan. This decline in the importance of the British silk trade was unquestionably a significant factor in the slow decline of British manufacturing of silk. It cannot be said that the British industry was seriously injured by French competition alone under the Treaty

[43] Pariset, *op. cit.*, pp. 349, 380.

of 1860. Swiss competition was also a factor of importance, as was German competition after 1870. The effects of the Anglo-French Treaty cannot be isolated from the effects of similar treaties subsequently negotiated by both countries with their continental neighbors. Neither can they be isolated from the changing trade routes that restored commercial supremacy to Lyons and then caused a struggle for supremacy between the French capital of the silk industry and the Italian; nor from the changes in fashion, which were probably more frequent and of greater significance in silk than in any other textile industry. Finally, we must consider the effect of the American Civil War, combined with the high protective tariff and the birth of an American silk industry, which made the United States less accessible as a market and thereby increased the intensity of the competition of the European countries among themselves.

The tables [44] at the end of this chapter give us some indications of the exportations of silk goods to the United States for the decade following the Treaty of 1860 with England, and they give us a very few such indications regarding exports to European countries for two years after the signature of the Anglo-French Treaty. The figures are too incomplete to justify many comments. It seems clear, however, that in 1860 the United States held second place among French foreign markets for silk goods; that in that same year of 1860 French exports to us decreased considerably, largely because of the disturbed state of the New York market; and that in 1861 the outbreak of the American Civil War and the enactment of the high protective tariff caused the United States to fall from second to fifth place among French foreign markets. After the close of the Civil War the exportation of silk goods to us recovered considerably, but up to 1873 at least it had scarcely come within measurable distance of the total exportation made in 1860. A comparison of the table of exports to the United States with that of exports to the principal European customers of France indicates that, with the possible exception of ribbons, for which we lack information because the figures given do not show the different classes of silk

[44] *U. S. Consular Reports*, 1860–73.

goods, the English market was not flooded with French silks when the Treaty admitted them free early in the year 1860. Whatever influence the Treaty of 1860 may have had in later years, it does not appear to have been the dominant influence in the silk trade between the two countries for the first two years of its existence. We would seem justified, therefore, in concluding that in the years just after 1860 the most important influences on the silk trade of France with England, as well as with other European countries, were the high price of raw silk resulting from the disease of the silkworms, the virtual loss of the American market during the period of the Civil War, and the change of fashions which deserted flowered and other fancy silks and ribbons in favor of simpler and cheaper pure silks and of mixed goods. It seems probable that the French silk industry adapted itself to the new demands of fashions. The rather large exportation of ribbons to the United States in 1870 and 1871 might show that ribbons were again becoming fashionable; but it might also be a result of the interruption of trade with Germany by the Franco-Prussian War causing the merchants of St. Étienne to ship a larger proportion of their normal output to the American market. St. Étienne reported as late as 1863 that fashions favored feathers and flowers and that between 1861 and 1867 her production of ribbons fell from 90,000,000 francs to 55,000,-000.[45] We know that the late 'sixties were a period of industrial depression in western Europe, so that French manufacturers could not hope to increase their sales greatly in their own or in neighboring markets. On the other hand, French merchants had expected the former Confederate States to take large quantities of French silks on the conclusion of the Civil War, and their failure to do so because of their economic exhaustion resulted in a serious crisis from overproduction in France and heavy losses to both manufacturers and merchants.

We might expect to find that in 1876, when the discussion of the commercial policy of France was resumed with a view to revising the general tariff of the country, the attitude of the silk industry would be less favorable to the policy of a low tariff

[45] Gras, *op. cit.*, pp. 609, 615.

than it had been in 1860. The disease of the silkworms might have caused such a change of opinion, as phylloxera did in the case of the wine industry. We find, however, that the sharp decline in the French silk crops made the silk industry favor not a less, but a more liberal policy, because that industry had been almost wholly dependent on the importation of raw silk. Lyons wanted this importation to be as large and as cheap as possible, and the Government gave its assistance by encouraging the organization of the Messageries Maritimes Shipping Company in 1862 [46] as a rival of the Peninsular and Oriental Company of England that brought silk directly from the Orient; and by opening the Suez Canal in 1869. Through these means Lyons rapidly recovered the position it had held before 1850 as the principal silk market of Europe. Another factor that made the French silk industry grow more liberal in its attitude toward the tariff was the continuance of the popularity of mixed goods which, combined with the loss of Alsace in 1871, necessitated a large importation of cotton, wool, and flax yarn.

International competition in silk goods was sharper in 1876 and 1877 than in 1860, yet the French silk industry had grown to fear it less because it had learned from experience that it was beneficial. The opening of the English market had been a great boon to the French when their American market had been nearly cut off by the Civil War and its value continued to be great when, with the return of peace, the sale of French silks in the United States remained somewhat restricted by the high tariff. Even St. Étienne, which had been so strongly protectionist in 1860, wrote to the French Government in 1877 that it wanted all the commercial treaties renewed, and it showed far more concern over the reduction of the duty on cotton yarn than it did over the competition of Switzerland in ribbons.[47] The general opinion in the silk industry of the effects of the Anglo-French Treaty of 1860 seems to be well expressed in a letter from the chamber of commerce of Lyons to the Minister

[46] Gueneau, *op. cit.*, p. 67.
[47] Arch. Nat., F 12–6196. Letter from the Chamber of Commerce of St. Étienne to the Minister of Commerce, May 28.

of Commerce, written, like that of St. Étienne, in the spring of 1877:[48]

> "Both sides are glad to testify that this reform has had marvelous results. It is praised everywhere. . . . It is universally admitted that without it our economic recovery would have been made far more slowly and our debt paid off with far less ease. In spite of the heavy taxes resulting from our disasters [in the war with Germany] our exports have increased continuously. Because of this would it not seem natural to go one step farther on the road which has proved so favorable to us? . . . We are now no longer concerned with an experiment; it would be simply the extension and development of what is now an accomplished fact which has been accepted as salutary by all industries."

The favorable opinion of the Treaty of 1860 with England and the similar treaties with other countries that followed it, expressed by the chamber of commerce of Lyons in 1877, coupled with favorable comments by the ribbon manufacturers of St. Étienne and the absence of complaints from other branches of the French silk industry, shows pretty clearly that the new commercial policy adopted by the Second Empire had no injurious effects on that industry. We know that the plain tulle industry of Lyons which dreaded English competition in 1860 met the test successfully.[49] There is also no indication that the manufacture of waste silk was injured by British competition, although we know that in England that branch of the silk industry was growing steadily in importance. If, then, we are justified in believing that the Treaty of 1860 did the French silk industry no harm, we may inquire whether its effects were notably beneficial. In general it can be said that they must have been, because, with the exception of a few branches, the French silk industry was far stronger than the British or than that of any of the other European countries. We must be careful, however, not to overemphasize the strength of the French silk industry and not to exaggerate its triumphs in England. The concessions made by England in 1860 were far more important in their effects on the French industry than the reductions made in the French tariff. But the opening of the

[48] Arch. Nat., F 12–6196. April 5 and April 21.
[49] Natalis Rondot, *L'Industrie de la soie en France* (Lyon, 1894), p. 96.

British market did not ruin the British industry, nor can it rightly be called the one great cause of its slow decline. Even in Coventry we cannot say that the ribbons of St. Étienne were the only cause of the severe crisis in the early 'sixties. It must be remembered that fashions deserted ribbons in about 1856, that the disease of the silkworms raised the price of all raw silk, and that the Civil War cut off almost entirely the rich American market. Coventry would have gone through a crisis even without French competition, but that competition made her sufferings far greater.

The French silk industry also passed through a series of crises beginning about 1856, crises that, on the whole, were more severe than the majority of those it had been called upon to meet at frequent intervals throughout its history. Lyons, for example, had often complained of changes in fashions and of the preference of the French and even the international public for cheap and inferior silks instead of the fine ones in whose production she excelled. Yet it cannot be denied that the situation of the French silk industry between 1856 and 1876 was very difficult. The combination of unfavorable factors was unusually serious. To the important and long-continued change in fashions were added the disease of the silkworms and the restrictions of the American market by the Civil War and the high tariff. All these factors, combined with the steady improvements in means of transportation and the general decline of prices, caused a steady increase in the intensity of international competition. In this struggle the Treaty of 1860 with England, and the similar treaties with other countries that followed, gave assistance in making important foreign markets in Europe more accessible and in stimulating to greater activity several branches of the French silk industry. This stimulation was felt not only in manufacturing, but also in trade, and it was unquestionably one of the factors that helped Lyons defeat London and recover her position as the greatest silk market in Europe.

The following tables show some of the effects of the changes in foreign markets on the French export trade in silk goods:

EXPORTS FROM THE LYONS DISTRICT (INCLUDING ST. ÉTIENNE) TO THE
UNITED STATES (IN THOUSAND FRANCS)

KIND OF SILK	1859	1860	1861	1862	1863	1864
Total..........	138,247	103,638	25,346	23,714	28,357	26,715
Raw silk........	....	....	....	....	....	....
Silk piece goods..	....	....	....	....	19,750	18,432
Taffeta ribbons...	....	....	....	....	....	5,307
Velvet..........	....	....	....	....	8,607	2,178
Tulles..........	....	....	....	....	....	798

KIND OF SILK	1865	1866	1867	1869	1870	1871
Total..........	48,691	48,814	35,798	51,756	66,933	74,321
Raw silk...... ⎫			2,348	1,143	2,274	3,217
Silk piece goods ⎬	33,157	27,810				
⎭			22,023	37,653	44,009	48,752
Taffeta ribbons...	9,774	14,813	5,875	8,839	12,849	12,153
Velvet..........	3,966	4,692	4,846	3,312	6,519	8,784
Tulles..........	1,795	1,499	705	809	1,282	1,415

EXPORTS FROM THE LYONS DISTRICT (INCLUDING ST. ÉTIENNE) (TO THE
CHIEF FOREIGN COUNTRIES (IN THOUSAND FRANCS)

COUNTRY	1858	1859	1860	1861	1862
England.......	104,000	163,298	156,514	122,883	154,692
U. S. A........	90,000	138,247	103,638	25,346	23,714
Belgium	34,400	36,690	35,975	30,422	28,344
Zollverein.....	34,300	49,337	51,860	52,873	57,050
Italy..........	22,000	20,895	17,482	27,722	21,469
Spain.........	20,400	17,956	15,450	17,402	17,751
Turkey........	8,400	7,238	4,611	3,581	7,201
Switzerland....	7,400	7,993	6,904	8,960	7,986

CHAPTER XIV

THE WINE INDUSTRY

WHEN England and France are compared as great exporting nations, it is seen that England has been noted largely for the unusual cheapness of her goods resulting from the economies obtainable through production on a large scale. The majority of the articles exported by France, on the other hand, are still luxuries of high price whose attractiveness to foreign consumers is the result of the remarkable artistic gifts of the French that enable them in cloth goods to show exceptional skill in color and design, and which make it possible for them to excel also in the manufacture of perfumes and in the preparation of food. Rarely are natural factors such as climate, or the monopoly or control of a large part of the raw material, among the decisive reasons for the exportation of manufactured goods from France.

The wine industry in France stands out in contrast to most of the other great exporting industries of the country because the superiority of its product depends to a great extent upon the climate and soil of certain restricted districts. It is fortunate in that dependence, however, for the gifts of nature have been so great that the wines of France have been sought by many peoples since the days of the Romans. No French industry has been in a stronger position to compete with its rivals in foreign markets and, in consequence, none has been more anxious to develop those markets. From the ministry of Vergennes, when the first important treaty of commerce with England was signed, to the period when the commercial policy of France was controlled by Méline, the wine industry led all others in its enthusiastic support of the efforts made to lower the French tariff.

As in the silk industry, the merchants were the controlling element, yet most wine merchants also owned and managed the vineyards whose products they sold. Though, as we have seen, the whole wine industry of France was anxious to export on a considerable scale, in actual fact only the finer qualities of wine were so exported. The greater part of the product of French vineyards was consumed within the country. The market for the *vins ordinaires* of the Midi could scarcely have been called even national until the railroads had made quick and cheap transportation between most parts of France an effective reality shortly before the signature of the Anglo-French Treaty of Commerce of 1860. In its attitude toward the tariff the wine industry resembled most that of silk, yet its policy changed, whereas that of the silk industry did not, despite the fact that both suffered from serious diseases which injured or destroyed the raw materials used. The silk industry solved its difficulties by using a smaller proportion of the raw silk produced in France and by importing to an ever increasing extent cocoons or raw silk from the Orient. As the merchants of the large centers like Lyons and St. Étienne dominated the industry, the appeals for help from the growers of silk were largely ignored.

The wine industry, on the other hand, was bound far more closely to the soil, and its leaders were really farmers as well as merchants. They could not import their raw material on a large scale because the excellence of their product depended on the climate and soil of France. Their enthusiasm for free trade survived the crisis caused by the attacks of *oïdium* at the beginning of the Second Empire, because the crisis was short, so that there was not time for countries like Italy and Spain to flood France with their wines and because Europe was not yet covered by a network of railroads that could facilitate the cheap transportation of wine. Their enthusiasm succumbed to the attacks of phylloxera because they lasted for many years and because the perfection of the railroads then made it possible for Italy and Spain and the French colony of Algeria to ship great quantities of their wines into France. Hence it is not surprising that, though the manufacturers of silks remained chiefly free traders, the wine merchants turned for a time to high protection and

helped to overthrow in 1892 the liberal tariff policy inaugurated
in France in 1860.

French wine merchants under the Second Empire, however,
had never suffered seriously from foreign competition in their
home market. They reigned supreme in France, as had their
ancestors for centuries, and they were interested chiefly in
increasing the sale of French wines in other countries. For many
years they had sought vainly to do this in England. They had
always been convinced of the superiority of their products to
the stronger wines of Portugal and Spain. They persevered,
therefore, in their efforts to introduce French wines into England on a large scale, convinced that the English public would
inevitably learn in time to appreciate their superiority if it
could obtain them at a moderate price. The fact that many
departments of France continued to prefer cider or beer to
wine was ignored, or the analogy to the English position was
not perceived. Even the manufacturers of the cheap and sour
wines of the Midi hoped fondly to introduce their product into
England, and complained loudly when they found that the
duties of the Treaty of 1860 favored the light wines of Bordeaux
and discriminated against the *vins ordinaires* because of their
high alcoholic content. The French wine industry remained
convinced that the English would become drinkers of wine in
good time if only they could be induced to admit French wine
freely. They could see only the financial problem, that England had virtually prohibitive duties on wines and other alcoholic liquors. They thought that through diplomatic negotiations
the British Government could be persuaded to repeal these
duties or reduce them to a point where they would no longer
exclude French wines and spirits. Neither they nor the French
Government recognized the fact that the excise taxes in
England really did produce a large revenue for the Government. In fairness we must admit, however, that British legis-
lators, so keenly appreciative of the advantages of free trade in
most commodities, could see no virtue in that doctrine when
applied to wine and spirits. They were not willing to admit
even that moderate excise taxes and low tariff duties might so

increase the sale of wine and spirits of foreign origin in Great Britain that the amount of revenue secured by the Government would be immensely greater.

The short-lived treaty of commerce negotiated between England and France in 1786, on the eve of the French Revolution, showed what might be expected if a heavy reduction of the British duties on French wine could remain in operation over a longer period. The reduction granted by England amounted to approximately 50 per cent [1] and resulted in a great increase in the shipments of wine from France. Dupont de Nemours, in a public letter written before the outbreak of the French Revolution, said that the increase in French exports of both wines and spirits to England was enormous, as proved by the records of the chamber of commerce of Bordeaux, which would indicate that the increase of exports consisted chiefly of the light clarets and *sauternes* of the Gironde.[2] Another writer based his estimate on the total annual consumption of wine in England between 1777 and 1792 and wrote that he found that the proportion of French wines rose from 2.6 per cent to 8.4 per cent.[3] Chaptal, Napoleon's Minister of Commerce, stated that in his opinion the British reductions granted in the Treaty of 1786 had doubled the exports of French wines to England and trebled the shipments of spirits.[4] In making his plans for a new treaty in 1802, which was never negotiated because of the renewal of the war between France and England in the following year, Chaptal emphasized the importance of inducing England to repeal the increases in her wine duties voted after the beginning of the French Revolution, so that France would receive

---

[1] Auguste Arnauné, *Le Commerce extérieur et les tarifs de douane* (Paris, 1911), p. 103. From 2.61 francs per liter to 1.21 francs. These figures are clearly for wines shipped in barrels, which were usually charged a lower rate than when shipped in bottles. They evidently include the British excise tax of 17 guineas per barrel.

[2] M. F. Dumas, *Étude sur le traité de commerce de 1786 entre la France et l'Angleterre* (Toulouse, 1904), p. 160.

[3] Arnauné, *op. cit.*, p. 106.

[4] Jean A. C. Chaptal, " *Un Projet de traité de commerce avec l'Angleterre sous le Consulat*," Revue d'économie politique, VI (February, 1893), 83–98. The writer is the grandson of Napoleon's minister.

again the favorable rates granted in 1786.[5] Scanty as this evidence is, it shows that a marked decrease in the British duties under the treaty negotiated by Eden and Rayneval had proved a great stimulus to French exports. While England had continued to prefer the stronger wines of Spain and Portugal, she showed that she could absorb a much greater quantity of French wines and spirits.

During the period between 1815 and 1849, when England was changing from high protection to practically free trade, further reductions in the British duties on spirits were made, although they were slight in comparison with the reductions made on most other articles in the British tariff. The Act of June 26, 1849, reduced the duty on French spirits from 619 to 412 francs per hectoliter, which resulted in an increase of French shipments of 50 per cent.[6] England had already become the principal foreign market for such spirits. No reduction affecting French wines was made, although England's almost complete adoption of free trade and her repeal of the Navigation Acts greatly stimulated commerce between the two countries and French exports of wines to England increased somewhat as a result. Yet the situation remained discouraging for the French Government and wine merchants.

Herbet, the French Consul General in London, wrote to the French Minister of Foreign Affairs in 1853 [7] that the increase in the consumption of French wines in England had not kept pace with the increase in the British population. He felt that the principal reason for this was the very high duties on all wines in the British tariff. He stated that a contributing factor was the decrease in the income of the aristocracy following the repeal of the Corn Laws in 1846, which made the economy secured through the consumption of wines of greater strength seem a matter of importance. It would be interesting if Herbet gave some evidence in support of his conclusion that the British

---

[5] *Ibid.*, p. 95.
[6] Arch. Nat., F 12–2684. Report of the Ministry of the Interior, Division of Foreign Trade, to the Minister of Foreign Affairs, November 17, 1852.
[7] February 11. See Arch. Nat., F 12–2684.

aristocracy was impoverished to an appreciable extent by the reforms of 1846. But even if this statement seems to be of doubtful validity, Herbet's recommendations to his government for future action were sound. He wrote that the high duties had prevented all British classes below the aristocracy from becoming familiar with French wines, and that even the nobility knew only the wines of Champagne and the Gironde. He stated that only a reduction of the British duty on French wines to a figure below one shilling per gallon would make it possible for the middle class in England to drink them. But he saw no prospect of England's consenting to so drastic a reduction; in fact, he doubted whether the British Government was prepared to consider any decrease of the wine duties, because it feared a decrease would result in a large loss of revenue for which there would be no compensation through equivalent concessions from France for the benefit of British goods. In the main-tenance of the high tariff on wines and spirits, the British Government, in Herbet's opinion, would be supported by the English liquor trade with its virtual monopoly of the home market and the large amount of its capital required because of the heavy excise tax and the high cost of licenses to sell liquor. Finally, there was no popular interest in England in the question of obtaining wine cheaply; in other words, there was no prospect of starting an agitation like that of the Anti-Corn Law League for cheap bread.

The drastic reduction of the British duties on French wines and spirits was certain to be one of the principal demands made by France in the negotiations that resulted in the Treaty of 1860. Chevalier requested it, as we have seen, in his inter-view with Gladstone on October 16, 1859, when he began the negotiations on his own initiative. He was strongly supported by Cobden, who wished to see as many of the French wines as possible admitted at a duty of one shilling per gallon. Glad-stone approved of a big reduction, but as Chancellor of the Exchequer he was troubled by the prospect of a considerable loss of revenue. Furthermore, he was not willing to consider a change in the traditional taxation of wines and spirits for revenue.

This meant that a low duty on all wines could not be granted, because of the fear that spirits, which were taxed at a much higher rate than wines in England, might be smuggled in as wines. Hence, the British Government insisted on keeping the old system of classifying wines according to their alcoholic content. In the case of French wines this meant that the new duties granted would favor the light clarets and *sauternes* of the Gironde and would discriminate against the stronger wines of Burgundy, and still more against the strong but cheap *vins ordinaires* of the Midi. The following schedule of duties was embodied in the treaty signed on January 23, 1860: [8] Up to 15 degrees proof spirit according to the Sykes hydrometer, one shilling per gallon, or 27.51 francs per hectoliter. From 15 to 26 degrees proof spirit by the Sykes hydrometer, one shilling and sixpence per gallon, or 41.27 francs per hectoliter. From 26 to 40 degrees proof spirit by the Sykes hydrometer, two shillings per gallon, or 55.03 francs per hectoliter. These rates applied to wine in casks or barrels. If wine was imported in bottles it must pay in all cases two shillings per gallon. The same rate of two shillings would also be charged on wine in casks or barrels unless entered at certain specified ports in Great Britain.

After the ratification of the French treaty, in February, 1860, the British Government took advantage of Article IX permitting an increase of the duties on French wines and spirits if the British excise tax was increased. In August, 1860, therefore, the duties on French wines were raised slightly and the classification modified as follows: [9] Up to 18 degrees, the duty was one shilling per gallon, or 27.51 francs per hectoliter. From 18 to 26 degrees, the duty was one shilling and ninepence per gallon, or 48.15 francs per hectoliter. From 26 to 40 degrees, the duty was two shillings and elevenpence per gallon, or 80.25 francs per hectoliter. As before, these rates applied to wine in casks or barrels only. Wine in bottles was now to pay two shillings and fivepence per gallon instead of two shillings.

This revision of the British tariff duties, while raising most of

[8] Article VI.
[9] *Economist*, August 11, 1860.

them, made the classification somewhat more liberal, particularly for the class of wine paying the lowest duty, where the limit of alcoholic content was raised from 15 to 18 degrees. This concession did not, however, satisfy most of the French wine growers who were opposed to the whole British system of classification on the basis of alcoholic content because it favored the wines of the Gironde as compared with those of Burgundy, or the *vins ordinaires* of the Midi, since the light clarets and *sauternes* of the region about Bordeaux came within the first class under the British system and consequently paid a duty considerably lower than that paid by the wines of Burgundy or the south, which came chiefly within the second class. The French Government found that no objection to the amount of the British duties was made in the letters and petitions it received from organizations of wine merchants.[10] They protested only against the advantage given the merchants of Bordeaux. The French Government itself appears to have found the British rates reasonable, but protests from Burgundy and the south continued to come in, and Cobden stated openly that he considered England morally bound by verbal promises to give a duty of only one shilling per gallon on most French wines.[11] Consequently, the Emperor's ministers thought that there might be a chance of persuading the British to lower their rates or change their classification so as to admit most French wines under the lowest duty. England was asked in the autumn of 1861 to grant a uniform duty on all French wines, but was informed that France would not accept a high rate and would like to see the new duty as low as one shilling per gallon.[12] It soon became clear, however, that the British Government was not prepared to

[10] Arch. Nat., F 12-2684. Memorandum of the Ministry of Commerce, Division of Foreign Trade, September 10, 1860.

[11] Cobden to Russell, November 11, 1860. F. O., 97-207. The reply by Lord John's secretary was dated December 27.

[12] Arch. Nat., F 12-6220. Russell to Comte de Flahault, French ambassador, September 13, 1861; French Minister for Foreign Affairs to Minister of Commerce (Rouher), September 27, and the reply, October 29, 1861; Minister for Foreign Affairs to Minister of Commerce, December 4, and the reply, December 13, 1861.

grant a uniform duty on French wines unless the rate was high. Since that would have injured the wine merchants of Bordeaux without helping those of other parts of the country, the French Government dropped the negotiations.

The effect of the reduction in the British duties on French wines under the Treaty of 1860 can be estimated only in a general way because of the lack of specific information regarding exports. We ought to have data regarding shipments of wine to England from the three principal districts producing wines of fine quality; namely, the Gironde, Burgundy, and Champagne; and also from the Midi as producer of the bulk of the *vins ordinaires*. Unfortunately, no complete figures are available from any of these districts, so that we are obliged to base such conclusions as can be reached on a few figures from the Gironde, and on a limited number of letters, petitions, and reports from various wine-growing regions in France. Such information is wofully inadequate, but even reasonably complete and reliable statistics would have to be interpreted with caution because of the great variation in the production of French vineyards in different years; while the exact effect of variations in production on exportation would be difficult to determine because wine of good quality is generally kept several years before being sold. A few statements seem to be justified, however, and we have very few figures regarding shipments to England. The exports from the Gironde to England were as follows: [13]

[13] Statistiques de la Douane: Commerce spéciale.

Year	*Vins ordinaires* in casks or other receptacles Hectoliters	*Vins ordinaires* in bottles Hectoliters	Year	*Vins ordinaires* in casks or other receptacles Hectoliters	*Vins ordinaires* in bottles Hectoliters
1850	8,027	4,903	1871	146,924	30,285
1851	9,255	5,655	1872	136,724	34,794
1852	10,174	4,970	1873	186,708	32,182
1853	10,548	6,337	1874	155,454	45,926
1854	14,922	5,784	1875	160,325	37,207
1855	11,719	4,843	1876	212,940	35,809
1856	12,176	7,831	1877	227,796	47,116
1857	16,485	7,643	1878	156,099	40,892
1858	12,610	6,993	1879	190,208	49,552
1859	19,413	9,136	1880	223,919	58,030
1860	41,439	14,245	1881	218,633	40,459
1861	51,111	9,799	1882	180,650	42,568
1862	45,641	9,018	1883	173,404	41,645
1863	50,303	12,298	1884	171,723	36,390
1864	59,999	11,508	1885	185,068	38,316
1865	68,365	9,887	1886	173,042	39,066
1866	106,092	14,009	1887	152,852	31,913
1867	99,565	18,528	1888	144,506	28,994
1868	143,262	19,552	1889	156,736	31,541
1869	127,883	23,514	1890	179,898	31,900
1870	151,963	28,405			

For the whole of France the exports to England were:

Year	Hectoliters [14]
1858	44,000
1859	66,000
1860	132,000
1861	118,000
1862	124,000
1863	134,000
1864	157,000

The wines consumed in England have been estimated by Professor Arnauné from the several countries as follows: [15]

[14] F. Convert, "La Viticulture et la vinification, 1800–1870; la viticulture après 1870, en crise phylloxérique," *Revue de viticulture* (September, 1899 — November, 1900), p. 580.

[15] Arnauné, *op. cit.*, p. 255.

	1859 Percentage	1880 Percentage	1885 Percentage
France	9.5	41.9	40.4
Portugal	27.8	12.8	21.0
Spain	39.6	30.3	28.4
Others	23.0	10.0	10.2

Incomplete as these figures are they indicate that French exports of wine to England increased greatly after the signature of the Treaty of 1860. When the French Republic in the years following 1875 was considering the revision of its general tariff, it consulted the various chambers of commerce regarding the renewal of the treaty with England and of the similar treaties with other countries that had been negotiated shortly afterwards. Bordeaux reported that since 1860 British consumption of her wines had increased tenfold[16] and Châlons-sur-Saône, representing the district of Burgundy, reported a similar increase.[17] The increase in the exports from Bordeaux is not surprising because the Treaty of 1860, as has been mentioned, discriminated in favor of the light wines of the Gironde; but the Burgundian wine merchants had protested with some warmth against the higher duties levied on their product in England, and had induced the French Government in the autumn of 1861 to ask vainly for a further reduction. Hence the statement from Châlons that Burgundian exports had increased greatly, despite the continued discrimination in the British tariff, is significant. While we have little other evidence from Burgundy, the complete absence of further complaints regarding British duties after 1860 seems sufficient confirmation of the statement from Châlons.

Montpellier, the principal center of the Midi, where most of the *vins ordinaires* were produced, reported in 1877, as well as in 1870, that there had been no appreciable increase in the shipments of the cheaper French wines to England.[18] Her mer-

[16] Arch. Nat., F 12–6196, May 2, 1877. Chamber of Commerce of Châlons to Minister of Commerce.

[17] *Ibid.*, July 28, 1877.

[18] Arch. Nat., F 12–6160. The Chamber of Commerce of Montpellier and the Société d'Agriculture de l'Hérault sent a petition to the Minister of Commerce, January 16, 1870, on behalf of two hundred and fifty-four communes in the Department of Hérault. See also F 12–6196, Chamber of Commerce of Montpellier to the Minister of Commerce, April 15, 1877.

chants blamed the high British duties on strong wines for the lack of expansion of their trade, but we may properly doubt whether under the most favorable tariff duties England would ever have consumed large quantities of *vins ordinaires*. It seems clear, therefore, that the Treaty of 1860, while not opening the British market to the cheap wines of the south, did cause a notable increase in French exports to England of the finer wines with which the English were already familiar. We have evidence of this for the wines of Bordeaux and Burgundy, and it seems safe to assume it for the wines of Champagne. But it is equally clear that the stubborn British continued to like the stronger wines of Spain and Portugal, as well as their own native beverages of whiskey, beer, and gin; and that no treaty could have changed them into a nation of drinkers of wine.

The devotion of the bulk of the French people to their national beverage never varied, but the supply provided by the bounty of nature and the care of the wine merchants varied greatly from year to year. Changes in rainfall or temperature frequently affected seriously the size of the crop of grapes or the flavor of their juice, particularly in the case of the wines of fine quality of the Gironde, Burgundy, and Champagne. Such variations caused extreme movements of prices, so that frequently the wine merchants had to suffer heavy losses. Those producing the *vins ordinaires*, which represented at least three quarters of the annual crop, were more fortunate, for, while their prices were always low, they were pretty steady because variations in flavor were not great and changes in temperature and rainfall occurred less frequently in the districts where the bulk of those wines was produced. The most extreme cases of variation in the size of the crop were not the result of the weather, however, but of a number of diseases of the vines, the most important of which were *oïdium*, which was very destructive for a few years, and phylloxera, which never cut the whole crop down as much in any one year, but which lasted for many years and, therefore, caused far greater havoc. These diseases injured all the vines in France, although phylloxera was probably felt most in the departments of the Midi producing the *vins ordinaires*. This disease is of particular interest to us in our study of the commercial policy of France after 1860, because the prolonged diminution of the wine crop for which it was responsible was one of the main reasons why the wine merchants finally deserted the cause of free trade about 1890. The following table [19] showing the acreage planted in vines and the size of the crop from 1850 to 1903 illustrates the effects of both *oïdium* and phylloxera, as well as of variations in weather. The contrast between the relative constancy of the acreage and the extreme variations in production is striking.

Year	Area planted (1,000 hectares)	Production (1,000 hectares)	Importation	Exportation
			Commerce Spécial in thousand hectoliters	
1850	2,182	45,266		1,911
1851	2,180	39,429		2,269
1852	2,159	28,636		2,439
1853	2,169	22,662		1,976
1854	2,173	10,824		1,330
1855	2,175	15,175		1,214
1856	2,170	21,294		1,274
1857	2,180	35,410		1,124
1858	2,184	53,919		1,619
1859	2,173	29,891		2,519
1860	2,205	39,558	183	2,020
1861	2,220	29,738	251	1,857
1862	2,236	37,110	121	1,893
1863	2,274	51,372	103	2,084
1864	2,256	50,653	120	2,336
1865	2,294	68,943	99	2,868
1866	2,288	63,838	81	3,273
1867	2,315	38,869	203	2,591
1868	2,332	50,110	395	2,806
1869	2,350	71,376	378	3,063
1870	2,238	53,538	127	2,866
1871	2,369	56,901	148	3,319
1872	2,373	50,823	518	3,429

[19] Étienne Antonelli, *Protection de la viticulture* (Paris, 1905), p. 265.

Year	Area planted (1,000 hectares)	Production (1,000 hectares)	Importation	Exportation
			Commerce Spécial in thousand hectoliters	
1873	2,381	35,716	654	3,981
1874	2,447	63,075	681	3,232
1875	2,421	83,836	292	3,731
1876	2,370	41,847	676	3,331
1877	2,347	56,405	707	3,102
1878	2,296	48,721	1,603	2,795
1879	2,241	25,770	2,938	3,017
1880	2,209	29,677	7,219	2,488
1881	2,070	34,139	7,839	2,572
1882	2,105	30,886	7,357	2,618
1883	2,096	36,029	8,980	3,093
1884	2,041	34,781	8,115	2,470
1885	1,991	28,536	8,182	2,580
1886	1,959	25,063	11,011	2,704
1887	1,944	24,333	12,277	2,402
1888	1,844	30,102	12,064	2,118
1889	1,818	23,224	10,470	2,166
1890	1,817	27,416	10,830	2,162
1891	1,763	30,140	12,278	2,049
1892	1,783	29,082	9,400	1,845
1893	1,793	50,070	5,985	1,569
1894	1,767	39,053	4,492	1,721
1895	1,747	26,688	6,356	1,696
1896	1,728	44,656	8,818	1,788
1897	1,689	32,351	7,529	1,774
1898	1,707	32,282	8,625	1,636
1899	1,698	47,908	8,466	1,651
1900	1,730	67,353	5,217	1,736
1901	1,735	57,964	3,708	1,957
1902	1,733	39,884	4,295	1,981
1903	1,689	35,402	5,874	1,726

Phylloxera, the worst of the diseases that attacked the vines of France, was caused by a small parasite, a kind of aphis that appeared in several different forms. The first form, *Phylloxera gallicola*, lived on the leaves of the vines and caused the formation of galls, which did not inflict serious damage. But from it came a second form, *Phylloxera radicola*, which took to the roots of the vines and multiplied there with great rapidity, killing the vines. From this form of phylloxera living on the root there came occasionally a small number of females which developed wings which enabled them to fly long distances to lay their eggs, thus spreading the disease with fearful efficiency. Phylloxera was first reported in 1863 at Roquemaure in the Department of Gard, one of the most important of the regions producing the *vins ordinaires*.[20] It is believed to have been brought over in the roots of vines from America, which had been imported at the time of the epidemic of *oïdium* between 1850 and 1855.[21] After the first appearance of phylloxera, it was reported occasionally from scattered points in the Mediterranean plain or the Gironde until after 1875, when it seems to have spread more rapidly and to have caused widespread havoc. Various remedies were tried such as sulphate of carbon or sulphocarbonate of potash introduced into the soil where they liberated a gas deadly to the insect; but they were difficult and costly to apply, and the result was often doubtful. The flooding of the vineyards was found equally unsatisfactory, certainly as a general remedy, and it was finally determined that the only adequate remedy was the importation of American plants whose roots were immune to the attacks of the insect.[22] This remedy required much time to apply and the disease continued to spread through the country, attacking Champagne as late as 1890, and the Meuse and Moselle region in 1896.[23]

As the table given above indicates, the decline in the production of the French vineyards caused by phylloxera was never as great in any one year as had been that caused by *oïdium*, but it was spread over a period of many years. From 1877 to 1900 the production of wine in France reached 50,000,000 hectoliters only once, and in most years the total production scarcely

[20] Convert, *op. cit.*, p. 662.

[21] Henri Sempé, *Le Régime économique du vin* (Paris, 1898), p. 14.

[22] Théophile Malvezin, *Histoire du commerce de Bordeaux, depuis les origines jusqu'à nos jours* (4 vols., Bordeaux, 1892), IV, 339.

[23] Sempé, *op. cit.*, p. 20.

reached 30,000,000. The wine merchants, therefore, had to go through a prolonged period of depression at just the time when other agricultural industries in France were clamoring for protection against the competition of American wheat and meat brought to Europe in ever increasing quantities through the opening up of the west in the United States, and through the declining cost of ocean shipping. Another cause of depression in the French wine industry, which our table shows, was the growth of the importation of wine from foreign countries, which attracted attention about 1878 and became serious two years later. Italy sent considerable quantities of wine, but chiefly of the finer qualities which were so different from the fine wines of France that their competition was not a very serious factor; but Spain sent large quantities of wine that was both cheap and strong and which, therefore, competed with the *vins ordinaires* of southern France, for it could either be drunk as wine or, because of its high alcoholic content, could replace French wine as raw material for French liqueurs and other spirits.[24] By 1888 Algeria also was shipping large quantities of cheap wine.[25] As the *vins ordinaires* were produced on a large scale in southern France, and on a smaller scale in many other parts of the country, there was an excellent field provided for protectionist propaganda. It is true that the serious competition of foreign wines with the French was in only a slight degree the result of the lowering of the French tariff under the Second Empire. It was essentially a new problem for the wine merchants and the French Government in 1880. No country had hitherto contested successfully the supremacy of France in the production and sale of wine. Now the French industry was assailed by the combination of phylloxera, which cut down production until the home crop could not meet the demands of French consumers, and of the flood of imported foreign wines, made possible chiefly by the low cost of transportation resulting from the development of railroads and ocean shipping. Cheap transportation, which had brought the growers of *vins ordinaires*

[24] Sempé, *op. cit.*, p. 185.
[25] *Ibid.*, p. 192.

more than twenty years of extraordinary prosperity, and which had aided also the producers of the finer wines, now became a means of bringing comfort to the thirsty French consumer, but acute distress to the wine industry of France. It is no wonder that that industry gave way under the assaults of disease and foreign competition and that it joined in the wholesale attack which destroyed the weakened system of the commercial treaties negotiated under the Second Empire.

CHAPTER XV

THE ATTEMPT OF PRESIDENT THIERS TO RESTORE HIGH PROTECTION IN FRANCE

THE Anglo-French Treaty of Commerce of 1860 was an economic reform of very considerable importance, for it compelled French manufacturers to meet the competition of the country that then led the world both in trade and in most of the industries using machinery driven by power. It forced the rapid introduction of a considerable amount of such machinery in France and a general improvement in methods of production and marketing. Unfortunately, however, the Treaty was forced upon the country practically without warning, by a despotic sovereign whose power had passed its zenith. Napoleon III cannot be held responsible for the American Civil War which broke out before all the clauses of the commercial treaty had become operative and brought suffering and loss to French industry and trade for many years; but he did undertake the disastrous expedition to Mexico in 1862, and then embarked on a series of diplomatic misadventures culminating in the war with Prussia, which brought defeat and humiliation to his country. Sir Louis Mallet, who had assisted Cobden at Paris in 1860 and never wavered in his defense of the policy then inaugurated, has left us a good summary of the effects of Napoleon's incompetence on this important economic reform of his reign. He wrote in 1871:

"Owing to the lamentable inconsistencies and shortcomings of the Imperial Government, the economic régime introduced in 1860 and which required a systematic policy of peace to enable it to take root, although attended with very remarkable success, had never been cordially accepted, either by the political classes or by the country at large, and when, from a combination of inevitable causes, the Imperial Government became unpopular, the selfish interests which had always protested against commercial reforms, acquired sufficient strength to present a formidable Parliamentary resistance to the Government in the maintenance and further prosecution of the Treaty system." [1]

Circumstances seemed favorable for an attack on the commercial policy of the Imperial Government in 1868. In addition to the American Civil War, the conflict between Austria and Prussia in 1866, and troubles in several of the republics of South America, which had interrupted trade by cutting off valuable markets for manufactures or supplies of essential raw materials, French industry and trade were depressed by the growing feeling of insecurity in Europe.

Furthermore, the rapid extension of the use of machinery and the improvements in transportation had contributed even more than the political factors mentioned to cause industrial depression by stimulating overproduction and speculation. Such economic factors, however, are difficult to explain and have rarely served to inspire orators in political assemblies. It was much easier to attribute industrial and commercial distress to foreign competition, made possible by what orthodox protectionists in France considered the criminal folly of an increasingly unpopular government. The time was approaching when the treaty of commerce with England could be denounced, an action devoutly desired by all opponents of free trade, because upon that agreement rested the whole system of treaties that bound together the principal states of western Europe. If, then, the Treaty of 1860 should be destroyed the whole network of commercial treaties would collapse and France would be free to regulate her own tariff. With such issues at stake it was no wonder that loyal protectionists roused themselves to use the weapons that destiny and the Emperor had thrust into their hands.

The attack on the commercial policy of the Second Empire was conducted by leaders of unusual vigor and ability. Thiers had been prominent in politics for more than thirty years, both as a deputy and as a leading minister of Louis Philippe. He hated Napoleon III and all his works, both political and economic, and opposed him and his government at every oppor-

---

[1] F. O., 146–1615. Memorandum of October 17, 1871.

tunity. Equally ardent in the cause of protection, and also
the possessor of personal ability in debate, was his lieutenant,
Pouyer-Quertier, a wealthy cotton manufacturer of Normandy.
Behind these leaders were large groups of manufacturers eager
for the return of high protection and large profits and ready to
write pamphlets, sign petitions, vote in the Corps Législatif,
or organize demonstrations by their workmen, according as they
were directed. The Emperor, who had sent them word in
January, 1860, that, if they organized strikes against the English
treaty, they, and not their laborers, would go to jail, was now
a sick man and increasingly unpopular. There seemed every
prospect of success if only the protectionists showed persistence
and determination.

In May, 1868, Thiers and Pouyer-Quertier in the Corps
Législatif asked permission to interpellate the Government on
the economic régime. Their request was granted and the unusual opportunity thus offered to criticize the Emperor's ministers and policies was fully used, the discussion covering not only
the tariff, but also railroad construction and administration,
financial speculation, taxation, and even foreign policy. The
Government was sustained by a large majority, as was inevitable,
for it was not yet responsible to the Corps Législatif and had
not yet allowed free elections.[2]   But an impression had been
made by the protectionist speeches and by the fact that the
Government had permitted the discussion, and the attack was
renewed at frequent intervals. Before the end of 1869 Thiers felt
strong enough to seek the denunciation of the Treaty of 1860
by France, and the complete revision of the French tariff, and
there seemed a good chance of his forcing the consent of the
Government to a modification of the Treaty. The Emperor
actually resigned his constitutional right to sign treaties without
the sanction of the Corps Législatif[3] and announced that the
Government had directed the Conseil Supérieur du Commerce

[2] Auguste Arnauné, *Le Commerce extérieur et les tarifs de douane* (Paris, 1911),
p. 276.
[3] Adolph Beer, *Allgemeine Geschichte des Welthandels* (5 vols. in 2. Vienna,
1860–84), II, pp. 38–39.   Also F. O., 27–1824.   Lord Lyons to the Foreign
Office, January 30, 1870.

to begin a formal investigation of the economic régime of France. This did not satisfy the protectionists, who realized that these concessions showed that the Imperial Government was afraid of them. Pouyer-Quertier, Schneider, the head of the great Creusot iron works, and other leaders refused to serve on the Conseil Supérieur on the ground that its proceedings would be controlled by the Government through the numerous officials that sat on the council by virtue of the positions they held, so that a fair judgment as between free trade and protection could not be expected. Again the Government yielded and consented to an investigation under the direction of a committee chosen by the new parliament that was to be freely elected.[4] When this committee of thirty-six was chosen in February, 1860, it was composed of only twelve declared free traders, of seventeen moderate protectionists, and of seven extreme protectionists. The free traders had succeeded in electing their leaders, de Forcade la Roquette, the former Minister of the Interior, and Jules Simon and Johnston of Bordeaux, but their representation was far smaller than was justified by their numbers in the Chamber because the protectionists had insisted that they would not accept the results of an investigation directed by a majority of free traders, on the ground that such an investigation could not be impartial.[5] The Enquête was never finished because of the outbreak of the Prussian War in July, but the hearings that had been held since the middle of March showed that the protectionists were very strong both in parliament and in the country. It is virtually certain that, had the Empire survived the war with Prussia, England would have been asked to consent to the revision of the Treaty of 1860 in the direction of higher protection.

France emerged from the war in the spring of 1871 with a weak government, a crushing war indemnity, a huge deficit, and a feeling of bitterness and humiliation that made her economic and financial problems seem almost insoluble. At the head of the

[4] F. O., 27–1768. Lord Lyons to the Foreign Office, November 23 and 26, 1869.

[5] *Ibid.*, 27–1825. Lord Lyons to the Foreign Office, February 15, 1870.

new government stood Thiers with the title of Chief of the Executive Power. He had led the struggle against the Germans after the capture of Napoleon III at Sedan until it was seen to be hopeless; he was now negotiating the best peace terms that he could; and he was striving to restore order throughout the country and to maintain peace between the rival political groups in the National Assembly until a form of government could be found that would be acceptable to the majority of the French people. The services Thiers rendered his country were great and despite the passions of politics they were appreciated by the National Assembly, which kept him in power after his political opinions had ceased to command its general support.

One of the main problems confronting Thiers was the raising of taxes to fill the deficit and pay the war indemnity, so that France could balance her budget and free her territory from military occupation. The amount needed was large and the Government attempting to raise it was weak, so that taxes must be found that would cause the least amount of resentment. Almost inevitably the choice of a tax that should raise a considerable part of the funds desired fell upon the tariff. Statesmen of all ages have used the tariff for revenue because the amount that could be obtained was frequently large and because few people felt the burden, since they paid the tax in the form of increased prices of commodities consumed and did not realize that they were paying a tax to the Government. The choice of Thiers and of his minister of finance, Pouyer-Quertier, therefore, seemed a wise one. It appeared that a large amount of revenue could thus be raised almost painlessly. Furthermore, a considerable increase of tariff duties was likely to be popular in a country that was still largely protectionist in sentiment. But a grave problem was created by this plan to raise a large part of the increased revenue through the tariff. France was bound by the network of commercial treaties, of which the English Treaty of 1860 was the foundation, with respect to most of the duties that could be increased. She would have to negotiate for the modification of these treaties or else denounce them a year before their expiration, at the risk of injuring her trade through reprisals, and possibly also her political relations. Neither remedy could be applied quickly, for only the treaties with England and Belgium could be denounced in 1871, and the need for increased revenue was urgent. The difficulty of raising duties was great, therefore, because of the diplomatic complications that were almost certain to be encountered. It was rendered even greater by the fact that in all the countries of Europe Thiers was known to be an ardent protectionist. He had defended the old system of prohibitions before 1860 and he had done his best to modify or destroy the whole system of commercial treaties at the end of the Second Empire. England, the most important country with whom negotiations must be undertaken, was devoted to free trade as a matter of principle. Could Thiers convince her that he wished to raise the French tariff for revenue and not for protection? And was that really his desire? Had he abandoned his life-long love of protection, or was he simply seeking another opportunity to undo the liberal work of the Second Empire?

In March, 1871, Thiers told the British ambassador, Lord Lyons, that the French Government did not plan to reverse the imperial policy of moderate protection; nor did it desire to denounce the Treaty of 1860. France wished only to modify the details of her treaty with England. He reminded Lord Lyons that some modification of the Treaty would have been asked for even by the Second Empire if it had lasted a few months longer. Later in the spring he spoke of his liking for the traditional British policy of letting each nation regulate its own commercial legislation, and he intimated that he hoped France would recover her freedom to do this. In short, he had already reached the point where he was willing to show the British ambassador that, in his opinion, France should get rid of the whole system of commercial treaties. He continued, however, to speak of the importance of making all changes by mutual agreement, and of the overwhelming need of more revenue, as if that were the principal reason why France should modify her commercial treaty with England. Yet, as early as July, he called attention to the serious errors he considered had been made in calculating many of the duties in the tariff conventions that supplemented the Anglo-French Treaty of 1860. Although protection was a small part of his scheme he wished to correct such errors and to see that in the future French manufacturers did not suffer from unfair competition, such as that endured by Roubaix at the hands of Bradford. Such a statement was neither tactful nor accurate. Lord Lyons knew, and Thiers should have known, that the manufacturers of Roubaix had been able to sell their cloths in the very streets of Bradford itself. But this was not all, for Thiers went on to show Lyons that he had sought an early agreement with England chiefly because her devotion to free trade was so well known that any increases of duties that she accepted would not be rejected as unduly protective by other states having treaties with France, such as Belgium and Switzerland. Thiers was to learn later that none of the treaty states were prepared to consider the modification of their agreements with France. But more important to us at this point is the fact that Thiers was showing more clearly every day that the need for raising the tariff in order to get more revenue for France was far less important in his eyes than the need for more protection. And he was expressing these views with amazing frankness to the accredited representative of the state in Europe that most strongly disliked protection.

In August, 1871, Thiers went a step farther. On the 10th, he sent for the British ambassador and informed him that England must choose between the modifications of the tariff that he had proposed and the denunciation of the Treaty of 1860. He even told Lord Lyons that he suspected that the French free trade party had been plotting against him with the British Government in London. If England should choose the denunciation of the Treaty, said Thiers, she need not expect to be treated by France as a most favored nation. Rather, as the strongest rival of France, she must expect to receive fewer concessions than other states, and the French Government would see to it that in the future goods being brought from French colonies to the mother country were carried directly to French ports, so that they should not pass through English warehouses. Before ending this tirade Thiers told Lyons that he had always thought the Treaty of 1860 disastrous for France, although beneficial to England, and that he had always wanted its denunciation. The position thus taken by the Chief of the Executive Power in an interview with the British ambassador was maintained publicly when, in December, 1871, Thiers asked the National Assembly to denounce the Treaty of Commerce with England. He could have denounced it himself by virtue of the powers he held under the existing laws of France, but he wanted the support of the Assembly on this issue as expressed by a formal vote of denunciation. In his speech Thiers made no allusion to the need of France for more revenue, but said that the sole reason for the proposal made to England to modify the Treaty and for the present request to denounce it, was to secure adequate protection for French industries. He declared that the modification of the Treaty would not have promoted the best interests of France; that it would now be inconvenient; and that he had proposed it only to please Great Britain. Thus did Thiers develop his tariff policy, beginning with an ostensible attempt to raise more revenue for a country that seemed to be in danger of bankruptcy, and ending in a determined effort to destroy the treaty with England in the hope of giving French industries high protection.[6]

Let us consider now the commercial policy of England and the attitude of Gladstone and his Cabinet toward the Treaty of 1860 with France and the network of agreements that had been built upon it. It will be remembered that Gladstone had been a follower of Sir Robert Peel who had hoped to complete his work of lowering the British tariff by the conclusion of treaties that should open up more markets to British goods. When, in September, 1859, Cobden came to Hawarden to tell Gladstone of Michel Chevalier's plan for the conclusion of a treaty of commerce between England and France, Gladstone welcomed the suggestion, as he saw in it an opportunity to complete the work

[6] F. O., 27. Vols. 1883 and 1884. Lord Lyons to the Foreign Office. Dispatches No. 11 of March 6, 1871; No. 27 of May 12; No. 49 of June 20; No. 89 of July 21; and No. 112 of August 11.

of Peel. A month later he received Chevalier privately in his office in Downing Street and in a single conversation reached an agreement that became the basis of the treaty signed on January 23, 1860. Gladstone, who was then Chancellor of the Exchequer, was the principal advocate of the treaty in the Cabinet and its most powerful champion in the House of Commons.

In 1871, Gladstone, as Prime Minister, was in an even more favorable position to determine the commercial policy of England than he had been in 1860. But, since Cobden's death in 1865, opposition to commercial treaties had become strong in England and Gladstone had gone over to it.[7] His reception of the French proposals to modify the tariff of 1860 by raising many of the duties was, therefore, distinctly hostile, for he felt that France was asking England to continue restrictions on her freedom to regulate her own tariff and, in addition, formally to indorse the principle of protection, to which England had long been opposed. He understood perfectly that Thiers was really more interested in securing high protection for French industries than he was in obtaining more revenue through the tariff. In a memorandum which served to guide the Foreign Office in its negotiations with France Gladstone expressed his views regarding the Treaty of 1860 and the modifications of it which Thiers now desired to make. He said that, in 1860, there were many weighty arguments against the conclusion of such a treaty and he specified the following: (1) long experience had shown it was useless to make such treaties: (2) a government should always retain liberty of action regarding its revenue which, in England's case, meant the right to levy duties on wines, spirits, and the exportation of coal; (3) England, by concluding a treaty with France, would interfere in the purely internal struggle in that country between protectionists and free traders. England had negotiated the treaty because the arguments in favor of it seemed stronger. It was expected that other states would follow the example of France; that France herself would take

[7] K. J. Fuchs, *The Trade Policy of Great Britain and her Colonies since 1860* (London, 1905), p. 35.

further steps toward reducing her tariff still more, so that with the passage of time the tariffs of Europe would progressively decline to the great advantage of trade and the promotion of peace.

"How strangely is the situation now altered," wrote Gladstone. "The arguments against the Treaty. . . remain in their fullest force. The arguments for the Treaty are turned upside down. We are now avowedly asked to sign a retroactive instrument in order that, once more, other States may act in the same direction as France; but it is now in the direction of restriction and pressure, not of Free Trade. Are we not also asked to do what may induce or encourage France, hereafter, to ask of us further measures in the same sense? . . . By this hypothesis, France will, if we agree, stop short of what she thinks her own interests require. She will not do this in order to obtain an equivalent from us: for she is acting in the full belief that whatever happens she is sure on our side in fact of what she now holds by covenant. . . . She is really making this arrangement with us . . . to work through us on foreign Powers . . . and thus we shall still be liable to be represented to French Protectionists as standing between them and their interests. She will still be able to point to sacrifices (in her own estimation) which she will have made to please us. . . . In my opinion there is little to be done in attracting or estranging Thiers, who will simply drive bargains and these Jews' bargains. . . .

"In sum, we made in the case of the Treaty of 1860 a great and marked exception to a well established rule for what we thought well defined and very strong reasons. We seem by this means to have given considerable force to the Free Trade movement on the continent of Europe. When these powerful considerations are removed, and not only removed but reversed, is not our safest course to fall back upon our old basis, namely, that the cause of freedom in commerce will, as a rule, be most effectively advanced by leaving each nation to consider the subject in the light of its own interests alone? " [8]

The views of the British Government, as expressed by the Prime Minister, show us that the reaching of an agreement between France and England was certain to be difficult. England realized that France must secure more revenue in her time of need, but she was firmly opposed to protection. She was convinced that any substantial increase of French duties on British goods would cut down seriously her exports to France, and such evidence as we have indicates that her conviction was justified. It is more difficult to sympathize with the prevalent opinion in England that protection was stupid, if not positively

[8] F. O., 146–1615. Memorandum of October 3, 1871.

immoral. We may agree that in general free trade is wiser and based on sounder economic principles. Many people in France were prepared to admit that, but they found the English assumption of superior wisdom, if not of superior virtue, distinctly irritating. The British Government, becoming rapidly convinced that the real object of Thiers was not the increase of French revenue, but the restoration of high protection, took little interest in his proposals to modify the Treaty of 1860 and was not frightened by his threat to denounce it. England might have refused to negotiate at all if she had not feared that she might be placed at a disadvantage as compared with other nations in her trade with France. If the treaty lapsed without being replaced by another agreement England could not expect to be treated by France as a most favored nation. In addition, she lacked protection for her merchant marine engaged in the indirect or carrying trade, which was large and profitable. The Treaty of Navigation of 1826 gave national treatment only to ships engaged in the direct trade between England and France, while the Treaty of 1860 and its supplementary conventions scarcely touched on questions of navigation and shipping dues. England's fear of discrimination against her shipping and of being placed in a less advantageous position than other nations, such as Belgium and Germany, in the trade with France was a factor of importance in the Anglo-French negotiations. Without this factor it seems probable that England would have allowed Thiers to break off the negotiations entirely.

The efforts of Thiers to persuade or threaten England to agree quickly to a modification of the Treaty of 1860 were rendered extremely difficult by the problem of controlling the National Assembly. As in his attempts to bend England to his will, so in his efforts to push legislation through the French Assembly Thiers displayed neither skill nor tact. He introduced proposals that were certain to arouse bitter opposition and when that opposition declared itself he was prepared to make only unimportant concessions. He expected to dominate the National Assembly through his political prestige, and such slight successes as he won in his tariff policy were secured by this means.

In addition, he tried to persuade the Assembly that Great Britain was willing to modify the Treaty of 1860 and that all he needed to carry his measures was the vote by the Assembly of the necessary taxes and duties. At the same time he told England that the Assembly was behind him in his tariff policy and that the only obstacles to his obtaining the money France needed so badly and the protection that French industries required, were British slowness in negotiating and the insistence of Her Majesty's Government in haggling over details. Many months passed before the National Assembly realized that England disliked Thiers' proposals, but the British Government knew from the start how the Assembly felt about his desired taxes and duties on raw materials. Lord Lyons had a wide range of acquaintances among Frenchmen in public life and kept his Government accurately informed regarding the debates on tariff policy in the Assembly and the opinions of important persons outside that body. The knowledge of the disinclination of the National Assembly to follow Thiers in the methods by which he chose to attempt the restoration of high protection in France was certainly responsible for many of the delays in the Anglo-French negotiations.

On June 12, 1871, Thiers had his bill to meet the deficit in the French revenue introduced in the National Assembly. It was proposed to raise 488,000,000 francs, of which 244,000,000 were to be obtained by the following tariff duties: [9]

	Francs
Sugar from colonies and abroad........	114,000,000
Coffee.............................	20,000,000
Petroleum...........................	10,000,000
Textile raw materials.................	70,000,000
Other raw materials..................	100,000,000
Manufactured goods..................	10,000,000
Export duties.......................	15,000,000
Navigation dues.....................	5,000,000

The duties on sugar and coffee were not new, but merely

[9] E. Rausch, "*Französische Handelspolitik vom Frankfurter Frieden bis zur Tarifreform, 1882*," Staats- und socialwissenschaftliche Forschungen, XVIII (1900), 6.

increased existing rates. They aroused practically no opposition in the National Assembly and, together with duties on chicory, tea, cocoa, chocolate, various spices, wines, spirits, and tobacco, were passed on July 8, by a vote of 477 to 4.[10] On the other hand, the export duties which were to be levied on wine and other foods were rejected by the Budget Committee after appeals had been heard from wine merchants and other exporters, and the Government did not venture to bring them before the National Assembly as a whole in defiance of its Committee.[11]

The Government's proposal for navigation dues was received in a very different spirit. It was generally felt that the French merchant marine had not increased in recent years, while the building of ships in French ports had decreased considerably. There was undoubtedly ample justification for this belief that the French merchant marine was declining in comparison with that of other states. The protectionists in the National Assembly attributed this relative decline to the liberal legislation of the Second Empire. They seized upon Thiers' proposal to raise 5,000,000 francs from wharfage dues of 1 franc per ton on all ships entering French ports from foreign countries or the French colonies, and proceeded to build upon it a whole new system of protection for French shipping. The Budget Committee, reporting through Ancel of Havre on August 10, 1871,[12] recommended the revival of the old tax on the cargoes of ships entering under foreign flags and the increase of the tax on cargoes composed of goods which were not brought directly from the country that had produced them, but from warehouses in other countries. These taxes were known as the *surtaxes de pavillon* and the *surtaxes d'entrepôt*. The Government had not included such taxes in the bill of June 12, 1871, because it knew that they would cause diplomatic complications, but this did not trouble the National Assembly, which included them in the Act of January 30, 1872. The judgment of the Government was soon

---

[10] F. O., 27. Vol. 1883, Lord Lyons to the Foreign Office, July 9, 1871.
[11] Rausch, *op. cit.*, p. 8. Also Auguste Arnauné, *Le Commerce extérieur et les tarifs de douane* (Paris, 1911), p. 277.
[12] *Ibid.*

vindicated. The *surtaxes de pavillon et d'entrepôt* had been virtually abolished by the Act of May 19, 1866, which, with respect to these taxes, was to take effect in 1869,[13] and on December 11, 1866, a navigation treaty had been concluded with Austria on this new basis, which, through the most favored nation clause, was extended to most of the other states of Europe. France requested Austria to give up her privileges under the Treaty of 1866, but Austria, under pressure from Bismarck, refused. This meant that the surtaxes voted by the National Assembly could not be applied to the ships of most European states. But England was a notable exception. Under the Treaty of 1826 [14] British ships were to receive the same treatment as French ships if they came directly from a British port, which meant that these *surtaxes de pavillon et d'entrepôt* could not be levied on British ships engaged in the direct trade. Under the Convention of November 11, 1860, they could not be levied on either jute and cotton from India or on wool from Australia which had passed through the British warehouses; [15] but, with these exceptions, these surtaxes could be levied on British ships engaged in the indirect trade; that is, on ships which did not come to France directly from a British port. Under the Act of January 20, 1872, the *surtaxe de pavillon* was collected on the cargoes of many British ships, which placed them in a disadvantageous position as compared with the ships of most other European nations trading with France.

Most of the questions raised by this surtax were highly technical, but the expense and loss which the surtax inflicted upon British shipping interests and the apparent discrimination against England because she was almost the only important European nation to pay the tax were among the most important factors that led England to resume negotiations with Thiers

---

[13] Arnauné, *op. cit.*, p. 267.

[14] Lewis Hertslet, *A Complete Collection of the Treaties and Conventions, and Reciprocal Regulations at present subsisting between Great Britain and Foreign Powers and of the Laws, Decrees, Orders in Council, &c., concerning the same* [etc., etc.] (24 vols., London, 1827–1907), III, 123.

[15] Rausch, *op. cit.*, p. 12.

after he had denounced the Treaty of 1860 and to conclude with him the Treaty of November 5, 1872.

The heart of the bill of June 12, 1871, from Thiers' point of view, was the section imposing duties on textile and other raw materials and on manufactured goods. On textile raw materials it was proposed to levy duties of approximately 20 per cent ad valorem, while on other raw materials, such as hides, wood, oily seeds and fruits, and dyestuffs the duties were to be somewhat lower. The duties on manufactured goods entering France were to be imposed in compensation for those on raw materials and were to be refunded through drawbacks if the manufactures on which they had been levied were subsequently exported. It was through these duties on raw materials and manufactured goods that Thiers hoped to restore a considerable part of the protective system as well as to collect a large amount of revenue. Much of the cotton and wool used by France could thus be taxed, for the chief markets for those raw materials were Liverpool and London, while the compensatory duties on the cloths made from them would give French manufacturers in those industries some of the protection which Thiers thought they needed so badly. Nothing was said about protection when the bill was introduced, but everyone knew that "compensation" was then the favorite word in the protectionist vocabulary, the contention being that French manufacturers should be "compensated" for the various elements in the cost of production of their goods, virtually all of which were alleged to be dearer in France than in England.

One might have expected that these proposed duties would be voted by the National Assembly with enthusiasm because the majority of its members were protectionists. The imposition of these would also have destroyed one of the most important parts of the economic reform of 1860, the free admission of raw materials. But instead of receiving the proposal with enthusiasm the Assembly showed strong opposition. Many deputies feared that the duties on raw materials would increase greatly the cost of production of French manufacturers and operate to diminish both the production and consumption of the goods made from the materials thus taxed. The compensatory duties on manufactures were not considered high enough to give the desired protection, and it was thought rightly that the commercial treaties would prevent their collection. The Budget Committee made its report on August 31, through Casimir-Périer, who had been a staunch opponent of the Treaty of 1860 and was one of the owners of the coal mines of Anzin. Instead of 170,000,000 francs the Committee granted between 50,000,000 and 60,000,000 francs to be obtained through a uniform duty of 3 per cent levied on all raw materials not covered by the Act of July 8, 1871, on colonial goods, with the exception of coal and cereals. The Committee refused to recommend any drawbacks on the ground that they had led to serious abuses in the period before 1860. To overcome the deficit in the budget that would result from reducing the duties on raw materials the Committee proposed an income tax whose yield was estimated at 80,000,000 francs.[16] Shortly after receiving this report the National Assembly adjourned so that the Government could take no further action until December.

Thiers had begun talking to Lord Lyons about changes in the French tariff in the spring of 1871, but no official communication had been made either to the British ambassador or to Her Majesty's Government through the French ambassador in London, the Duc de Broglie, when the bill for taxing imported raw materials was introduced on June 12. Not until July 1 did Broglie call at the Foreign Office to inform Lord Granville that the new French duties would be for revenue only and that England would have to choose between negotiating regarding their amount and having France denounce the Treaty of 1860. On July 17 the duke called again and brought with him Ozenne, the director of the Bureau of Foreign Commerce, who evidently gave more information about the proposed French duties, which Lord Granville considered very high. No definite or complete proposals which could serve as an adequate basis for negotiation were made on either occasion.[17] We can understand that Thiers

[16] Rausch, *op. cit.*, p. 26.
[17] F. O., 27. Vol. 1882. Foreign Office to Lord Lyons, June 17, July 1, and July 17, 1871.

could not make such proposals when he did not know what duties the National Assembly would sanction, yet we can hardly be surprised at England's reluctance to negotiate a settlement without them. Thiers, however, was determined to have his way, and would not wait. He informed Lord Lyons that he wanted the negotiations completed before the British Parliament was prorogued or the National Assembly adjourned.[18]

In replying to the letter of its ambassador transmitting Thiers' request, the Foreign Office said that the Board of Trade would consult the chambers of commerce in Great Britain, but that they could not advise the British Government until France made the definite proposals which had been asked for in vain.[19] Thiers then threatened England with denunciation of the Treaty of 1860 and reprisals against British trade, hoping in this way to end the negotiations and present the National Assembly with a *fait accompli* that would make it easier to force through the bill for taxing raw materials. Lord Lyons advised his Government to ignore the threats of the French President and accept his rather vague proposals, on the condition that France agree to treat England as a most favored nation. In this way England could stop further increases of duties in the French tariff and could prevent the indefinite repetition of Thiers' maneuver.[20] Lyons thought she was entitled to such treatment, because, according to Article XI of the Treaty of Frankfort, France had promised to treat Germany as favorably as she treated England, Austria, Russia, Belgium, Holland, or Switzerland, which meant, of course, as a most favored nation.[21] This proposal was rejected by Thiers in a way that showed Lord Lyons was correct in fearing that the French demands would be renewed and probably raised in the future. The President said that he could not give England most favored nation treatment

[18] F. O. 27. Vol. 1883. Lord Lyons to the Foreign Office, July 25 and July 29, 1871; also Vol. 1884. Lord Lyons to the Foreign Office, August 1, 1871.

[19] *Ibid.* Vol. 1882. Foreign Office to Lord Lyons, July 29, 1871.

[20] *Ibid.* Vol. 1884. Lord Lyons to the Foreign Office. Nos. 112 and 113, August 11, 1871.

[21] *Ibid.*, and also Vol. 1883. Lord Lyons to the Foreign Office, May 14, 1871.

for an unlimited period because that would prevent him from increasing the French tariff in the future by compelling him, either to get the consent of all the other powers with whom France had commercial treaties, or to wait until those treaties had expired.[22]

The negotiations between France and England for the modification of the Treaty of 1860 broke down at this point. France had made written proposals,[23] but they were not complete and could not be because the Government was not certain as to the exact changes in the tariff which the National Assembly would authorize. As England quite naturally insisted on knowing just what increases in duties she would be asked to accept, a satisfactory agreement could not be reached. The French point of view was well expressed in a verbal note given Lord Granville by the Duc de Broglie on November 30,[24] in which he said that France had assumed that when England, after receiving the general French proposals in July, 1871, had asked for details, that she meant she had no objections to make to the main features of the proposals. Now that England, three months later, did make such fundamental objections, the French Government felt that she wished to break off negotiations. France maintained that her proposals did not constitute an attack on the principle of free trade, as England had alleged, since they called for only a few increases in duties. If the British Government would be willing in the future to take a fairer view of these questions, the French Government would renew the negotiations. In the meantime, it felt that its only course was to ask the Assembly for authority to denounce the Treaty of 1860. Granville replied that the British Cabinet felt that, if France could propose conditions that were quite different from the protection-

[22] *Ibid.* Vol. 1884. Lord Lyons to the Foreign Office, August 22, 1871.

[23] See especially F. O., 27. Vol. 1887. Memoranda of the Duc de Broglie to Lord Granville, July 18, August 4, and September 13, 1871; Note of Gavard, French chargé d'affaires, August 15, and replies to Lord Granville August 4, 5, and 21, 1871; also Vol. 1882. The Foreign Office to Lord Lyons, October 20, November 1 and November 2, 1871.

[24] *Ibid.* Vol. 1887. The note was written by de Rémusat, the French Minister of Foreign Affairs, at Versailles, November 15, 1871, but was not presented in London until November 30.

ist views of Thiers, the two governments might reach an
agreement; [25] but Broglie assured him that Thiers would not
change his views and that there was no chance of reaching an
agreement. Thiers obtained the sanction he sought from the
Assembly and denounced the Treaty of 1860 on March 15,
1872.[26]

We must now return to the National Assembly which resumed its session on December 4, 1871. Two bills for increasing
the French tariff were presented for its consideration. The first
was the report made by Casimir-Périer for the Budget Committee
on August 31, which proposed a uniform duty of 3 per cent on
raw materials which were not covered by the Act of July 8, 1871,
regarding colonial goods, with the exception of cereals and coal.
This bill was so bitterly attacked from all sides that it was never
brought to a vote. The second bill, brought in on December 9,
was virtually the same as that introduced by the Government on
June 12, and gave only a slight reduction in the amount of the
duties on raw materials. This bill was discussed after the Christ-
mas holidays, the debate lasting from January 10 to January 19,
when the National Assembly passed a resolution introduced by
Feray, the well-known linen manufacturer and ardent protectionist, which declared that the Government's bill should be
submitted for further consideration to a committee of fifteen
with instructions that it should not be approved if any other
means could be found to balance the French budget. Thiers
promptly resigned, but as the Assembly still had confidence in
him he was requested to remain in office, which he did until late
in the spring of 1873.[27]

A new bill providing for the collection of 126,000,000 francs
from duties on raw materials instead of 155,000,000 francs, the
amount named in the former bill, had been sent to the National
Assembly by Thiers only three days after his resignation as

[25] F. O. 27. Vol. 1934. The British Government sent a formal reply January 10,
1872, to the verbal note presented by de Broglie on November 30, 1871; but its
views are expressed most clearly in Vol. 1882, Foreign Office to Lord Lyons November 1 and 2, 1871, the latter note giving the views of Gladstone.

[26] *Ibid.* Vol. 1934. The Foreign Office to Lord Lyons, March 15, 1872.

[27] Arnauné, *op. cit.*, p. 283, and Rausch, *op. cit.*, p. 41.

president of the Republic, on January 20, had been refused. But even this amount seemed excessive to many deputies and some of the proposed duties were still high. The Assembly's Commission reported on May 10, after attempting to reach a compromise between high duties on raw materials with drawbacks on the exportation of manufactured goods made from them, and low duties without drawbacks. It was estimated that these duties would yield 93,000,000 francs when France had freed herself from all treaty engagements, but that the articles on which the duties could be imposed at once, without waiting for the expiration of treaties or their modification, would yield a revenue of only 42,000,000 francs. Thiers secured the promise of this small sum only through his great political prestige. It was quite clear that the majority of the National Assembly disliked the idea of duties on raw materials because they feared they would injure French trade and industry. Even that staunch protectionist, Pouyer-Quertier, who had been Minister of Finance since the opening of 1871, resigned in June, 1872, and shortly afterward introduced an amendment to the tariff bill providing that none of the duties on raw materials might be levied until compensatory duties of an equivalent amount had been imposed on goods manufactured from those or similar raw materials. In this emasculated form the bill for which Thiers had fought for more than a year was passed on July 26, 1872.[28] The victory had been won, but only through protracted negotiations whose success was most uncertain could it be made fruitful.

Negotiations between England and France were resumed shortly after the passage of the law on raw materials. Lord Lyons advised his government to allow the provisions of the law to be included in the new treaty because this would be the only real inducement to France to negotiate it. Unless England yielded on this point before the Treaty of 1860 expired on March 15, 1873,[29] Thiers would be legally free to tax British goods and ships in French ports as much as he liked and Eng-

[28] Arnauné, *loc. cit.*, Rausch, *op. cit.*, pp. 41, 44–45.
[29] F. O., 27. Vol. 1941. Lord Lyons to the Foreign Office, July 31, 1872; also *ibid.*, Vol. 1942. Lord Lyons to the Foreign Office, August 13, 1872.

land would find herself in a very disadvantageous position as compared with other nations with whom France had treaties of commerce and navigation. Her only security then would lie in making the French fear that she would levy duties on their goods in reprisal. Yet it would be difficult to arouse that fear, because England could not actually make such reprisals, since they would violate the principle of free trade to which she had declared herself firmly attached. The advice of Lord Lyons to negotiate on the basis of the new law on raw materials was wise, but the Foreign Office was in a mood for legal quibbling and sent de Rémusat, the French Minister of Foreign Affairs, a note denying the right of France to levy the proposed duties on raw materials.[30] The denial was based on Article IX of the Treaty of 1860,[31] which stipulated that, if either France or England found it necessary to establish an excise tax on an article of home production, an equivalent duty might be imposed on the importation of articles of the same description produced abroad. England argued that this meant that France could not impose a new import duty or increase an old one without first imposing an equivalent excise tax upon such articles produced in France. Thiers, on the other hand, justified the imposition of the new duties by the terms of Article III of the Supplementary Convention of November 11, 1860,[31] which provided that, if France granted new drawbacks on the exportation of articles, import duties on similar articles produced in England could be raised by an equal amount. The position taken by Thiers may have been in accordance with the letter of the Treaty, but it was certainly contrary to its spirit.

Fortunately, England changed her mind and withdrew from her position in order to reach an agreement with France before the Treaty of 1860 expired. It was clear, as Lord Lyons had said, that she must accept such duties as France could impose under the law of July 26, 1872, and that she must refrain from increasing her duties on wines from France as well as from

---

[30] F. O., 27. Vol. 1935. The Foreign Office to Lord Lyons, August 2 and 9, 1872.
[31] H. Reader Lack, *The French Treaty and the Tariff of 1860* (London, 1861); also Arnauné, *op. cit.*, p. 281.

imposing a duty on the exportation of coal. If England would accept these conditions Thiers was anxious to sign the new treaty quickly. This explains why he was now willing to agree to protect England from discrimination by giving her most favored nation treatment. He was ready, also, to give British shipping in the indirect trade the same status in the ports of France as shipping in the direct trade, which meant giving up the collection of the *surtaxe de pavillon*. This was because loud protests were coming in from the French ports against that surtax, which was seriously injuring their trade by diverting cargoes from French to Belgian or other foreign ports from which they reached France overland. Thiers realized that this surtax would have to be given up, and it should be remembered also that it had never been recommended by him, but had been imposed by the National Assembly on its own initiative. His position would be strengthened, however, if the surtax could be given up as a gracious concession to England. The negotiations resulted, therefore, in the Treaty of November 5, 1872, by which England accepted the duties on raw materials under the Act of July 26, while France in return granted her most favored nation treatment and exemption from the *surtaxe de pavillion*.[32]

During the remainder of Thiers' term of office there were no further developments of importance in the commercial negotiations between France and England. A mixed commission, under the chairmanship of Mr. Kennedy, of the Board of Trade, worked out the details of the new French tariff as applicable to British goods, and settled various other technical questions, all of which were embodied in the protocol signed January 29, 1873,[33] and annexed to the Treaty of November 5, 1872, as had been provided in that instrument. The only change of interest to us was the reduction by the Mixed Commission of many of the compensatory duties of manufactures in the Act of July 26, 1872, until the majority of them ceased to give French industries

[32] F. O., 27. Vol. 1942. Lord Lyons to the Foreign Office; and Vol. 1944, the Foreign Office to Lord Lyons. These volumes give various memoranda and the text of the Treaty of November 5, 1872, which was never ratified.

[33] *Ibid.* Vol. 2002. Lord Lyons to the Foreign Office, January 14, 16, and 25, 1873.

high protection and became compensatory in fact as well as in name.[34] The treaty thus modified was presented to the National Assembly for ratification on February 4, 1873, and referred to a hostile committee of fifteen under the chairmanship of Pouyer-Quertier. Still further reductions of the duties in the Act of July 26 were made in a treaty signed with Belgium February 5, 1873,[35] and presented for ratification on February 19. As a result the Assembly's Committee, twelve of whose fifteen members were high protectionists, was reluctant to recommend the ratification of either treaty. The National Assembly voted on March 14 that the conventional tariffs then in force, which were those of the treaties of 1860 and 1861 with England and Belgium respectively, should remain in force until new ones had been put into operation.[36] No further action had been taken when, on May 24, Thiers resigned again, principally because of his conviction that the government of France should remain a republic, while the majority of the National Assembly favored a monarchy. On this occasion his resignation was accepted and the presidency was assumed by Marshal MacMahon.

Within two months of his fall from office Thiers saw all his efforts to change the tariff policy of France checked. By the Treaty of July 23, 1873,[37] which replaced his treaty of November, 1872, which the National Assembly never ratified, the whole system established by the Anglo-French Treaty of 1860 and its supplementary conventions was restored. The entire Act of July 26, 1872, imposing duties on raw materials and compensatory duties on goods manufactured from them or from raw materials like them, was repealed. England was left in possession of the moderate tariff duties in France to which she had been entitled before Thiers assumed office, and, in addition, she retained two concessions which he had reluctantly given her, most favored nation treatment for her goods, and exemption of

---

[34] F. O., 27. Vol. 2003. Lord Lyons to the Foreign Office, February 27, 1873.

[35] Arnauné, *op. cit.*, p. 285.

[36] F. O., 27. Vol. 2004. Lord Lyons to the Foreign Office, March 11, 13, and 15, 1873.

[37] Hertslet, *op. cit.*, Vol. 14.

her carrying trade from the *surtaxe de pavillon*. Yet neither the French nor the British Government was satisfied. Despite the fact that it had insisted on the restoration of the Treaty of 1860, the administration of President MacMahon and the Duc de Broglie favored increased protection for French industry and trade. It rejected the work of Thiers, partly because it felt the duties on raw materials would do much harm by increasing the cost of production in France, and partly because the compensatory duties on manufactures were not high enough to give the protection desired. Still more important was the fact that the duties in the Act of July 26, 1872, could not be applied to England and Belgium alone, for they would have yielded far too little revenue to justify the impairment of political relations that would have been the inevitable result of such discrimination. The treaties of commerce with the other states of Europe remained in force and those states had signified their refusal to consent to their modification. Nothing effective could be done, therefore, toward a general revision of the French tariff before 1877 at the earliest.

England was not pleased by the Treaty of 1873. She secured equality of treatment for her goods and ships as compared with the other nations of Europe in the trade with France. She was thus assured of remaining on a plane of equality with Germany, as she wished, and need not fear seeing Germany derive further profit from Article XI of the Treaty of Frankfort at her expense. But she had been obliged to consent to the revival of the system of 1860. Her reluctance to do this was incomprehensible to the Duc de Broglie, who reminded Lord Lyons that when Thiers had denounced the Treaty of 1860 the year previous England had wished to keep it. Why, then, did she now object to the revival of the Treaty of 1860 and desire only to be assured of treatment as a most favored nation? Lord Lyons, expressing the views of Gladstone and Lord Granville, replied that England did not want any more commercial treaties. She believed that each country should be free regarding its own tariff, but she wanted security against special disfavor in trade and navigation. England had wished to keep the Treaty of 1860 when Thiers denounced it simply in order to avoid the disturbance of trade sure to be caused by the uncertain result of new negotiations undertaken after the system had been in operation for twelve years. But the Treaty had always been regarded in England, said the ambassador, as a compromise forced by peculiar circumstances and far from wholly correct in principle or satisfactory in detail.[38]

Thiers seems to have been as ignorant of England's indifference to the Treaty of 1860 as was the Duc de Broglie. He might have succeeded early in his negotiations with her if he had played on this indifference. Another argument that might have been very effective was the crying need of France for revenue. Thiers began with this argument, but he did not stick to it, although the attitude of the British Government showed that it was not merely courteous, but also probably sincere in expressing a desire to aid France. If Thiers had not made such help too costly to England, he might have secured it. Another method by which success might have been attained would have been to make it clear to England that, without flagrant discrimination against her alone, her trade and shipping could be placed in a disadvantageous position as compared with those of other countries in their relations with France. England's sensitiveness regarding the security given Germany by Article XI of the Treaty of Frankfort, which stipulated that in commercial matters she must be treated as favorably as England, Belgium, Austria, Switzerland, Italy, or Russia, and her anxiety to stop the losses to her carrying trade from the *surtaxe de pavillon*, indicated that pressure could have been brought to bear effectively by such means, provided the pressure was applied with skill and courtesy, according to the traditions of diplomacy. But Thiers was too impatient and lacking in finesse to continue long either the method of persuasion or that of pressure. He changed rapidly and frequently from one to the other, and after a struggle that lasted nearly a year and a half he won only a barren victory in the Treaty of November 5, 1872.

In fairness to Thiers it must be admitted that there were

[38] F. O., 27. Vol. 2007. Lord Lyons to the Foreign Office, July 15, 1873.

great obstacles in his path. It is doubtful whether any tariff policy could have pleased both England and the National Assembly, for the British Government disliked protection in both theory and practice, while the majority of the French parliament clearly favored a return to high protection. The policy Thiers actually adopted, however, was sure to antagonize both. It was distinctly protective, and thus obnoxious to England, while to French merchants and manufacturers it seemed certain to injure trade and increase greatly the cost of production. Thiers had had ample warning through speeches in the Assembly, newspaper articles, and petitions from chambers of commerce that the duties he proposed were most objectionable to the leaders of the industrial and mercantile classes in France. Yet he insisted on them and refused to consider alternatives. As a result, he estranged the very groups in the National Assembly that had most influence in economic affairs and that sympathized most strongly with his desire to increase protection for both industry and trade. But even if, by the use of wiser methods, Thiers had won the support of the National Assembly, the most serious obstacle to the restoration of high protection would have remained. France was bound by her treaties of commerce until 1877. In order to avoid flagrant discrimination against England and Belgium, who had reluctantly negotiated new agreements, Thiers would have had to secure the modification of the treaties of France with the other states of Europe. His supreme error was his failure to realize that none of the states to whom France was bound was willing to modify her treaty in a protectionist sense. By even the most skilful diplomacy, therefore, Thiers could not have secured a large amount of revenue from duties on raw materials in 1871 or even in 1873. The imposition of such duties should never have been attempted. The restoration of high protection could have been secured by patient waiting, for in 1877, when the last important treaty expired, France would be free to change completely her whole tariff policy.

CHAPTER XVI

THE ABANDONMENT OF THE TREATY

THE negotiation of the Anglo-French Treaty of 1860 has often been called an economic coup d'état, because it was effected suddenly and with determination by the despotic government of Napoleon III. The attempt made by the Emperor's bitter opponent, Thiers, to overthrow the imperial tariff policy was characterized by similar determination, although circumstances prevented rapid success or failure. In the earlier case Chevalier knew what he wanted and secured it, and Thiers, although he failed, was just as certain of what he wished to accomplish. But the period following the fall of Thiers and the repudiation of his tariff policy stands out in sharp contrast. It is characterized primarily by indecision. No strong leader appeared with the requisite combination of a definite commercial policy and the political strength to put it into execution. The chief reason for this lay in the political situation. France was torn by the struggle between Legitimists, Orleanists, and Republicans until the resignation of President MacMahon in 1879, and even after that ministries continued to be weak and short-lived. Consequently, the tariff, always the football of politics, was tossed about between rival groups until nearly eight years elapsed before even an unsatisfactory compromise could be reached.

For the supporters of a truly liberal tariff policy this political instability was a tragedy. From the economic point of view the situation in France was far more favorable in 1874 and for two or three years afterward than it had ever been before or was to be later. The country had recovered from the economic effects of the War of 1870 with amazing rapidity, showing once more its characteristic vitality. This period of recovery in France coincided, happily, with an era of general industrial prosperity through most of western Europe. As a result the disposition of the French Government in 1875 to continue the policy of commercial treaties that had been begun in 1860 met with general approval. The Comte de Meaux, who was then Minister of Commerce, wished to make the tariff schedules established by this series of treaties the basis for the new general tariff whose enactment everyone realized was necessary. Had the political situation been normal, so that a ministry could have remained in power for a reasonable length of time, this could almost certainly have been accomplished. It is true that de Meaux was far from being an economic statesman, as a study of the circular he addressed to the chambers of commerce of France in April, 1875, will show; [1] yet he certainly favored making the treaty tariff the basis for the drastic revision of the general tariff of France with its many exorbitant duties and its numerous prohibitions. Had this been accomplished, the protectionist reaction that was so largely responsible for the Act of 1881 would have encountered an obstacle so serious that it would probably have been checked for several years at least.

The correspondence between the French Ministry of Commerce and the chambers of commerce or *chambres consultatives* throughout the country caused by the issuance of the Comte de Meaux's questionnaire in April, 1875, throws some light on the condition of various French industries at that period. It also helps us to see more clearly their attitude toward the tariff policy of the country, and the reasons that caused them to take that attitude. In 1875, as previously, the silk and wine industries and the merchants of the principal ports favored a very moderate tariff and, in some cases, even actual free trade. The diseases of the silkworms in France had not changed the attitude of the industry as a whole toward the tariff, because that attitude was determined by the merchants of Lyons, whose domination was stronger than ever. Lyons had profited, as we have seen, by the increase of trade with the Orient facilitated by the founding of the *messageries maritimes* in 1862 and still more by the opening of the Suez Canal in 1869, so that her supremacy as a market was far more clearly established in 1875 than it had

[1] Arch. Nat., F 12–6196. April 7, 1875.

been in 1860. Furthermore, the merchants of Lyons had formed a new organization in 1869, the Union des Marchands de Soie, under the direction of Marius Morand, a zealous free trader who fought protection at every turn.[2] Even St. Étienne, the principal seat of the ribbon industry, which had been rather protectionist in 1860, was now in favor of a very moderate tariff. This change was probably due in part to the fact that neither British nor Swiss competition in ribbons had proved as serious as had been feared. It was probably due even more to the persistence of fashions favoring mixed silks which affected Lyons as well. This meant that other textile yarns, such as cotton, wool, and flax, were used on a considerable scale and that their importation under the lowest possible duties was a matter of real concern to the manufacturers of silk cloths and ribbons. The attitude of the wine industry toward the tariff was unchanged in 1875. While France had then begun to suffer from the ravages of phylloxera, the destruction of vines as yet had not been great. French vintages had been unusually large and importations of wine had remained a factor of negligible importance. Several years were to pass before the wine growers turned toward protection.

Of the industries which had objected most strongly to the conclusion of the treaty with England in 1860 the most important, it will be remembered, were those of cotton and iron. In 1875 the attitude of the cotton industry was the same, although it had shown sufficient vitality to repair a considerable part of the loss caused by the cession of Alsace to Germany in 1871. The position taken by the iron industry, on the other hand, was distinctly more moderate. The depression of the late 'sixties was, of course, attributed by the Comité des Forges to the effects of the commercial treaties and the losses incurred were dwelt upon eloquently, although no satisfactory evidence regarding them was given. The industry clearly shared in the industrial prosperity which began shortly after the conclusion of the Franco-Prussian War and it seems probable that, like most manufacturers, the French ironmasters increased their pro-

---

[2] Louis Gueneau, *Lyon et le commerce de la soie* (Lyon, 1923), pp. 71–75.

duction unduly. The point of greatest interest in the attitude of the French iron industry about 1875 is the change in emphasis from importations to exportations. In 1860 ironmasters declared that France would be flooded by British iron and that their industry would probably succumb to its injuries; but in the middle 'seventies little was said of this danger and the ironmasters complained bitterly of the expansion of the iron industries of other European countries and of the United States, not because they were afraid that those countries would flood the French market, but because they were becoming increasingly able to satisfy their own needs without asking for iron or steel products from France. In short, the leaders of the French iron industry were now concerned primarily with the loss of foreign markets. It is obvious, therefore, that they felt confident of maintaining control of their own home market and that their industry was so strong that it was absolutely dependent on selling a considerable part of its annual production abroad. While between 1875 and 1877 they asked for the conversion of ad valorem to specific duties, there was no general expression of a desire for a notable increase in the amount of protection; emphasis was placed rather on the maintenance of the *status quo*.

The woollen and worsted industries, on the whole, were opposed to the renewal of the commercial treaties unless the duties on their products were raised; yet it is difficult to make a general statement as to their attitude because different branches of the industries and sometimes different manufacturing centers had quite divergent opinions. The worsted industry, using chiefly combed wool, was well developed with good methods of production and adequate equipment. Its principal centers, such as Reims and Fourmies, controlled not only the home market, but also various foreign markets because of the excellence of their products. They were interested, therefore, in developing foreign trade still further and consequently favored a low tariff. The woollen industry, using chiefly carded wool, was not as well developed as the worsted. Many of its centers, such as Reims,[3] Roubaix, Elbeuf, Louviers, and Sedan, felt that they

[3] Reims was an important center for both worsteds and woollens.

were still in some danger from foreign competition between 1875 and 1877 and they finally induced the French Government to grant a heavy increase in the duties on carded wool yarn and woollens, while leaving the duties on the yarn of combed wool and on worsteds almost unchanged.[4]

The distinction thus made was not fully justified by the facts. While it is true that France did show conspicuous superiority as compared with many other countries in the manufacture of many worsteds, the inferiority of the woollen industry was not universal nor was it irremediable. We should recall how bitterly the manufacturers of the mixed cloths of Roubaix complained at every opportunity of the competition of Bradford in Yorkshire, despite the fact that they were able to sell their goods in the very streets of the English town. We cannot, therefore, accept at their face value the statements of centers like Louviers and Elbeuf in the middle 'seventies that their industry was in a critical condition and liable to succumb to foreign competition at any moment unless the Government granted a notable increase of protection. While our evidence is scanty it appears to justify quite different conclusions. It seems probable that in the case of Elbeuf at least, the manufacturers were installing looms driven by power and improving the rest of their equipment and their methods of production. It was natural that these changes should be made on a considerable scale about 1875, because the industrial boom of the preceding three years had resulted in general overproduction and a great increase in the intensity of competition. The manufacturers of Elbeuf were compelled to make costly improvements in order to avoid even more costly losses. The competition of which they complained bitterly to the Government, as had long been their custom, was far from being wholly foreign, as they alleged. It seems certain that in 1875 centers like Roubaix and Reims were well equipped with good machinery, that their mills were large and that they reduced their operating costs by pro-

---

[4] *Économiste français*, July 22, 1876. Report of Balsan to the Conseil Supérieur du Commerce; also Arch. Nat., F 12–619 , Chamber of Commerce of Elbeuf to the Minister of Commerce, April 7 and August 18, 1877, and the Chamber of Commerce of Louviers·to the Minister of Commerce, March 31, 1877.

ducing on a large scale a limited number of articles. We have definite information that at Elbeuf, Louviers, and Sedan the change from machines run by hand to those driven by power proceeded very slowly. At Elbeuf, and probably at the other centers also, many kinds of cloth were made, so that only a small amount of each could be produced. In addition, we know that at Elbeuf, at least, the mills were numerous and small. In short, the manufacturers there produced at a high cost because they did so on a small scale without specialization. They may have suffered from foreign competition. We lack the evidence either to prove or disprove the accuracy of their statements in this respect. It seems certain, however, that they suffered from competition in the home market from which the tariff could not protect them, and it is probable that they suffered severely. We are told by the Chamber of Commerce of Yorkshire in 1881[5] that, through the competition of Reims and Roubaix with their power-looms and modern improvements, Elbeuf was losing each year trade worth 20,000,000 francs. The existence of this strong competition between woollen centers within France undoubtedly was known to the Government, but did not, unfortunately, influence its policy. The allegation that the French woollen industry was in a critical condition because of foreign competition was accepted and, as we have seen, a large increase was granted in the duties on carded yarn and woollens.

The attitude of the French linen industry toward the French tariff policy in the years 1875–77 resembled that of the woollen industry, but we are fortunate in having more information from the principal manufacturing centers sent to the government chiefly in response to a second circular issued to the chambers of commerce in the spring of 1877. The spinners of flax were very anxious to secure higher import duties on yarn, while the weavers, with equal energy, demanded lower duties on yarn and higher duties on cloth. The Government offered a compromise by recommending the maintenance almost unchanged of the existing

[5] Parl. Paper, Commerc. No. 38, 1881; also No. 41, Memorial of the Joint Tariff Commission of the Yorkshire Chambers of Commerce on the French General Tariff, March 22, 1881.

duties on both yarn and cloth which, quite naturally, satisfied no one.[6] The position of the French linen industry was certainly difficult, but it is quite clear that the principal pressure on French manufacturers did not come from excessive importations of either yarn or cloth. Importations of flax had been increasing for some time, but, as Raoul Duval pointed out in his report to the Conseil Supérieur du Commerce in 1876, this showed, not that the French industry was declining, but that it needed a larger supply of raw material. Northern France produced flax of excellent quality, but it had to meet the competition of Belgium, where conditions for the cultivation of flax were equally favorable, and it had also to meet the competition of Russia, where flax was grown on a large scale at a cost far below that in either France or Belgium. This meant that the French, like the Belgians, were being forced to grow only the finest qualities of flax and to use the very best methods of preparing it for spinning. The growing of flax was coming to be restricted in France to the districts of the north and, as we have seen, it was being limited to the finest qualities, the manufacturers importing coarser flax chiefly from Russia. Duval was right, therefore, in saying that the increase of imports was a benefit, not an injury, to the French industry.

The spinning and weaving of flax in France had probably never fully recovered from the severe crisis at the close of the American Civil War and, as in most countries, they necessarily shared in the decline of the linen industry caused chiefly by the increasing use of cotton. The French linen industry was forced to specialize and to use more machinery, as were the industries of northern Ireland and Scotland. As in the case of cotton, the French linen manufacturers had proved their ability to spin coarse yarn very well and needed no protection against the competition of Ireland and Belgium either in the French or in foreign markets. In the spinning of fine yarn the superiority of Belfast was uncontested, but, in the opinion of Duval, no increase in duties would help the French spinners of fine yarn, because the excellence of the

[6] *Économiste français*, July 22, 1876. Report of Duval to the Conseil Supérieur du Commerce.

Irish spinning was the direct result of high specialization and unusually skilled labor. The principal effect of such an increase of duties would be to raise the price of fine linens and thus injure their exportation from France, which continued to be considerable. The growing intensity of international competition was forcing the increasing use of machinery in the weaving of linens in France. As in the woollen industry of Elbeuf, we find complaints from the linen weavers of Armentières. In the spring of 1877 the Chambre Consultative of Armentières wrote to the French Government that the linen industry there was going through an acute crisis due to the rapidly increasing use of the power-loom, which was driving out weaving by hand. The effect of this change was most unfortunate, wrote the chamber, because it was crowding the weavers into the towns and making it impossible for them to find other work when the looms were stopped. It was also causing the concentration of the linen industry in a small number of manufacturing centers. The chamber remarked, in conclusion, that, while it realized that the Government could not stop such industrial crises because they were universal, it hoped that by watchful care it could prevent them from causing the destruction of the French linen industry.[7] This letter from Armentières illustrates the evolution of the linen industry in the late 'seventies. It shows that the increasing tendencies to the use of machinery and to specialization were causing concentration into a small number of towns, with the restriction of production chiefly to coarse yarn and fine cloth in whose weaving the French had long excelled. The industry was evidently adapting itself to the decreased demand for most linens and was apparently as prosperous as could have been expected. We have sufficient evidence to show that this evolution of the French linen industry resembled closely that of the industries of northern Ireland and Scotland, and that it was not affected seriously by excessive foreign competition.

The report of the Commission on textiles to the Conseil Supérieur du Commerce in the summer of 1876[8] gives the opinion of

---

[7] Arch. Nat., F 12–6196. April 28, 1877.

[8] *Économiste français*, July 15, 1876.

two men well qualified to determine the position of the French textile industries with respect to British competition. One of the authors, Fernand Raoul-Duval, was a capitalist with investments in various enterprises, including cotton mills, and with strong convictions in favor of free trade; the other, Balsan, was a protectionist manufacturer of woollens. After a careful study of both French and British industries, they came to an agreement, despite the difference in their views regarding tariff policy. They found some elements of the cost of production favorable to France as compared with England and others adverse. After considering them all, they concluded that France had a disadvantage of only 4 per cent, although in many cases this was compensated for by the cost of transporting British goods to France. The French manufacturer had to pay more for coal, but the British had the disadvantage of higher wages and shorter hours for their workmen, although this was partly offset by the greater productivity of British labor through better education and greater specialization. England had other advantages which the French could well afford to consider. Her trading organization was superior, which, with other factors, meant that the rate of interest was lower in Great Britain than in France and capital or credit easier to obtain. English railroads were more abundant and their service was so much faster that British freight moved as rapidly as express in France. Finally, the equipment of practically all British ports was admirable and far superior to that of the French.

The textile commission ended its report with recommendations so constructive that they deserved the serious attention of the French Government. Like their study of the factors of British superiority in credit and transportation, these recommendations might well have been embodied in a new commercial policy and applied to many non-textile industries in France. Duval and Balsan advised the abolition of nuisance taxes levied in order to help fill the deficit caused by the recent war with Germany, especially the tax of 5 per cent on freight and that on commercial paper. They suggested the free importation of coal, machinery, and tools; the construction of more railroads and the more efficient exploitation of all French railroads, both old and new, and the improvement of the equipment of French ports. Finally, they recommended that the existing conventional or treaty tariff be made the new general tariff applicable to countries that did not have commercial treaties with France of the type of the Chevalier-Cobden Treaty of 1860. Although this was a pretty strong statement, they went farther and said that the treaty tariff was one of the most complicated and protective in Europe and should be simplified. The aim of the Government, said the commission, should be a tariff for revenue only.

The report of the textile commission may have gone farther than the Government could safely have ventured when it recommended the free admission of coal, machinery, and tools, and a tariff for revenue only. Such radical changes would appeal to an economic statesman like Chevalier rather than to a minister dependent upon a shifting political majority. Yet the Comte de Meaux in 1875 thought along similar lines even if he did not go quite so far, and the bulk of the recommendations in the report of 1876 could have been accepted by the Government without any important modification of its policy. Above all, the recommendation for improvement in railroad service and in the equipment of the ports could have been acted upon with perfect safety and with results of far greater significance than would have been obtainable by changes in tariff schedules. But this part of the Duval report seems to have made no impression on the Government.

The liberal but weak tariff policy of the Minister of Commerce in that year is shown most clearly by his letter to the president of the Chamber of Commerce of Macon and Charolles on June 2, 1875.[9] Here he stated that the Government did not wish to decide French commercial policy until the chambers of commerce had been consulted. Yet no need for so general a consultation was shown by the minister, for he said that the Cabinet did not wish to change radically the system under which, despite severe trials, French industry and trade had developed for fifteen years. Instead of proposing a new commercial policy, the

[9] Arch. Nat., F 12–6196.

Comte de Meaux asked for the consideration of certain details in the tariff that might be changed, such as the increase of some duties and the decrease of others. Would the president of the Chamber decide between ad valorem duties which were fairer and less burdensome to the poorer classes and specific duties which, because of greater ease of collection, would form a surer source of revenue for the Government? There was grave need of an increase of revenue and of a less burdensome means of collecting it than existed in certain new taxes which injured industry and trade, an allusion to the taxes on freight and commercial paper denounced in the following year by Duval and Balsan.

The circular which the Minister of Commerce had sent out on April 7, 1875,[10] to all the chambers of commerce and the less important *chambres consultatives* resembled closely the letter to the president of the chamber at Macon, and the replies were as disappointing in their failure to make constructive suggestions as we may presume the answer from Macon to have been. The minister asked four questions in his circular: (1) What increases or decreases in rates should be made in the revision of the tariff? (2) Should there be ad valorem or specific duties? (3) Could the tariff be so revised as to increase the revenue? (4) Would the conventional régime, or treaty system, be preferable to a new general tariff established by law? A small amount of useful information was obtained by the Government in the replies to its circular. It was made clear that virtually all the chambers of commerce favored the maintenance of the *status quo;* that is, the retention of a network of tariff treaties with a general tariff applicable to countries such as the United States, which did not conclude tariff treaties with France. It was shown also that nearly all the chambers wished the duties in the treaty tariff to remain approximately the same. This was far more important because it showed the absence of a widespread demand for a return to high protection as late as the year 1877. Even to protectionists the treaty system built upon the agreement with England in 1860 was of value because it gave them security for a definite term of years against changes in tariff duties. They

[10] Arch. Nat., F 12–6196.

felt also that such treaties were of greatest benefit to the nation that was most advanced in industry and that, in the case of most of the agreements, the country in that fortunate position was France.

The majority of the chambers of commerce desired three modifications of the existing situation: (1) that all tariff treaties should expire on the same date and that in every case the term of validity should be ten years; (2) that the revision of the old general tariff should begin promptly, regardless of treaty negotiations; and (3) that the most favored nation clause be abolished. The recommendation of the second change was frequently accompanied by the request that the rates of the new general tariff be approximately the same as those of the existing treaties. Few chambers seem to have realized that that would mean inevitably reduction of duties in the treaties to be negotiated, since otherwise the conclusion of a treaty would give a country no advantages which it could not obtain from the general tariff. The reason for the recommendation of the third change, the abolition of the most favored nation clause, was generally stated to be that it would diminish greatly the principal benefit derived from the treaties which was felt to be that they insured the stability of the tariff for a stated period. Although they did not name other reasons for their opposition to this clause, it is certain that many chambers of commerce realized clearly that it had been responsible for the reduction of many duties and that it facilitated the granting of reductions by the Government without the consent of French manufacturers. Every time a country with which France had signed a treaty of commerce negotiated a treaty with a third state any concession granted in the new treaty was automatically extended to France. Similarly, France would be virtually compelled also to grant concessions in any new treaty she negotiated, because practically all the important states of Europe between 1860 and 1870 had negotiated with each other commercial treaties containing the most favored nation clause.

Despite the general lack of constructive suggestions there were many things in these replies of the chambers of commerce and the *chambres consultatives* that must have gratified the Comte de Meaux. We know that he wished the treaties of commerce renewed and this desire was echoed in most of the replies. He favored also a further reduction rather than an increase of duties, and the chambers showed that in the main they wanted the continuance of the *status quo*. Had he been able and ready to give France a lower tariff through legislation or a series of treaties, there is little doubt that he could have done so even as late as 1877. But to the specific questions he asked the replies were largely unsatisfactory because the chambers did not have the ability to discuss financial details and lacked the statesmanship which he himself had failed to show. How could he expect definite statements regarding changes in individual tariff duties when none of the principles of future tariff policy had been agreed upon? It was equally unreasonable to expect from bodies like the chambers of commerce a clear-cut decision between ad valorem and specific duties on the grounds he had laid down, the interests of the poor and the financial needs of the Government. The chambers could see the problem only in the light of the interests of the most important industries of their districts, because their leaders were usually local manufacturers or municipal officials. Why should they care whether a revision of the tariff could bring more revenue to the Government? The question which interested them was whether such a revision would diminish or increase the profits of their leading industries or crops. Finally, the question asking whether France should have a new series of treaties or a new general tariff established by law was ambiguous because France actually possessed both, and had become accustomed to both during a period of fifteen years. Since the minister did not want to destroy the whole network of commercial treaties, it would have been far wiser not to raise this question.

It was a pity that the Comte de Meaux did not put clearly before the chambers of commerce the tariff policy he appears to have wanted and ask for its approval or rejection. The country in 1875 was disposed to accept a policy of real moderation in the tariff, so that it is almost certain that such a proposal by the minister would have been indorsed. Instead of that the minister's circular raised either unimportant questions or asked important ones ambiguously. Hence the replies contained a futile discussion of the relative merits of a treaty tariff and of a general tariff when there was no serious intention of abolishing either. They dwelt upon the comparative advantages of specific and ad valorem duties without reaching any valuable conclusions. Yet the Minister of Commerce cannot justly be held solely responsible for the character of the circular of April 7, 1875, or for the largely unsatisfactory nature of the replies. To an accusation of personal ineptitude he could have replied that the political situation made it impossible for him or any other member of the Cabinet to advocate a strong economic policy. This will appear even more clearly if we study the diplomatic negotiations for the modification of the Anglo-French Treaty of Commerce of 1873, which had revived almost unchanged the instrument negotiated thirteen years earlier by Chevalier and Cobden.

In the autumn of 1875 the French Government was confronted by the approaching termination of its commercial treaties with the chief states of Europe. The agreement with Italy had been denounced by the government of Victor Emmanuel and would expire in July, 1876, the Swiss treaty denounced by the French would terminate in November of that year, while the treaties with Austria-Hungary, Great Britain and Belgium would expire in the year 1877. As on previous occasions, the French wished to negotiate with Great Britain first. On November 18, 1875, Lord Lyons, the British ambassador, reported to the Foreign Office that the Duc Decazes had asked officially whether England would consider negotiating a new treaty of commerce to replace that of 1873.[11] France would like to have a treaty lasting for ten years, said her Minister of Foreign Affairs, and he intimated that such a treaty, serving as a basis for similar treaties with the other European governments, would be the only means of preventing frequent changes in the French tariff, because free trade was not as firmly rooted in France as in England. Lord Lyons supported the French advance, saying that both the Minister of

[11] F. O., 27–2220. No. 336.

Finance and the Minister of Commerce were strongly in favor of it. The former was Léon Say, grandson of the well-known economist and free trader, Jean Baptiste Say, and son of Horace Say, one of the leaders of the free trade cause in 1860; while the latter was still the Comte de Meaux, with whose desire for a very moderate tariff we are now familiar. Lyons argued that when three of the principal French ministers were free traders the opportunity of securing a treaty agreeable to Great Britain was so good that it ought not to be lost. He knew as well as anyone that the term "free trade" in France did not have the same significance as in England; that it meant only a moderate tariff. Yet he felt the opportunity was unusually favorable because most French officials were in favor of high protection. As French ministries were then very unstable, the existing government which wanted a low tariff might give place at any moment to a group of extreme protectionists.

The Foreign Office replied with its usual conservatism.[12]   It said that ending the Treaty of 1873 before the normal date of expiration would disturb trade and raise complications regarding existing contracts; that England ought not to begin the negotiation of a new treaty before notice had been given to end the old. England felt also that negotiations with France should be deferred until the other French treaties had expired and a general arrangement had become possible. Back of these official statements was the fact that English trade was then suffering severely from depression, which made the Government feel that the disturbance of trade by commercial negotiations would be undesirable. Two factors, however, induced the Foreign Office to change its mind within a month. Lord Lyons wrote[13] that delay would make a general arrangement such as England wished impossible because, in the opinion of Decazes, it was virtually certain that neither Italy, Switzerland, nor Austria would agree to it simply to please Great Britain. An Anglo-French treaty, on the other hand, could serve again as a basis for a network of treaties, as it had in 1860. The only difference would be that

[12] F. O., 27. Vol. 2220. No. 266.
[13] *Ibid.*, No. 365. December 12, 1875.

now those treaties would be negotiated almost simultaneously. The second factor which influenced Downing Street was that several states denounced their commercial treaties with England.[14] Hence the British Government decided that it could not wisely await the end of the existing commercial depression. It accepted the proposal of the Duc Decazes and requested the French to submit definite proposals.

Instead of rapid negotiations, as in 1860, there followed months of diplomatic maneuvering and unofficial conversations. Despite the facts that they had made the first advance and that the Duc Decazes had urged quick action, the French now sought delay for two reasons. They wished to replace ad valorem duties by specific and they wanted to have the new general tariff passed by the chambers, so that it could serve as a basis for bargaining. The British replied that their fiscal policy of recent years made it impossible for them to bargain with France regarding tariff duties, and that a new French tariff law would hardly be a suitable basis for diplomatic negotiations. They contended that the failure of negotiations during the presidency of Thiers proved the justice of their argument. They indicated also that specific duties would be too burdensome for British exports to France, which were generally heavy, coarse goods of slight value; and that, in consequence, they would be unwelcome to Great Britain. They could not see that it was futile to refuse to bargain with a government which was determined to do so, and that it was equally useless to insist upon free trade as a sacred principle when to the French it was purely a matter of expediency. This was shown with refreshing clearness many years later by Lord Salisbury, who said in a speech to the Associated Chambers of Commerce of the United Kingdom:

" This matter of commercial tariffs is singularly unfitted for the exercise of that magic spell of remonstrance and objurgation of which the people of this country are so fond. The object of a foreign power in raising its tariffs is to exclude your commodities and when you tell them in reproachful tones that the effect of their policy will be to exclude your commodities, the only result is that they say, 'Thank you, I am very much obliged to you. That is just what I intended.'

---

[14] *Ibid.*, No. 273. December 22, 1875.

And they give another turn of the screw to the tariff in order that the effect may be quite unmistakable and leave you to your reproaches. I therefore hope that whatever other policy may be recommended to Her Majesty's Government by these enlightened Chambers, they will not go back to the somewhat antiquated policy of remonstrance, which will do the very reverse of what they intended." [15]

Negotiations for a new Anglo-French treaty of commerce were actively renewed in March, 1877, on the initiative of the British Government, because the Treaty of 1873 was due to expire within four months. The outlook was not bright, for the points of view of both governments regarding the tariff were as divergent as before. Furthermore, the ministry in France was exceptionally weak and, in consequence, was preoccupied with politics. Yet there were some faint rays of hope. Jules Simon, the French premier, was a noted free trader, while the Duc Decazes, who was well disposed, was still in charge of foreign affairs. The Minister of Commerce, Teisserenc de Bort, appears to have been a politician without fixed convictions regarding the tariff. On the British side the chief commissioner sent to Paris was Sir Louis Mallet, a strong free trader who had helped Cobden in the negotiation of the tariff conventions of 1860. He hoped to renew the Treaty of 1860 and possibly to obtain even greater reductions in the French tariff, both because of his personal convictions and out of loyalty to the memory of his friend. Such a victory would have been a fitting culmination to a long career of service under the Board of Trade. The French commission consisted of Amé, the director general of customs; Ozenne, a veteran in commercial negotiations, but, unfortunately, a personal rival of Amé; and Léonce de Lavergne, the well-known economist and writer on agriculture. All three were free traders and might have accomplished much if they had been given a fairly free hand. But the premier, Jules Simon, had yielded to the request of the Délégués de l'Industrie de France to add a manufacturer to the commission. In his anxiety to please he had gone even farther than he was asked to and appointed an advisory commission to guide the official negotiators. This consisted of Pouyer-Quertier,

[15] K. J. Fuchs, *The Trade Policy of Great Britain and her Colonies since 1860* (London, 1905), p. 71.

Feray, Balsan, Reverchon, and Jullien.[16] The last two were not important figures and Balsan, who had sat on the textile commission with Duval in 1876, was a moderate protectionist; but Pouyer-Quertier and Feray were senators with great political influence, and ever since its inception in 1860 they had fought bitterly against the policy of reducing the French tariff through commercial treaties.

The letters of Sir Louis Mallet show that difficulties arose almost as soon as the French and British commissions met, although for some time they did not appear to be insoluble. It can be said, in fact, that there was a reasonable chance of negotiating a satisfactory treaty if the political situation in France did not grow worse. The difficulties encountered arose partly from inadequate preparation for the conferences on both sides and partly from the inevitable differences in the aims of the two governments. Thus Sir Louis wrote to the British Foreign Secretary, Lord Derby, two weeks after the first meeting of the commissions:

> " I can not help much regretting that some general understanding as to the outlines of any new treaty had not been come to before our commission was appointed; but, as Lord Lyons says, it is possible that points of view so different raising very broad and distinct issues at the outset might have cut short all negotiation, if negotiation be desirable. As it is we must make the best of it and avoid on the one hand anything which might appear abrupt or peremptory and on the other protracting unduly a discussion which can only end in mutual disappointment." [17]

The first great difference of opinion between the French and British came over the question of the British duties on French wines, which had been one of the most important issues in 1860 when it had been settled by the statesmanship of Gladstone on the insistence of Cobden and Chevalier. Shortly afterward, the French had discovered that the duties of the British tariff under the Treaty of 1860 would exclude most of the cheaper wines of

[16] Chevalier to Sir Louis Mallet, April 1, 1877. Mallet Papers. Also Dispatches of the British Commissioners, March and April, 1877, No. 4, April 2, 1877. Privately printed for the Foreign Office and the Board of Trade. Mallet Papers.

[17] Sir Louis Mallet to Lord Derby, April 6, 1877. Mallet Papers.

France, and they persuaded Cobden to ask for a further decrease, which was refused by the British Government. The French continued to cherish the illusion that the English people would acquire a taste for their cheap wines quickly if they could buy them at moderate cost. It became, therefore, good politics for the French Government to demand vigorously a drastic reduction of the British duties in 1877. The French commission indicated at the start that it would ask to have the duty of one shilling per gallon on wines below 15 degrees proof spirit substantially cut in half for the reason that it amounted to about 100 per cent on most French wines. Sir Louis wrote to the Chancellor of the Exchequer, Sir Stafford Northcote, asking approval of a reduction. His personal opinion was that a considerable reduction could be made without risk to the revenue of the British Government, but Sir Stafford did not agree with him. He replied that England had no revenue to spare and that an attempt to readjust British taxation to meet the needs of a commercial treaty would be unpopular. He added that, if England gave France a further decrease in wine duties, both Spain and Portugal would ask for similar favors, which would cause a further loss of revenue. He suggested that the French treaty be renewed for a year or two, evidently without any concession regarding wine, and that, if the French refused, England could get on without a treaty. In conclusion he wrote: "You may tell your French friends with perfect truth that there is more of a protectionist feeling growing up here than at any time within the last twenty years." Sir Louis replied: "I fear that at present there is little hope of our finding a basis which will admit of a new treaty unless something can be done for wine and it is lamentable that this was not ascertained before the two governments embarked on this blind negotiation. France is much to blame for not stating distinctly as a preliminary this condition, and I am afraid that on our side there was a certain remissness in not clearing the ground before accepting the French proposal for a commission." [18]

Other difficulties over economic questions arose between the

[18] Sir Stafford Northcote to Sir Louis Mallet, April 23, 1877, and the reply of Sir Louis, April 26. Mallet Papers.

two commissions. Thus the French insisted upon a stipulation by Great Britain that she would not reimpose any duties which she had abolished, nor raise any duties now in force during the continuance of the proposed treaty. Sir Louis Mallet described this demand as largely a matter of form and we have no direct evidence as to the light in which it was regarded by the British Government. It can be said only that in 1860 England had resented a request that she agree not to levy any export duty on coal in the future and that she had stipulated that any increases made in her excise taxes, which were levied chiefly on wines and spirits, would justify a proportionate increase in her tariff duties. It seems reasonable to surmise, therefore, that Downing Street would dislike this request of the French commission and because of it feel less inclined to conclude a new treaty. England, on her side, made requests that the French felt quite unable to accept. Mallet told some of the French ministers that his government would regard as indispensable large reductions in the French duties on iron, coal, steel, machinery, metal manufactures, and textiles. On the last item of textiles he wanted a decrease of 50 per cent on both yarn and cloth. Teisserenc de Bort, the Minister of Commerce, replied promptly that France could grant no such concessions; that she was not prepared to promise more than slight decreases on iron and coal. The French commission, however, subsequently granted considerable reductions on iron, coal, and machinery, and 20 per cent on textiles, provided the duties were made specific and the reduction spread over a period of five years.

Despite these differences of opinion on purely economic matters, Lord Lyons reported on May 1 that the British commission had prevented the French from introducing their proposed new general tariff as a basis of discussion and had stopped also the universal conversion of ad valorem into specific duties. On the whole, he regarded the French proposals as a distinct improvement on the Treaty of 1860. But he felt uneasy regarding the political situation in France, saying that the French free traders were timid and poorly organized; but the protectionists were well organized and were growing more popular. He said that

there was no chance of a decisive economic reform in France because of this and the fact that the Government did not possess a
solid majority in either Chamber, while the taxes were so heavy
that even a temporary loss of revenue could not be borne.[19]
Shortly afterward there began a constitutional crisis in France,
when on May 16 President MacMahon virtually dismissed the
republican ministry of Jules Simon and replaced it by a monar-
chistic ministry under the Duc de Broglie. For a month more the
letters of Sir Louis Mallet and Chevalier and the dispatches of
Lord Lyons show that there were occasional conversations between the British ambassador and the French ministers regarding
the proposed treaty, but that the French and British commissions did not meet again. The new French government, as
Chevalier wrote, was absorbed by the difficulties of its minis-
terial existence and by its efforts to prepare the way for a restoration of the monarchy. The conclusion seems justified, therefore,
that it allowed the tariff negotiations to lapse while being careful
to avoid any appearance of a definite rupture between the French
and British governments. Thus, through lack of interest and
determination in France, and to a lesser extent in England also,
the last opportunity to improve, or even effectively to preserve,
the Anglo-French Treaty of 1860 was lost. Before negotiations
could be resumed industrial depression and protectionist propaganda had rendered the French free traders impotent.

In their successful struggle, which may be said to have begun
in 1877, the French protectionists were led as before by the iron
and textile industries which had long been controlled by a few
strong firms and through them had developed an efficient organization for influencing both the voters and the French parliament.
Their efforts were directed chiefly toward winning the support of
the agricultural interests, particularly the producers of wheat,
meat, and wine, who were slowly becoming discontented. The
task of the industrial protectionists was to persuade the farmers
and wine growers that the real cause of their troubles was foreign
competition and that the sovereign remedy was a tariff wall so

[19] Dispatches of the British Commissioners. Also No. 184, Lord Lyons to
the Foreign Office. Mallet Papers.

high that it could not be scaled even from the United States. The task was thoroughly congenial, but took many years to accomplish because French agriculture had not suffered perceptibly from foreign competition under the moderate tariff established by the Second Empire. The farmers were accustomed to great variations in agricultural prices and had not yet realized that American shipments of grain and meat had become factors of some importance in the depression of prices. The wine growers had been very prosperous indeed in the decade between 1860 and 1870 and for some time afterward. For many years they had sought to develop chiefly their foreign markets and had, therefore, desired free trade. They had only just begun to suffer much from phylloxera, and the invasion of the French market by wines from Italy and Spain was not a serious factor for several years after that. The protectionist reaction in France, therefore, began too soon to win the prompt support of either the farmers or the wine growers.

The most striking thing about the French return to high protection is that it was very gradual. The industrial protectionists were well organized, as we have seen, and had found an able leader in Méline. They did not encounter serious opposition from the free traders in the Government and the French parliament because the free traders had neither an effective organization nor really strong convictions. There had not been an urgent demand for real free trade in France even in 1860; in fact, the phrase "free trade" did not have the same meaning as in England, but signified rather moderate protection. The attitude of the French "free traders" was negative, therefore, rather than positive. They felt that protection in their country had been carried too far, but were not really hostile to its principles. When the protectionist reaction began in 1877 they did not start a vigorous offensive to secure free trade, but tried only to retain the system of commercial treaties and the fairly moderate tariff which rested upon them. They were able to save the treaty system in 1881, after a struggle of four years, by preventing the union of the industrial and agricultural protectionists. But this apparent victory was really only an armistice, and was not won by the eloquence of the free trade leaders in the Chambers, able as many of them were. It was chiefly the result of the slow development of the economic forces that gave strength to the protectionists, and of the fortunate coincidence that a brief respite from economic depression began in 1880, when the tariff bill was under consideration in the Chamber of Deputies.

While the protectionist reaction was slowly gaining strength in France, opposition to the renewal of the commercial treaty of 1860 was growing in England. After a few years of reviving trade which had followed the severe depression beginning in 1868, British merchants suffered again from depression which seriously affected both industry and agriculture from 1874 to 1880. In consequence, there arose an agitation of some importance against the prevalent policy of free trade. The leaders of this "Fair Trade" movement declared that they wished to put the domestic on an equal footing with the foreign producer with respect to artificial conditions of production, such as export bounties, protective duties, and other forms of indirect taxation. This agitation was in full force when France denounced her commercial treaty with England in December, 1878, and it was soon directed against a renewal of that treaty. The fair traders argued that the Treaty of 1860 had been made to favor French trade more than British in the hope of converting France to free trade. Since France had not seen the light, but had shown unmistakable signs of wishing to bury her head still more deeply in the sands of protection, there was no justification for sacrificing British interests any longer. Furthermore, prices continued to fall, so that the burden of the duties in the French tariff grew steadily heavier. Consequently merchants and manufacturers brought pressure to bear on the Board of Trade against any further concessions to France. They demanded a further decrease in French duties and few were willing to accept the maintenance of the *status quo*, which would have been as much as a strong French government could have granted, and was beyond the power of the weak ministries that continued to succeed each other with bewildering frequency. The British chambers of commerce were opposed to the increase of any French duties whatever, even if the average level of the French tariff on British goods was not raised. They protested also against the conversion of ad valorem into specific duties on the ground that they would bear hardest on coarse goods, which formed so large a part of British exports to France.[20]

There seems to be no clear evidence that British interests were sacrificed to French by the Treaty of 1860, as the fair traders claimed, although France probably gained more from the effects of the treaty than did England. This argument against the renewal of the treaty was not sound; but the other arguments made to the Board of Trade were sound enough in principle. There can be no question that falling prices made the burden of the French duties greater. It seems clear also that the general conversion of ad valorem into specific duties would in effect have constituted an increase in the protection given French manu-facturers and that this was one of the reasons why the French Government insisted upon it. It was unfortunate, however, that these views were pressed upon the British Government at that moment. The French Government was sincerely desirous of reaching an agreement and was prepared to offer as great conces-sions as it could while struggling against the slowly rising tide of protection. A willingness on England's side to accept a com-promise might have made possible an agreement of some value. Instead of that the pressure of the fair trade movement stiffened the attitude of the British Government to such a degree that an agreement became virtually impossible.

The first action since negotiations had broken down in the spring of 1877 was taken by the French Government when, on December 31, 1878, it denounced the Anglo-French Treaty of Commerce of 1873. Under the terms of that agreement, which provided for twelve months' notice if either party wished to recover its freedom, the treaty would expire on January 1, 1880. The official reasons for denunciation given by the French Gov-ernment were two. In the first place, it wished the Chambers, which were to meet in ten days, to be entirely free to revise the

[20] Fuchs, *op. cit.*, pp. 188–196. An excellent summary of the fair trade agita-tion.

French tariff. Then, commercial relations between France and Austria-Hungary had just been broken off. It seemed a good time, therefore, to terminate all the commercial treaties by which France was bound and prepare to negotiate new ones in connection with the new French general tariff which was still being prepared.[21] It is probable that these factors had much to do with the sudden action of the Cabinet in Paris, but there is reason to believe that the decision may have been due chiefly to protectionist propaganda. Lord Lyons reported to the British Government on January 19, 1879, that the real cause of denunciation was a demand made by the French protectionists led by the cotton spinners. This opinion is corroborated by an editorial published on January 17 in the *République française,* the organ of Gambetta, which declared the denunciation to be a maneuver of the protectionists. It pointed out that the step was taken secretly without authorization of the Chambers, which made it even more reprehensible than the action of Napoleon III in signing the Treaty of 1860 without consulting the Corps Législatif. Lyons gave it as his opinion that the denunciation of the Treaty of 1873 by the Cabinet without the authorization of the French parliament was illegal and cited as a precedent the action of President Thiers and his Minister of Finance, Pouyer-Quertier, who were sworn enemies of the Treaty of 1860, but did not venture to denounce it until they had obtained the sanction of the National Assembly.[22] The British Government, however, accepted the denunciation of the Treaty of 1873 as due and legal notice on the part of the French Government. A few months later, in August, 1879, when it was clear that the new general tariff of France could not be enacted for some time, the French Chambers passed a law authorizing the Government to extend the validity of the Anglo-French Treaty of 1873 for six months after the promulgation of the new French tariff. England sig-

---

[21] Parl. Paper, Commerc., No. 2, 1879; Dispatch No. 1, December 31, 1878, Count de Montebello to Marquis of Salisbury; No. 3, January 3, 1879, Lord Lyons to Lord Salisbury; and No. 6, January 7, Lord Salisbury to Lord Lyons.

[22] *Ibid.* Lord Lyons to Lord Salisbury in Dispatches No. 12 of January 17, and No. 14 of January 19, 1879.

nified her willingness to accept this decision also and the two governments signed a declaration to that effect on October 10, 1879, at Paris.[23]

Not until June of the following year did an exchange of views take place between the two governments regarding the commercial treaty that should replace the one denounced by France eighteen months before. The French ambassador, Léon Say, then presented to the British Foreign Secretary, Lord Granville, a note stating that France was ready to reopen negotiations with England on the following bases: (1) England should grant a decrease in duty on some class of French wines; (2) livestock and agricultural products should be outside the scope of the negotiations, as France wished to place them entirely in her new general tariff; (3) both parties should seek a means to stop frauds committed in passing goods through the customs; (4) both should seek also to improve the *status quo* with a view to increasing Anglo-French trade.[24] The British Government replied immediately that it would be glad to reopen negotiations. It made no mention of the first three bases for negotiation proposed by the French, but showed a keen interest in the fourth, which it interpreted as an offer by France to decrease the duties on the chief products of British industry. This interpretation was not the one the French Government had in mind and it soon proved a fertile source of misunderstanding, for the British insisted upon it throughout the negotiations. The British counter-proposals which were handed to the new French ambassador, Challemel-Lacour, in August, dealt only with the last of the four French bases of negotiation. They showed that England expected a general reduction in the French duties on British goods, that she would fight every case where France sought to convert ad valorem into specific duties, and that she would seek to have the treaty extended to cover the colonial trade of both countries.[25]

The French memorandum of September 24, 1880, showed how

[23] Parl. Paper, Commerc., No. 28, 1879. Document No. 1 of August 7; and Paper No. 3, 1880.

[24] *Ibid.*, No. 24, 1880. Document of June 6, and reply of same date.

[25] *Ibid.*, No. 37, 1881. Document No. 1, Sir Charles Dilke to Mr. Adams, August 6, 1880, and No. 7, Sir Charles Dilke to Challemel-Lacour, August 23.

serious was the divergence in the views of the French and British governments. France stated plainly that she could not grant reductions from the future general tariff to England unless she received favors from the British in return, because she was bound by Article XI of the Treaty of Frankfort in 1871 to give Germany any concessions granted to Great Britain. She made it clear that the French senate, which must coöperate with the Chamber of Deputies in the ratification of any future treaty, was strongly protectionist and hostile to treaties of commerce; that because of agricultural, industrial, and commercial depression the French Government must maintain virtually intact the existing level of tariff duties and that it had promised the Chambers that it would do so. While many of the arguments with which the French note was embellished could be refuted, its conclusions were sound. The tide of protection was rising in France and any French government which ignored that fact was simply courting disaster.[26] The British Government should have recognized this and have tried simply to protect British trade from undue discrimination without wasting months in a futile attempt to negotiate a detailed tariff treaty. Instead of that England raised objections to the French plan of making specific as many duties as possible.[27] While the matter had not been stated clearly in either of the French memoranda, it was common knowledge that most of the duties in the new French general tariff would be specific. England had intimated in her original counter-proposals that she would seek to keep ad valorem duties in the proposed treaty. By bringing the matter to the front a second time she compelled the French Government to state firmly that specific duties would be substituted for ad valorem.[28] Thus before real negotiations began the two governments took antagonistic positions on two of the most important questions to be dealt with, the general level of duties on British goods in the

[26] Parl. Paper, Commerc., No. 37, 1881. Document No. 9, Sir Charles Dilke to Lord Granville, October 14, 1880.

[27] *Ibid.*, No. 37, 1881. Document No. 17, Lord Granville to Lord Lyons, January 11, 1881.

[28] *Ibid.*, No. 37, 1881. Document No. 29, Lord Lyons to Lord Granville, March 3, 1881.

future French tariff and the form in which those duties were to be levied.

On May 8, 1881, the French ambassador, Challemel-Lacour, notified Lord Granville of the promulgation of the new French general tariff, and on the 26th of the same month the British and French commissioners met in London to discuss the details of the French tariff and seek to establish upon it the basis for a new commercial treaty between the two countries. The discussion continued through sixteen conferences, but served only to increase the divergence in the points of view of the French and British governments. The British commissioners wished to make the proposals of Say in June, 1880, the basis of negotiation and sought to persuade the French delegates to inquire into the decrease of prices since 1860 and to readjust the specific duties in their new tariff to the present values of goods. The French declined firmly but courteously to do anything of the kind. They insisted upon the maintenance of the *status quo*, upon the general conversion of ad valorem into specific duties, and upon the substantial retention of most of the rates in their new general tariff, subject to a reduction of 24 per cent offered to all states signing commercial treaties in return for favors received. The discussions at London were, therefore, futile, and the British commissioners recommended to their government that the French offer to resume negotiations in Paris late in the summer be declined unless further communications from the French Government should indicate that there was a reasonable prospect of the conclusion of a satisfactory treaty.[29]

The British Government, realizing that an agreement could be reached only after long negotiations, asked the French Government to extend the validity of the Treaty of 1873 for three additional months, which it had been authorized to do by a recent vote of the French parliament. The French refused at first and accordingly the British broke off negotiations on August 18; but on September 15 the French reversed their position and consented to prolong the duration of the treaty from November 8,

---

[29] *Ibid.*, No. 37, 1881. Document No. 101 of July 11, 1881.

1881, to February 8, 1882. Meantime, on unofficial assurances of the change in French views, the British had consented to renew negotiations, and sent a commission to Paris, which reopened discussions on September 19. The new conversations proved as futile as the old. Each side made minor concessions, but refused to change its position regarding nearly all matters of real importance to the other side. Thus the British found the French proposals regarding duties on cottons and woollens as unsatisfactory as ever, while on their side they refused a French request to lower some of their duties on French wines on the old ground that they could not afford the loss of revenue. On November 4 the British commissioners reported that they had been unable to reach any agreement with the French which they could advise their government to accept. Conversations were resumed from time to time until the middle of February, 1882, when both governments finally admitted that there was no hope of agreeing on the details of a commercial treaty.[30]

After many dreary months the Anglo-French commercial negotiations had thus come to their inevitable conclusion. Neither government was willing to agree to a compromise on matters of real importance because in each country public opinion was clearly hostile to such a compromise. The hands of both governments were really tied and their agreement to disagree was no indication of ill will on either side of the Channel. This was shown by the fact that on February 16, 1882, Lord Lyons, the British ambassador, proposed to the French Government the conclusion of a treaty whereby each country should grant to the goods of the other most favored nation treatment; that is, neither France nor England would receive the goods of any other country on terms more favorable than those granted to the goods of the other signatory to this treaty. This would give England, in particular, assurance that France would not discriminate against her goods in favor of those of Germany. The French Government received the British proposal somewhat coldly on the ground that a most favored nation agreement would leave England free to raise her duties on wines and silks at any time

[30] For the negotiations in Paris see Parl. Paper, Commerc., No. 9, 1882.

and thus inflict a serious injury on two important French industries. While the two governments were arguing about this the
French Cabinet presented to the Chambers a bill granting most
favored nation treatment to British goods, which was passed
promptly and promulgated on February 28. In the meantime
the French Government had evidently reconsidered its position
and realized that British trade was so valuable to France that it
would be unwise to offend the British Government. Hence, on
the very same day, the French prime minister, de Freycinet, and
the British ambassador, Lord Lyons, signed a declaration
whereby each government granted the goods of the other most
favored nation treatment until February 1, 1892. The date of
termination chosen was that of the treaties France had recently
signed with Belgium, Italy, Sweden and Norway, Spain, and
Portugal. It meant that British goods would enter France on
the same terms as the goods of Germany, to whom France was
bound to grant as favorable treatment as she gave to the other
important countries in Europe. In effect, it gave England the
conventional or treaty tariff of France just as if she had signed a
commercial treaty with detailed tariff clauses like the treaties
France had signed with Italy and several of the smaller European
states.

Superficially the commercial relations of England and France
were to continue for another decade unchanged, but funda-
mentally they were sadly altered. The Treaty of 1860, renewed
in 1873, had been repudiated because England wished to go
beyond it and France to draw back. The compact negotiated
by Michel Chevalier and Richard Cobden with the greatest
secrecy, and forced upon a reluctant people by the Emperor
Napoleon III, had been far more significant than most commercial
agreements because it had not been an exclusive bargain for the
advantage of the two signatories at the expense of other countries. Its principal author, Chevalier, had intended it to be the
first link in a chain of commercial agreements which would bind
together all the great nations. The treaty provided expressly for
its extension to other countries and both France and England
had concluded similar agreements with the principal states of

Europe. Each new treaty brought down a certain number of tariff duties and contained the same clause as the parent treaty of 1860, by which every decrease granted by either France or England to a third party should automatically be extended to the other. In this way the tariff walls in Europe were slowly being lowered to the advantage of the entire continent. Now the most important link in the chain had been broken, but elaborate precautions had been taken to conceal the break. To all appearances the chain was as strong as ever, but in reality it was certain to snap whenever the protectionists were ready to renew their assault. Three of the four great authors of the Treaty of 1860, Chevalier, Cobden, and Napoleon III were dead. No one in France was able to carry on their work and the sole survivor in England, Gladstone, who was now prime minister, had long since lost interest in the achievement of which he had once been proud. The next decade was to witness the growing indifference of England and the continued rise of protection in France, as in the other countries of continental Europe, until in 1892, Méline, the successor of Mimerel, Thiers, and Pouyer-Quertier, was able to destroy the whole network of commercial treaties.

CHAPTER XVII

THE RÔLE OF CHEVALIER AND THE SIGNIFICANCE OF THE TREATY

THE Anglo-French Treaty of Commerce of 1860 can be given its proper place in economic history only if it is considered as the most important feature of a well-conceived but imperfectly executed plan for the development of French industry, trade, and agriculture. After the Revolution of 1848, which was intimately connected with the development of the industrial revolution in France, industry and trade had increased with great rapidity, yet many observers felt that their increase was far less than it should have been because manufacturers, relying upon the protection given them by a prohibitive tariff, continued to use antiquated methods. The government of the Second Empire realized clearly, as the July Monarchy had understood somewhat dimly, that the system of prohibitions and of virtually prohibitive duties in France must go, so that French industry might develop in a free and healthy manner. It took various steps to achieve this object, such as granting temporary licenses for the importation of rails or reducing certain tariff duties slightly by decree. It showed a certain amount of courage and energy and it spoke with a new accent of authority. It even decided to repeal the prohibitions in the French tariff, and made one ill-advised attempt to carry out its decision. But it did not display the requisite combination of courage with vision until a statesmanlike plan was provided for it by the engineer and economist, Michel Chevalier.

The terms of the Treaty of 1860 and of the Emperor's letter to Fould [1] announcing far-reaching economic reforms are well known, and the ideas of Chevalier regarding tariff reform had

[1] *Moniteur*, January 15, 1860.

351

been published in his *Examen du système commercial connu sous le nom de système protecteur* in the year 1852. Chevalier was believed to have had a share in the negotiation of the Treaty, but it was not known that in the archives of the French Government lay a plan embodying his ideas which served as a basis for the Emperor's letter and the treaty signed with England eight days later. This plan is contained in an anonymous and undated document. We cannot say positively when it was presented to the Emperor, nor even when it was first shown to Cobden, who took so active and prominent a part in the negotiation of the Treaty and who was the intimate friend of Chevalier. Yet no one who has seen and studied this document can doubt that the ideas it contains provided the Emperor and his ministers with the plan they needed to free French industry and trade from the shackles of the prohibitive system, to aid agriculture, and to increase and cheapen the means of transportation by land and water.

This anonymous plan in the archives of the French Government [2] resembles the Treaty of 1860 in six significant points. Both seek the abolition of prohibitions, the author of the plan making a positive recommendation to that effect and the Treaty carrying out the recommendation by substituting for prohibitions duties that might not exceed 30 per cent after 1861 or 25 per cent after 1864; both forbid the prohibition of the exportation of coal by England; and both provide for a marked decrease in the French import duties on coal which, according to the plan, were to be at the uniform rate on all French frontiers of 10 centimes per 100 kilograms, and in the Treaty, of 15 centimes. According to the plan British duties on French silks were to be cut in half and in the Treaty they were admitted free, owing to an unexpected concession offered by Gladstone to Chevalier in their confidential discussion of October 15, 1859.[3] With regard to wine the plan asked for a reduction of British duties on French products to two shillings on July 1, 1861, and to one shilling on July 1, 1866, while the Treaty stipulated that there be a scale of

[2] See Appendix, p. 369.
[3] Arch. Nat., F 12-2482.

duties based on alcoholic content ranging from one to two shillings and applicable on April 1, 1861. Finally, the plan asked that the British duties on French spirits be reduced 33 per cent and the Treaty granted a decrease from 15*s*. to 8*s*. 2*d*. per gallon.

The similarity of several of the important provisions of the anonymous plan to the provisions of the Emperor's letter to Fould of January 15, 1860, is quite as marked as in the case of the commercial treaty with England. Both documents call for the abolition of prohibitions and of the import duties on raw wool and cotton; both demand a heavy reduction of the import duties on coffee and sugar; and both suggest, as means of facilitating the execution of the proposed economic reforms, the use of the balance remaining from the loan of 500,000,000 francs and from the suspension of the amortization of the public debt. Slight differences in wording between the two documents do not alter the essential identity in them of these five important provisions.

The date of the anonymous plan can be determined within a period of six weeks by means of two statements in the text. Mention is made of reducing by one half the duties on textile raw materials on October 1, 1859; and the use is suggested of the remnant of the loan of 500,000,000 francs. A loan of that amount was issued on May 7, 1859, for the war in Italy, and was heavily oversubscribed. As the war was much shorter than had been expected, there remained, as late as January, 1860, a balance of nearly 160,000,000 francs in the French treasury. It can be said, therefore, that this document was certainly written between May 1 and October 1, 1859. In addition, two assumptions seem justified: first, that so thorough a reform would not have been planned during the war in Italy; and, second, that until the war was over no other use would be considered for any important part of a loan raised to carry on the military operations. Hence the statement seems warranted that the anonymous plan was written after the signature of the Peace of Villafranca on July 11, 1859, and it is the belief of the writer that it was written about the end of that month.

Many considerations point to Michel Chevalier as the author of the anonymous plan. In the first place he was the principal author of the treaty of January 23, 1860. As we have seen he proposed the negotiation of such a treaty in a series of letters to Cobden as early as 1856. His correspondence shows also that he repeated his proposal late in the summer of 1859, at just about the time at which the plan was written, that he succeeded in converting Cobden to the idea in September, and that in October he joined Cobden in England and proposed the conclusion of the treaty to Gladstone, the Chancellor of the Exchequer.[4] In the second place the anonymous plan resembles strikingly Chevalier's plan for reforming the French tariff which forms the conclusion of his *Examen du système commercial connu sous le nom de système protecteur* published in 1852. In this early plan, Chevalier recommended the abolition of prohibitions, import duties that should never exceed 30 per cent, the admission free of raw materials, and the classification as raw materials of cotton, wool, dyestuffs, and chemicals used in dyeing. All these recommendations are made also in the anonymous plan.

Other ideas of Chevalier are found in the anonymous plan and two of them give further evidence of his authorship. Both are named as among the compensations to be offered the French manufacturers to get them to accept the abolition of prohibitions. It is suggested that to provide good foremen for the manufacturers the state give 500,000 francs to each of the chief manufacturing cities of the empire to create schools on the model of La Martinière of Lyons. This idea of founding technical schools was one which Chevalier expressed frequently in his writings and in his lectures at the Collège de France. Even more significant is the recommendation that the sum of —— millions, spread over eight years, including 1859, be put at the disposal of the Minister of Commerce to make loans to manufacturers wanting to buy better equipment. These loans were to be repaid in ten annual instalments, beginning two years after the loan was

---

[4] The best account of the interview is in Chevalier's letter to Gladstone of June 19, 1872. The original is in the Gladstone Papers and a copy in the Flourens Papers.

granted, and were to bear interest at 3 per cent. Chevalier was the only prominent economist in France who openly expressed his approval of loans by the Government to promote the development of industry and agriculture after the publication of the Emperor's letter to Fould. In addition, as has been shown, a law was passed August 1, 1860, setting aside the sum of 40,000,-000 francs for such a loan. As in the plan, repayment was to be made in ten annual instalments beginning two years after the granting of the loan. Only the rate of interest was changed from 3 per cent to 5 per cent. Finally, it should be noted that the report in which the Council of State recommended to the Corps Législatif the passage of this law was written and signed by Michel Chevalier.

It may be asked why the anonymous plan in the French archives was not signed by Chevalier. The explanation is that it was a rough draft written in the characteristic hand of a clerk. It certainly is not the document presented to the Emperor or his ministers, but, like the majority of the papers in the Government archives shown to investigators, is the manuscript from which the finished document was copied. It would be natural for Chevalier to have such a draft written out for him. We know that he had a private secretary and that, as a member of the Council of State, he was entitled to the services of the clerks in the government offices. Further evidence that the document in the Archives Nationales is a rough draft is the fact that in two places there are corrections in another hand, and this provides us also with further evidence that the author of the plan was Chevalier. A study of these corrections and a comparison of them with samples of the handwriting of Chevalier, Cobden, Rouher, Fould, Baroche, and other possible authors of the plan, was made by M. M. Charles Schmidt and Léon Gauthier of the Archives Nationales and the writer, and it was agreed that the handwriting was that of Chevalier.[5]

The evidence from all these sources seems to justify the con-

---

[5] In the list of concessions to be made by England in Section I there appear between the lines, and in pencil, the words *Idem pour les eaux de vie*. In paragraph three of Section II there is, also in pencil, the word *Garance*.

clusion that Chevalier was the author of the anonymous plan for the treaty of commerce with England and for several economic reforms which were designed to aid agriculture, to improve the French system of transportation, and to help the manufacturers prepare themselves to meet a moderate amount of foreign competition. These reforms and the extent to which they were carried out deserve to be considered in conjunction with the effects of the Anglo-French treaty and the other treaties which followed it; but before this can be done another question regarding the part played by Chevalier must be answered. The uncertainty of the date when Chevalier's plan was put before the Emperor makes it necessary to produce evidence to show that Chevalier did not take the initiative in the treaty negotiations as a secret agent of the French Government. The natural assumption would be, in the case of negotiations which remained unofficial for some time, that the men who conducted them were acting as private persons under the orders of their governments seeking a basis for an agreement which would justify the opening of formal negotiations. One of the most eminent of French historians in a brief discussion of the treaty negotiations has referred to both Chevalier and Cobden as agents of their governments [6] and Rouher, who was Minister of Commerce at the time, subsequently stated that Chevalier would not have ventured to act except under the orders of the Emperor. These statements, however, are not supported by any evidence. The historian referred to made no serious study of the negotiations of 1859, and in consequence, his statement that both Chevalier and Cobden were secret agents was merely a plausible assumption. Rouher,

---

[6] See Lavisse, *Histoire de la France Contemporaine*, VII, 7–10. Seignobos states that Chevalier's interview with Gladstone took place October 25 instead of October 15; that the Treaty was signed January 22 instead of 23; and the Second Tariff Convention November 15 instead of 16. He speaks of Cobden's reception by the Emperor and does not mention that of Chevalier. Furthermore, he states that Napoleon III offered England a commercial rapprochement in order to win for the Francophile Palmerston the support of the Manchester School; whereas Palmerston had, in June, 1859, offered the presidency of the Board of Trade to Cobden and, on his refusal, had secured its acceptance by Milner Gibson. Both Cobden and Bright supported the Palmerston government on its assumption of office.

on the other hand, knew the facts almost from the beginning, for he was the first member of the Imperial Government consulted by Chevalier and it was he who advised the distinguished economist to lay his proposal before the Emperor. His primary interest, however, was in politics and in strengthening his influence with his sovereign. He made this statement to an Englishman[7] in 1863 when he was at the height of his power and enjoying the almost complete confidence of his imperial master. He knew that the Emperor appreciated flattery and that Chevalier could safely be ignored because he had no political power and was too outspoken and independent in his views to be *persona grata* for any length of time to Napoleon III.

On the question of the spontaneity of the initiative taken by Chevalier in proposing the Treaty direct light can be thrown only by his own words, although his authorship of the plan in the French archives should be considered as corroborative evidence. Nassau Senior, the English economist and well-known conversationalist, quotes him as saying on May 12, 1860: [8] "I related to the Emperor the substance of my conversation with Gladstone. I said I had had no previous communication on the subject with any ministers, that mine was a totally unauthorized proceeding, and would fall to the ground without inconvenience if His Majesty disapproved it." The impression given by this account is that Chevalier was making a new and startling proposal to his sovereign, and not a report on the carrying out of a suggestion received, and this is borne out by the letters he wrote to his wife in October, 1859. In his letter of the 17th from London, he said: "Si cela aboutit . . . et il n'y manque plus que le consentement d'une personne, la plus intéressée de toutes à adopter . . . ce sera la plus grande chose que j'aurai faite de ma vie." Again, on the 21st, he wrote: "Les meilleures choses avortent souvent. Les obstacles semblent tous levès, mais un hazard, l'insouciance de celui-ci, le

---

[7] April 6, 1863. Nassau Senior, *Conversations with Distinguished Persons during the Second Empire, from 1860 to 1863* (2 vols., London, 1880), II, 206.

[8] Nassau Senior, *Conversations with M. Thiers, M. Guizot, and Other Distinguished Persons during the Second Empire* (2 vols., London, 1878), II, 314.

caprice de celui-là font tout avorter. Je ne me fais pas illusion. Ce sera un devoir rempli. Nul ne pourra dire que c'est mon intérêt qui m'a poussé." This is hardly the language of an agent who had been eminently successful in the mission on which he was sent.[9]

If Chevalier had been sent to England by the Emperor, or had gone with the Emperor's knowledge and approval, and had secured the object for which he crossed the Channel, he would not have been reluctant to see Napoleon on his return, nor would he have been likely to seek the advice of one of the Emperor's ministers before making his report. As a member of the Council of State he could ask for an audience at any time without attracting attention because of an unusual request. But Chevalier was reluctant to see the Emperor. He wrote to his wife from Paris on October 23: "Je me demande si je ne devrais pas aller chez l'Empereur pour lui parler de la situation des esprits en Angleterre. Mais je suis peu porté à me porter près de lui présentement." On the following day he wrote again: "M. Rouher m'a engagé à voir l'Empereur: il croit la chose utile. Je me suis rendu à cet avis."

Chevalier's letters to his wife show that he was extremely doubtful of the Emperor's approval of the plan with which he returned from England and that that was the reason why he was not anxious, for the present, to see Napoleon. His conversation with the Emperor on October 27, as reported by Senior, contains the statement that his proceeding in England was "totally unauthorized." Similar statements were made by him in his letter to his friend M. Devinck in 1867,[10] in his letters to Bonamy Price in 1868 and 1869,[11] and in his memoir on Cobden in Frond's *Panthéon*.[12] It might be alleged that Chevalier concealed the truth because he did not wish to say openly that he

---

[9] The letters of Chevalier to his wife in October, 1859, are in the Renaudin Papers.

[10] Paris, April 19, 1867. Cahier 4. Flourens Papers.

[11] May 3, 1868, and January 8, 1869. Cahier 4, p. 951 and Cahier 5, Flourens Papers.

[12] Frond, *Panthéon des illustrations françaises du XIXᵉ siècle*, 16 vols. Paris, 1869. Vol. XVI.

was sent to England by Napoleon III while the Emperor was still the ruler of France, but in 1872 he made an even stronger statement in a letter to Gladstone in which he described their conversation at Downing Street on October 15, 1869. "Ce Français vous dit: . . . Je n'ai aucune mission de l'Empereur: il ignore que je suis en Angleterre. Mais diverses circonstances me font penser qu'en ce moment il accepterait la proposition d'un traité de commerce avec vous . . . ."

In closing his letter, Chevalier said:

"Dans votre discours du 14 juin et dans d'autres antérieurs, vous vous êtes abstenu de prononcer mon nom parmi ceux des auteurs et initiateurs du traité. Je l'attribue à ce que vous avez pensé que je ne faisais qu'exécuter un ordre de l'Empereur en me rendant à Londres en Octobre, 1859. La supposition est plausible, mais la réalité est qu'en cette circonstance je n'ai eu mission que de moi-même. Je ne parle point ainsi pour déprécier l'Empereur. Il fut alors plein de bonne volonté; il rendit un très grand service à la cause. Il est aujourd'hui malheureux et calomnié. Mais la vérité est que si, personellement, il a beaucoup contribué au traité, il n'en eut pas l'initiative, et dans celle-ci je suis fondé à revendiquer une bonne part." [13]

Important as was the part played by Chevalier in beginning and carrying through the negotiations for the treaty of commerce with England in 1860 this was not the only service which he rendered. As has been demonstrated in his anonymous plan, he intended that the Treaty should be accompanied by various economic reforms because he did not regard the Treaty as an end in itself, but rather as the means of promoting the free and healthy development of French industry, trade, and agriculture. In addition to the Treaty, he recommended the free admission of certain raw materials, such as wool and cotton, which was effected by the Law of May 5, 1860; the heavy reduction of duties on other raw materials or their admission free of duty; loans to manufacturers for the purchase of machinery and other equipment, and the improvement of means of transportation with a reduction in their cost. Finally, it is almost certain that he had in view not merely a commercial treaty with England, but a whole network of treaties that should break down tariff barriers throughout Europe. No such recom-

[13] Chevalier to Gladstone, June 19, 1872. Gladstone Papers.

mendation was made in his anonymous plan, however, although it appears in the Emperor's letter to Fould dated January 5 and published in the *Moniteur* January 15, 1860.

The negotiation of treaties of commerce with the other states on the European continent required no great effort on the part of the French Government, because those states were placed at a disadvantage as compared with France and England by the conclusion of the agreement negotiated by Chevalier and Cobden. Before the definite duties provided for by the Anglo-French Treaty had been agreed upon, King Leopold had expressed to the French ambassador at Brussels his desire for the negotiation of a similar treaty between France and Belgium [14] and this treaty was signed in the following year. Other treaties followed in rapid succession until France had agreements with all the important states of Europe except Russia, and with many of the smaller states, while England found it to her advantage to conclude a similar series of commercial treaties. The British would have preferred to see their continental neighbors adopt free trade of their own accord as England had, but since they did not do so some means had to be found of securing for Great Britain the commercial advantages accruing to France as a result of her network of treaties. While England had few tariff concessions left to grant, she stood out as the strongest nation in trade, in finance, and in naval armament, so that her friendship was valuable and her enmity dangerous. She was able, therefore, to secure treaties with most of the important continental states on a most favored nation basis, which meant that her merchants and manufacturers profited by nearly all the tariff concessions granted by other states to each other by which the level of duties in Europe was steadily lowered from the conclusion of the treaty of 1860 to the outbreak of the Franco-Prussian War.

The most effective means of aiding French manufacturers to meet the foreign competition to which they were to be subjected by the commercial treaties was the improvement of transportation. In his letter to Fould the Emperor recommended both the

[14] Min. Aff. Étr. Negociations Commerc. Série C. Carton 22 D, Dossier 1.

development of the existing system and the reduction of rates, with particular emphasis on the navigation dues on the canals. Chevalier also was keenly interested in transportation and was anxious to increase its speed as well as to lower freight rates, although he emphasized the need of making more efficient the railroads rather than the waterways. Despite the Emperor's emphasis on waterways in his letter to Fould, his government did little to extend or improve them because public opinion did not demand it, since it had become absorbed in the development of the railroads. Differences in the width and length of locks remained a serious impediment to through traffic, but the cost of transportation was lowered considerably by the decrees of August 22, 1860, and February 9, 1867, reducing the navigation dues until they became insufficient to pay for the upkeep of the waterways.[15] It is clear that the Emperor's promise in his letter to Fould to reduce navigation dues was carried out and that the Government acted on the principle that after the signature of the commercial treaty with England it should make the use of the waterways as nearly free as possible.

The government of the Second Empire showed great interest in the building of railroads, but less anxiety to increase the speed and decrease the cost of service. The mileage of railroads in France was increased from 3,868 kilometers in 1852 to 8,246 in 1858 and 16,887 in 1870.[16] Most of this mileage was in lines radiating from Paris. The need of transverse connecting lines was great, but little seems to have been done to meet it because it was virtually certain that such lines would not be profitable. The Government did push through the Law of July 12, 1865, authorizing the construction of a whole series of little lines of local interest and offering to pay from one fourth to one half the cost of construction. Most of these, however, were narrow gauge lines and many of them steam trams rather than real railroads.

---

[15] Alfred de Foville, *De la transformation des moyens de transport et ses conséquences économiques et sociales* (Paris, 1880), p. 135.

[16] *Ibid.*, p. 18. Also Alfred Picard, *Les Chemins de fer, aperçu historique; résultats généraux de l'ouverture des chemins de fer, concurrence des voies ferrées entre elles et avec la navigation* (Paris, 1918), pp. 15, 26.

After passing this statute the Imperial Government did not urge the construction of the local lines and no real progress was made until several years after the close of the Franco-Prussian war.[17]

Many complaints were made by French manufacturers that the Imperial Government did not carry out its promise to help them meet the foreign competition created by the commercial treaties by giving them faster, cheaper, and more abundant transportation. It seems clear that little was done to increase the speed with which freight was handled by the French railroads and that there was no notable reduction in freight rates. It can be said also that, while the navigation dues on the waterways were greatly reduced, little was done to improve the waterways themselves, so that it is doubtful whether their efficiency was increased appreciably. There seems, therefore, to have been some justification for the complaints of the manufacturers, but there are also powerful arguments that can be used in the defense of the Government. Complaints from manufacturers to the Government on some subject were of daily occurrence and had become so habitual that in most cases they had little significance. The manufacturers rarely thought of the French proverb *Aide-toi et le ciel t'aidera.* Also they showed little understanding of the financial problem that faced both the Government and the railroad companies. The territory to be served by the railroads was large and the industrial centers frequently small and scattered, so that there were relatively few regions in which there was any great density of traffic. Without such density of traffic it was unreasonable to expect quick service at a low cost. Improvements could undoubtedly have been made, for the rules governing the making of rates and the conditions of service were rigid, as was almost inevitable when the railroads were operated under government control. The fundamental difficulty, however, was beyond the control of the manufacturers, the railroads, or the Government. Despite the tendency to concentration in modern industry which has been felt in France, as elsewhere, the tendency toward the persistence of small-scale and rural industry in France has never been overcome.

[17] Foville, *op. cit.*, p. 18, and Picard, *op. cit.*, p. 22.

It is less powerful now than in the past, but it was a potent force in the period of the Second Empire, when it constituted a serious obstacle to the development on a large scale of the cheap and rapid transportation of goods.

The persistence of small-scale and rural industry in France was not only a force that checked the development of transportation, but one which served also to keep alive the belief in high protection, and which helped powerfully to bring about its restoration when economic and political conditions were favorable in the period beginning about 1877. There is no evidence that any important French industry suffered unduly from foreign competition created by the treaties of commerce. As we have seen, the wine industry, which was practically crippled for a number of years, owed its troubles entirely to phylloxera, which caused so great a destruction of vines that the French growers could not supply the demand of even their home market. The silk industry went through several crises after 1860, but the difficulties were clearly due to changing fashions, diseases of the silkworms, and competition from the Orient, which was facilitated by the development of ocean transportation. The linen industry was declining in all the countries of western Europe because of the competition of cottons and cheap woollens, and the decline of European freight rates put an end to the cultivation of flax except in districts where conditions were unusually favorable or where labor was remarkably cheap, as in Russia. The woollen and the cotton industries survived and grew stronger in France and the crises through which they passed were caused partly by normal economic factors which affected the industries in other countries as well, and partly by the American Civil War and the loss of Alsace and Lorraine. The iron industry was not destroyed by British competition, as had been predicted by Thiers and by many ironmasters. The absence of complaints regarding the domestic market after 1870 shows that the home industry retained control of that market. It could hardly have failed to do so, because high duties on iron and steel and their manufactures were retained in all the treaties of commerce.

The commercial treaties should be studied not from the point of view of the tariff alone, but from that of industrial evolution. It cannot be said that these treaties formed the most powerful force causing either prosperity or depression. Certain benefits to French industries were clearly brought by the more liberal tariff policy. Methods of manufacture were improved under the stimulus of foreign competition, the tendency toward industrial concentration and large-scale industry was strengthened, and the use of machinery was enormously increased, while in those industries or processes of manufacture where machinery had been employed before 1860 the types of machinery were improved until in many cases the French used the best. But generalizations in such matters are dangerous. Every student of French industry knows that in several particulars French manufacturers set the pace for the world before 1860. France was supreme in the silk and wine industries and was noted for some of her linens and woollens and for a few of her cottons, and other examples of French skill could be cited. But in general in 1860 she was far behind England in her mechanical equipment, in the construction of her factories, and in her methods of selling her products both at home and abroad. In all these things the influence of the Treaty of 1860 and its successors was beneficial.

The critics of the treaties of 1860 have rarely faced the facts squarely. Most of them have been protectionist manufacturers seeking large profits from a restricted market. Their views were expressed in the tariff policy of the country before 1860 and after 1892. Another argument used with sincerity by some lovers of freedom, and for their own ends by protectionists like Thiers, was that the treaties were forced upon France by a despotic emperor. There is much force in this argument and it proved distinctly embarrassing to many advocates of the moderate protection offered by the treaties when the Second Empire displayed its incompetence and left the French people a legacy of hardship and humiliation. Yet, in the last analysis, the forces which caused the overthrow of the treaty policy were mainly economic, for many of the republicans who detested Bonapartism favored very moderate protection. These forces, protectionist propaganda, the absence of any strong movement in France for real free trade, and depression in industry and agriculture, have been discussed in an earlier chapter. What merits our consideration here is the study of the difficulties encountered during the maintenance of the treaty policy from the point of view of industrial evolution. This study has rarely been made by critics of the treaty policy because, when industrial difficulties arose, it was easier to blame foreign competition and appeal for help to the Government. It is still easier to do this even in the most prosperous country in the world. It must be admitted, however, that the tendency has been for students of the industrial revolution to dwell exclusively on its beneficial results. We all worship "progress" as a sort of fetish and assume that it is necessarily good. Yet it creates difficulties as does any process of growth.

In few cases were the real difficulties faced by French manufacturers created by the commercial treaties, but in many cases they were intensified by them. There were first the difficulties of war and the fear of war which were present almost continuously during the first eleven years of the new tariff policy beginning with the American Civil War, 1861–65, and ending with the Franco-Prussian War of 1870–71. But economic factors were more important and influential. With the progress of the industrial revolution there came inevitably the intensification of industrial competition. This was increased by the development of transportation which brought to an end many a regional monopoly of an industrial center. Thus the industry of *indiennes* at Rouen suffered both from the competition of similar cotton goods made in Alsace and from that of cheap and light woollens produced at Reims. Its principal enemies were not the British, as alleged, but rather protectionists equally zealous for the defense of national labor in France. The use of machinery created new difficulties for both employer and workman in France as elsewhere. The investment of capital was enormously increased, which meant larger profits in times of prosperity and greater losses during industrial crises. To the workman the change meant specialization in one occupation. It was more frequently impossible for him to be both farmer and spinner or weaver. On the other hand there was some compensation in the fact that his wages rose and that he was less likely to be thrown entirely out of work in the factory, because the loss from idleness of machinery and from depreciation was so great that the employer could not close his factory as easily as before.

The progress of the industrial revolution in France meant that French industry felt more quickly and completely the effects of industrial booms and depressions. Thus the terrible crisis of 1868–69 in the textile industries, which was largely the economic liquidation of the American Civil War, was felt almost as keenly in France as in England. While this crisis was chiefly the result of war rather than of normal economic forces, other crises which followed were not. France had become a part of the industrial world which was growing steadily smaller as markets widened with the development of international trade and transportation. When she suffered from declining prices her manufacturers and farmers, like those of other countries, blamed foreign competition. There was much truth in the contention, but one may doubt whether the remedy of high protection, which was finally adopted by France and most of her continental neighbors, was the best for her people as a whole. The increasing volume of production and the increasing speed and diminishing cost of transportation were the factors that were bringing down prices in nearly all countries. This brought temporary hardship to many producers, but the loss was not permanent or irremediable to them, while to the far larger mass of consumers there was a long enduring benefit in the reduction of the cost of living.

The function of commercial legislation is rarely to create or to destroy, but rather to fulfill. Its scope is conditioned by economic forces whose effects it can hope only to soften or stimulate. If it is wisely framed and executed, its results will be more beneficial than harmful. Experience has shown that this was the case with the Anglo-French Treaty of Commerce of 1860 and the other agreements which followed. The treaty with England was negotiated in secret and forced upon an unwilling country by its despotic emperor. But it was the result, not of a sudden decision or caprice, but of carefully matured plans made by an eminent engineer and economist, Michel Chevalier. It did not replace the French system of prohibitions and a prohibitive tariff by free trade, but by moderate protection. It encountered great difficulties from the beginning. The ruler by whose authority it had been signed proved wasteful in finance and reckless and incompetent in war and diplomacy, and ended his reign by bringing disaster and humiliation to France. The treaty came into force in the year that saw the beginning of the American Civil War, which made the period of transition, for the textile industries at least, one of acute difficulty. But there is no evidence that any important French industry was seriously injured by the tariff policy which it inaugurated. On the contrary, most French industries were strengthened through the stimulus of a moderate amount of competition. They renewed and improved their equipment and adopted better methods of manufacturing and of selling their goods. These gains were kept after the treaty policy had been modified in 1881 and repudiated in 1892. Its abandonment was the result, not of misfortunes of its own creation, but of industrial and agricultural depression which were felt throughout Europe, and of the powerful appeal of protection to the governments and peoples of nearly all countries. France, which did the most to create the system of commercial treaties, was not the first, but the last of the important continental states to abandon it. We cannot say, therefore, that the instrument negotiated by Chevalier and Cobden was a failure. It remained legally in force for more than twenty years and was really effective for thirty-two. During most of this time it set an example which was followed by nearly all the states of Europe. To French industry it applied the additional pressure needed to achieve maturity. Through it the country entered resolutely upon the path of progress and, although it encountered new hardships, it secured new and greater benefits.

APPENDIX

BASES D'UN TRAITÉ DE COMMERCE ENTRE LA FRANCE ET L'ANGLETERRE EN 5 PARTIES

(Archives Nationales, F 12–2482)

I

L'Empereur abolit les prohibitions à partir du 1er juillet 1861 (date antérieurement fixée par l'Empereur), et les remplace par des droits n'excédant pas 25% (qui, avec le double décime, feraient 30%).

Le chiffre de ces droits serait établi d'après le montant des valeurs actuelles, telles qu'elles sont consignées d'après le dernier Tableau du Commerce.

Le gouvernement impérial se proposant d'abolir les droits sur les matières premières, ou de les remplacer par de simples droits de balance, il ne serait rien ajouté aux susdits 25% en raison de ces droits.

Le gouvernement de l'Empereur réduirait dès à présent le droit sur la houille et le coke à 10 centimes par 100 kilogrammes (droit actuel sur la frontière prussienne), sans distinction de zône. Au 1er juillet 1861, le droit sur la houille et sur le coke serait supprimé.

Au 1er juillet 1861, le droit sur les fers en feuilles et tôles, les fers en petites barres rondes, carrées ou méplates, et les fils de fer serait remplacé par le droit actuel sur les fers en barres; dans un délai de cinq ans à partir de là, ce dernier droit serait mis à 50 francs.

Disposition analogue pour l'acier en feuilles, en petites barres et en filés.

DE LA PART DE L'ANGLETERRE

Au 1er juillet 1861, l'Angleterre réduirait le droit sur les vins à deux shillings par gallon. Au 1er juillet 1866, le droit serait réduit à un shilling.

Au 1er juillet 1861, le droit sur les soieries serait réduit de moitié.

Idem, $\frac{1}{3}$ sur les esprits et eaux de vie.

369

On pourrait joindre à cela diverses dispositions de moindre importance, comme celle-ci:

Le droit sur les œufs subirait une réduction (totale ou de moitié) à la condition que la France supprimerait le droit qu'elle perçoit à la sortie de cet article.

L'Angleterre s'interdirait d'établir un droit de sortie sur la houille et le coke.

II

COMPENSATIONS À OFFRIR AUX MANUFACTURIERS FRANÇAIS POUR QU'ILS ACCEPTENT LA LEVÉE DES PROHIBITIONS

Les droits sur les matières premières textiles et notamment le coton brut et la laine en masse seront réduits de moitié à partir du 1er octobre 1859 et supprimés ou réduits à un droit de balance de 25 centimes par 100 kilogr., à partir du 1er juillet 1861.

Même disposition pour les matières tinctoriales exotiques. (A).

Garance, idem.

Réduction analogue sur l'impôt indirect qui frappe le sel destiné aux fabriques de soude.

Au 1er juillet 1861, réduction à 25% au maximum des droits sur les acides, les sels et autres produits chimiques. (B).

Une somme de   millions, répartie en trois ans, y compris 1859, serait mise à la disposition du Ministre du Commerce pour faire des avances aux manufacturiers qui voudraient acheter un matériel perfectionné.

Ces avances seraient remboursables en dix annuités, dont la première ne courrait que deux ans après le versement des avances par le Trésor. Les annuités seraient calculées sur la base d'un intérêt de trois pour cent.

Une convention serait passée avec les compagnies de chemins de fer, pour qu'elles transportent la houille et le coke au tarif minimum de quatre centimes par tonne et par kilomètre, sous la condition que ces matières se présentent par wagons complets.

Dans l'intérêt de l'industrie métallurgique, même stipulation pour le minerai de fer, pour la fonte en gueuses et le fer en barres de tout échantillon.

On obtiendrait cette concession des compagnies de chemins de fer par différents moyens, dont le plus simple serait peut-être de les affranchir pendant dix ans d'une partie des impôts qu'elles supportent, et notamment de la taxe sur leurs revenus.

On pourrait même, l'expérience le montre, obtenir un tarif plus bas que quatre centimes.

Pour fournir de bons contre-maîtres aux manufactures, une somme de cinq cent mille francs serait donnée par l'État à chacune des vingt plus grandes villes manufacturières de l'Empire, afin de créer une école sur le modèle de la Martinière de Lyon. Les écoles d'arts et métiers n'ont jamais satisfait à ce besoin.

L'industrie du sucre indigène aurait la faculté d'exporter ses produits avec un drawback, sur la base d'un rendement particulier, c'est à dire différent de celui qui existe pour le sucre étranger et le sucre colonial. (Elle souscrirait à un rendement plus élevé).

NOTA. Les dispositions (A) et (B) entreraient dans le traité de commerce negocié avec l'Angleterre.

III

AVANTACES À FAIRE PARTICULIÈREMENT À L'AGRICULTURE

Autoriser immédiatement (selon la demande faite par le Corps législatif), l'entrée libre du guano sous tout pavillon.

Supprimer les formalités attachées à l'entrée des machines agricoles, formalités qui ont rendu illusoire la modération du droit.

Lever la prohibition sur la sortie des écorces à tan, la remplacer par un droit modéré.

Lever la prohibition sur la sortie du minerai de fer. Un certain nombre de propriétaires en tireraient du revenu.

Modifier les formalités requises pour l'obtention des sommes destinées au drainage. Avec les règlements actuels, la loi des 100 millions reste sans effet.

IV

MOYENS DE RENDRE LA RÉFORME POPULAIRE

Abaisser à 25 francs par 100 kilog. le droit sur le sucre brut.
Même réduction sur le café.

V

VOIES ET MOYENS

1. Le reliquat de l'emprunt de 500 millions.
2. La dotation de l'amortissement pendant un temps nécessaire.
3. L'emprunt s'il y a lieu.

PETITION OF MANUFACTURERS TO EMPEROR JANUARY 20, 1860

(Archives Nationales, F 12–7109)

SIRE,

Lorsque le Gouvernement de Votre Majesté annonça par une note insérée au Moniteur le 24 juillet 1856, le premier ajournement du projet de la loi relative à la levée des prohibitions, il promit en même temps, sur les réclamations des chambres de commerce, de procéder à une enquête afin de constater le degré de protection nécessaire à nos diverses industries.

Lorsque le 11 mai dernier, M. le Ministre du Commerce écrivait à la Chambre de Commerce de Lille que la date de juillet 1861, assignée à la solution de la question du retrait des prohibitions, se trouvait reculée par les évenements, il ajoutait encore en parlant de l'enquête:

« Le Gouvernement avait l'intention de commencer vers le mois d'octobre prochain l'enquête par l'examen des produits, à l'égard desquels le projet de lever la prohibition semble ne devoir surélever aucune contestation sérieuse; ces produits sont au nombre de dix-sept.

« A la suite de cette enquête, c'est à dire en 1860, le Corps législatif aurait été saisi du projet de loi spécial à ces divers produits. Pendant la même année on aurait procédé à l'enquête relative aux articles plus vivement contestés qui, vous le savez, comprennent les industries textiles, de telle sorte que, pour celles-ci, le projet de loi pût être présenté en 1861.

« Mais le Gouvernement reconnait, sans difficulté, que les complications récentes de la politique extérieure rendent inopportune l'étude de cette réforme douanière; il est naturellement amené à ajourner l'enquête, et par cela même la solution de la question du retrait des prohibitions. Le programme que l'administration s'était tracé et la date de juillet 1861 qu'elle avait fixée, se trouvent donc modifiés par les évenements.''

Ainsi la promesse avait été faite et renouvelée, il y a peu de mois encore, que la question ne serait pas tranchée sans qu'une enquête préalable eût permis d'entendre les représentants de l'industrie nationale.

Qu'arrive-t-il cependant? Votre Majesté va changer de four en comble les articles les plus importants de notre législation douanière, non pas seulement ceux qui protègent le travail national par la prohibition, mais ceux qui le protègent par de simples droits, de telle sorte que toutes nos grandes industries seront atteintes à la fois; elle va opérer ces changements si énormes, et cela sans qu'aucune enquête ait eu lieu, sans que nous ayons pu nous faire entendre.

Ayant appris que l'Empereur daignait admettre quelques manufacturiers, désignés par M. le Ministre du Commerce, à lui présenter leurs observations, nous lui avons aussitôt adressé une demande pour obtenir à notre tour cette faveur. Nous étions nombreux. Plus de quatre cents industriels délégués étaient à Paris, car nous avons de grands intérêts à défendre. Il nous a été répondu que les occupations de Votre Majesté ne lui permettaient pas de nous recevoir, et nous avons éprouvé le douloureux regret de ne pouvoir faire connaître à l'Empereur la situation réelle du travail national.

Nous vous demandons, Sire, ce que devient alors cette promesse d'enquête à laquelle nous avions du nous fier. Car l'industrie française ne saurait prendre pour une enquête sérieuse et complète de courtes paroles échangées avec M. le Ministre du Commerce, et l'audition, par Votre Majesté, de quelques manufacturiers qui ne représentent qu'une bien minime partie des diverses branches de notre production. Nous n'avons pu être admis à débattre nos intérêts; nous allons être condamnés sans avoir été entendus.

Or dans quelle circonstance Votre Majesté supprime-t-elle cette enquête qui devait précéder la levée des prohibitions et qui nous avait été promise d'une façon si solennelle? Précisément, lorsqu'il serait le plus nécessaire de s'entourer des lumières et de l'expérience de tous les corps spéciaux, ainsi que de tous les hommes compétents. Car, chose bien grave, il s'agit de se lier par un traité de commerce avec l'Angleterre. Certes, il est bien loin de notre pensée de vouloir contester le moins du monde le pouvoir que l'Empereur tient de la constitution. L'Empereur a le droit de faire les traités de commerce sans soumettre à la sanction législative les modifications de tarifs qui y sont stipulées; mais nous ne croyons pas sortir des limites d'une soumission respectueuse en rappelant les paroles suivantes extraites du rapport fait par l'illustre Président du Senat, par M. Troplong, à l'appui du senatus-consulte du 23 décembre 1852, portant interprétation et modification de la constitution.

Voici comment s'exprimait M. Troplong.

« Votre commission a la conviction intime que plus le Gouvernement est armé d'un droit éminent pour faire les traités, plus il sent la nécessité de s'environner des lumières des hommes spéciaux pour n'entrer dans la voie des modifications diplomatiques de tarifs qu'avec de grandes précautions.

« Les traités de commerce touchent à ce qu'il y a de plus délicat dans les intérêts de notre navigation, de notre industrie, de notre commerce, et de notre agriculture. En cherchant à faire le bien, on peut se laisser entrainer à des mesures fatales; et il y a tel traité de commerce assez dangereux pour porter la plus grande perturbation dans tous nos intérêts, pour ruiner la production agricole, pour anéantir nos fabriques, et bouleverser le système entier de notre économie politique. Par un traité de commerce irréfléchie, rien ne serait plus facile que de compromettre la richesse intérieure du pays, aussi profondément qu'un traité de paix, portant imposition de subsides ou cession de territoire, porterait atteinte à l'honneur national. »

M. Troplong disait plus loin:

« Le célèbre traité de 1786 ne produisit des effets si désastreux sur certaines branches de l'industrie française que parce que le Gouvernement ne s'environna que de lumières partielles, laissant à l'écart un grand nombre des organes naturels du commerce et de la fabrication. Le Gouvernement de l'Empereur sait, au reste, dans sa haute sagesse, que ces questions sont hérissées de difficultés, qu'on y marche à côté de pièges adroits et de théories d'autant plus funestes qu'elles sont plus séduisantes. »

Nous n'ajouterons qu'on mot. Les mesures que Votre Majesté se prépare à prendre ne sont rien moins qu'une révolution économique et sociale. Il nous paraît impossible qu'en touchant à tant de choses sans consulter les représentants de nos cités manufacturières l'administration ne commette pas de nombreuses et importantes erreurs. L'existence d'un nombre plus ou moins considérable de nos industries nationales se trouvera donc compromise. Où sera le remède, si on est lié par un traité ? Il nous faudra de deux choses l'une; ou bien en subir les désastreuses conséquences, ou bien recourir à la guerre pour le briser à coup de canon. Telle est la terrible alternative dans laquelle on va se placer.

Il était de notre honneur et de notre devoir, Sire, de soumettre ces observations à Votre Majesté, au nom des populations qui nous ont envoyés vers Elle. Puissent-elles être entendues ! Car elles sont inspirées par le dévouement le plus sincère à l'Empereur et au pays.

Nous avons l'honneur d'être, Sire, de Votre Majesté,
les très-humbles, très-obéissants
et très-fidèles sujets.

[Signed by 165 manufacturers]

Paris, January 20, 1860.

PETITION OF THE OCTAVE FAUQUET COMPANY TO THE MINISTER OF COMMERCE

(Archives Nationales, F 12–6221)

Monsieur le Ministre,

J'ai le plaisir de vous présenter par écrit les demandes que j'ai eu l'honneur de vous adresser de vive voix dans votre réception du dimanche 4 courant;

La Société Octave Fauquet et Cie. demande l'introduction libre de tous droits à partir du mois d'octobre 1860, de tout l'ensemble des machines de filature de coton et de quelques autres accessoires destinés à la formation d'une filature de coton modèle, à Oissel près de Rouen.

Pour obtenir une semblable faveur, la Société présente à Son Excellence le Ministre de Commerce, les motifs suivants. Étant obligé d'importer de machines anglaises, puisqu'elle ne peut trouver présentement en France les mêmes avantages, elle sera obligée de faire venir en même temps des hommes aptes à la règle et à en enseigner le maniement aux ouvriers; néanmoins ces derniers auront encore besoin d'un apprentissage qui rendra la marche des machines moins régulière et moins productive, tandis que les frais d'entretien en seront plus couteux les premières années de la création. Le prix des matériaux de construction en général, et notamment des métaux pour supports et charpentes, bois ouvrés, matériaux composés, etc.; n'étant pas encore diminué des abaissements de droits sur les matières premières vont être employés en ce moment à des conditions désavantageuses, relativement à celles qu'on obtiendra un peu plus tard, lorsqu'une main d'œuvre couteuse remplacée par des moyens mécaniques, le plus grand emploi des matières joint à la facilité des transports en modifiera les prix en les rendant plus uniformes dans les différents pays.

Voulant en outre faire des bâtiments incombustibles pour être à l'abri d'un incendie, la Société sera obligée d'employer des moyens nouveaux pour éviter de faire des constructions trop couteuses, en s'arrangeant aussi de manière que la santé des ouvriers n'ait point à souffrir des grandes variations de température si pénibles à supporter dans la plupart des ateliers; elle fera pour toute l'industrie des expériences nouvelles dont elle paiera les frais. S'il nous est permis, Monsieur le Ministre, de faire valoir, que solidarisant nos intérêts et concourrant à la création de cette entreprise, nous tous qui touchons aux diverses branches de la grande industrie de coton, nous formons un ensemble de connaissances pratiques et de capacités qui garantissent suffisamment la bonne exécution du modèle que nous voulons présenter à l'industrie, et prouvons que ce n'est point par hasard ou par contrainte mais par conviction et confiance que nous entrons dans la lutte. J'ose croire, Monsieur le Ministre, qu'il vous sera suffisamment démontré que les désavantages de la position actuelle, les quelques risques que nous courrons, les frais supplementaires que nous ferons, enfin l'exemple que nous donnons doivent compenser la valeur intrinsèque de la bonification que nous sollicitons et qui représente à peu près dix pour cent du montant de toutes les dépenses.

Les capitaux du commerce n'osant pas généralement en ce moment s'immobiliser dans l'industrie, surtout pour des sommes assez importantes, nous voudrions, Monsieur le Ministre, obtenir du Gouvernement de l'Empereur, une part des capitaux qui doivent être mis à la disposition de l'industrie et connaître les conditions des prêts et les garanties exigées.

Vous promettant, Monsieur le Ministre, la plus entière discretion sur ces démarches que j'ai fait près de vous sans informer mes coassociés, j'attendrai selon l'avis de votre Excellence, des communications ou l'ordre de me rendre près d'elle, ayant bon espoir dans la protection que vous m'avez offerte avec tant de bienveillance, afin de décider quelques conditions fondamentales qui doivent en dépendre et que le temps me force d'arrêter le plus tôt possible.

Soyez assez indulgent, Monsieur le Ministre, pour me pardonner cette nouvelle insistance et croire au plus profond respect de votre serviteur très reconnaissant et très devoué.

Signé: OCTAVE FAUQUET.
Rouen, 5 mars, 1860.

BIBLIOGRAPHY

DESPITE its great significance and the eminence of its authors, no history of the Cobden-Chevalier Treaty of 1860 has ever been written. This omission is partly the result of the unpopularity of the Treaty in France and of the secrecy with which it was negotiated, but it is to an even greater extent the consequence of the belief in England that the Treaty was negotiated almost single-handed by Richard Cobden. The first great book on the subject was Morley's *Life of Richard Cobden* and the last is Hobson's *Richard Cobden, the International Man*. No real biography of Michel Chevalier has ever been written, and Morley's brilliant *Life of William Ewart Gladstone* devotes only five pages to the Treaty. Lord Morley's volume on Cobden remains the ablest single work, yet even it is not based on a thorough study of sources. No use was made by him of either the Chevalier or Gladstone papers, nor is there any evidence that he obtained important information from the men themselves, although they were both alive when the first edition of his book was published. The Cobden papers were thoroughly studied, as his marginal notes prove, but no mention is made of three letters in which Chevalier proposed a treaty of commerce as early as February, 1856. Lord Morley certainly did not think that Cobden was virtually the sole author of the " Cobden Treaty," though he gave that impression to most of the later writers who have used his book. Hobson, like Morley, has studied only the Cobden papers and, though he throws new light on the Treaty as an achievement in the cause of international peace, he follows his predecessor in giving Cobden credit for converting the Emperor. Yet in 1878 there had appeared Nassau Senior's *Conversations with M. Thiers, M. Guizot, and Other Distinguished Persons during the Second Empire*, giving an account of a talk with Michel Chevalier in May, 1860, in which the distinguished Frenchman stated that he had seen the Emperor and induced him to accept the idea of a commercial treaty with England before Cobden had been admitted to the palace.

Among political and economic historians a few give more than passing notice to the Treaty of 1860. De la Gorce in his *Histoire du second empire* gives a brief and inadequate account of the secret negotiations, based only on the rather unsound Greville journals and on Jules Simon's short *Notice sur Michel Chevalier*. He does not give any of the

377

real facts concerning the origins of the Treaty, although Simon was pretty well informed. Of the French economic historians Levasseur and Amé must have known Chevalier personally and have been in a position to obtain accurate information; yet neither of them gives a good account of the secret negotiations. Levasseur does give Chevalier credit for the idea of the Treaty and quotes freely from his letter to Bonamy Price, one of the most important of the original sources, but makes the serious mistake of saying that the decisive interview in October, 1859, was between Gladstone and de Persigny, instead of Chevalier. He also quotes Duruy to the effect that Rouher was opposed to the Treaty and worked for it only to please the Emperor, whereas every other source testifies to Rouher's enthusiastic support and Chevalier states that he was the first person in whom he confided on his return from England. Arnauné, on the other hand, gives a pretty good account of the negotiations, based chiefly on Chevalier's Memoir on Cobden published in 1865 in Frond's *Panthéon des illustrations françaises du XIXᵉ siècle*. This is not as good a source as the letter to Price, but in using it Arnauné makes no mistakes. He seems also to have read Simon, although he does not give him as a reference. Percy Ashley, in his *Modern Tariff History*, although he has used only secondary sources, gives what is probably the best of the brief accounts of the Treaty and of the reasons for its conclusion.

A few minor works should be mentioned here, such as those of Devers, Reybaud, Lack, Leroy-Beaulieu, and Dumas. Louis Reybaud, in his *Économistes modernes*, 1862, has articles on Cobden and Chevalier, in which he gives to Cobden all the credit for starting the negotiations; but he deserves our gratitude, for his book called forth an admirable memoir from his appreciative colleague in the Institute in which Chevalier gives the facts in great detail. We can only regret that this memoir was never published. H. Reader Lack, in *The French Treaty and the Tariff of 1860*, gives the text of the Treaty and subsequent Tariff Conventions in a convenient form. The author was secretary to the Tariff Commission and published his book in 1861. A brief biographical sketch of Chevalier has been written by his son-in-law, Paul Leroy-Beaulieu, in the *Nouveau dictionnaire d'économie politique*. Though shorter than that of Jules Simon, it is far more accurate in its account of the history of the Treaty. Dumas' *Étude sur le traité de commerce de 1786 entre la France et l'Angleterre*, is an able book, showing thorough and accurate research. Had it dealt with the Treaty of 1860 there would be nothing left to write about. It is, however, invaluable for a comparison of the two treaties.

On the conclusion of the Cobden-Chevalier Treaty many of the protectionists in France could not resist the impulse to express their feelings in print. A few of them really had something to say and there should be mentioned the anonymous author of the *Historique du traité de commerce de 1860 et des conventions complémentaires,* Goldenberg (a friend of Chevalier with moderate protectionist views, despite his iron foundries in Alsace), Casimir-Périer (one of the owners of the Anzin coal mines), and Feray (a linen manufacturer and one of the leaders of the protectionists).

Chevalier's letter to Price has already been referred to. It is the only one of his important letters on the Treaty that has been published, having been printed in the appendix to Bonamy Price's *The Principles of Currency,* and also in the *Journal des économistes* for February, 1869. Important facts are given also in Boiteau's *Les Traités de commerce,* published in 1863. The author was a well-known writer on economic subjects and a personal friend of Chevalier, from whom he must have obtained much of his information, which is more complete than that of any other writer, with the possible exception of Lord Morley. Another collection of memoirs resembling Frond's *Panthéon* was published in 1869 under the title *Les Contemporains célèbres,* and Chevalier again wrote the article on Cobden, giving a number of facts not included in the earlier article. Finally there is Gladstone's article on " The History of 1852–60, and Greville's Latest Journals," in the *English Historical Review,* April, 1887. Gladstone gives a great deal of valuable information on many different aspects of the Treaty, but he is the most unfair of all English writers to Chevalier, whom he does not even mention as one of the authors of the Treaty. His injustice is surprising because he and Chevalier were personal friends after 1860 and because Gladstone knew more about the history of the Treaty negotiations than any other man except Cobden and Chevalier. It can only be said that Gladstone was perfectly sincere in his conviction that the principal authors of the Treaty were Cobden and the Emperor, and that no one else ought to be mentioned in that capacity.

The material in the newspapers and periodicals on the Treaty of 1860 throws no real light on the negotiations, but does illustrate the growth of the free trade movement in France as well as that of the protectionist opposition; and it also records the debates on the Treaty in the English and French parliaments. The most valuable of the economic journals, which was also the organ of the French free trade party, is the *Journal des économistes;* the organ of the opposition was the *Moniteur industriel.* Compared with these periodicals the *Economist* is of slight value, and its views on matters relating to free trade are so rigidly orthodox that it might almost be classed among the organs of the Opposition. Chevalier was on the staff of the *Journal des débats*, which is the most useful of the French newspapers; one might almost say the only one of any use. Its views are liberal on economic matters, but do not necessarily represent the ideas of Chevalier, for each editor expresses his personal opinions with perfect freedom. Among the English papers the *Morning Post* (Palmerston) is the best informed and is the source from which most of the French press derives its information. Despite Palmerston's indifference, the *Post* was favorable to the Treaty from the very start. The position of the *Times* varied, but in general it was moderately favorable. The *Morning Star* (Cobden and Bright) was, of course, enthusiastic, but it gives far less information than the *Post.* All the British papers give useful information on the debates in Parliament, but, of course, none of them are as valuable as Hansard. In France, reports of the proceedings of the Chambers are given in the *Moniteur.*

The material in the Government archives is abundant and valuable, the most important collection being that of the Archives Nationales (Série F–12). Here there is a series of reports on commercial negotiations with England from 1840 to 1860, of which the two most important were written in 1852. They give not only a history of previous negotiations, but also an estimate of the concessions which the French Government, just before the establishment of the Second Empire, felt it could offer England without danger to French industries. Details are fully discussed and there are some valuable statistics. A collection of drafts of the Treaty of 1860 shows the different steps in the negotiations, although its value is lessened by the lack of signatures and dates, so that only by a comparison with the drafts in the British archives can a rough chronology be established. The voluminous report of Rouher and Baroche on the Treaty (both the MSS. and the completed report) does not give any information of great importance and makes no attempt to describe adequately the real negotiations; it is purely an official document intended for publication. There are several letters by Rouher, Baroche, Cobden, and Chevalier. They are all short and are important chiefly as samples of handwriting, but one by Cobden to Rouher is interesting as explaining his objections to the French Government's proposal to present the Treaty for ratification by the French Chambers. The longest of Chevalier's letters, which is also addressed to Rouher, states that he sends with it a translation of Cobden's letter and adds an explanation of the position of the British Government regarding its duties on French wines. A collection of petitions to the Emperor from all parts of France concerning the Treaty and the letter to Fould is most valuable as being the best indication of the state of public opinion. Though in the Gironde petitions were carefully recruited by the Chamber of Commerce of Bordeaux, and in the Drôme by a zealous prefect, the majority were spontaneous expressions of opinion by industrial or municipal bodies whose interests were affected. Further information of the utmost importance is contained in a series of reports on French industries by government agents sent out by the Conseil Supérieur du Commerce, in the early summer of 1860, and in a few reports on earlier industrial investigations. The data given show the exaggeration of the protectionist claims and their frequent falsification of statistics. Finally there are two papers written to show the importance of the Treaty and win for it popular support, of which one is by Chevalier; and a plan for a treaty of commerce with England written probably in August, 1859, by Chevalier. The determination of its authorship is most important because its chief clauses bear a striking resemblance both to many features of the Treaty and to the Emperor's letter to Fould announcing sweeping economic reforms which were to include the Treaty.[1]

The Quai d'Orsay has a set of the reports published in the *Moniteur* of the debates of the Chambers on bills or petitions resulting from the Treaty. These are really only summaries, and are far less satisfactory than stenographic reports, but they are the best available. The debates show clearly the hostility of both the Senate and the Corps Législatif to the Treaty policy, although the Treaty itself did not come before them. The Ministry of Foreign Affairs has also the despatches of the Count de Persigny and its instructions to him. These deal chiefly with the ratification of the Treaty by the British Parliament, which was complicated by the diplomatic crisis called forth by the Emperor's decision to annex Savoy. The official account by the French Government of the Treaty negotiations is important as it is the only record of the formal deliberations of the plenipotentiaries at Paris in January, 1860, but its explanation of the origins of the Treaty can be regarded only as evidence of the fertile imagination of its author, Alexis de Clercq. In an appendix are given Cobden's letter to Baroche of January 13, 1860,

---

[1] After my investigation had been completed the Series F 12 was partly reclassified. Most of the documents dealing with the actual negotiations of the Treaty are now in No. 2482.

stating his opinion that the minimum duty on British goods imported into France should not exceed 10 per cent and the maximum should be 25 per cent; and the reply of Baroche of January 22, giving the maximum as 30 per cent and the minimum as variable, but approximately 10 per cent. This correspondence led to an acrimonious discussion between Cobden and Rouher in the Tariff Commission over the minimum duties, which Cobden contended could never exceed 10 per cent. Finally there is a complete set of the Procès Verbaux of the sessions of the Tariff Commission from August 20 to November 16, 1860, together with a few reports on technical diplomatic or industrial questions.

In the Public Record Office is a useful memorandum by Hertslet on commercial negotiations with France from 1821 to 1855. This is a more complete account than that given in the reports in the Archives Nationales, but is purely diplomatic. The correspondence of the Foreign Office with Lord Cowley and Cobden concerning the Treaty is most valuable, since it appears to be complete. It includes drafts of the Treaty, reports of the negotiations, and the Cabinet's instructions to the negotiators. All these papers are signed and dated and many of them have marginal notes by Gladstone, Palmerston, or Russell. The correspondence of the Foreign Office with Lord Cowley concerning Italy and Savoy is of interest to us only because of the influence of the annexation crisis on the ratification of the Treaty. Finally, there are the somewhat technical correspondence of Cobden with the Board of Trade regarding the Tariff Conventions and a duplicate set of the Procès Verbaux of the Tariff Commission. F. O. 27 gives the ordinary diplomatic correspondence with Lord Cowley; F. O. 97 deals solely with the Commercial Treaty of 1860 and the Tariff Conventions.

We now come to the richest of all the sources of new evidence, the private papers of Cobden, Gladstone, and Chevalier. The Cobden letters shown to investigators are copies of the originals made at the direction of Mrs. Cobden shortly before her death in 1877. The copies I saw were the same that were studied by Lord Morley, as shown by the marginal notes in his hand. The most important of them are Cobden's Diary kept during his stay in France 1859–60, and his correspondence with Chevalier, Gladstone, and Sir Louis Mallet. It should be noted, however, that neither the Chevalier nor the Gladstone correspondence is complete. The Mallet letters deal only with minor points connected with the Tariff Conventions and with the dispute between Cobden and the British Government over the British duties on French wines which was never settled in a manner satisfactory to Cobden.

In the Gladstone papers at Hawarden is a complete set of the Cobden-Gladstone correspondence in the original on both sides. These letters form the most important source on the British side for the history of the Treaty negotiations, for Cobden's letters to Gladstone are full and frank and Gladstone's replies disclose the policy of the British Government, Gladstone having been given complete charge of the negotiations by the Cabinet as long as they should remain secret and unofficial. Even after the active intervention of the Foreign Office this private correspondence continued, for Cobden never gave his full confidence to any of the other British ministers. Gladstone's letters were returned to him by Mrs. Cobden after her husband's death on the ground that he could keep them better than she. In the Hawarden papers there is also the original of a letter from Chevalier to Gladstone written in 1872, which contains one of the three most important accounts by him of the early part of the secret negotiations and also the unqualified statement that he came to England in October, 1859, entirely on his own initiative and without the knowledge of the Emperor. This statement carries particular weight because it was made after the fall of the Second Empire when there was no reason why Chevalier could not speak frankly. Correspondence between Gladstone and Lord John Russell shows the sympathetic attitude of Lord John toward the treaty negotiations and indicates the opinions held by some of the other members of the Cabinet.

The Chevalier papers are partly in the possession of his granddaughter, Mme. Maxim Renaudin, one of the children of his second daughter Cordelia, who married Paul Leroy-Beaulieu and who acted frequently as her father's secretary. Mme. Renaudin has the letters Chevalier wrote to his wife during his trip to England in October, 1859, to negotiate the Treaty of Commerce. These letters were found in a locked drawer in Chevalier's desk, which the family broke open after I had asked for papers. In general they are very short, but they mention the more important interviews with Cobden, Gladstone, Bright, and de Persigny in England, and with Rouher and the Emperor after his return to France. They show that Chevalier dreaded meeting the Emperor; that Rouher was the first person in France to whom he confided his plan for the Treaty; and that not until Rouher had urged him to do so did he ask for an audience with the Emperor. Mme. Chevalier very wisely did not burn the most important of these letters as her husband asked her to do. Mme. Renaudin has also the MSS. of her grandfather's memoir to Louis Reybaud refuting his account of the treaty negotiations in his *Économistes modernes*.

But the greater part of Chevalier's papers is in the hands of another granddaughter, Mlle. Flourens. It seems clear that a good many papers must have been lost, and it is known that many were burned after Mme. Chevalier's death in 1913; but Mlle. Flourens has many letters and notes of great value. Generally these are copies made by her mother and her aunts and corrected by their father. The most important are Chevalier's letters to Devinck (a manufacturer and municipal councillor of Paris), Price, and Gladstone, which contain his most complete accounts of the treaty negotiations. There are also two letters from de Persigny and one or two from Bright, all these referring to the debates on the Treaty in the British Parliament; the final draft of the Memoir to Reybaud already referred to; the MSS. of several drafts of the Treaty, together with many notes and statistics made when working with Cobden; and finally about one hundred letters from Cobden, the greater part of which were not copied by the Cobden family when Chevalier sent them to Mrs. Cobden for that purpose. They are chiefly short notes making appointments, or dealing with the many questions of detail that arose during the negotiations in Paris; but they are valuable because they give us, in conjunction with Cobden's other letters and his Diary, some scrap of evidence for practically every day of the negotiations. They also show what an active part was played at every stage by Chevalier.

For the six industrial studies a few books of fairly general scope proved valuable, such as Clapham's *Economic Development of France and Germany, 1815–1914* and Ballot's *L'Introduction du machinisme dans l'industrie française*, but the majority of the printed sources are books which deal with only one industry, such as the excellent study of the cotton industry of Alsace by Robert Lévy. Little could have been written, however, without the two great French Enquêtes of 1860 and 1870, the records of both of which are in the Bibliothèque Nationale, and the many valuable letters, reports, and petitions in Série F 12 of the Archives Nationales and F. O. 27 of the British Foreign Office. For the French iron industry there is the book of the Comité des Forges, *La Sidérurgie française 1864–1914*. This is privately printed, is not to be found in any of the great public libraries, and cannot be purchased. Consequently it gives information of great value because the writers felt free to speak frankly. The book goes back far beyond 1860.

On the commercial negotiations between England and France from 1870 to 1882 I have used freely such printed sources as Amé, Arnauné, Fuchs, and Rausch; but the most important source, which was not open

Bibliography 385

to investigators until recently, is Series F. O. 27 at Chancery Lane. On the negotiations in 1876 and 1877 interesting information is to be found in the papers of Sir Louis Mallet, who was devoted to the memory of his former chief Cobden and was a personal friend and correspondent of Michel Chevalier. In addition to the personal correspondence of Sir Louis Mallet, there is the whole official correspondence on the negotiations of those two years, which is not yet available to investigators, at the Public Record Office. For material after 1877 I have had to rely for official information chiefly upon the British bluebooks in the British Museum. On the French side nothing official is yet available, but there are scraps of information and some reports on French industries and the work of French tariff commissions in the *Économiste français*.

Books, Documents, and Articles

ADAMS, E. D., Great Britain and the American Civil War. 2 vols. New York, 1925.

ALCAN, MICHEL, Fabrication des étoffes. Traité du travail de la laine cardée: notions historiques — progrès techniques — développement commercial. 2 vols. Paris, 1866. Contains a good introduction on the history of the woollen industry.

AMÉ, LÉON, Étude économique sur les tarifs de douanes. 1 vol. Paris, 1859. 2d edition, Paris, 1860. 2 vol. edition, Paris, 1876.

ANTONELLI, ÉTIENNE, Protection de la viticulture. Paris, 1905.

ARNAUNÉ, AUGUSTE, Le commerce extérieur et les tarifs de douane. Paris, 1911.

—— La Monnaie, le crédit, et le change. Paris, 1894.

ARNOLD, R. A., History of the Cotton Famine. London, 1864.

ASHLEY, PERCY, Modern Tariff History. 2d edition, London, 1910.

BALLOT, CHARLES, L'Introduction du machinisme dans l'industrie française. Lille, Paris, etc., 1923.

BEAUMONT, GASTON DU BOSCQ DE, Industrie cotonnière en Normandie. Paris, 1901.

BEAUQUIS, A., Histoire économique de la soie. Grenoble, 1910.

BEER, ADOLPH, Allgemeine Geschichte des Welthandels. 5 vols. in 2. Vienna, 1860–84.

BOITEAU, PAUL, Les traités de commerce; texte de tous les traités en vigeur, notamment des traités conclus avec l'Angleterre, la Belgique, la Prusse (Zollverein) et l'Italie, avec une introduction historique et économique, des renseignements sur les monnaies, les

mesures, les douanes, les usages, et un catalog alphabétique des
principaux articles tarifés dans les divers pays du monde. Paris,
1863. Contains a valuable introduction on the Treaty of 1860.

BOUCHIÉ DE BELLE, A., Bastiat et le libre-échange. Paris, 1878.

BURNLEY, JAMES, History of Wool and Woolcombing. London, 1889.

Cambridge History of British Foreign Policy, 1783–1919. *See* Ward.

CASES, COMTE DE LAS, Mémorial de Sainte Hélène. 2 vols. Paris 1842.

CHAPTAL, JEAN, A. C., " Un Projet de traité de commerce avec l'Angleterre sous le Consulat," Revue d'économie politique, VI (February,
1893), 83–98.

CHARLÉTY, SÉBASTIEN, Histoire du Saint-Simonisme (1825–64). Paris,
1896.

CHEVALIER, MICHEL, " Richard Cobden," in Les Contemporains célèbres. Paris, 1869.

—— Cours d'économie politique fait au Collège de France. 3 vols.
Paris, 1842–50.

—— Élections dans le Département de l'Aveyron, 1846, 1846.

—— Examen du système commercial connu sous le nom de système
protecteur. Paris, 1852. 2d edition, Paris, 1853.

—— (editor) Exposition universelle de Londres. Paris, 1851.

—— (editor) Exposition universelle de 1862. 7 vols. Paris, 1862–64.

—— (editor) Exposition universelle de 1867. 13 vols. Paris, 1868.

—— History of Political Economy, to which is added an Account of the
Negotiation of the Commercial Treaty between France and England. Translated by W. Bellingham. London, 1869.

—— L'Industrie moderne, ses progrès et les conditions de sa puissance.
Paris, 1862.

—— Des Intérêts matériels en France. Travaux publics. Routes,
canaux, chemins de fer. Paris, 1838. 4th edition, Paris, 1839.

—— " Du Système prohibitif en France dans ses rapports avec les
classes ouvrières et avec les intérêts Britanniques," Revue des
deux mondes, VI (December 1, 1856), 616–647.

——Religion saint-simonienne. Politique industrielle et système de la
Méditerrannée. Paris, 1832.

—— Le Renouvellement des traités de commerce. Paris, 1876. Also
Revue des deux mondes, CXXIII (June 15, 1876), 721.

CLAPHAM, J. H., The Economic Development of France and Germany,
1815–1914. Cambridge, 1921.

CLARENDON, LORD, Ten Years of Imperialism in France: Impressions of
a " flaneur." Edinburgh, 1862.

Comité des Forges, La Sidérurgie française, 1864–1914. (Privately printed), Paris, 1920.

CONVERT, F., "La Viticulture et la vinification, 1800–1870; la viticulture après 1870, en crise phylloxérique," Revue de viticulture, September, 1899 — November, 1900. Valuable also for the effects of the Treaty of 1860 and the railroads on the French wine industry.

COQUELIN, CHARLES, "Les Douanes et les finances publiques," Revue des deux mondes, XXII (May 1, 1848), 356; XXII (May 15, 1848), 557, XXII (June 15, 1848), 861.

CORDIER, ALPHONSE, La Crise cotonnière dans la Seine Inférieure. Rouen, 1864.

—— Exposé de la situation des industries du coton et des produits chimiques dans la Seine Inférieure et l'Eure, 1859–69. Rouen, 1869.

DEVERS, A. (Devers is a pseudonym used by Auguste Arnauné), "La Politique commerciale de France depuis 1860," Verein fur Sozialpolitik, XLVII (1892), 507.

DOLLFUS, JEAN, De l'industrie cotonnière, etc., à l'Exposition de 1855. Paris, 1855.

—— De la Levée des prohibitions douanières. Paris, 1860.

DOWELL, STEPHEN, History of Taxation and Taxes in England from the Earliest Times to the Present Day. 4 vols. London, 1884. 2d edition, London, 1888.

DUMAS, M. F., Étude sur le traité de commerce de 1786 entre la France et l'Angleterre. Toulouse, 1904. An excellent sketch, sound, and well presented.

DURUY, VICTOR, Notes et souvenirs, 1811–1894. 2 vols. 2d edition, Paris, 1902.

ELLISON, T., The Cotton Trade of Great Britain. London, 1886.

Enquête: Traité de commerce avec l'Angleterre. 7 vols., Paris, 1860. The valuable seventh volume is to be found only at the French Ministry of Commerce.

Enquête parlementaire [1870] sur le régime économique en France. Paris, 1872. This Enquête covers cotton, wool and linen, with one session on silk. It was stopped by the war.

Exposé de la situation de l'Empire présenté au Sénat. Paris, 1861–69.

FERAY, ERNEST, Du Traité de commerce de 1860 avec l'Angleterre. Paris, 1881. Valuable on the Enquête of 1860 and the tariff conventions.

FOVILLE, ALFRED DE, La France économique; statistique raisonnée et comparative; territoire, population, propriété, agriculture, industrie, commerce, moyens de transport, postes et télégraphes, monnaie, crédit, finances, richesse, colonies. Année 1889. 2 vols. Paris, 1890.

—— De la transformation des moyens de transport et ses conséquences économiques et sociales. Paris, 1880.

FROND, VICTOR, Panthéon des illustrations françaises du XIXᵉ siècle. 16 vols. Paris, 1869.

FUCHS., K. J., The Trade Policy of Great Britain and her Colonies since 1860. London, 1905. Valuable on both the treaty of 1860 and the Fair Trade movement.

GILL, CONRAD, The Rise of the Irish Linen Industry. Oxford, 1925.

GLADSTONE, W. E., " The History of 1852–60, and Greville's Latest Journals," English Historial Review, II (April, 1887), 281–302.

GORCE, PIERRE DE LA: Histoire du second empire. 7 vols. Paris, 1899–1905.

GRAS, L. J., Histoire de la rubanerie et des industries de la soie à St. Étienne et dans la région stéphanoise. St. Étienne, 1906.

GREVILLE, CHARLES F., The Greville Memoirs (third part); a journal of the reign of Queen Victoria, from 1852 to 1860. 2 vols. London, 1887.

GUENEAU, LOUIS, Lyon et le commerce de la soie. Lyon, 1923.

GUYOT, JULES, Étude des vignobles de France pour servir à l'enseignement mutuel de la viticulture et de la vinification françaises. 3 vols. Paris, 1868. 2d edition, Paris, 1876.

HERTSLET, LEWIS, A complete Collection of the Treaties and Conventions, and Reciprocal Regulations at present subsisting between Great Britain and Foreign Powers and of the Laws, Decrees, Orders in Council, &c., concerning the same: so far as they relate to Commerce and Navigation, [etc., etc.,]. 24 vols. London, 1827–1907.

Historique du traité de commerce de 1860 et des conventions complémentaires. Paris, 1861. (Anonymous book.)

HOBSON, J. A., Richard Cobden, the International Man. London, 1918.

HOTTENGER, G., L'Ancienne Industrie du fer en Lorraine. Nancy: Société industrielle de l'Est, 1927.

HOUDOY, JULES, La Filature du coton dans le nord de la France. Paris, 1903.

JERROLD, BLANCHARD, The Life of Napoleon III. Derived from state records, from unpublished family correspondence, and from personal testimony. 4 vols. London, 1874–82.

KAUFMAN, RICHARD. Eisenbahnpolitik Frankreichs. Berlin, 1897. French translation published by Librairie Polytechnique, Paris, 1900.

LACK, H. READER, The French Treaty and the Tariff of 1860. London, 1861.

LEROY-BEAULIEU, PAUL, " Michel Chevalier." In Nouveau dictionnaire d'économie politique (2 vols. and supplement, by Say and Chailley, Paris, 1893–97), I, 410–416.

LEVAINVILLE, J., Rouen, étude d'une agglomération urbaine. Paris, 1913. Useful in the study of the development of the Norman cotton industry.

LEVASSEUR, ÉMILE, " De l'Esprit des tarifs français." Journal des économistes, 2d series, XXVI (1860), 176. Valuable survey of French tariff history.

—— Histoire des classes ouvrières et de l'industrie en France de 1789 à 1870. 2 vols. 2d edition, Paris, 1903–04.

—— Questions ouvrières et industrielles en France sous la troisième république. Paris, 1907.

LEVI, LEONE, History of British Commerce and of the Economic Progress of the British Nation. 1763–1870. London, 1872. 2d edition (1763–1878), London, 1880.

LÉVY, ROBERT, Histoire économique de l'industrie cotonnière en Alsace; étude de sociologie descriptive. Paris, 1912.

MALVEZIN, THÉOPHILE, Histoire du commerce de Bordeaux, depuis les origines jusqu'à nos jours. 4 vols. Bordeaux, 1892.

MANTOUX, PAUL, La Révolution industrielle au XVIIIe siècle. Essai sur les commencements de la grande industrie moderne en Angleterre. Paris, 1906.

MEREDITH, H. O., Protection in France. London, 1904. A very useful book.

MORLEY, JOHN, The Life of William Ewart Gladstone. 3 vols. in 2. London, 1911.

—— The Life of Richard Cobden. London, 1879.

NAPOLÉON III, Œuvres de Napoléon III. 5 vols. Paris, 1854–69.

OLIVIER, ÉMILE, L'Empire libéral; études; récits, souvenirs. 18 vols. Paris, 1895–1918.

PARISET, E., Histoire de la fabrique lyonnaise. Étude sur le régime social et économique de la soie à Lyon depuis le XVIe siècle. Lyon, 1901.

—— Les Industries de la soie. Lyon, 1890. There are good sections on English, German, and Swiss industries as well as on French.

Périer, Casimir, Le Traité avec l'Angleterre. Paris, 1860.

Picard, Alfred, Les Chemins de fer, aperçu historique; résultats généraux de l'ouverture des chemins de fer, concurrence des voies ferrées entre elles et avec la navigation. Paris, 1918.

Price, Bonamy, The Principles of Currency; six lectures delivered at Oxford, by Bonamy Price . . . with a letter from M. Michel Chevalier on the history of the treaty of commerce with France. Oxford and London, 1869.

Rausch, E., "Französische Handelspolitik vom Frankfurter Frieden bis zur Tarifreform, 1882," Staats- und socialwissenschaftliche Forschungen, XVIII (1900), 354.

Renouard, Alfred, Histoire de l'industrie linière. 3 vols. 1879.

Reybaud, Louis, Le Coton: son régime — ses problèmes — son influence en Europe. Nouvelle série des études sur le régime des manufactures. Paris, 1863.

—— Économistes modernes. Paris, 1862.

—— Études sur le régime des manufactures. Condition des ouvriers en soie. Paris, 1859.

—— La Laine. Nouvelle série des études sur le régime des manufactures. Paris, 1867.

—— "Du Tarif des douane et de l'inconvénient des réformes à titre provisoire," Journal des économistes, IX (January, 1856), 31.

—— "L'Exposition de l'industrie de 1855 et ses conséquences économiques." Revue des deux mondes, XII (December 15, 1855). 1284–1321.

Rondot, Natalis, L'Art de la soie. Les soies. 2d edition. 2 vols. Paris, 1885–87.

—— L'Industrie de la soie en France. Lyon, 1894.

Saint Marc Girardin, Des traités de commerce selon la constitution de 1852. Paris, 1860.

Schmidt, Charles, "La Crise industrielle de 1788 en France," Revue historique, XCVII (January–April, 1908), 78.

Schwabe, Mme. J. L. (editor), Cobden. Notes sur ses voyages et correspondence. Paris, 1879.

Sempé, Henri, Le Régime économique du vin. Paris, 1898. Useful on imports and on the change to protection.

Senior, Nassau, Conversations with Distinguished Persons during the Second Empire, from 1860 to 1863. 2 vols. London, 1880.

—— Conversations with M. Thiers, M. Guizot, and Other Distinguished Persons during the Second Empire. 2 vols. London, 1878.

SIMON, JULES, " Notice sur Michel Chevalier." Speech before the French Academy, December 7, 1889. Published in Journal officiel, December 9, 1889, page 6132.

THAYER, W. R., The Life and Times of Cavour. 2 vols. Boston, 1911.

USHER, A. P., The Industrial History of England. Boston, 1920.

VADOT, NAPOLÉON, Le Creusot. Le Creusot, 1875.

WARD, SIR A. W., AND GOOCH, G. P. (editors), The Cambridge History of British Foreign Policy, 1783–1919. 3 vols. New York, 1922–23.

WARDEN, A. J., The Linen Trade, Ancient and Modern. London, 1864.

WARNER, SIR FRANK, The Silk Industry of the United Kingdom. Its Origin and Development. London, 1921. Badly organized, but very useful.

WEILL, GEORGES, L'École St. Simonienne, son histoire et son influence jusqu'à nos jours. Paris, 1896.

WOLOWSKI, L. F. R., " La Réforme douanière," Journal des économistes, Series II, XXV (January, 1860), 435.

INDEX

References to various industries, the tariff, etc., apply to France, unless otherwise noted. Less important references are given by page numbers only and follow the final item in each entry.

A

Abbeville, woollen industry of, 218–219; linen industry of, 236.

Agriculture, favored by the Physiocrats, 4; protective tariff extended to, 9; tariff proposals on products of, 72; Napoleon III on, 83–84; government loans to, 84; and the protectionist reaction of 1877, 340–342.

Algeria, wines of, 292.

Allier, Dept. of, iron industry of, 166.

Alsace, cotton industry of, 181, 184, 365; cotton spinning in, 186–187; cotton weaving in, 189–190; crisis of 1861–65 in, 197, 199; crisis of 1869 in, 202–204; concentration of cotton industry in, 211–212; woollen industry of, 222, 226; ribbon industry of, 263; loss to France of, 273.

Amé, quoted on tariff reform, 25; on Enquête of 1860, 137 note; on iron industry, 173, 175 and note; on cotton industry, 192; on linen industry, 247; negotiator of treaty with England, 336; 135.

American Civil War, effect on cotton industry, 193–198; effect on woollen industry, 203, 223–224, 232, 234; effect on linen industry, 238–239, 246–247, 250–251; effect on silk industry, 271–273, 275; effect on French commercial policy, 295; 366.

Amiens, cotton industry of, 155–158, 183, 190, 210; woollen industry of, 218, 226; 126.

Anglo-French Alliance, plan for, 76–77 and note, 78.

Anjou, 239.

Anonymous Plan for Economic Reform, 1859, Chevalier author of, 143 and

note, 234, 352, 354–356; provisions of, 351–352; date of, 353; text of, 369–372.

Anti-Corn Law League, 16, 28, 123, 282.

Anzin, coal mines of, 309.

Arkwright, 240.

Armentières, 327.

Arnauné, Auguste, quoted on French and English industry, 17; quoted on English wine consumption, 286–287.

Articles de Paris, 13.

Artois, Comte d', 184–185.

Association for Free Trade, organized by Bastiat, 16; disappears, 17; 40.

Aube, Dept. of, 210.

Austria, influence on negotiations for the Treaty of 1860, 76, 77 and note; war with, 62, 118; Treaty of 1866 with, 307, 333, 344; danger of war with France, 76, 77 and note, 78.

Aveyron, Dept. of, Chevalier elected Deputy from, 34.

Avignon, 256.

B

Bâle, ribbon industry of, 262.

Ballot, Charles, 152, 181, 240–241 note.

Balsan, 328, 337.

Baril, Amiens manufacturer of Utrecht velvet, 155; secures government loan, 155–156; his experiences as a cotton manufacturer, 157–158.

Baroche, Minister of Commerce, 60; Minister of Foreign Affairs, 62, 75, 98, 132–134; 192.

Bastiat, Frédéric, leader of free trade cause, 15; organizes Association for Free Trade, 16; death, 18 note.

Beauvais, woollen industry of, 218.

Béhic, 151.

DATE DUE

19 Oct 82			